Strategic Social Media

Strategic Social Media

From Marketing to Social Change

L. Meghan Mahoney and Tang Tang

WILEY Blackwell

This edition first published 2017
© 2017 John Wiley & Sons, Inc.

Registered Office
John Wiley & Sons Ltd, The Atrium, Southern Gate, Chichester, West Sussex, PO19 8SQ, UK

Editorial Offices
350 Main Street, Malden, MA 02148-5020, USA
9600 Garsington Road, Oxford, OX4 2DQ, UK
The Atrium, Southern Gate, Chichester, West Sussex, PO19 8SQ, UK

For details of our global editorial offices, for customer services, and for information about how to apply for permission to reuse the copyright material in this book please see our website at www.wiley.com/wiley-blackwell.

The rights of L. Meghan Mahoney and Tang Tang to be identified as the authors of this work has been asserted in accordance with the UK Copyright, Designs and Patents Act 1988.

Library of Congress Cataloging-in-Publication Data applied for.

ISBN Hardback: 9781119259190
ISBN Paperback: 9781118556849

A catalogue record for this book is available from the British Library.

Cover image: cosmin4000 / Gettyimages and ktsimage / Gettyimages

Set in 10/13pt Minion by Aptara Inc., New Delhi, India

1   2017

Contents

Introduction

The social media revolution has undoubtedly brought limitless guides on how to maximize the new technology towards a desired outcome. The inherit definition of social media is grounded in its ability to support interactive dialogue across various media platforms (Baruah, 2012). However, the majority of social media references measure success by its ability to maximize profit or become a viral sensation. As social media scholars we wonder, if the entire premise of social media is the ability to hold a conversation online, wouldn't a successful social media endeavor be to successfully engage the intended audience through interactive dialogue rather than top-down diffusion? Thus, the idea for *Strategic Social Media: From Marketing to Social Change* was born.

Inspiration was further ignited by a futile search for a textbook to use for a college-level social media course. While numerous social media texts intend to offer a step-by-step "how to" manual in social media marketing practices, few provide theoretical explanations for the role social media play in facilitating behavior change in audiences. It was important to create a reference that covers the many opportunities that social media affords users in breaking down barriers with institutions of power, achieving greater transparency, and encouraging dialogue to mobilize users. Our hope is that this book provides a balance between best social media marketing practices and the application of traditional communication, behavior change, and marketing theories.

Social media are able to inspire human behavior change, whether that behavior change is intended to inspire marketing decisions or social change. We believe it is important to provide social media strategies that readers can apply to any past, present or future social media platform. The intersection of theory, practice, and mindfulness will help practitioners make better decisions regarding brand objectives and the world they impact, and make them more valuable than a professional who is only familiar with social media tools and marketing business models.

Strategic Social Media: From Marketing to Social Change, First Edition. L. Meghan Mahoney and Tang Tang.
© 2017 John Wiley & Sons, Inc. Published 2017 by John Wiley & Sons, Inc.

This book is divided into five distinct sections: 1. Social media landscape; 2. Social media users and messages; 3. Social media business models and marketing strategies; 4. Social responsibility and cause marketing; and 5. The future of social media technologies.

We begin by exploring the role of social media in today's convergence culture by asking questions such as: What is the current social media landscape? How are individuals and organizations utilizing new media tools? The section introduces three primary functions of social media – diffusing information, providing a sense of community for audiences, and mobilizing users into action. These functions will build the foundation for all social media strategies outlined in later sections of the book.

The second section of the book focuses on constructing social media messages that reach intended audiences and ignite dialogue and behavior change. It examines how social media alter the way we view the audience. Rather than viewing users as a passive entity who only consume online messages, we favor theoretical assumptions about how users participate and negotiate in the information-exchange process. By transforming social media messages from modes of information diffusion towards more interactive sites for mobilization, we are able to establish a sense of community among users.

Third, the book examines various social media business models and marketing strategies. Classic marketing literature has focused on how to best compete with similar products. This section explains the importance of collaborating and communicating with your competitors to promote mutual gain. It also offers insights on how to best evaluate and monitor social media marketing efforts.

Next, this book explains why marketing for social good is more important than ever. By examining case studies in public health, civic engagement, and cause marketing, we identify the potential of social media to make a positive difference on the world. Social media users demand increased transparency with how products are manufactured, sold, and reviewed by other consumers. By taking control over social media narratives, practitioners are able to increase their return on investment, while also promoting social good.

Finally, this book explores the future of social media landscape. The section explains how to integrate traditional media with new, incorporates a more sustainable mindset, and argues for a general framework for social media scholarship. The book concludes by offering insights on Web 3.0 and the future social media technologies.

In writing this book, we were fortunate to receive enormous help and support from family, friends and colleagues. We are particularly grateful to Roger Cooper, Ryan Mahoney, Rafael Obregon, Pat Peirce, Patti Peirce, Paul Peirce, Jie Tang, Mingtang Wang, Xu Wang, and Sichun Yang, who have been a tremendous support since the first day of this project. The faculty members at the West Chester University and the University of Akron who have helped us along the way, including Timothy Brown, Elizabeth Graham, Chih-Hui Lai, Edward Lordan, Andrew Rancer, Julia Spiker, Philip Thompsen, and Heather Walter. Our gratefulness is extended to the anonymous reviewers who read the manuscript in various stages of development. There is no doubt that the book becomes a stronger effort as a result of implementing their comments. We would especially like to thank Wiley-Blackwell and its editors for their constant support and guidance. Finally, to our kids – Beatrice Mahoney and Maxx Tang Yang – who were born in the middle of this project, thanks for motivating and enriching us every day.

Ultimately, the goal of this book is to share with our readers – students, social media practitioners, and current/future generation of social media users – the power and positive possibilities that social media hold in influencing personal relationships and social change. While it would prove impossible to predict all of the new media changes that we will see in our lifetime, we hope this book can shed light on the future of social media landscape – a world where marketing and social change will no longer exist in mutually exclusive entities. We hope that *Strategic Social Media: From Marketing to Social Change* is a valuable resource for anyone interested in successfully persuading audiences through social media messages.

Reference

Baruah, T.D. (2012). Effectiveness of social media as a tool of communication and its potential for technology enabled connections: A micro-level study. *International Journal of Scientific and Research Publications*, 2(5), 1–10.

Part I

Social Media in Convergence

1

Understanding Social Media and Social Behavior Change

Learning Objectives

After reading this chapter, you should be able to:

1 Explain how social media has been able to transform audiences into more participatory, globalized and civically engaged users by changing the ways in which they gather, interact with, and disseminate information.

2 Distinguish between audience assumptions in historic linear mass communication models and social media transactional processes.

3 Understand the role of behavior change theory in the marketing process.

Introduction

Digital natives, or individuals who have been born and raised in a digital world, are often referred to as alien outliers to society (Bauerlein, 2009; Palfrey & Gasser, 2010). In 2009, Professor Mark Bauerlein released the book *The Dumbest Generation: How the Digital Age Stupefies Young Americans and Jeopardizes Our Future (Or, Don't Trust Anyone Under 30)*, and posits the millennial generation (i.e., individuals born between 1982 and 2002) as less informed and knowledgeable than previous generations due to their constant use and interaction with digital technologies. The book condemns millennials for their disinterest in reading print books, erosion of basic grammar skills, lack of memory recall ability,

Strategic Social Media: From Marketing to Social Change, First Edition. L. Meghan Mahoney and Tang Tang.
© 2017 John Wiley & Sons, Inc. Published 2017 by John Wiley & Sons, Inc.

and a fascination with distributing mundane status updates through social networking sites.

While Bauerlein's criticisms suggest that technology is detrimental to the future of society, the purpose of this book, *Strategic Social Media: From Marketing to Social Change*, is to offer a different position. Undoubtedly millennials, just like previous generations, are different from their predecessors. They think and process information differently and prefer multiple streams of information with frequent interaction with content (Oblinger & Oblinger, 2005; Prensky, 2001). Perhaps one reason why we speak about digital natives as alien and unlike previous generations is due to the unmatched potential that they hold in shaping the world for the better (Palfrey & Gasser, 2010).

The authors of this book believe that technology creates better-informed and more knowledgeable citizens of society, leading towards greater opportunity for positive social change than ever before. Specifically, this book hopes to outline the underlying communication strategies that inspire behavior change in social media audiences, whether that behavior change is intended to inspire business decisions or positive social changes. Additionally, under the guidance of related communication theories, this book aims to show readers how to develop social media marketing messages.

Individuals today have more frequent interaction with information about a wider range of issues, making them more engaged with events happening around the world. Many are concerned about the negative influence social media has on our youngest generations. However, each era of new media comes with a strong and vocal wave of fear and resistance. While it is possible to inspire behavior change through media, new technologies are not inherently good or evil. Take a look at the following items. Which are examples of new media?

(a)   The Internet during the late twentieth century
(b)   Magazines during the colonial era
(c)   Paperback books during World War II
(d)   All of the above.

The answer is (d) All of the above.

The definition of what new media includes is perpetually changing. To say that one generation's media use is better than another is ill-informed. Most often, individuals fear the unfamiliar and unknown when it comes to technology. With adults spending more than 8.5 hours per day in front of screens (Zackon, 2009), it is only natural to question what type of influence media has on everyday lives. However, this reflection must consider the complicated process of igniting behavior change through media content.

Years of communication research have taught us that the cause-and-effect process is not as simple as previously thought. The media is often identified as the cause for negative behavior, whether it is making us more violent, obese, or over-sexualized members of society. However, the process of audience behavior change is far more complicated than a direct media effects model suggests. It is easier to blankly assume that because person A consumed media B that they were led towards behavior C. These types of causal relationships seem justified, especially when the media message in question is something unfamiliar or scary. However, this type of assumption is sometimes referred to as "hypodermic-needle theory" (Scheufele & Tewksbury, 2007), and is an outdated notion of how media directly influences behavior through a linear cause-and-effect process. A strong understanding of behavior change research outlined in this chapter will help illustrate this process.

Social media is defined as a group of Internet-based applications built on the ideological and technological foundations of Web 2.0 that allow the creation and exchange of user-generated content (Kaplan & Haenlein, 2010). It is right to turn to social media when attempting to inspire behavior change in audiences through media messages. The user-generated profile feature of social media is the closest connection many media producers will ever have to the individual personality of an audience member. Social media does not fundamentally change the ways in which audiences make decisions about their everyday actions, but simply maximizes the opportunity for marketers to reach and interact with consumers. This book therefore investigates how individuals turn to social media as a space to create and recreate personal and perceived identities, thus helping social media marketers understand how social media tools are used by their audiences and how to inspire behavior change through social media content.

Many alternative social media references teach users the specifics about how to use various platforms. They share information about how Facebook status updates are different than Twitter posts. However, the authors of this book believe that it is more useful for marketers to have a strong understanding of how social media is able to inspire human behavior change than it is to know about platform-specific tools. Rather than constantly looking ahead at what is new or trendy in social media, it is more practical to learn about how humans make decisions based on their own life experiences, including media content consumption. Marketers can then use this knowledge to develop social media strategies through whatever social media platform they choose or emerge as the next trendy platform in the future.

Through an understanding of foundational communication theories, one will be able to apply the tools of behavior change to any past, present or future social media platform. It is better to understand the link between media and behavior change than it is to know the differences between platform interfaces. By the end of this book, it should be clear that regardless of your goal as a social media strategist, whether it is for social media marketing, personal social media use, or creating large-scale social change campaigns, the process through which audiences are inspired towards permanent behavior change is the same.

Thus, the authors believe that rather than viewing digital natives as *The Dumbest Generation*, a bridge must be built between traditional communication theories and social media practitioners. This will help individuals utilize technologies to meet their goals. This chapter aims to discuss how social media has been able to push individuals towards more participatory, globalized, and civically engaged spaces by changing the ways in which users gather and disseminate information (Castells, 2001; Scheufele, 2002; Jenkins, 2006; Levine, 2007). While this chapter provides a substantial overview of communication theories, future chapters will help guide readers towards developing specific social media strategies, and thus illustrating the promising opportunities brought by social media.

Bridging Communication Theories and Social Media Practitioners

persuasion
behavior change

This chapter provides a basic communication theoretical framework for individuals look- ing to advance their career through the effective creation and dissemination of social media messages. One basic definition states that communication is "who says what to whom and with what effect" (Lasswell, 1948; Griffin, 2011). This definition of communication intrinsically links the construct to persuasion. Whether it be the source of the mes- sage (who), the content of the message (what) or audience characteristics (whom), the process of communication is all about behavior change (Griffin, 2011). Understand- ing human behavior is one of the most crucial things that social media communi- cation specialists need to learn before developing successful social media marketing campaigns.

Because this book is interested in constructing social media messages, it will mostly examine the communication process through the mass communication paradigm. Tradi- tional models of mass communication were long thought of as a *"one-to-many" model*, where one message was crafted to appeal to as many people as possible, and broadcast through a mass medium to reach a large audience. Here, mass communication is able to disseminate a single message multiple times in a much more efficient manner than any other type of communication (Dominick, 2008). Mass media audiences were seen as homogeneous, individually anonymous and geographically dispersed. With a simple click of a button, an advertisement could be broadcast to the masses in print, over the radio or on television. However, just like the other types of communication, scholars and communication special- ists quickly learned that this top-down linear model that posits one individual as a sender of a communication message and another as a receiver was not the most effective at persuading audiences.

A more nuanced outlook of the role that audiences play in the mass communication reception process proved necessary. Persuasive communication models began to integrate the interaction between senders and receivers of messages. These range from linear mod- els of communication, where information is transferred from the sender to the receiver in a step-by-step process, to a more transactional process where the information exchange is fluid and takes participation from both sides. It is important to understand the differences between these models in order to best persuade audiences towards desired behavior change outcomes via social media messages.

Linear Communication Models to Modern Transactional Processes

Theoretically, our understanding of communication models has gone through great trans- formations over the past 100 years. This chapter suggests that these transformations and trends are a guide for emerging communication contexts, specifically those in the digital and social age. The 1947 *Shannon–Weaver model of communication* (Figure 1.1) is used as the foundation for much of our knowledge of communication today. It highlights many important takeaways for effective communication. The model identifies eight concepts as

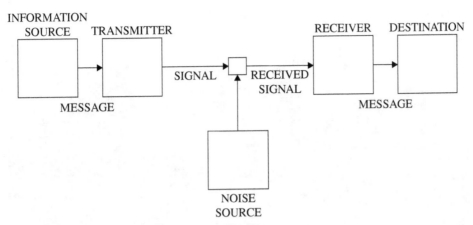

Figure 1.1   Shannon–Weaver model of communication. Source: Shannon, 1948. Reproduced with permission of The Bell System Technical Journal.

key elements for information transfer: source, encoder, message, channel, decoder, receiver, noise, and feedback.

In this model, shared meaning is imperative for effective communication. Most importantly, it provides an explanation for miscommunication. The receiver of a message could walk away without the intended message not only due to external noise, but also due to the encoding and decoding process. This applies to social media conversations as well.

For example, a friend may write a message on your Facebook wall. Your friend knows that the wall is a public space where others are likely to see the message. She wishes to be discreet about the meaning of her message, so she uses personal jokes and acronyms in her message, rather than being forthcoming. The message is so secretive that even you, the intended receiver, don't understand the meaning of the message. In this example, there was no external noise to cause the miscommunication; the technology worked appropriately and there was no language barrier between sender and receiver. However, the encoding and decoding process did not align, thus resulting in miscommunication. This is one of the first models of communication that included an explanation for why miscommunication occurs even without external noise.

Regardless of the foundational importance of the Shannon–Weaver model of communication, researchers came to realize that the process of communication is much more transactional in nature than the Shannon–Weaver model illustrates. Rather than communicating through a linear process, which posits one individual as a sender of a communication message and another as a receiver, a *transactional model of communication* (Figure 1.2) accounts for all participants as senders/receivers in a simultaneous and fluid exchange.

The quality of this exchange depends on the ability and willingness of communicators to gather necessary information and disseminate in an appropriate manner for the target audience. While one individual is speaking, the other communicator is providing simultaneous

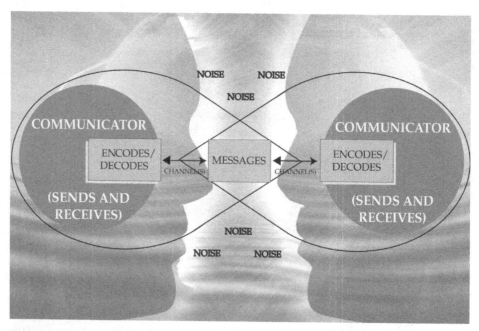

Figure 1.2   Transactional model of communication. Source: Reproduced with permission of the National Communication Association.

feedback through nonverbal cues, relational history, and the setting of the communication exchange. People constantly shape their communication patterns based on real-time events in the communication environment.

While the linear model of communication gives limited power to the receiver of the message, the transactional model equalizes their role, as communication can only take place when the two meet on an agreed-upon meaning. In the example above, the subtle Facebook message causes miscommunication between the sender and the receiver of the message. However, you don't just examine Facebook wall posts as a singular communication process. You consider the relational history with the person who constructs them, the time of day that the message was posted, and the technology through which the message was constructed. Maybe you see that the message was posted through your friend's new iPhone and assume that the autocorrect spelling function of the new technology made the message unreadable. Each of these pieces of information influence how you interpret the message and are just as vital to the communication process as your friend's intended meaning.

Regardless of the communication process, whether it be communication between two friends, a public address in front of hundreds, or a 140-character tweet, the better message is able to account for this gathering and dissemination process, the more effective the message becomes. Through this transactional lens, a more inclusive view of communication studies emerges. This leads us to our first action plan for social media communication strategists. Each chapter will include a similar action plan to help you apply concepts to real-life marketing strategies.

Transactional Communication Action Plan

There are three steps towards maximizing communication between the sender and receiver of social media messages.

1   Be certain that you are not just creating social media messages based on your own goals and objectives.
2   Determine who the members of the target are, the technologies that they utilize, and their own needs and gratifications.
3   Identify any barriers to an effective communication process, such as competence, access or complicated relational history.

Your friend's decision to write a subtle message on your Facebook wall was based on her or his own predetermined objectives. The message contained private content, and despite Facebook being a more public forum, it was chosen as the medium for dissemination. Rather than considering the message target, technology options and the audience decoding process, your friend only considered ways in which the message could be altered for his or her own purposes. Instead, she should have chosen a more appropriate medium where the message could have been more forthcoming and easier to interpret, such as a private mobile messaging application, like Snapchat.

Now that you understand the differences between linear and transactional models of communication, it is important to take a deeper look at the ways in which the human decision-making processes influence marketing. Social media technologies have made it more important than ever to understand how audiences make sense of media messages. This information exchange navigates the items we purchase, the groups we join, and the recommendations we share with friends. Human behavior change is an essential area of study for anyone who is interested in marketing.

Marketing and Behavior Change Theory

The American Marketing Association defines *marketing* as the activity, set of institutions, and processes for creating, communicating, delivering, and exchanging offerings that have value for customers, clients, partners, and society at large (American Marketing Association, 2013). The definition is intrinsically linked with marketing research, which helps connect customers to the market through monitoring and evaluation efforts. Ultimately, marketing practitioners are responsible for designing and implementing a strategic plan in order to reach specific objectives. Marketing, advertising, public relations, and branding all fall under the broader umbrella of strategic communication. In today's ever-changing digital landscape, a strategic communication vision is more vital than ever to a company's brand (Howard, 2012).

Behavior change communication is an evidence- and research-based process of using communication to promote certain predetermined behaviors through an appropriate mix of

Public health interventions

social marketing

interpersonal, group and mass media channels (Manoff Group, 2012). Traditionally, behavior change theories have been utilized to develop public health interventions. The hope is that through strategic mass media dissemination, pro-social messages are able to prompt human behavior change so that individuals may engage in more positive and healthier lifestyles. These messages are important to the safety and well-being of mass audiences. Mass media provides the most efficient and cost-effective means for dissemination. However, the messages do not always prove the most persuasive. Often, these messages are up against hundreds of years of cultural rituals and practices that prove antagonistic to their health goals. While inciting this type of permanent behavior change in lifestyle can prove very difficult to achieve, this area of research has made great strides in our understanding of how to best persuade human behavior through mass media messages.

It wasn't until the early 1970s that marketers began using human behavior change theories to explore how to influence consumer behavior through mass media messages. Before this time, the focus was on the product and brand itself. Very little research went into the preference and lifestyle of target audiences. *Social marketing* emerged as a systematic way to design, implement, and control programs that are calculated to influence the acceptability of social ideas, including product planning, pricing, communication, distribution and marketing (Kotler & Zaltman, 1971). Here, marketers began to see that it was much more effective to sell an idea and lifestyle, rather than a product.

Since the inception of social marketing, several alternative frameworks have been offered. Researchers have explored the possibilities for persuasion through target audiences, a change in mind-set process, and a more planning-centered approach (Thackeray & Neiger, 2000). Each of these approaches offers unique challenges and benefits for using mass media to influence human purchasing behavior. However, they all take into account the transactional role that audiences play in the communication process. Rather than focusing solely on the product or the media message, marketers have begun to realize the potential of considering audience lifestyle and preferences as a central ingredient to behavior change.

Hybrid is best

Social marketing and behavior change theory are complementary methods for understanding how consumers make purchasing decisions (Thackeray & Neiger, 2000). The best approach to marketing is a hybrid process. Strong media messages are able to influence human behavior, but only if they speak to the goals and experiences of their audiences. Consumers have their own preferences and life experience, and the more that they are able to identify with media messages, the stronger that the message will speak to them. Though the media is able to reach a mass audience, audiences don't like being seen as a member of a larger homogeneous crowd. The efficient and cost-effective nature of disseminating messages through mass media was making the content less individualized, thus proving less persuasive. Social media has made it easier than ever for marketers to integrate these two approaches.

positive reinforcement in all purchasing stages

It is the role of marketers to ensure that consumer behavior is positively reinforced at every point of engagement. As the marketplace grows with new products, brands and services, it is essential to the survival of businesses to have a steady core of loyal customers. In fact, the industry named this cognitive procedure *shaping*, where the product is seen as a positive or negative reinforcer to the consumer purchasing behavior (Rothschild & Gaidis, 1981). It is the goal of marketing to ensure that purchasing is positively reinforced at every stage, including in retail stores, as well as its consumption at home.

Shaping procedures are used so that consumer purchasing trials become more than a random process. Rather than ensuring that customers choose your product or service when faced with the endless options available in a global marketplace, marketers hope to shape consumers so that there is no question as to which product they purchase in the future. This helps marketers rely on a sale before consumers ever walk into a store. Consumption is much more than a one-time transaction. Shaping leads to long-term patterns of consumer behavior.

For a long time, it has been difficult to track longitudinal patterns of consumer behaviors and consumption. Traditional market research, such as surveys and focus groups, were unable to capture audience data over time. However, advances in technologies, such as customer loyalty reward cards, credit history and scanner data, have made long-term tracking easier. While these are effective ways to understand the history of products customers buy, this book argues that social media technology is the most important tool for marketers to use when interested in shaping consumer behavior.

The use of social media for transactional communication with audiences is critical to any marketing practitioner. Today, 46% of online users turn to social media when making purchasing decisions (Karr, 2014). Research has found that social media increases brand recognition and customer loyalty, generates greater exposure for business, increases audience traffic, improves search ratings, results in new business partnerships, reduces marketing expenses, and yields a higher conversation rate (Stelzner, 2011; DeMers, 2014). Rather than secretly tracking purchasing behavior with technology, social media allows marketers to engage directly with audiences through an open transactional process. This is especially useful as customer concerns for privacy and data security increase.

Companies are now able to utilize numerous platforms to engage customers, including company websites, blogs, discussion forums, email, Facebook, Twitter and Pinterest. While it is important for marketers to reach out to their customers, it is equally important for sales and customers to be able to communicate with one another via social media (Mangold & Faulds, 2009). This develops a strong community among members, a concept discussed in detail in Chapter 3. Social media provides an ideal way to communicate with customers without disrupting their everyday rituals.

Once transactional communication is in progress, and consumers are shaped by positive social media reinforcement, they are more likely to return for repeat business. The positive reinforcement no longer just comes in the form of purchasing or product experience. Social media allows marketers the ability to check-in, monitor, and listen to audiences at every step of the consumption process, including the period of time before they ever make a purchase and long after they bring it home. Social media can prompt consumers to think about a product or brand when they otherwise would not.

For example, as a consumer, you may put great thought into a purchase of a new pair of athletic shoes. There are a lot of competing brands to choose from. You may examine consumer blogs or reviews to determine which pair best suits your particular lifestyle. Maybe you will use it primarily for walking, and it is something that you may use fairly regularly in your daily life. Social media helps guide your decision based on your particular lifestyle and price point, helping to personalize the consumption process to suit your individual needs.

Once the purchase is made and you wear the shoes a few times, you are likely not to think about them very often. This is what consumers want in a product. If the shoe is meeting the purchase goals, it becomes a part of your daily routine and habit. The only time you are likely to consider the shoe purchase again is if something goes wrong and the experience is negatively reinforced, such as the sole wearing thin and the shoe hurting your foot.

This is an unfortunate challenge faced by marketers in the consumption process. How can repeat brand loyalty be encouraged when customers only buy new products because their previous purchase no longer meets their needs? Social media allows the opportunity for marketers to build a relationship with consumers during that critical time period when the product is working well for consumers. Marketing practitioners can ask customers to share pictures of the purchase, provide information about local hiking trails, or offer exclusive promotions for being such a good customer. All of these help to positively reinforce, or shape the way consumers feel about their purchase. In fact, it makes it easier for transactional dialogue at every point along the consumption process: before, during and after the sale. That way, consumers are thinking about your brand when their experiences are positive.

Humans have always exhibited markedly habitual behavior with regard to their marketing decisions. We tend to buy the same brand of products, eat similar types of food, and go to the same stores when shopping. We even tend to spend the same amount of time and money in stores each visit. Knowledge of these patterns of human behavior can prove very lucrative for marketers. This information is missed when marketers only focus on media messages and products. Social media provides new opportunities for getting to know your consumers on a much more intimate level.

Generally, *consumer habits* are a form of automaticity that is guided by past experiences (Wood & Neal, 2009). This is why shaping is so essential to repeat business. Repetition is central to all facets of human life, including our daily media consumption. Humans tend to have a limited *media repertoire*, or the entirety of media channels that a person regularly uses (Hasebrink & Domeyer, 2012). Though a larger supply of media content from multiple media sources exists, your consumers tend to only use a very limited number of media sources in their everyday lives. The notion that millennials have all of the information in the world at their fingertips is true. However, they tend to only visit their favorite websites on a routine basis. This helps to organize all this information, but also drastically decreases the amount and type of content received.

Repetition is also an important facet of consumer purchasing. It helps ease the uncertainty of such a saturated marketplace. In fact, the more bogged down individuals feel by time pressures, distraction and self-control depletion, the more heavily they rely on routines (Hasebrink & Domeyer, 2012). This proves true of our consumption rituals and mass media routines. Often, these are the very same negative moods and attitudes that guide media-seeking behavior. If you are feeling stressed out or bogged down at work, you may be more likely to come home and watch hours of television to relax. Repetition helps ease stress in our everyday lives.

In order to break consumer habits, mindful decisions must be made by audiences that interfere with their current routines. Communication theory tells us that it can be very difficult to change the daily routines of individuals. The theory of *cognitive dissonance* helps to explain the discomfort that individuals experience when they are confronted by new information that is contradictory to their current beliefs, attitudes and ideas (Festinger, 1962). Humans do not like their daily repertoires disrupted.

When met with media messages that are not consistent with current practices, audiences use communication to make things more consistent and reduce dissonance. Humans strive for internal consistency. Dissonance reduction is achieved in one of four ways: (i) to change the behavior or cognition; (ii) justify the behavior by changing the conflicting cognition; (iii) justify the behavior or cognition by adding new cognitions; or (iv) deny any information that conflicts with existing beliefs.

Dissonance reduction methods

Let's assume that you read a media message that states a new brand of athletic shoes recently introduced to the market is better than the one that you just purchased. You have already invested substantial time researching social media prior to your purchase to determine which brand would be best for your lifestyle. However, this new information is not consistent with your purchasing decision.

There are many ways that you may try to reduce the dissonance that this new media message brings. You may decide that you will no longer purchase the brand of shoes that you just bought, justify all of the money that you saved by buying a pair of lesser quality shoes, or decide that the new shoes are probably not better at all and are just a new fad that will go away. All these are ways that you communicate to make things more consistent with your previous behavior.

The cognitive dissonance process often leads individuals avoiding or ignoring situations and information that are likely to increase dissonance. This helps to explain why consumers ignore so much of traditional media marketing. Because of a limited media repertoire, it is unlikely that consumers actually receive these media messages unless they are being broadcast on media platforms that audiences are already visiting as part of their daily routine. This is especially true now that media users are able to fast-forward or skip commercials/advertisements all together.

Social media provides a space where marketers and consumers coexist. It allows marketers to focus their attention on customers who are already interested in their behavior and would be more impacted by media messages that are consistent with their current cognitions.

Based on this understanding of human behavior, it is clear that marketers need to consider behavior change theory when developing a social media marketing strategy. This book will help practitioners understand how to best research audiences to craft social media messages, choose an appropriate social media platform, and monitor the resulting information exchange. Moreover, it encourages the social media strategy to fit within a larger marketing campaign to reach product goals. This will help transform customers into lifelong brand advocates.

While the majority of the book focuses on crafting social media messages for marketing purposes, Part IV explains why it is a smart idea to use social media to market for social good. This is consistent with the roots of behavior change theories. A more socially conscious brand strategy can prove mutually beneficial for businesses, audiences, and the globalized world alike. Now that we understand the benefits of using behavior change theory in marketing strategies, let's examine a case study of a start-up company that provides audiences with an alternative marketing narrative to fight dissonance with a habitual consumer behavior.

Case Study: Warby Parker

In 2010, classmates at the Wharton School of the University of Pennsylvania, Neil Blumenthal, Andrew Hunt, David Gilboa, and Jeffrey Raider, were dissatisfied with the options available for individuals in need of prescription eyeglasses. Costs of lenses and frames were high; eye doctors require advance appointments; and travel to showrooms to try on frames can be far, especially for rural consumers. The traditional way of doing business was not working for everyone in the marketplace. While it can be difficult to change the behavior of customers who are used to purchasing a certain way, the classmates decided to try to disrupt the market with an innovative strategy. Through a small $2500 program seed investment, the classmates launched Warby Parker, a new brand and way of selling prescription eyeglasses and sunglasses (Warby Parker, 2015).

Warby Parker is not like other eyeglass retailers. Their business model focuses on online distribution, rather than showrooms that sell outside manufacturer merchandise. By designing glasses in-house, and selling only directly to consumers, the company is able to drastically lower the purchasing cost of glasses. This alternative way of buying and selling eyeglasses was new to the marketplace, and initially audiences may have felt great dissonance. They may have believed that eyeglasses were too important a purchase to make online, or that the cost of frames was so low because the quality wasn't great. The company was able to effectively utilize social media to communicate with customers, change these narratives, reduce the dissonance, and eventually capture their loyalty. Today, Warby Parker has shipped more than 500,000 pairs of glasses in and employs over 100 people.

Individuals may have been concerned with purchasing eyeglasses through an online distribution because they would not be able to walk into a showroom and try on frames as at a traditional retailer. To mitigate these concerns, Warby Parker developed a "Home Try-On Campaign" where consumers are able to order five pairs of glasses online, which are shipped to the customer's home to try on at no charge. Consumers are then able to pick the pair that best suits them and return the remaining pairs at no charge. Beyond this remote business transaction, Warby Parker uses technology to engage the customers to make this exchange feel like a more personalized experience.

Warby Parker encourages transactional communication by consistently communicating with, and responding to, customer comments on their social media platforms. They regularly prompt customers to participate with user-generated content by asking them to post pictures of themselves wearing the glasses on Facebook, Twitter and Instagram. The Home Try-On Campaign encourages customers to share the purchase with their personal social networks. This communication with individuals that consumers already know and trust likely helps to reduce customer dissonance with the new product. In fact, customers who post photos of themselves in frames are buying at twice the rate of those who don't (Shandrow, 2013).

The company also uses social media to provide information that consumers are searching. In addition to the Home Try-On Campaign, social media is used to offer expert advice on eyeglasses. The company creates informative YouTube videos and asks fans to do the same (Tobin, 2013). Rather than just creating media messages based on the goals and objectives of selling eyeglasses, the company has directed attention towards the challenges consumers have with the traditional eyeglass market. This direct communication creates meaningful and personalized transactional communication that leads to brand loyalty (Shandrow, 2013).

Furthermore, Warby Parker has included marketing for social good in their business strategy. By teaming up with the company VisionSpring, the company is able to provide a pair of eyeglasses for a person in need for every pair of Warby Parker glasses that a consumer purchases. To date, Warby Parker has given away 500,000 pairs of glasses. This socially conscious business strategy makes people feel good about changing their purchasing habits. It has proven a mutually beneficial strategy for the Warby Parker business, its audiences in need of eyeglasses, and the globalized world alike.

Here you see how social media provides an opportunity for businesses to reach out to potential customers and provide an alternative narrative for reducing dissonance. Even if a new customer is skeptical about the business model, the free shipping and Home Try-On Campaign limits the risk. Social media is also used to prompt users to share their positive experiences with friends. Not only does this become a part of their new schemata of interpretation, it allows new customers to hear about the product through an already trusted source, rather than through a business's self-promotion. This is just one example of how social media helped a new business to disrupt a traditional marketplace. Each chapter of this book will explore additional case studies where social media helped in reaching business goals.

Discussion questions

1   How does social media technology aid Warby Parker's alternative business model for selling prescription eyeglasses? What challenges would the company have faced in a traditional media environment?

2   How is Warby Parker using social media to promote transactional communication with customers, rather than more linear advertising? What role does user-generated content play in this process?

3   What elements of Warby Parker's social media marketing strategy help reduce dissonance for consumers that are considering switching eyeglass brands? How does the socially conscious business strategy help provide an alternative narrative that they can share with their social network?

Summary

There is much to learn about how we utilize new media to make decisions in our daily lives. It also remains unclear exactly how we interact with and are affected by media texts. Throughout this chapter, we have discussed the complexities of this process and identified the role that audiences play. Most importantly, we have learned how mass communication is no longer viewed as a vehicle for "one-to-many" messages. Selective targeted messages are most effective in establishing behavior change no matter which type of communication specialty you are interested in engaging. This shift from viewing a mass audience to targeting individuals is essential to successful social media marketing.

Because of social media, audiences are now seeing themselves as generators of content, rather than passive receivers of media texts. Businesses need to personalize content and allow room for participation. People are no longer shocked when a website addresses them by their first name, and it will not be long, if we have not reached the point already, where this level of individuality and customization is expected. Social media makes it easier than ever to encourage this type of transactional communication. It is an efficient and cost-effective way to reach your business objectives, as well as the goals of your audiences.

Social media has brought forth new opportunities for information gathering, dissemination and socialization. However, these new technologies have not completely altered our purposes for doing so. The tools for behavior change are the same, and once you understand the theoretical underpinnings, you will be better equipped to create and disseminate efficient and effective messages for your social media campaigns. This chapter has presented the first rule of an effective social media marketing strategy: stop thinking about communication in a linear fashion. Ask questions about the interests of your target audience, rather than wondering how to get media messages to reach the largest number of people possible.

This book is interested in guiding strategy for producers of social media messages that inspire behavior change in audiences. This chapter has laid the foundation for how communication theories approached audience behavior change in the past. Hopefully, a stronger understanding of the complexities of the relationship between media content and subsequent behavior change has been gained.

Through the use of behavior change theory, marketers are able to create media messages that meet the goals and experiences of their audiences. Through a mindful strategy, consumer behavior can be positively reinforced at every point of engagement. This will reduce dissonance in the behavior change and result in more loyal and long-term brand advocates. These customers will then influence their own social network to continue increasing your return on investment.

Today, an entire generation has grown up utilizing new media technologies, but has never taken the time to examine their influence critically in order to maximize its potential. A strong practitioner is the one who is able to apply technological competence and critical thinking skills to a long-term strategic plan. The following chapters will examine historical shifts in behavior change literature and the opportunities and challenges of information diffusion, community and mobilization. These three constructs will become the core of your social media strategy, and will set you apart from other social media experts in the field.

Key Takeaways

1   Communication theories help teach social media communication specialists how to gather necessary information, package it towards a specific target audience, and disseminate it through an appropriate medium.
2   Our understanding of the communication process has shifted from a linear model towards a more transactional process that accounts for all participants as senders/receivers in a simultaneous and fluid exchange. Determine who the target of the message is, the technology that they utilize, and their needs and gratifications.
3   Marketers are turning towards behavior change theory to better understand the lifestyle and experiences of consumers. This focus on consumer behavior helps transform customers into lifetime brand advocates.
4   Social media should be used to engage in dialogue to help build relationships with customers. This positive reinforcement will keep them coming back.
5   Humans exhibit markedly habitual behaviors. A strong understanding of these routines will help practitioners better construct social media marketing messages that appeal to consumer lifestyle.

References

American Marketing Association (2013) http://www.ama.org (accessed June 8, 2016).

Bauerlein, M. (2009) *The Dumbest Generation: How the Digital Age Stupefies Young Americans and Jeopardizes Our Future (Or, Don't Trust Anyone Under 30)*. New York: Tarcher/Penguin.

Castells, M. (2001) *The Internet Galaxy: Reflections on the Internet, Business, and Society*. New York: Oxford University Press.

DeMers, J. (2014) The top 10 benefits of social media marketing. *Forbes Magazine*. Available at http://www.forbes.com/sites/jaysondemers/2014/08/11/the-top-10-benefits-of-social-media-marketing/ (accessed June 8, 2016).

Dominick, J. (2008) *The Dynamics of Mass Communication: Media in the Digital Age*. New York: McGraw Hill.

Festinger, L. (1962) *A Theory of Cognitive Dissonance*, Vol. 2. Stanford, CA: Stanford University Press.

Griffin, E. (2011) *Communication: A First Look at Communication Theory*. New York: McGraw Hill.

Hasebrink, U. & Domeyer, H. (2012) Media repertoires as patterns of behaviour and as meaningful practices: a multimethod approach to media use in converging media environments. *Participations: Journal of Audience and Reception Studies*, 9(2), 757–779.

Howard, S. (2012) The changing face of strategic communication. Available at http://cla.umn.edu/sjmc/news-events/news/changing-face-strategic-communication (accessed June 8, 2016).

Jenkins, H. (2006) *Convergence Culture: Where Old and New Media Collide*. New York: New York University Press.

Kaplan, A.M. & Haenlein, M. (2010) Users of the world, unite! The challenges and opportunities of social media. *Business Horizons*, 53(1), 59–68.

Karr, D. (2014) 2014 statistics and trends for businesses on social media. Available at https://www.marketingtechblog.com/2014-statistics-trends-businesses-social-media/ (accessed June 8, 2016).

Kotler, P. & Zaltman, G. (1971) Social marketing: an approach to planned social change. *Journal of Marketing*, 35, 3–12.

Lasswell, H.D. (1948) *The Structure and Function of Communication in Society*. New York: Harper & Bros.

Levine, P. (2007) *The Future of Democracy: Developing the Next Generation of American Citizens*. Lebanon, NH: University Press of New England.

Mangold, W. & Faulds, D. (2009) Social media: the new hybrid element of the promotion mix. *Business Horizons*, 52(4), 357–365.

Manoff Group (2012) Defining social and behavior change communication (SBCC) and other essential health communication terms. Available at http://manoffgroup.com/documents/DefiningSBCC.pdf (accessed June 8, 2016).

Oblinger, D. & Oblinger, J. (2005) Is it age or IT: first steps toward understanding the net generation. Available at http://www.educause.edu/research-and-publications/books/educating-net-generation/it-age-or-it-first-steps toward-understanding-net-generation (accessed June 8, 2016).

Palfrey, J. & Gasser, U. (2010) *Born Digital: Understanding the First Generation of Digital Natives*. New York: Basic Books.

Prensky, M. (2001) Digital natives, digital immigrants. Available at http://www.albertomattiacci.it/docs/did/Digital_Natives_Digital_Immigrants.pdf (accessed June 8, 2016).

Rothschild, M. & Gaidis, W. (1981) Behavioral learning theory: its relevance to marketing and promotions. *Journal of Marketing*, 45, 70–78.

Scheufele, D.A. (2002) Differential gains from mass media and their implications for participatory behavior. *Communication Research*, 29(1), 45–64.

Scheufele, D.A. & Tewksbury, D. (2007) Framing, agenda setting, and priming: the evolution of three media effects models. *Journal of Communication*, 57, 9–20.

Shandrow, K.L. (2013) 3 innovative ways startups are driving results over social media. Available at http://www.entrepreneur.com/article/227399 (accessed June 8, 2016).

Shannon, C.E. (1948) A Mathematical Theory of Communication. *The Bell System Technical Journal*, 27, 379–423.

Stelzner, M. (2011) Social Media Marketing Industry Report. How marketers are using social media to grow their businesses. Available at http://www.socialmediaexaminer.com/SocialMediaMarketingReport2011.pdf (accessed June 8, 2016).

Thackeray, R. & Neiger, B.L. (2000) Establishing a relationship between behavior change theory and social marketing: implications for health education. *Journal of Health Education*, 31(6), 331–335.

Tobin, A. (2013) Social justice: Warby Parker, clever marketing, and the power of doing good. Available at http://arcompany.co/social-justice-warby-parker-clever-marketing-and-the-power-of-doing-good/ (accessed June 8, 2016).

Warby Parker (2015) Buy a pair, give a pair. Available at https://www.warbyparker.com/buy-a-pair-give-a-pair (accessed June 8, 2016).

Wood, W. & Neal, D.T. (2009) The habitual consumer. *Journal of Consumer Psychology*, 19(4), 579–592.

Zackon, R. (2009) Grounding-breaking study of video viewing finds younger boomers consume more video media than any other group. Available at http://www.researchexcellence.com/files/pdf/2015-02/id124_vcm_pressrelease_3_26_09.pdf (accessed June 8, 2016).

2

Information Diffusion

Learning Objectives

After reading this chapter, you should be able to:
1 Explain Rogers' diffusion of innovations theory and be able to determine the opportunities and challenges of social media message diffusion.
2 Distinguish the differences between Web 1.0 and Web 2.0 technology structure.
3 Analyze the construct of transparency and understand how to utilize it to maintain control of your social media messages.

Introduction

Chapter 1 explored how our conceptualization of the communication process has shifted from a linear model towards a more transactional process, and examined basic assumptions regarding the role audiences play in the sense-making process. This chapter introduces the basic structures and content of social media technologies. These structures have gone through a similar trend, where audiences have been transformed from passive entities that simply consume online messages (Web 1.0) into active users (Web 2.0) that participate, negotiate and generate content in the information-exchange process.

As a marketer, there is little you can do to account for how your consumers will negotiate and make sense of media texts. You have very little control over personal preferences, life experience, personalities, and internal or external audience noise. However, what you

Strategic Social Media: From Marketing to Social Change, First Edition. L. Meghan Mahoney and Tang Tang.
© 2017 John Wiley & Sons, Inc. Published 2017 by John Wiley & Sons, Inc.

can do is to gain a better sense of how to maximize messages for persuasion. The next three chapters will focus on three historical shifts in behavior change literature: diffusion (Chapter 2), community (Chapter 3), and mobilization (Chapter 4). Each chapter will discuss the significance and takeaways of utilizing social media to prompt behavior change in consumers.

There are many opportunities and challenges for using diffusion, community or mobilization strategies in social media messages. In general, an inverse relationship exists between user participation and message control. Therefore, it is important to make informed decisions about when to use more top-down media approaches for tight control over media messages, and when more participatory approaches are necessary for audience mobilization. To begin, let's focus on Rogers' diffusion of innovation, a foundational linear theory for utilizing mass media for behavior change.

Diffusing Your Message

Marketers and communication specialists have long been interested in how and why new ideas spread through cultures. Have you ever wondered why some trends become popular, while other ideas never take off? It is challenging to predict just how your consumers will respond to a message, in particular when messages are distributed through a mediated channel, rather than through face-to-face communication. When creating a social media message, whether it be promoting a new product or inviting friends to a party, you are hoping that they receive the message and follow through with a desired behavior change. While the process seems simple enough, there are many things that could go wrong along the way. How do you ensure that the message actually reaches the target audience? How do you make the content of the information appropriate and understandable for all members of the audience? What can you do to ensure that the content is enticing enough to prompt behavior change? Everett Rogers (1962) explored this process in his book, *Diffusion of Innovations*. Diffusion of innovations (also referred to as *diffusion of innovations theory* and/or *diffusion*) explains how new ideas spread through media outlets over time among members of a targeted community (Haider & Kreps, 2004). Researchers identified five stages of diffusion of innovations to explain the process: (i) awareness, (ii) interest, (iii) evaluation, (iv) trial, and (v) adoption. This process highlights how important the basic assumptions, preferences and life experience of audiences are to the effectiveness of media messages prove effective. If adoption is successful, individuals will follow through with the new desired behavior change (Rogers, 1976; Haider & Kreps, 2004). A strong understanding of this theory will help marketers, media organizations, political candidates, or even just everyday citizens better understand the diffusion, adoption or rejection of new ideas.

Let's use Apple's launch of the tablet computer, iPad, in 2010 as an example. How does a brand's new innovative technology, unlike any other tablet computer, become a universally known and trusted product? Through Rogers' diffusion of innovations process:

Step 1   Users need to become aware of the iPad's existence. Generally, this is achieved through traditional means of advertising, 'show and tell' displays, or word-of-mouth techniques.

Step 2   Users would have to believe that the message was something that was both <u>targeted</u> <u>to them, targeted to them, and a benefit their everyday life.</u> Prior to Apple's iPad, most tablet computers proved bulky and had limited storage capacity. In order for the iPad to transcend this step, it must offer something unique from alternative products.

Step 3   Users would complete an <u>evaluation of the product</u>. Evaluation can come in many forms, such as buying the product and evaluating whether or not they are satisfied with the results. However, with a high-ticket technology item like an iPad, this is unlikely. More realistically, users would want to do some research on their own. They may search customer reviews online, visit their local Apple store to play with the interface, or ask a friend if they could borrow theirs to see if the technology meets expectations.

Step 4   The <u>trial stage</u> of the diffusion process is the <u>most critical and time-consuming.</u> During this period, users may consider themselves as current satisfied customers of the iPad, but may still be open to alternative products, or disengage if there is social backlash. No one wants to use a previously popular technology that has become unpopular and their friends are going to tease them for it (think of outdated social networking sites here, such as Friendster or Myspace).

Step 5   Finally, a <u>point of saturation</u> is reached where users adopt the technology, in this case the Apple brand. Users may switch their personal computer to an Apple, or invest in a new secondary device, such as the iPhone. Through the diffusion behavior change process, users have transformed into loyal brand advocates. In this final stage, it is the user (consumer) that becomes the disseminator of the brand message to their personal social network.

While this theory does a nice job of explaining the diffusion process, criticisms of this dominant media-centric approach exist (Melkote & Steeves, 2001). Many believe that the diffusion structure allows little room for audience feedback and participation. However, we know from Chapter 1 that audiences are participatory in the information-exchange process. Diffusion of innovations theory demonstrates how unlikely it is for individuals to complete all five stages of the adoption process. They could fall off of the process at any point. Only a small percentage of your audiences will actually reach the adoption phase. Therefore, social media practitioners must learn as much as they can about their audiences to ensure whether audiences actually desire the information that they are hoping to disseminate.

Despite the low likelihood that audiences will reach all five stages of the diffusion process, most advertisers and corporations continue to use linear top-down techniques to reach consumers, such as tweeting messages like "We're having a sale. Buy now!" This could be because these types of messages often prove the most efficient and cost-effective method to reach large audiences, especially through traditional mass communication channels like radio or television commercials. They can reach a large number of individuals with a single message, often referred to as *"push and pray" marketing* (Stratten, 2012).

"Push and pray" marketing indicates that traditional media campaigns distribute their message to as many people as possible to create awareness-only campaigns. Message producers can only hope that message receivers follow the remainder of the behavior change process. Most often, these producers never receive any feedback from their audiences and are unaware whether consumers follow through with the desired behavior change (i.e., purchasing behavior).

While the "push and pray" strategy helps to increase awareness, the importance of interpersonal communication in the decision-making process cannot be overemphasized. A friend's recommendation earns much more than an expert's endorsement. This has always been a struggle that mass media campaigns have dealt with: how can they compete with an interpersonal network of community and friends? Not only do satisfied customers have strong brand loyalty, but they also bring in their own personal network of friends. This is why a community-centric technique is so critical to a successful behavior change campaign (the community-centric technique is discussed in Chapter 3). Nonetheless, today, the interactive nature of social media allows new opportunities for diffusion-centric campaigns. It is easier than ever before for friends to share recommendations through mediated channels. Therefore, let's take a more detailed look at the structural shift in technology use from Web 1.0 to Web 2.0.

Web 1.0 to 2.0 Technology Structure

Technology structure plays a critical role in how we respond, interact with and create media content. Once you understand opportunities and challenges between various media structures, more can be done to manipulate social media messages for behavior change. How does social media differ from traditional mass communication, or even alternative new media platforms? You often hear the term "social media" interwoven between buzzwords such as "user-generated content," "online interactivity" and "Web 2.0." All of these point to the structures and opportunities of social media, but none explicitly explain its definition.

Social media

Chapter 1 explained how social media includes any Internet-based applications that build on the ideological and technological foundations of Web 2.0 and allow the creation and exchange of user-generated content (Kaplan & Haenlein, 2010). *User-generated content* includes everything from blogs, collaborative projects such as Wikipedia, social networking sites such as Facebook, content communities such as YouTube, and virtual game worlds such as World of Warcraft. While social media is an umbrella term that includes all forms of online audience exchange, participation and dialogue, user-generated content is a more specific type of social media that allows audiences to work together to create online content.

Some main characteristics of social media include an online space where users are able to create, share and evaluate content for the purpose of social interaction through social software (Lietsala & Sirkkunen, 2008). These spaces are personalized and hold individual URLs that link to external networks. Often these spaces serve as ever-changing communities, where members post messages free of charge through a tagging system. In addition, there are many functions of social media, including improving identity, conversations, sharing, presence, relationships, reputations and groups (Kietzmann *et al.*, 2011). Marketers who are interested in developing a social media strategy must first understand these various functions and structures and seek for the appropriate balance between each in achieving their marketing goals.

Mass media

Mass media is defined as a group of technologies that allows one-to-many communication through mediated channels (Pearce, 2009). In the context of mass media communication, the audience is seen as large, anonymous and homogeneous, making it an ideal form for information diffusion. If you are interested in broadcasting a message to thousands of users, why not turn to a mass medium such as radio or television? Even as the Internet became a commercial service in the 1990s, most content only addressed audiences in a top-down manner with little interactive features for feedback. If you wished to seek out additional information about a company, you could go to the company's index page and read whatever content they had created. As a user, your role was primarily a passive receiver of information, where you could access information, but not change or respond. However, you were still able to negotiate and make sense of the message according to your own life experiences, preferences and personality, even within the traditional mass media environments, which is why the concept of a "passive audience" was never really true.

The World Wide Web was initially created as a platform to facilitate information exchange between users (Kaplan & Haenlein, 2010). Mangold and Faulds (2009) explain how the first purpose of Internet communication is consistent with traditional mass media tools – to communicate to a large audience. In the early 1990s, most online content resembled traditional published mass media material, where users accessed content created by a relatively small number of publishers who had control over the content. A decade later, in the early 2000s, as participatory technology became more readily available, users began interacting with the content, rather than just consuming the content. Today, we are well into an era of content creation among users. The role of social media (i.e., users communicating with one another) brings about the most opportunities for information distribution (Agichtein *et al.*, 2008). This timeline of interactivity progression from the 1990s to the present is the shift from Web 1.0 content to Web 2.0 distribution (Figure 2.1).

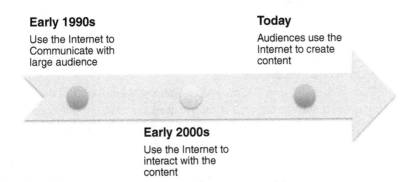

Early 1990s
Use the Internet to Communicate with large audience

Today
Audiences use the Internet to create content

Early 2000s
Use the Internet to interact with the content

Figure 2.1   Timeline interactive progression.

Shift to Web 2.0

Web 1.0 is identified as the era where the Internet was used as a one-to-many model (Cormode & Krishnaumurthy, 2008). Though the Internet was always designed for users to participate with messages, the tools to do so were not always available to audiences. In its initial inception, Internet content tended to mirror traditional mass media structures, where audiences used websites to gain information, not interact with the content. It was not until advancements in interactivity and participation that social media emerged. *Web 2.0* allows any participant to be a content creator, and is exemplified by a large number of niche groups who exchange, tag, comment and link content. These advancements in technology allowed users to share stories, recommendations and communicate directly with a product source.

Indeed, Web 2.0 extends beyond just providing users with the ability for feedback. Wirtz *et al.* (2010) proposed four fundamental constructs to the Web 2.0 phenomenon. Each of these constructs allow for increased participation among users:

- social networking;
- interaction orientation;
- personalization/customization;
- user-added possibilities.

Social networking is the ability for users to find and keep in contact with a personal community, including interpersonal contacts or interest-based networks. Users are able to share thoughts, pictures and events. *Interaction orientation* identifies the interactivity nature of Web 2.0. Users are able to provide feedback and engage with content according to the structure that producers allow. This is one step beyond the individual negotiation and sensemaking process, as users can physically alter the media content. Don't like what you read on Wikipedia? Web 2.0 allows you to change it.

Personalization/customization is the ability for users to pick and choose the content that is of most interest to them. Users can block information, set up personal toolbars and bookmarks, and deny Facebook friends they do not wish to communicate with. All these are ways in which users are taking control of their own Web 2.0 experience. Users demand this feature in almost everything that they access online now, including customized content on CNN.com, Amazon, and ESPN.com (Krishnamurthy *et al.*, 2001). Finally, *user-added possibilities* transform users into producers of Internet content. Audiences are no longer just seeking information/content, but are creating it through Wikis, blogs, video and photo-sharing sites. All these features were not possible in a Web 1.0 environment and maximize behavior change potential in audiences.

This shift from Web 1.0 to Web 2.0 not only allows users more control over their web experience, but it also influences the type of content available. O'Reilly (2007) explains how this user-controlled space allows for collective intelligence, where the blogosphere represents the voice Internet users used to only hear in their heads. For the first time in history, the audience is able to decide what is important, thus turning the concept of a traditional mass media gatekeeper upside down. Web 2.0 allows users the ability to change the media landscape within their society (O'Reilly, 2007). Today's social media users have unlimited opportunities to receive, create or ignore online content, and are proving more empowered and motivated than ever before (Buenting, 2006; Boulos & Wheeler, 2007; Dijck, 2009). This undoubtedly changes historical notions of who and what deserves media and marketers' attention and which groups are left muted.

There are certainly many opportunities for today's Internet users to participate. In fact, it would seem unusual, and perhaps even frustrating, for new media content not to have a participatory feature for feedback, comment or interactivity. Marketers who create mass media campaigns used to struggle between reaching large numbers of individuals and allowing the option for audience participation and dialogue. However, social media resolves this conflict between user participation and message control. There are many times when limiting the amount of participation users have over content may actually be appropriate in order to retain control over the message. In this case, it becomes a choice from marketers to utilize a diffusion approach to behavior change.

For example, the President of the United States of America may choose to limit the amount of participation users have on the White House's official Facebook page. This is an elected office that represents the voice of a country and message control is very important. Moreover, it would prove impossible to create messages that all members of the audience agreed upon. The audience is much larger than the average niche social media site. Although audience participation and engagement are great in terms of behavior change, if the content of your message is critical, it may be wiser to go the route of message diffusion.

Web 2.0 allows the opportunity for increased participation. It is up to the producer of the message to understand when it is best to increase participatory options and when it is best to keep strong control over content. Additionally, every organization should have a space online that diffuses information about the product. Generally, this is the home index page of your organization's website, a place for users to go if they would like to gain more knowledge about your product. Without this "home base," users may begin to distrust your brand. It is critical for every online agency to have a clear transparency strategy and control plan for their brand.

Transparency, Control and Public Relations

In 2010, the household cleaning product company SC Johnson announced its new media campaign, "Family standard of transparency." The first advertisement in the series, "Honesty," emphasizes the company's commitment to disclosing the ingredients in all of its products. CEO Fisk Johnson explains,

> The truth is, companies often don't have to tell you everything that's in their products. But we're a family company that believes in working hard to do what's right for the families who buy our products – and one of the things that means is being transparent with what's in our products.

In a bold move, SC Johnson decided to be more forthcoming about the ingredients in its products, beyond what was regulated and required by government. The hope of this type of marketing move is to bolster ethos with consumers.

The company launched the website www.WhatsInsideSCJohnson.com (SC Johnson, 2010) that diffuses all of the ingredients in the company's products, including fragrances, dyes and preservatives. Why might a cleaning company, in a time when consumers are more critical and conscious of chemicals than ever before, choose to provide a public space to display the ingredients of the products when no one is forcing them to do so? Jensen (2001) explains how there is no better time for marketers to promote their organizations through greater social accountability and transparency.

Amidst an information environment where individuals hold the expectation of accessing *anything* in just a few keystrokes, it is a strong decision for SC Johnson to be in control of how this disclosure reaches its consumers.

Create additional transparency

One of the foundational communication theories, the *theory of social penetration*, explains the relationship between self-disclosure and trust. Researchers demonstrate how the development of relational closeness ranges from individuals with whom we feel a superficial bond to those with whom we feel a more intimate connection. One of the most significant indicators of relational closeness is self-disclosure. The more willing one party is to open up and disclose personal and private information, the closer the receiving party feels towards their relationship. In order for people to trust and connect, both parties must be willing to engage in a level of transparent disclosure (Altman & Taylor, 1973; West, 2009).

Not only is self-disclosure beneficial for interpersonal relationships, but this increased transparency is the expected norm for today's social media marketers. With so many conversations happening online, if a consumer seeks information that a marketer is not willing to disclose, he or she most likely will be able to find it from someplace else. You must take control and not let others write your own brand narrative.

Wright and Hinson (2008) point out how social media creates alternative information channels, making it difficult for organizations to manage and control information diffusion. The more marketers are able to control the transparency, authenticity and accountability of their product, the more opportunities there will be for listening and true dialogue. *Transparency* implies openness, communication and accountability (Phillips & Young, 2009), and the more you are willing to do this, the more your consumers will begin to trust your products.

This idea of transparency is important for all aspects of a company, not just ingredients within a product. In 2008, Apple came under fire for the working conditions of their manufacturing plant, Foxconn, in China. The online public sphere erupted, linking the production of the iPhone with underpaid workers, unpaid overtime hours, extreme working hours, violent supervision, and worker suicides (Warren, 2012). Many Apple users were sharing petitions urging other consumers to boycott Apple within their online social networking circles. This outrage went viral in just a few days.

However, many of the claims presented in the investigative reporting of Foxconn proved exaggerated and false (Smith, 2012). Apple communication specialists found themselves in the middle of a public relations crisis, with little to do but push out traditional press releases stating that claims were untrue. However, users curious in learning more information were not satisfied with the official press releases and found little to no information on Apple's website regarding the company's product production. Therefore, they were relying on alternative media outlets to construct Apple's production narrative. The new CEO of Apple, Tim Cook, seemed unable to answer many of the questions consumers were asking about the scandal.

Having little transparency into the production of Apple products was a mistake by the company. Consumers expect to be able to find out unlimited information regarding merchandise, and if Apple was not going to provide it, others could effectively push forth this narrative, no matter how exaggerated. Fortunately, Apple was able to turn this public relations crisis into a key case study of image rebranding through transparency.

Cook eventually called for a voluntary inspection of Foxconn factories by the Fair Labor Association. This vow to ensure safe business practices was crucial, even though the initial story of wrongdoing was admittedly proven exaggerated. Moreover, Cook personally visited production factories and posted many of his thoughts, findings and pictures from the trip on the Apple website (Apple Press Info, 2012). Now if you were to search the production of Apple products on the Internet, you would encounter a very different narrative. You would see pictures and reports detailing how Apple products are made in a safe and responsible environment. Increased transparency grants corporations the chance to tell their own story.

Apple is not the only company to face a public relations crisis regarding the production of their goods. For nearly four decades Nike was under fire for outsourcing manufacturing plants to lessen costs (Rothenberg-Aalami, 2004). Human rights activists criticized Nike for taking advantage of child workers and for having destructive and unsafe working environments, while making billions of dollars in profit (Hill, 2009). The Nike brand was tarnished by this reputation of being associated with sweatshops.

In 2013, Nike became one of the most transparent companies in the industry. Simply by visiting their webpage, you can find information on annual reports, supply chains, supplier certifications, standards for compliance, and employee training (Figure 2.2). This increase in transparency is just one step in the rebranding efforts of Nike, and part of the reason why it continues as the world's largest athletic shoe and apparel company. It is important that your company also provides this level of ethical consideration and transparency to prevent a public relations crisis.

Though it's easy to assume that these narratives of child workers, sweatshops and unsafe factory working conditions are those from previous generations, it is certainly a human rights issue that garners more and more attention as we continue to grow as a globalized and connected marketplace. While it was once possible to remain ignorant on how consumption decisions impact the world we live in, social media magnifies the lives around us. Unfortunately, oftentimes this attention usually comes as the result of a horrible tragedy.

In April 2013, over 1000 garment workers died and over 2500 were injured when the eight-story Rana Plaza factory building near Dhaka collapsed (BBC, 2013). This tragedy has been referred to "deaths by negligence" as the building had failed a number of safety regulations in prior inspections. Many social media boycotts emerged as news of the tragedy spread (O'Donnell, 2013). This boycott targeted companies such as The Gap, Wal-Mart and other American retail stores that had not yet signed a labor-backed plan to improve factory safety, but instead work on their own alternative plans. In fact, The Gap was one of the

Figure 2.2   Nike transparency website. Source: Screen Capture from Nike's Website.

leading entrepreneurs seeking global *corporate social responsibility* programs, where companies voluntarily incorporate a social good campaign into their business strategy. European companies such as Abercrombie & Fitch that had agreed to the labor-backed plan were not subject to the same public scrutiny after the tragedy, possibly due to the transparency of their production plan over others.

This case demonstrates how social media has become the leading platform for consumers to voice their frustrations and solutions to the products that they buy. Nine out of ten consumers report that they are willing to boycott socially irresponsible companies (O'Donnell, 2013), and many experts believe such tragedies could be avoided if the cost of garments increased by just 10 cents (Covert, 2013). The National Consumers League took this concept and created a Facebook campaign where users were able to pledge to companies that they would be willing to pay 10 cents more for socially responsible garments. Hopefully, as more individuals become aware of such irresponsible business practices, more policies and regulations will be put in place that force companies to make more ethical and transparent decisions regarding the production of their products. It is important to consider a transparency action plan to maintain control over your brand narrative and prevent a public relations crisis.

Transparency Action Plan

There are three steps to create greater social accountability and transparency for your company.

1   Create additional transparency regarding the production, consumption and profit of your product. Ensure that it is visible on the index page of your website.
2   Be transparent about the planned and perceived obsolescence (explained below) of your product.
3   Decide other elements of brand transparency, which will lead to a stronger emotional connection with consumers.

Transparency of your product

Transparency extends beyond just the production of goods, but this is the crucial first step when developing a diffusion plan. It is easy to be transparent about the everyday tasks within an organization such as the employees and wages, but is more challenging when it comes to out-of-house stages, such as manufacturing, shipping and environmental impact. Nonetheless, transparency should also include the mission statement, the consumption and the profit of your products, and long-term satisfaction and customer service.

Organizational *mission statements* come in many formats with various purposes. Swales and Rogers (1995, p. 228) define mission statements as "a management tool for projecting corporate integrity and instilling loyalty and normed behavior in the corporate workforce" but noted the complexities between genres. When crafting a mission statement, it is important to be succinct and consider your organizational goals and objectives. Mission statements should be between one and three sentences in length. Here you should be clear to the audience why you are in your line of business, who your customers are and what you can do for them, and how you differ from your competitors. It is critical to differentiate the mission statement from a company's branding efforts (discussed further in Chapter 3). Mission statements need to focus on ultimate transparency instead of getting too creative with messaging.

It is also important that your organization is forthcoming with the price of your product. Nothing is more frustrating than making your consumers take the time to visit your organization's website and not finding any information regarding how much a good or service costs. Consumers will assume that the price is too expensive to list or that it is negotiable. Even if these assumptions are true of your product, be forthright with consumers on why. Be transparent. Tell your consumers directly that even though your product may cost more than competitors, it is worth the extra money, or why you encourage them to negotiate the price based on their personal needs. Don't leave your customers guessing.

The price of your product goes beyond just a monetary price tag. Whatever it is that you are selling to consumers (yourself to a potential employer, an invitation to a party, or a Facebook status to "like"), you need to be forthcoming about what the cost and benefits are if they follow through with your prompt. How much time are you asking for? Will you be willing to share any information provided? What future obligations are involved? This is the golden rule of communicating: Do unto others as you would have others do unto you. Not doing so will catch up with you eventually, and will leave a lingering impression on how your audience views you.

It is also important to consider the "price" of your product with regard to the global environment. This is a great chance to showcase some of the socially responsible decisions that you made during the production stage of your goods to differentiate yourself from other competitors. Is the packaging of your product recyclable? Be sure to take extra steps to prompt users to do so. Does your organization sponsor local charities or causes in the community? Provide that information too. Tell consumers what social issues are important to you. Disclosing these individual preferences is meaningful to consumers and helps build rapport and trust. Customers prefer to see their hard-earned money go to responsible individuals, not a salesperson who is only interested in selling a product. Finally, in terms of creating transparency of your product, you want to provide information regarding the long-term satisfaction of your product. What lasting impact does your product have on the world?

Planned and perceived obsolescence

When creating a transparency action plan, you also want to consider the planned obsolescence and perceived obsolescence of your product. *Planned obsolescence* is the production of goods with uneconomically short useful lives that force customers to make repeat purchases (Bulow, 1986; Fitzpatrick, 2011). Selling a product that breaks too quickly will turn consumers away and prompt them to buy from someone else. Selling a product that never breaks means that the consumer will never have the need to return for business because their original product is still working. If your product obeys the concept of planned obsolescence, your customers will trust the product after it breaks and will pay additional money to fund a replacement.

The premise behind planned obsolescence is that most rational consumers are short-term oriented when it comes to purchases, meaning they pay for the present value of a service or product. Therefore, in order to maximize profit, some companies construct products to actually break after a period of use. The ethics of this type of business practice has been debated for years. This is another opportunity for complete transparency, especially if you have risen above some of your competitors. Also, encourage your customers to share their experiences with your product or service through social media.

Even though the desirability for a product is a little more difficult to measure and control, it is still an important factor to consider. Kaspar (2004) describes how *perceived obsolescence* is the limitations of products based on social appeal, rather than function. Even though a product may still function correctly as your customers intended with purchase, it is no longer fashionable or appropriate for modern society. This explains why some people upgrade to the newest model of phone or computer even though their previous model still works and serves its intended purpose. If customers are willing to invest in your product, especially if the investment proves substantial, the social desirability of your product may be something worth addressing. How invested is your company in customer loyalty and keeping up with modern updates?

Additional elements of brand transparency

In addition to fostering the transparency of your products and their planned and perceived obsolescence, it is important to consider the profit transparency of your brand. You may want to share information with your customers about the wages and benefits for your employees. This is the most overlooked stage of transparency, as many do not believe it is the business of everyday consumers to know how much employees and CEOs make. However, one of the biggest fuels of the Nike scandal was how huge the margin was between the lowest-level employees and the employees at the top. Companies should strive to empower all members of their organization to feel as though they are a meaningful part of the success. When the organization benefits, all employees should feel as though they benefit as well.

Consumers want to know where their money goes, even once it is out of their hands. Let's refer back to The Gap social media boycott as an example. Say that you work for The Gap. Your consumers received a social media message that asked them to boycott The Gap because the company did not sign a labor-backed plan to improve factory safety for production employees. They then went online to The Gap's website to learn more about the production of your goods. On the website, your consumers learned more about your efforts to seek global corporate social responsibility programs on an individual level. Moreover, they also learned that the company that owns The Gap also owns the garment stores they trust such as Old Navy, Banana Republic, PiperLime and Athleta. Transparency regarding the production of goods and ownership of businesses makes them trust the brand even more. Instead of boycotting The Gap, your consumers may decide to share this information with their social network and support you.

It is important to be transparent about the identity of the head of your organization and what his or her affiliations include. During the summer of 2012, Chick-fil-A's owner Dan Cathy stated in a publicized interview that he opposed same-sex marriage. This prompted many to look into the company's charitable endeavor, the WinShape Foundation (Cline, 2012). Social media erupted when information emerged that millions of dollars from the WinShape Foundation have been made to political organizations that oppose lesbian, gay, bisexual, and transgender (LGBT) rights. Because of this, Jim Henson Co. pulled its Muppets toys from Chick-fil-A's kid meals, and the Mayors of Boston and Chicago publicly expressed opposition to new Chick-fil-A's opening in their cities. Many were outraged to learn about these donations. Others supported the owner's right to free speech and organized a "Chick-fil-A Appreciation Day." While it is not illegal for a CEO to have political or religious views, many loyal customers did not want to contribute their money to such campaigns. It would have been less of a public relations crisis public relations crisis if information was more accessible by the company for audiences.

Perhaps a more surprising political comment made by a CEO was John Mackey of Whole Foods. The mission statement of Whole Foods demonstrates concern for the community, environment and the whole planet, but has come under public scrutiny for high prices and low wages for employees (Mukherjee, 2013). In an interview, Mackey linked Obama's mandatory healthcare program to fascism. He later retracted this statement, saying it was a "bad choice of language." However, the statement proved a costly mistake, as 89% of Whole Foods stores in the United States are in counties that support Barack Obama and likely support the mandatory healthcare program (Stolbert, 2011). It is important to again note that there is nothing illegal or even unethical about the head of a company having political affiliations or religious beliefs. However, it was the lack of transparency that consumers felt slighted by in both of these examples.

There are many companies that have utilized social media to provide transparency regarding their employees' wages and working conditions. Some simply disclose in job postings under the "human resource" tab on their home page. Others allow employees to blog about their experiences on the company's website. These extra efforts allow consumers to feel good about putting their money towards these organizations and the individual lives that they are helping by doing so.

Zappos.com has taken this transparency strategy one step further and allows consumers to take a 60-minute tour through their Zappos headquarters in Las Vegas, Nevada to learn about the Zappos Family culture. During the tour, consumers experience "how a values-based organization uses strong culture to live out every day." They can also take a free (and funny) virtual tour through the Zappos website at http://www.zapposinsights .com/tours/virtual. When consumers order a pair of shoes from Zappos, they are introduced to an actual employee from Zappos, making it a more personal experience.

Finally, and perhaps most importantly, companies should be transparent about the societal benefits of their organization. This is, if nothing else, a smart branding and marketing strategy. While we will explore the marketing benefits and how to link these societal benefits to socially responsible business models in later chapters, it is important to note here that societal benefits should be as specific and tangible as possible. Use social media to provide pictures of the actual people, places or initiatives that your customers are benefiting from your service. Don't just say that your product is "green"; demonstrate visually and specifically state what that means for your organization. If your product is linked to a cause or charity, be specific about the percentage of profits that are donated. This will increase sales, while keeping your organization out of trouble.

You should also consider including a blog in addition to a home index page for increased transparency. This blog should not necessarily be centered around the promotion and selling of your products, but instead be a place that consumers want to visit, even if they have no interest in purchasing your products. It is important to remember the value of forming relationships with individuals outside your niche audience. Whole Foods, an American food supermarket specializing in natural and organic food, has a blog that shares healthy eating recipes; PetSmart, a retail of pet supplies, has a blog for pet safety; and Lowe's, a home improvement and appliance store, has a blog for "Do It Yourself" ideas. Each of these offers something for people who are not just looking to buy products.

It is also important to implement this strategy even, and perhaps especially, when the product you are promoting is yourself. For example, when Philippe Dubost, a web product

Figure 2.3   Amazon résumé. Source: http://phildub.com. Reproduced with permission of Philipee Dubost.

manager from Paris, was looking for a job, he decided to develop a social online résumé that resembled the infrastructure of an Amazon product page (Phil Dub, 2014) (Figure 2.3). The résumé was traditional in many senses; it provided the usual professional content, including experience in the field, education and recommendations (found under the "Product reviews" section of an Amazon page). However, Dubost was able to give employers a better sense of his own skills and characteristics by increasing the amount of transparency regarding many professional and personal elements in his life. Rather than simply stating that he is open to traveling for work, Dubost included a link to his personal travel blog, where employers were able to see pictures, read about travel experiences and see a proficiency in multiple languages. He also provided snippets of private sphere information regarding personal hobbies, by pairing his product with a favorite pair of running shoes and a link to his personal Tumblr blog. Interested companies can even add his résumé to their cart to see his price of hire.

Of course, these additional links all showcased Dubost in a positive manner – who wouldn't want to be associated with marathon running? Technology allows an opportunity for job seekers to increase the amount of positive information employers are able to receive in an easy-to-navigate and interesting way. Be forthcoming with this information so that employers do not feel that they have to search alternative platforms to find out more. By taking control of your own online content and being transparent with private information, you are providing your own narrative with the public information that you want to be included. The online Amazon-style résumé received over 1.3 million unique visitors from 219 countries and landed Dubost a job working with BirchBox in New York City.

In sum, increasing transparency is a necessary step in today's digital landscape. Your consumers have unlimited access to information at their fingertips, and if you don't provide information regarding your product, someone else will. Moreover, increased transparency leads to a stronger connection with consumers. Transparency should be considered at every level, including production, consumption and profit.

Case Study: Shell *Arctic Ready*

This chapter has discussed the importance of transparency, and how an increase in openness, communication and accountability leads to an increase of trust and connection. Diffusing social media messages can be the best strategy for marketing practitioners who primarily wish to stay in control over their brand narrative. Though message diffusion does not have the greatest likelihood for behavior change, it is the safest option for preventing a public relations crisis. Greenpeace and the Yes Lab understood this control continuum, and really wanted to ignite behavior change in their audience. Therefore, they purposefully offered a limited amount of transparency to users in their campaign *Arctic Ready*. While a strong diffusion strategy is usually a good thing for organizations, this case study demonstrates how a lack of communication and transparency, and an increase in user control with social media messages, led to a public relations disaster for Royal Dutch Shell's drilling venture.

In 2012, Greenpeace, the self-proclaimed "largest independent direct-action environmental organization in the world" (Greenpeace, 2013), and the Yes Lab, an organization devoted to "helping progressive organizations and individuals carry out media-getting creative actions around well-considered goals" (Yes Lab, 2013), teamed up in protest to create a social media campaign *Arctic Ready* (http://arcticready. com/). The campaign was designed as a protest against Royal Dutch Shell for their $4 billion investment in Arctic drilling after Royal Dutch Shell had announced plans to begin exploratory drilling efforts in the Beaufort and Chukchi seas (Zeller, 2012).

Greenpeace and Yes Lab were looking for ways to inspire behavior change in audiences to protest the venture. They knew that an informative website that simply diffused information about the dangers of drilling in a top-down fashion was a strong way to control the flow of information, but it would likely bore audiences and would not prove very viral in nature. Instead, they decided to create a Web 2.0 *Arctic Ready* social media campaign. The *Arctic Ready* website had the appearance of being produced and managed by Royal Dutch Shell, including the logo, colors, format and language of the oil corporation's website. However, it wasn't run by Royal Dutch at all. It purposefully diffused very little transparency about who was in charge of the website and instead gave users control of content features that appeared to be advertisements for Royal Dutch Shell. This lack of control undoubtedly created a public relations disaster for Royal Dutch Shell.

Users of the site believed that the website was designed by the Royal Dutch Shell Corporation, and could not believe that a company with such a controversial product would allow interactivity and participation from consumers. They happily participated with the campaign, writing disparaging comments about Royal Dutch Shell Corporation over the photos of cute animals, such as polar bears and other wild animals (Figure 2.4). Audiences also played "Angry Bergs," a game designed to melt icebergs before they got too close to oil rigs, and take an online pledge to sponsor a failed drilling platform. This unconventional hoax campaign prompted user interaction over diffusion on almost every page.

ONCE UPON A TIME, OUR HOME WAS CLEAN AND BEAUTIFUL. THEN SHELL SAID LET'S GO.

Figure 2.4   *Arctic Ready* campaign. Source: http://articready.com/artic. Reproduced with permission of Mike Bonanno.

By giving up control of their message, *Arctic Ready* was met with the snark of everyday Internet users. Users shared their messages with their social network, believing it to be a public relations disaster for the company. The *Arctic Ready* campaign garnered 1.8 million page views in just two days (Stenovec, 2012). Though this campaign purposefully neglected the amount of transparency in their social media messages with the purpose of creating public relations backlash in order to hurt Royal Dutch Shell Corporation, you do not want to do the same for your company.

One big takeaway from this online campaign hoax (and public relations disaster for Royal Dutch Shell) is that if you give users just enough space to participate with your message, you're going to hear what they think of your product. If you utilize a strong diffusion strategy with a strong amount of transparency, you will regain more control over your brand narrative. Greenpeace and Yes Lab knew this, and rather than just diffusing information in a top-down manner about Royal Dutch Shell, they decided it would be much more effective if users were able to create the messages themselves. While you may get many messages that you're not looking for when you open up the channels for communication, it is an opportunity to gain a sense of how the public feels towards a brand or initiative. This type of participatory feedback can be invaluable for marketers.

Discussion questions

1   One of the greatest advantages of utilizing a diffusion approach in your communication strategy is that you are able to maintain tight control over message content. How was the *Arctic Ready* campaign able to utilize Web 2.0 components to shift the Royal Dutch Shell website from a diffusion-centered space to a place where audiences had more control of the message?

2   Consider the amount of diffusion-centric messages that you receive in a day, including billboard, radio, television, and online advertisements. Why were users more likely to share a participatory campaign such as *Arctic Ready* than they would be to share a diffusion-centric message, causing it to go viral?

3   When designing the *Arctic Ready* campaign, Greenpeace and Yes Lab decided that it would be more effective to have users create satirical messages poking fun at Royal Dutch Shell, rather than just transforming the website to reflect their position on environmental issues. Based on what you know about the behavior change process, why are Web 2.0 structures so much more powerful in enticing long-term behavior change?

Summary

This chapter focuses on the structure and content of social media. Specifically, it has explored how audiences have transformed from passive entities that consume online messages (Web 1.0) into active users (Web 2.0) that participate, negotiate and generate content in an information-exchange process. Diffusion of innovations explains how a new idea is able to spread through media outlets over time among members of a targeted community via a process of awareness, interest, evaluation, trial, and adoption.

There are many challenges with a diffusion-centric approach to a successful social media marketing campaign and behavior change. We learned in this chapter that if just one of the steps is not met, adoption becomes less likely. In general, an inverse relationship exists between user participation and message control. However, message diffusion does allow for tight control over media messages. If you are unsure of the public dialogue surrounding your product, or you are in a position where message dissemination is crucial (i.e., the White House), strict message diffusion may be the most appropriate option (Table 2.1).

Regardless of your product, you should always allow an online space where users can go to find out more information that is controlled by the message source. This "home base" is generally the index page on your company's website. In addition, alternative social media platforms need to be included to provide additional participatory features, and to answer any transparency questions your consumers may have. Companies with limited transparency

Table 2.1 Diffusion: a single media message designed for homogeneous mass audience dissemination.

Pros	Cons
Efficient way to reach a mass audience	Not a personalized method of distribution
Cost-effective	Limited audience participation
Disseminates large amount of product information in one place	Top-down content is less interesting to audiences
Allows tight control over media message	Low likelihood of audience adoption

begin to lose control over their own narratives, and as more users participate, the message becomes more and more diluted. Transparency is necessary in today's social media landscape, and should be considered at every level of your product process. If you choose not to make this transparent move, you are allowing others to control your brand narrative.

If you are willing to give up some of the control that strict message diffusion allows and encourage more participation from your audience, you will begin to increase the chances for behavior change. However, this is a much riskier marketing strategy that requires a solid understanding of community building and identification development. Let's explore these participatory approaches more in Chapter 3.

Key Takeaways

1 Diffusion of innovations is a foundational model for behavior change, which allows tight control over media messages, providing consumers with increased information and disclosure about your product.
2 A diffusion strategy is ideal for practitioners who are introducing a new product, managing a public relations crisis, or disseminating a message with high importance.
3 Diffusion strategies should disclose information about all three stages of a product life cycle: production, consumption, and the profit.
4 Your company's website should include a mission statement, the cost of the product, long-term satisfaction, customer service, the message source, wages and benefits for employees, planned and perceived obsolescence, and societal benefits.
5 Message transparency is important. Today's consumers are expecting more disclosure about the products and organizations than ever before. There is a strong correlation between self-disclosure and feelings of trust in a relationship. This trust will keep consumers coming back to a message source.

References

Agichtein, E., Castillo, C., Donato, D., Gionis, A. & Mishne, G. (2008) Finding high-quality content in social media. In: *Proceedings of the International Conference on Web Search and Web Data Mining*, pp. 183–194. New York: Association of Computing Machinery.

Altman, I. & Taylor, D. (1973) *Social Penetration: The Development of Interpersonal Relationships*. New York: Holt.

Apple Press Info (2012) Fair labor association begins inspections of Foxconn. Available at http://www.apple.com/pr/library/2012/02/13Fair-Labor-Association-Beg ins-Inspections-of-Foxconn.html (accessed June 8, 2016).

BBC (2013) Bangladesh factory collapse toll passes 1,000. Available at http://www.bbc.co.uk/news/world-asia-22476774 (accessed June 8, 2016).

Boulos, K. & Wheeler, S. (2007) The emerging Web 2.0 social software: an enabling suite of sociable technologies in health and healthcare education. *Health Information and Libraries Journal*, 24(1), 2–23.

Buenting, D. (2006) *Audience involvement with Yellow Card, an entertainment-education initiative promoting safe-sex behavior among African youth*. Dissertation, Regent University, Virginia Beach, USA.

Bulow, J. (1986) An economic theory of planned obsolescence. *Quarterly Journal of Economics*, 101(4), 729–749.

Cline, S. (2012) Chick-fil-A's controversial gay marriage beef. Available at http://www.usnews.com/news/articles/2012/07/27/chick-fil-as-controversial-gay-marriage-beef (accessed June 8, 2016).

Cormode, G. & Krishnamurthy, B. (2008) Key differences between Web 1.0 and 2.0. *First Monday*, 13(6).

Covert, B. (2013) Bangladesh factory upgrades could cost consumers as little as 10 cents per garment. Available at http://thinkprogress.org/economy/2013/05/07/1972201/bangladesh-factory-upgrades-consumers (accessed June 8, 2016).

Dijck, J. (2009) Users like you? Theorizing agency in user-generated content. *Media, Culture and Society*, 31, 31–58.

Fitzpatrick, K. (2011) *Planned Obsolescence: Publishing, Technology, and the Future of the Academy*. New York: New York University Press.

Greenpeace (2013) Greenpeace USA. http://www.greenpeace.org/usa/en/ (accessed June 8, 2016).

Haider, M. & Kreps, G. (2004) Forty years of diffusion of innovations: utility and value in public health. *Journal of Health Communication*, 9, 3–11.

Hill, C. (2009) *International Business: Competing in the Global Marketplace*. New York: McGraw-Hill/Irwin.

Jensen, I. (2001) Public relations and emerging functions of the public sphere: an analytical framework. *Journal of Communication Management*, 6, 133–147.

Kaplan, A.M. & Haenlein, M. (2010) Users of the world, unite! The challenges and opportunities of social media. *Business Horizons*, 53(1), 59–68.

Kaspar, R. (2004) Technology and loneliness in old age. *Gerontechnology*, 3(1), 42–48.

Kietzmann, J., Hermkens, K., McCarthy, I. & Silvestre, B. (2011) Social media? Get serious! Understanding the functional building blocks of social media. *Business Horizons*, 54(3), 241–251.

Krishnamurthy, B., Wills, C. & Zhang, Y. (2001) On the use and performance of content distribution networks. In: *Proceedings of the 1st ACM SIGCOMM Workshop on Internet Measurement*, pp. 169–182. New York: Association of Computing Machinery.

Lietsala, K. & Sirkkunen, E. (2008) Social media: introduction to the tools and processes of participatory economy. Available at http://tampub.uta.fi/bitstream/handle/10024/65560/978-951-44-7320-3.pdf?sequence=1firstmonday.org/htbin/cgiwrap/bin/ojs/index.php/fm/article/viewArticle/2138/1945 (accessed June 8, 2016).

Mangold, W.G. & Faulds, D.J. (2009) Social media: the new hybrid element of the promotion mix. *Business Horizons*, 52(4), 357–365.

Melkote, S.R. & Steeves, H.L. (2001) *Communication for Development in the Third World: Theory and Practice for Empowerment*. New Delhi: Sage Publications.

Mukherjee, S. (2013) Whole Foods CEO: Obamacare is "like fascism". Available at http://thinkprogress.org/health/2013/01/16/1456571/whole-foods-obamacare-/ (accessed June 6, 2016).

O'Donnell, J. (2013) Most would boycott irresponsible company. Available at http://www.usatoday.com/story/money/business/2013/05/21/consumers-boycott-companies-bad-behavior-gap-protests/2343619/ (accessed June 8, 2016).

O'Reilly, T. (2007) What is Web 2.0: design patterns and business models for the next generation of software. *International Journal of Digital Economics*, 65, 17–37. Available at http://mpra.ub.uni-muenchen.de/4578/ (accessed June 8, 2016).

Pearce, K. (2009) Media and mass communication theories. In: S.W. Littlejohn & K.A. Foss (eds) *Encyclopedia of Communication Theory*, pp. 623–627. Thousand Oaks, CA: Sage Publications.

Phil Dub (2014) Philippe Dubost: Web product manager. http://phildub.com/ (accessed June 8, 2016).

Phillips, D. & Young, P. (2009) *Online Public Relations: A Practical Guide to Developing an Online Strategy in the World of Social Media*, 2nd edn. London: Kogan Page.

Rogers, E. (1962) *Diffusion of Innovations*. New York: Free Press.

Rogers, E. (1976) Communication and development: the passing of the dominant paradigm. *Communication Research*, 3(2), 213–240.

Rothenberg-Aalami, J. (2004) Coming full circle? Forging missing links along Nike's integrated production networks. *Global Networks*, 4(4), 335–354.

SC Johnson (2010) SC Johnson debuts its new family standard of transparency. Available at http://www.scjohnson

.com/en/press-room/press-releases/11-24-2010/SC-
JOHNSON-DEBUTS-ITS-NEW-FAMILY-STANDARD
-OF-TRANSPARENCY.aspx (accessed June 8, 2016).

Smith, C. (2012) "This American Life" retracts Mike Daisey story about Foxconn factory visit. Available at http://www.huffingtonpost.com/2012/03/16/this-american-life-mike-daisey-retraction-foxconn_n_1353933.html (accessed June 8, 2016).

Stenovec, T. (2012) Shell Arctic Ready hoax website by Greenpeace takes Internet by storm. Available at http://www.huffingtonpost.com/2012/07/18/shell-arctic-ready-hoax-greenpeace_n_1684222.html (accessed June 8, 2016).

Stolbert, S. (2011) You want compromise? Sure you do. Available at http://www.nytimes.com/2011/08/14/sunday-review/you-want-compromise-sure-you-do.html?_r=0 (accessed June 8, 2016).

Stratten, S. (2012) *UnMarketing: Stop Marketing. Start Engaging*. Hoboken, NJ: John Wiley & Sons, Inc.

Swales, J.M. & Rogers, P.S. (1995) Discourse and the projection of corporate culture: the mission statement. *Discourse and Society*, 6(2), 223–242.

Warren, C. (2012) Petitions demand Apple improve Foxconn conditions. Available at http://mashable.com/2012/01/31/apple-supplier-petitions (accessed June 8, 2016).

West, R. (2009) *Introducing Communication Theory: Analysis and Application*, 4th edn. New York: McGraw-Hill.

Wirtz, B., Schilke, O. & Ullrich, S. (2010) Strategic development of business models: implications of the Web 2.0 for creating value on the Internet. *Long Range Planning*, 43(2–3), 272–290.

Wright, D. & Hinson, M. (2008) How blogs and social media are changing public relations and the way it is practiced. *Public Relations Society of America*, 2(2), 1–21.

Yes Lab (2013) What's the Yes Lab? Available at http://www.yeslab.org (accessed June 8, 2016).

Zeller, T. (2012) Shell's Arctic Drilling venture stumbles toward reality. Available at http://www.huffingtonpost.com/tom-zeller-jr/shell-arctic-drilling_b_1679697.html (accessed June 8, 2016).

3

Establishing Community

Learning Objectives

After reading this chapter, you should be able to:
1 Explain the importance of community and user dialogue exchange.
2 Understand the power of social networks in the behavior change process.
3 Define authenticity and message branding in order to incorporate them into a strategic marketing proposal.

Introduction

Chapter 2 focused on the structure and content of social media technologies. We learned how audiences have transformed online content from Web 1.0 messages into more interactive Web 2.0 messages. Despite the increased options for interactivity and participation, most behavior change strategies still utilize diffusion approaches, where a single message is disseminated to a mass audience with limited opportunity for active participation. This method proves best if your primary objective is maintaining tight control over your media message. However, a more effective and empowering approach to incite behavior change in audiences is to build interest and dialogue through communities.

This chapter explores the power of community persuasion and why individuals are so influenced by their own-networked community. Imagine a world where all mass media were social in nature. What if you turned on your television set, and your best friend was on the screen encouraging you to buy the same brand of yogurt that she eats every day. For the first time in history, social media makes this type of personal network promotion possible.

Strategic Social Media: From Marketing to Social Change, First Edition. L. Meghan Mahoney and Tang Tang.
© 2017 John Wiley & Sons, Inc. Published 2017 by John Wiley & Sons, Inc.

Remember that social media is built around principles of interactivity, participation, creation, and exchange (Kaplan & Haenlein, 2010). These structural features are the reason that 67% of online adults utilize social networking sites (Pew Internet Research, 2013). It is more exciting to receive media messages from those you know interpersonally and have already built a relationship with, than strangers who are trying to sell you products for profit. We tend to call the second types of messages spam.

Humans naturally seek community. Hopefully, you cherish those in your own social network and have filled it with individuals that you identify with, admire, and model, as these are the people through which you are socially constructing your own world. This chapter explores how these same people are fueling your own consumption habits and behavioral decisions. More importantly, it explains how a marketing practitioner is able to utilize these social media communities to fulfill the needs and expectations of consumers.

Community Development Theory

Individuals are unable to escape the culture in which they live. You may be able to resist certain cultural rituals or expectations, but you are still very much influenced by the world and people around you. These cultural norms shape who we are and how we behave. Therefore, it is important for social media marketing practitioners to take great efforts in getting to know as much as possible about how their audience lives through a thorough audience analysis. An *audience analysis* helps practitioners identify pertinent elements regarding audience demographics and psychographics. Generally, this research helps practitioners construct media messages that are appropriate and appealing to their target audience. These culturally specific messages are an important part of the behavior change process.

Cultural theorists have long examined cultural insights in order to best identify how individuals make meaning out of situations, events and relationships (Thompson *et al.*, 1990). This body of research demonstrates how individuals socially construct themselves through the world around them. Media is a large institution of power within this social system. Therefore, it is a powerful vehicle for behavior change, provided producers understand the role of media audiences.

Bandura's *social learning theory* helps explain the power media has in influencing our everyday behaviors. This theory views audiences as self-developing, proactive, self-regulating, and self-reflecting. Though media does influence the way we behave, it is just one small piece of a much larger equation. Humans are not just reactive in nature (Bandura, 2004). People are producers of social systems, rather than merely products. We are able to comprehend and regulate our environment and make meanings regarding what we see (Bryant & Oliver, 2009). Through these experiences, we process symbols into cognitive models that serve as guides for judgment and action. How influential these experiences can be depends on personal determinants, behavioral determinants, and environmental determinants.

Social learning theory also suggests that humans learn through modeling the behaviors of others. We are very much influenced by the people in our daily lives. While media can present images and behaviors of characters to model, the real-life interpersonal relationships and cultural norms around us provide much stronger models for how we act. It is much more persuasive to hear a recommendation from a friend than from a character on a television commercial. This is why the power of community is of such great importance to social media marketing practitioners.

Often, society loses sight of the complex sense-making process and credits media effects for poor decision-making by others. Playing one violent video game will not prompt someone to act violently in real life, even if cable newscasters continually make this connection in their broadcasting coverage. A person's social network and life experience play a stronger role in how they subsequently behave. However, this does not mean that as a practitioner you should not be concerned with audience behavior change. It is just important to realize how difficult it is to influence behavior change through a single mass media message. This is why diffusion techniques so often fail to prompt change.

Organizations have always been concerned with ways to create the strongest media messages to spark behavior change. Social learning theory highlights the importance of identification in this decision-making process. People are more likely to model behavior if they identify with the person they are viewing, and if it results in valued outcomes (Bryant & Oliver, 2009). Audiences may not necessarily need to experience those same behaviors in order to make a change (Bandura, 2004). Instead, they see that someone with whom they identify enjoy success when behaving in a certain manner, and that experience becomes a part of their own cognitive process. Identification with media messages is a crucial step in the modeling process. This is why it is essential for social media marketing practitioners to develop messages that are consistent with their target consumers' life experience.

The greatest advantage to social media marketing is that the characters portrayed on social networks are actually those within our interpersonal network. We already identify and relate with them. Social media allows you to see the behaviors of your social network in a new way. You can see your friends conduct product reviews on YouTube, brag about the large discount they received at a department store, or rave about a new restaurant that opened in town. You identify with these individuals and are prompted to engage in the same behaviors. This community dialogue is able to promote collective action that produces a change in behavior (Figueroa *et al.*, 2002).

Word-of-mouth marketing, where current satisfied customers recommend a service to other potential customers, has always proved a strong vehicle for sales/promotion. However, previous generations were bound by proximity to target audiences through this strategy. Marketing practitioners could only rely on current satisfied customers to promote products to those who live a reasonable distance from the marketplace. Today's social media landscape allows for a global marketplace where people are able to seek the products and merchandise that best suit their needs, without the constraints of proxemics.

Community is a natural necessity for humans. It guides how we perceive our daily decision-making processes and ourselves. We grow looking to others as a model for our own behavior, and this continues as we grow. Your audience is going to talk to each other about their experiences with your product no matter what. By only promoting messages through a diffusion strategy, you allow these conversations to happen behind a closed door. By promoting dialogue through social media, you allow for increased word-of-mouth marketing and are able to rectify any unpleasant experiences your customers may have. Diffusion

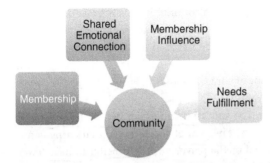

Figure 3.1   Community dimensions.

strategies allow marketers to talk with a mass audience with a single media message. Community strategies allow audiences to talk with each other through mediated channels.

There are many structural elements of social media that make community dialogue possible. A discussion forum is a great place for users to communicate with one another about shared goals. Other social media platforms also have their own dialogue features. One of the best places to encourage conversation is on your product's Facebook wall. Here you can ask your audience questions about their lifestyles and interests. Try not to use this space as a place to sell your product. Keep the focus as much on your audience as possible so that they feel as though it is their place to achieve community.

There are four dimensions to establishing this sense of community: membership, shared emotional connection, influence, and needs fulfillment (McMillan & Chavis, 1986) (Figure 3.1). As a social media marketing/communication practitioner, it is imperative that you meet each of these dimensions for your audiences when trying to promote a space for community, as they allow individuals to share in an identity, the conditions and constraints of power, and a set of social representation, as well as allow participation from members (Campbell & Jovchelovitch, 2000).

Individuals must feel as though they have done something to become a member of an organization before they can feel they are a part of the community. Many organizations establish a sense of membership through frequent-buyer clubs or by sending people exclusive benefits. Traditional public relations professionals conduct audience analyses to determine which demographic, or niche, is most likely to buy their product, and then explore like-minded characteristics (age, gender, education level, ethnicity) among these audiences to help make target decisions. While this is an effective way to target a group of individuals, with the new technologies social media professionals today can take the audience analysis one step further and actually target individuals.

As a marketer, you should try not to get too caught up in targeting individuals who are already likely to purchase your product or follow through with an intended behavior change. Instead, you should focus your energy on a secondary audience, which does not yet know that they would benefit from your service. It is very likely that the individuals most inclined to seek out and buy your product will continue to do so. You want to capture the latent niche, or potential audience. We will discuss this process further in Chapter 9.

The second critical step to establishing membership is building emotional connectedness between members. Think about the many groups and organizations that you belong to on your own social media. Chances are you have joined a community where you do not know anyone else in the group. Perhaps you only joined because a friend sent a request and the cause was important to him or her. While there is no harm in joining, you may not feel emotionally vested in the purpose of the group or the people inside. Even though you are a member of the community, you do not identify yourself within it. Simply being a member of an organization does not make it a community.

As you begin to target consumers online, be sure that you're not getting too obsessed with having high numbers of fans or followers. The goal of social media marketing is not to become the most popular kid on the social media playground. It is better to have fewer emotionally vested members than to have thousands of people who do not identify with your product. It is easy to gain members online. There are numerous sites you can go to, pay a sum of money, and they will increase your numbers depending on the amount of money paid. However, what does this really do for business or your organizational goals?

We learned in Chapter 2 about social penetration theory. One of the most significant indicators of relational closeness among humans is self-disclosure. The more willing one party is to open up and disclose personal private-sphere information, the closer the receiving party feels towards their relationship. Therefore, you must provide a space for dialogue that seems safe enough that community members feel emotionally safe to disclose.

Often media is seen as a *public sphere*, a place people gather to discuss "water cooler" issues of civic activity, such as news, politics, weather, and sports (Habermas, 1991). However, social media allows a chance for media content to center around *private sphere* issues, such as family, relationships, goals, values, and health. If a community member feels comfortable disclosing at this intimate level of disclosure, members will be more likely to feel emotionally connected to the organization. There certainly is a complicated balance with the quantity of ideal social media disclosure. We all know someone in our social network who we feel discloses too much information. It can be unsafe to ask people to disclose personal information on a public forum. Thus, social media marketers need to find a balance between public and private sphere to create this emotional connectedness for their consumers.

A great way to establish this balance is to promote member influence within your organization. Make members feel as though their participation and contribution within your community matter. Ask them to share recipes, experiences and pictures. Feature a fan of the week. Let them know that you value their opinion and input. Ask for critical criticism and then embrace it.

One example of a company that rebranded itself through community influence is Dominos Pizza. In 2010, Dominos launched a marketing campaign that depicted video clips of customers criticizing how their pizza tasted. This footage took clips from their focus groups and illustrated disheartened reactions about the taste and quality of their product. CEO J. Patrick Doyle admitted in these advertisements that changes needed to be made to their pizza recipe. This risky approach to marketing certainly cut through the noise of other advertisements, as it was able to reinvent a brand and show authenticity in customer care (Oches, 2010). Over a series of stages throughout the year of Dominos Recipe Reinvention, sales rose by 14.3%, a jump almost unheard of in an established food industry. This case demonstrates an important lesson for marketers: Show customers that you're really listening to what they have to say, and you will be rewarded.

The final stage in establishing community is needs fulfillment. Hopefully you are confident that your product serves a purpose. This stage of community building should draw from your mission statement (see Chapter 2). Ask your audience questions often so that you are able to hear how being a member of your community benefits them. Be sure to keep attention on your audiences, not your product, when communicating.

As discussed in Chapter 1, people prefer routine in their lives. It is incredibly difficult to prompt individuals to change their status quo, especially if the benefits of doing so are not presented clearly. Remember how the theory of cognitive dissonance demonstrates how humans seek consonance between their expectations and reality (Festinger, 1962). This means that we become uncomfortable when our ideas, beliefs, values, or emotional reaction expectations are not met. If your loyal customers receive information that is not consistent with that brand loyalty, they will have a motivational drive to reduce dissonance by adding new cognitions or reducing importance of the dissonance element.

One of the founding goals of communication is to spark interpersonal dialogue that promotes cultural identity, trust and commitment (Waisbord, 2001). Imagine how difficult these constructs are for an organization that audiences know is just trying to sell them a product. By relying instead on an individual's social network, you allow a sense of ownership to community members through the sharing and reconstructing of experiences. Rather than disseminating information from the top to the bottom, communication becomes a process where everyone discusses possibilities together. This more human-centered approach believes that the role of media and technologies should be used to supplement rather than dominate interpersonal methods (Gray-Felder & Deane, 1999; Waisbord, 2001). Based on this understanding, an action plan for establishing community through social media is outlined below.

Sense of Community Action Plan

There are five steps towards maximizing a sense of community.

1 Establish criteria that individuals must meet in order to join your social network. Though you may lose some audience members, those that do commit will feel that it holds exclusivity.

2 Focus audience research on a slightly less obvious secondary niche audience. These users are likely not targeted by any of your competitors and could increase your return on investment.

3 Prompt dialogue between users as much as possible by asking questions. Try centering conversation on private-sphere issues, rather than public, when appropriate.

4 Identify key members of your community and promote them often through giveaways or feature stories.

5 Continuously monitor and evaluate how satisfied customers are with your service.

Community participation is empowering and allows individuals to reclaim their interests in the public sphere, reaffirms their identity in relation to other social groups, and allows for better decision- making (Campbell & Jovchelovitch, 2000). As you can imagine, individuals hate being told what to do, particularly if they feel as though they are being talked down to. Remember this when creating your social media messages. Value your audiences and promote community rather than top-down advertising. Perhaps most importantly, social capital values human diversity and uses participation and empowerment as formative goals of communication (Kretzmann & McKnight, 1993). Thus, once you reach a place where communication is exchanged naturally within a community, members begin to trust in one another (Perkins & Long, 2002).

Behavior Change and the Power of Social Networks

Millennials are often criticized for having too many social networks with too many acquaintances. For example, Facebook users who are 18–34 years old had an average of over 300 friends (Pew Internet, 2012); the Russian young adult social networking sensation LiveJournal, or Zhivoy Zhurnal (ZheZhe), has a monthly audience of 8.7 million users (Greenall, 2012); and 70% of the users of China's popular microblogging site, Weibo (Sina Weibo), are those aged 19–35 years old (Nakao, 2012).

Putnam's (2001) book *Bowling Alone* criticizes young generations for having the lowest trends of civic engagement and social capital, citing new technologies as an eroder of social capital. It is filled with statistics showing decreased numbers of individuals marching on Washington, enrolling in the army, and volunteering at local charity organizations. However, millennials should take issue with this claim. It's not as though younger audiences care less about the world they live in. Instead, their sense of community has simply shifted with the opportunities of new technology.

Today's social media users have access to more information, more people and more cultures than any previous generation. Though they may not be volunteering at the local community Red Cross, this does not mean that they are not engaged in the world. Consider your own passions and philanthropies. Maybe you are concerned with bringing clean water to developing countries (charitywater.org) or invested in the end of human trafficking (PEHT) around the world. Your sense of the world in which you live is much larger than your parents' and grandparents'. It is easy for you to find socially positive organizations that fit within your own schemata of experience today. These online causes may be far removed from your personal proxemic community, but it is still possible to feel strongly attached to the community goals and mission.

Community is no less important to the millennial generation than it was to any previous generation. Bandura (2002) explains how personal agency operates within a broad network of sociostructural influences. We see and construct ourselves in relation to others. More importantly, our sense of mattering and importance also hinge on those we surround ourselves with. This has not changed. We need the community of others in order to have an understanding of our own selves. The ideals of our own culture help us see who we are and how we fit within it.

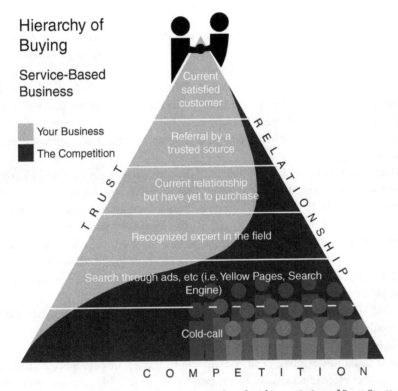

Figure 3.2 Hierarchy of buying. Source: Reproduced with permission of Scott Stratten.

As consumers, we rely on others' opinions to make purchasing decisions for the majority of our transactions (Trusov *et al.*, 2009). Word-of-mouth marketing is 30 times stronger than media marketing. There is no other marketing technique that provides returns this high. In particular, word-of-mouth marketing proves influential when it comes to obtaining new customers. Regardless of what you are trying to promote online, you must be concerned with network endorsements.

In 2012, search ads brought in $8.1 billion and represented 48% of the overall interactive advertising market (Parker, 2012). Companies are competing to land the number one spot in search engines. However, Stratten (2012) explains, through his hierarchy of buying, why this may not be the best business strategy. In order of importance, marketing strategies that bring the highest *return on investment* (ROI), or the benefit of an investment divided by the cost of the investment, include (Figure 3.2):

1 current satisfied customers;
2 referral from a trusted source;
3 current relationship but have yet to purchase;
4 recognized expert in the field;
5 search through ads;
6 cold calls.

Individuals make purchasing decisions based on their trusted personal network over experts in the field. Marketers spend millions of dollars on search engine optimization (SEO), celebrity endorsements, and traditional mass media advertising. However, marketing and communication theories demonstrate how few times these methods actually lead to human behavior change. We are much more influenced by our friends, family and trusted social network. Diffusion techniques are not the strongest strategy for prompting permanent behavior change in audiences. Let's use one of the standard lessons that a parent must teach their child as an example to illustrate how much more influential community messages are than diffusion.

Consider how you learned not to touch a hot stove when younger. Chances are it was done through a top-down diffusion fashion. Your guardian saw you approaching the hot stove, knew that it would hurt you, and relayed that information to you: "Don't touch that hot stove. It will hurt you." You did not need to experience this lesson on your own. Instead, it was diffused through a person you strongly identify and trust, and who holds great power over you. For many, this would be a persuasive enough message to follow through with the desired behavior change of not touching the hot stove. For others, their personality is such that it would just make them want to touch it more.

As a child, your social network is quite small. You identify and know a very small number of individuals. What they say and how they behave play a huge role in how you will model your own behaviors. If your mom speaks with an accent that differs from your immediate proxemics community, it is likely that you will acquire it at a young age too, even if the accent is not from your place of residence. As you begin going to school and meeting new people, some of whom you identify even more strongly with, her linguistic power over your own behavior begins to lessen.

This is why even if a trusted source of information diffuses a message in an authoritative top-down fashion, it may not be persuasive enough to promote behavior change in a community setting. If all of your new friends that you strongly identify with, feel connected to, and are invested in emotionally, take turns touching a hot stove, you may be likely to touch it yourself, despite your guardian's previous warnings. We enjoy feeling as though we are part of a community and do not want to do anything to jeopardize this. Even though a very strong diffusion message from a trusted source was effective, a social community provides a stronger call to action.

The potential of community messages is great news for social media practitioners. Social media is cost-effective, efficient and easy. Regardless of your industry, it is not only important that users feel as though they play an important role in your community, but that you also play an important role in theirs. One way you can do this is by increasing your authenticity and message branding.

Brand Authenticity

Chapter 2 discussed the importance of transparency when it comes to media messages. Transparency helps build trust and connection between the source and receiver of messages. However, while constructing these messages, it is important to consider your authenticity and brand. Brand authenticity will help your consumers better understand who you are and what you are trying to market.

Authenticity is about being yourself and harnessing what you uniquely bring to the table. As Stratten (2012) says, "If you're your authentic self, you have no competition." There are unlimited companies and products being sold online. Chances are, whatever it is you are trying to sell (your employment, a service, merchandise) someone else is already selling it. However, there is something unique and special about your contribution to the field. Thus, focus on your uniqueness.

Authenticity deals with a company's object, ownership, consumer experiences, identity construction and confirmation (Leigh *et al.*, 2006). It has many definitions in psychology, communication and marketing literature. Every organization has a story to tell. Consider how your story reflects the values and personality that you are trying to relay to your audience. You want your customers to feel a certain way about you whenever they read or see your media messages. These decisions should engineer how people think and feel about your brand whatever product you are selling (Holt, 2002). Once you have a sense of your organizational authenticity, you can begin your message branding strategy.

The American Marketing Association (AMA) defines *branding* as the name, term, design, symbol, or any other feature that identifies one seller's goods or service as distinct from those of other sellers. Think of authenticity as what makes your organization unique from other competitors and your brand as how you are going to demonstrate your uniqueness to consumers.

Consumers should be able to distinguish your products and services from other companies through six variables: physique, personality, culture, relationship, reflection, and self-image (Kapferer, 1997). If they are not able to do this, there is more work to be done on your branding strategy. Be sure to monitor and evaluate your brand often (Figure 3.3).

It is important that there is integrity behind your brand. Most often, if you are not honest with yourself, there will be a disconnection between your authenticity and the brand you are putting forward. One great way to ensure the authenticity of your brand is through storytelling.

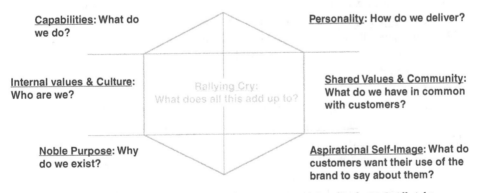

Figure 3.3 Brand identity framework. Copyright © 2015 Brand Amplitude, LLC. All rights reserved. Adapted from the 'Brand Identity Prism' by J.-N. Kapferer, *The New Strategic Brand Management*, 2012, p. 156. Source: Reproduced with permission of Carol Phillips.

Importance of Storytelling

Folklore

Social media should focus on community and dialogue and participation

Storytelling has evolved as one of our most primary, powerful and persuasive forms of communication (Ohler, 2008). Individuals have always told narratives based on the culture of folklore passed from generation to generation. Stories are a reflection of the values and ideologies within society, and therefore become incredibly valuable to how we make everyday life decisions. Through the deepest roots of humanity, stories were told orally and passed down through generations of families. Today, media has allowed us to record these retelling of stories, and there are huge numbers of them. Just because these stories are being told through a different medium, their value is not at all diminished; in fact, many would claim social media amplifies our desire to narrate our own stories.

Folklore is the art of storytelling within a culture. Through folklore, a similar lesson, theme or structure pattern is resembled, recycled and retaught, providing cultural continuity (Patterson, 2006). Folklore consolidates the interaction of literary and oral, professional and nonprofessional, formal and informal, constructed and improvised creativity (Degh, 1994). These media messages represent similar structure and content that provides guides for the way a culture behaves. The more you are able to understand your target audiences' culture, the more you are able to tap into these patterns of behavior.

People learn through stories, so it only makes sense that you provide one for your company. Discuss who you are, what goals you have, and why they are important to you and your audiences. Many successful organizations have started with a story. For example, TOMS Shoes began when the owner traveled to Argentina in 2006 and witnessed the hardships of children without shoes. Ikea owner, Ingvar Kamprad, began selling matches from bulk to neighbors in Småland, Sweden. These stories stay with people and create a much longer-lasting and emotional connection than would a bullet point list. Determine your authenticity and then build a brand that helps tell your story. Finally, and most importantly, allow your audience to share their experiences and narratives through social media.

Move beyond the constant top-down diffusion of your message. Remember that your social media sites really shouldn't focus on you or your product. Your diffusion site (likely your home website) is the space for these types of messages. Social media should be about community dialogue and participation. People do not want to be sold to all of the time. Having a designated place where individuals can go to learn as much information about your product as possible allows you to use social media as a place to build relationships and have dialogue with customers. Social media sites should be filled with questions for audiences to answer. Most of these questions should have nothing to do with your product, but instead should build your authenticity.

For example, if you work for a restaurant that only sells organic food, ask customers questions such as "Why is eating organic food important to you?" or "Share your favorite all-natural food recipe." Your role is not to be an expert, but to facilitate authentic dialogue and help create a space for community. By allowing your audiences to talk to each other, you are allowing the possibility for these cultural dialogue patterns to emerge naturally.

It should be noted that increasing participation and dialogue by audience members on your social media sites does require you to give up some control over your message. Your audience will likely not say the exact things that you would like them to say. In fact, sometimes they will say things that you really wish they wouldn't. Use these moments as a time to reflect on the services that you are providing. If it is a strong service, users will relay that information in this dialogue. Try your best not to edit or censor user dialogue, unless of course it is obscene and/or disrespectful to other community members. The more you are able to facilitate the direction of conversation through prompts the better. Of course, the more natural the conversations that take place, the bigger insight you have into how your target audience thinks, acts and values. When used correctly, social media is inexpensive market research into the cultural norms and expectations of your audience (we will discuss more about social media monitor and research in Chapter 12).

Case Study: Grey Poupon

As discussed, community is established through four dimensions: membership, shared emotional connection, influence, and needs fulfillment (McMillan & Chavis, 1986). Most marketers fall into the trap of using social media to increase the membership of their community. However, this is not a very effective strategy if the other three dimensions of community are absent.

The mustard company Grey Poupon took a different approach to establishing community through social media. Understanding the influence of exclusivity to membership, the company launched a new online marketing campaign on Facebook that pre-screens fans that attempt to "like the page." This screening measures whether the individuals have good enough taste to become one of the company's Facebook fans (Fiegerman, 2012). While most other businesses beg audiences to become fans of their social media pages, Grey Poupon audiences only become fans if they pass a series of steps.

In order to become a member of the Grey Poupon Facebook page, individuals must apply through an application called "The Society of Good Taste." Through an analysis of your interests, friends and writing style, the application determines whether your tastes are refined enough to be a Grey Poupon fan. Your membership with the Facebook group is then either accepted or denied.

This exclusivity screening works for Grey Poupon because the elite qualities that they are portraying are positive associations that individuals want to be identified with on their own social networks. Who wouldn't want to be associated with refined tastes and interests? If your organization is associated with something less culturally appealing, this may not be the best marketing strategy.

There are hundreds if not thousands of mustard brands across the world. It is important for Grey Poupon to find its authenticity in order to reach the niche of individuals who may become brand advocates for their product. Heinz yellow mustard authenticity centers on being the most global and convenient mustard available (Heinz, 2013); Plochman's identifies as being a family-owned organization (Plochman, 2013); and French's mustard is made with only all natural ingredients

(Frenchs, 2013). Grey Poupon found its niche within this market by branding its award-winning flavor with exclusivity and sophistication. Their audience is willing to pay a little higher price for these qualities.

Their website reads, "Grey Poupon quickly turns any dish into a gourmet offering – even a simple sandwich. So much so, that patrons are willing to pay a premium price for sandwiches that feature this sought-after mustard" (Kraft, 2013). This is a very different brand narrative from the other lower-priced mustards. It also helps the company remain transparent about why customers may be paying more, which may help explain why it has been around since 1777 (Figure 3.4).

Figure 3.4   Grey Poupon Facebook page. Source: facebook.com/greypoupon.

Discussion questions

1   How is Grey Poupon able to meet the four criteria of community (dimensions of membership) through their Facebook page? Which dimension is "The Society of Good Taste" application best able to fulfill?

2   What is the authenticity of Grey Poupon and how does it differ from other mustard brands? How is Grey Poupon able to capitalize on this niche through social media in ways not possible through traditional mass media?

3   How might Grey Poupon lose fans who are willing to pay a premium for their product if they marketed towards a more general mass audience?

Summary

It has always been difficult for marketers to promote community among audiences because there was no efficient or cost-effective manner for dialogue to take place. Marketing practitioners were only able to measure the success of their messages by sales or direct audience feedback. Social media has changed the exclusivity of mass media, and now individuals are able to communicate on an intimate level with organizations online.

Social learning theory shows us how individuals make decisions through modeling the behaviors of others. Mass media messages have always been a part of this process, but those messages included characters that were not a part of our own real-life social network. Social media has allowed this distinction to merge as well, as users are able to receive messages from individuals that they are already networked with on a personal level. These messages become a part of the cognitive process and help to construct reality.

Our sense of membership, shared emotional connection, influence and needs fulfillment are all crucial factors to how influenced we are within a community. One of the most significant indicators of relational closeness within a community is self-disclosure. The more willing individuals are to opening up and discussing private-sphere issues, the more emotionally vested they, and the other members of the group, will feel.

The value of member participation and contribution cannot be understated. One must constantly seek feedback and critiques from community members so that they feel as though they are a critical part of its success. However, this requires organizations to give up some level of control that strict diffusion allows. Social media marketing practitioners must be confident in the authenticity and brand of their message in order to engage on this level of participation.

One way to ensure success is to share your personal narrative. This narrative will help audiences to identify with your story, and provide the chance for you to explain your authenticity, or niche within the market. This more human-centered approach supplements, rather than dominates, interpersonal networks. Be sure to consider how this story reflects the individuals and personality, or brand, of your product.

Research demonstrates the power of word-of-mouth advertising through current satisfied customers. Social networks are creating personal agency through sociostructural influences. Your consumers are more likely to make purchasing decisions based on their trusted personal network than they are through experts in the field or information that they seek through search engines.

The power of social network in our everyday decision-making is huge. Social media allows marketers a space to harness this networked power and allows consumers the chance to talk to each other about their experiences. Don't waste your chance by only diffusing information in a top-down fashion. Be confident enough in your product to lose a little control so that your community is able to become empowered and participatory (Table 3.1).

Social learning theory taught us how individuals make meanings and decisions regarding their lives based on what they see. These cognitive models serve as guides for judgment and action. Yes, media do present images, messages and behaviors, but these experiences tend not to be as powerful vehicles for behavior change as actual real-life lived realities.

Table 3.1 Community: an online space where users engage in transactional dialogue about a shared topic or interest. Source: Author.

Pros	Cons
Out-of-the-box feedback	More niche audience
Strong audience identification with brand	Requires careful monitoring and frequent feedback
Higher behavior change yield	Loses some control over message

Consider the example above of the parent teaching a child not to touch a hot stove. While a person's individual community is a stronger form of persuasion than a top-down diffusion message, social learning theory taught us that the biggest driver of decision-making is personal experience. That is why most people don't touch a hot stove more than once. Once you've experienced the painful feeling of getting burnt, it does not matter what information a person in power diffuses, or what your individual social network says. You make the decision based on your own schema of events. You touched the hot stove. You know what it felt like. You know that there is little, if any, reward in doing so. You're not going to do it again.

These types of experienced decisions are much more likely to be permanent models for behavior change and are one of the most difficult constructs to establish through social media. How do you get someone to have a real-life experience through a computer screen? This construct is also the furthest to the right on our social media continuum, meaning that it lends very little control of the media message to the producer. However, if you are successfully able to mobilize your audience, there is nothing more powerful for permanent behavior change. Let's now turn our attention to social media mobilization in Chapter 4.

Key Takeaways

1 When prompting behavior change through media, it is important that individuals identify with your message. A comprehensive audience analysis can help ensure this.
2 Social media allows a unique opportunity for an individual's social network to share their product experiences with the general public and with each other.
3 Community is a more participatory approach to marketing, and thus it is a more powerful tool than diffusion-centric techniques in behavior change. It includes four dimensions: membership, shared emotional connection, influence, and needs fulfillment.
4 Be confident in your product to lose a little control and encourage more participatory and community-oriented social media marketing efforts.
5 Your social media sites should not focus on you or your product. Tell your brand story and invite your consumers to share their stories/experiences with your product.

References

Bandura, A. (2002) Social cognitive theory of mass communication. In: J. Bryant & D. Zillmann (eds) *Media Effects: Advances in Theory and Research*, pp. 121–153. Mahwah, NJ: Lawrence Erlbaum Associates.

Bandura, A. (2004) Health promotion by social cognitive means. *Health Education and Behavior*, 31, 143–164.

Bryant, J. & Oliver, M.B. (eds) (2009) *Media Effects: Advances in Theory and Research*, 3rd edn. New York: Routledge.

Campbell, C. & Jovchelovitch, S. (2000) Health, community and development: towards a social psychology of participation. *Journal of Community and Applied Social Psychology*, 10(4), 255–270.

Degh, L. (1994) *American Folklore and the Mass Media*. Bloomington, IN: Indiana University Press.

Festinger, L. (1962) *A Theory of Cognitive Dissonance*, vol. 2. Stanford, CA: Stanford University Press.

Fiegerman, S. (2012) Grey Poupon wants to be the most exclusive page on Facebook. Available at http://mashable.com/2012/09/13/grey-poupon-facebook-marketing-campaign/ (accessed June 8, 2016).

Figueroa, M., Kincaid, D., Rani, M. & Lewis, G. (2002) Communication for social change: an integrated model for measuring the process and its outcomes. New York: The Rockefeller Foundation. Available at http://www.communicationforsocialchange.org/pdf/socialchange.pdf (accessed June 8, 2016).

Frenchs (2013) The natural truth. Available at http://www.frenchs.com/our-promise (accessed June 22, 2016).

Gray-Felder, D. & Deane, J. (1999) Communication and social change: a position paper and conference report. New York: The Rockefeller Foundation. Available at http://www.communicationforsocialchange.org/publications-resources?itemid=14 (accessed June 8, 2016).

Greenall, R. (2012) LiveJournal: Russia's unlikely Internet giant. Available at http://www.bbc.co.uk/news/magazine-17177053 (accessed June 8, 2016).

Habermas, J. (1991) *The Structural Transformation of the Public Sphere: An Inquiry into a Category of Bourgeois Society*. Cambridge, MA: MIT Press.

Heinz (2013) A world of good food. Available at http://www.heinz.com/our-company/about-heinz.aspx (accessed June 8, 2016).

Holt, D.B. (2002) Why do brands cause trouble? A dialectical theory of consumer culture and branding. *Journal of Consumer Research*, 29(1), 70–90.

Kapferer, J.-N. (1997) *Strategic Brand Management*. London: Kogan Page.

Kaplan, A.M. & Haenlein, M. (2010) Users of the world, unite! The challenges and opportunities of social media. *Business Horizons*, 53(1), 59–68.

Kraft (2013) Products and brands. Available at http://www.kraftfoodservice.com/ProductsandBrands/Spreads/Grey Poupon/BrandAppeal.aspx (accessed June 8, 2016).

Kretzmann, J. & McKnight, J. (1993) *Building Communities from the Inside Out: A Path Toward Finding and Mobilizing a Community's Assets*. Chicago: ACTA Publications.

Leigh, T.W., Peters, C. & Shelton, J. (2006) The consumer quest for authenticity: the multiplicity of meanings within the MG subculture of consumption. *Journal of the Academy of Marketing Science*, 34(4), 481–493.

McMillan, D. & Chavis, D. (1986) Sense of community: a definition and theory. *Journal of Community Psychology*, 14, 6–23.

Nakao, T. (2012) Social media and mobile in China. Available at http://socialmediainasia.blogspot.com/2012_03_01_archive.html (accessed June 8, 2016).

Oches, S. (2010) The many acts of Domino's pizza. Available at http://www.qsrmagazine.com/menu-innovations/many-acts-domino-s-pizza (accessed June 8, 2016).

Ohler, J. (2008) *Digital Storytelling in the Classroom: New Media Pathways to Literacy, Learning and Creativity*. Thousand Oaks, CA: Corwin Press.

Parker, P. (2012) IAB: Search still on top, accounting for nearly half of interactive ad spending. Available at http://searchengineland.com/iab-search-still-on-top-accounting-for-nearly-half-of-interactive-ad-spending-136426 (accessed June 8, 2016).

Patterson, B. (2006) Historical viewpoint on television, folklore. Available at http://houstonianonline.com/2006/02/16/historical-viewpoint-on-television-folklore/ (accessed June 8, 2016).

Perkins, D. & Long, D. (2002) Neighborhood sense of community and social capital: a multi-level analysis. In: A. Fisher, C. Sonn & B. Bishop (eds) *Psychological Sense* of Community: Research, Applications, and Implications,* pp. 291–318. New York: Plenum.

Pew Internet (2012) Mean size of Facebook friends network. Available at http://pewinternet.tumblr.com/post/23177613721/facebook-a-profile-of-its-friends-in-light-of (accessed June 8, 2016).

Pew Internet Research (2013) Social networking fact sheet. Available at http://pewinternet.org/Commentary/2012/March/Pew-Internet-Social-Networking-full-detail.aspx (accessed June 6, 2016).

Plochman (2013) Mustard facts history and myths. Available at http://www.plochman.com/FHM.htm (accessed June 8, 2016).

Putnam, R. (2001) *Bowling Alone: The Collapse and Revival of American Community.* New York: Simon & Schuster.

Stratten, S. (2012) *UnMarketing: Stop Marketing. Start Engaging.* Hoboken, NJ: John Wiley & Sons, Inc.

Thompson, M., Ellis, R. & Wildavsky, A. (1990) *Cultural Theory.* Boulder, CO: Westview Press.

Trusov, M., Bucklin, R.E. & Pauwels, K. (2009) Effects of word-of-mouth versus traditional marketing: findings from an internet social networking site. *Journal of Marketing,* 73(5), 90–102.

Waisbord, S. (2001) Family tree of theories, methodologies and strategies in communication for development. Prepared for the Rockefeller Foundation. Available at http://www.communicationforsocialchange.org/pdf/familytree.pdf (accessed June 8, 2016).

4

Mobilizing Your Audience

Learning Objectives

After reading this chapter, you should be able to:
1   Mobilize your audiences into action through social media messages.
2   Understand how user-generated content empowers audiences into action.
3   Create a strategy that encourages audiences to interact with your social media site and engage in offline advocacy.

Introduction

Social media is designed for users to engage in dialogue and participate with each other. However, the goal of most mass media campaigns is to get audiences offline and mobilize them towards real-life behavior change. Most notably, companies are hoping to prompt audiences to purchase their product. Previous chapters have demonstrated the potential of social media in equalizing relationships between previous institutions of power and everyday citizens (Raftery, 1991; Weisbrod, 1991; Neuhauser & Kreps, 2003). Though the relationship between consumers and marketers may never be equalized, social media is certainly changing expectations.

Top-down diffusion messages are able to reach a large mass audience. Though the potential for behavior change is not great, it is the most secure way to control your message. However, by always playing it safe, you may be missing the real potential of social media

Strategic Social Media: From Marketing to Social Change, First Edition. L. Meghan Mahoney and Tang Tang.
© 2017 John Wiley & Sons, Inc. Published 2017 by John Wiley & Sons, Inc.

marketing. Community strategies allow audiences the ability to provide feedback and communicate directly with each other about issues they are vested in. This increases the amount of trust that they have in a product, and allows recommendations to come from a personal network, rather than a top-down source.

Participatory social media has transformed audiences into more educated, empowered and motivated Internet users (Boulos & Wheeler, 2006). This change in social media users provide social media marketers an opportunity to make a huge difference in their consumers and the world around them through mobilization techniques.

This chapter explores various methods for social participation. How can marketers get consumers offline and use social media to prompt real-life interaction and promote products? Chapters 2 and 3 explained how most behavior change interventions fail because of the oversaturation of media, with very little options for user feedback and interaction. While traditional media are limited in their ability to encourage interpersonal dialogue and reach a mass audience at the same time, social media is able to bridge this gap. By allowing audiences to take control over social media messages, everyday consumers could be transformed into lifetime brand advocates.

Social Media Mobilization

One of the greatest advancements of social media is the ability for collective action. Often, social movements fueled through new communication technologies are called cyberactivism, which changes the landscape of collective action (Eltantawy & Wiest, 2011). Howard (2011) defines *cyberactivism* as the act of using the Internet to advance a political cause that is difficult to advance offline. This concept of collective action has been studied for half a century, guided by the *resource mobilization theory*. Though often criticized, the premise of resource mobilization theory is that desire, dissent and attitude change are not enough to spark social change, but resources such as time, money and organizational skills are critical for a successful social movement (McCarthy & Zald, 1977; Jenkins, 1983).

Mobilization is defined as the process by which candidates, parties, activists, and groups induce other people to participate (Rosenstone & Hansen, 2003). Mobilization research generally examines large social movements and activism, and deals with the planning, execution, and facilitation of these actions. Mobilization is an important concept to turn to if you are interested in inciting behavior change through social media messages, because the premise for any successful behavior change through media messages requires both the advancing of media messages and an execution/facilitation strategy.

It is not enough to simply pique someone's interest in your product. While in isolation your message may be interesting enough to prompt behavior change, unfortunately consumers are bombarded with media messages all day. They will read your social media message while waiting at the bus stop, on their way to work, while simultaneously answering emails and looking at a friend's pictures. By the time they have any free time, they have heard hundreds of additional requests and have forgotten all about the message. Thus, marketing practitioners must provide enough resources to make mobilization as easy as possible right there and then, when consumers first come into contact with your message.

While social media has undoubtedly reinvented activism, it has also made it easier for audiences to hide behind a screen. Malcolm Gladwell (2010) argues that the weak ties of social connections seldom leads to high-risk activism. This is partly due to the comfort that users feel when sticking to their technology, and the discomfort when leaving it to experience new and uncertain behaviors. Social media makes it easy for users to diffuse messages, but harder for these messages to have a lasting impact on human behavior change.

Universities struggle with this premise in their recruitment. In order to experience university life, students must complete a long, arduous and sometimes expensive application process. For years, university recruiters have attempted to bridge this gap through media messages that promote community. They disseminate brochures showing current students "just like you" have a great time in their facilities. However, rather than diffusing information about a student "just like you," why not use social media to actually encourage "you" to have those experiences. Admission departments are now seeing the power of using social media to prompt individuals to put down the brochure, come to campus, and attend free open houses, sit in on classes, and try out feature facilities like state-of-the-art rock climbing walls. These experiences do so much more for individual decision-making processes than a single brochure would. It's clear that media messages cannot compete with a great real-life experience.

For decades, mass media was primarily used as a vehicle to get the message out to hundreds of thousands of audiences with just a single message (Stone, 1993). This process has been dubbed "push and pray" in the marketing realm (Stratten, 2012). As we learned in Chapter 2, push-and-pray marketing (Figure 4.1) is when practitioners try to reach as many users as possible (cold calling, radio broadcast, television commercials, email spam) in the hope that a small portion of that audience will follow through with the requested message.

Nonetheless, social media allows us the chance to use media for critiquing, disrupting and organizing. Why not provide audiences the chance to use the media in a way that they choose? Pull-and-stay marketing (Figure 4.2) allows practitioners to use media to listen and engage conversation. This facilitation will bring the right audience to you with a strong sense of trust and connection. Handing control over to users will empower them towards much larger and more impactful behavior change tactics. Let's take one of the most popular

push & pray

pull + stay marketing

Figure 4.1 Push-and-pray marketing. Source: Author.

Figure 4.2   Pull-and-stay marketing. Source: Author.

Internet revolutions as an example for how social media proved a mobilizer to permanent behavior change.

For 30 years Egyptian President Hosni Mubarack served under a one-party authoritarian state of emergency. Beginning January 25, 2011, demonstrations, marches and nonviolent civil resistance demanded the overthrow of the regime of the President. The Egyptian revolution has been characterized by the instrumental use of social media, especially Facebook, Twitter, YouTube, and text messaging by protesters, to bring social change. It was led by a loose network of young individuals that demonstrated a capacity for organization, discipline, restraint, and integrity (Khamis & Vaughn, 2011). However, individual Egyptians, for the first time in history, were able to find, communicate with, and organize like-minded individuals through social media and mobile devices. After just 18 days of demonstrations, Mubarak resigned on February 11, 2011. All of this happened because users were able to connect and facilitate action through social media.

Social media provides the tools for mobilization, by connecting individuals with a larger social network that feels the same way and is ready to take action. It has distinct inherent properties for facilitating real-life participation. One of the oldest social media platforms, Meetup.com, is built on the premise of interest-based networking. Individuals with the same interests are able to find each other, locate based on proximity, and facilitate real-life gatherings that would have otherwise been very difficult to organize. The website's tagline describes Meetup as "neighbors getting together to learn something, do something, share something," which clearly demonstrates the power of social media to get people offline and create interpersonal experiences.

Boyd (2011) explains how social media technology enables user action through its design of three types of integrated affordances: profiles, friends list, and tools of communication. Profiles constitute the space where conversations, both synchronous and asynchronous, take place. These profiles allow individuals the opportunity to create their own identity, whether real or idealized. Here, users can provide as much information as they choose, and tell others what they feel is most important about themselves and their interests.

Friends' lists are the audience and public of the social media user. This is the most critical part of social networks, as simply creating a Twitter profile does not constitute social media. Often, users who create profiles but do not follow or participate with others' posts are called media lurkers (Crawford, 2009). They do not contribute or take anything from the social media, and have little value to marketers.

You may remember the hype and excitement surrounding the release of the social networking sites Google+ and Ello. However, regardless of the innovative features for network and connection of the social media platforms, many users found little use and value in the sites because of their limited friends' lists. A social media site is only as good as the people we are able to connect with. That is why it is so difficult to launch a new successful social networking platform that is able to compete with the more established ones, such as Facebook or Twitter.

In addition to user profile and friends list, the tools of communication are really what allow users to communicate and organize themselves in a public or semi-public forum. These functions allow networks to connect local and the global, and lead to collective outcomes (Enjolras *et al.*, 2013). In the meantime, these communication tools provide some regulation to the spaces of communication. Without regulation, communities are likely to succumb to spam and "trolls," persistent posters of malicious or purposefully distracting comments (Gowers & Nielsen, 2009).

Once these structures are put into place (profiles, friends list, and tools of communication) the possibilities for mobilization are endless. The result of these features creates a more empowered and motivated action, as users do not feel as though they are being forced or prompted to do something. The action is the result of users' own ideas, collaboration and efforts. These collective outcomes are the most powerful kinds of behavior change and should be the goal of every social media marketer.

The Power of User-Generated Content

We have discussed in great length the inverse relationship between control and participatory messages. The more control you have over the message, the less participatory it proves in nature. However, it is important to note that these are not mutually exclusive entities. A social media message should be good at message diffusion, community *and* mobilization.

We have also discussed how participatory means promoting the greatest likelihood for behavior change in audiences. *Participatory communication* includes any process through which people define themselves, what they need and how to get there, through dialogue (Byrne *et al.*, 2005). It utilizes dialogue that leads to the collective problem identification of solutions to development issues. Social media provides a great resource for this initial step.

It is very easy to go into a community and tell individuals what they should do. However, if you are searching for a lasting and even permanent behavior change, this is not the best persuasion tactic. In a study by Husain and Shaikh (2005), a village was given condoms free of cost. While many users took advantage of this opportunity, researchers found that the likelihood of using the condom actually increased if the individual had to pay for it, rather than receiving it for free. This is consistent with the premise of participatory communication, because by purchasing the condom an individual is actually taking part and becoming an advocate for the cause. Individuals want an egalitarian solution, and to be a part of the change (Dutta, 2006). Active participation is critical to the readjustment of structural forces that exist as the core of the problem. Social participation, a combination of mass dissemination and media engagement, has proven the most efficient and effective way to spark behavior change in communication and development literature (Waisbord, 2001). Here, audiences are addressed in a bottom-up manner, rather than talked down to by media messages (Gray-Felder & Deane, 1999; Morris, 2003).

Sterne (2010) describes social media participation in marketing as providing audiences the opportunity to visit, click, retweet, post, comment, rate, and bookmark products. While this type of transactional feedback interaction is important, it also mirrors the same traditional top-down communication process (Bandura, 2004). Users have much more to offer than simply interacting with predetermined text. Allowing users to engage in transactional feedback is not enough to ignite permanent behavior change, especially in a media context where this type of engagement is expected and the norm for today's audiences. Social media marketing must mirror the same trends and involve participant dialogue and audience engagement in every step of the process, including product and message design, transforming consumers into message advocates (Waisbord, 2001). We must encourage consumers to move beyond content participation and move towards content creation.

In previous chapters, we have learned that individuals learn best through modeling the behaviors of their own culture and environment. While some of these behaviors are learned through media messages, the majority of our behaviors are learned from direct observation of those in our interpersonal lives and our own lived experiences. We used the example of learning not to touch a hot stove to demonstrate how once you live out the experience of getting burnt, there is little message diffusion or community persuasion that will convince you to touch the hot stove again. The goal of social media marketing should thus be to provide users with a real-life lived experience that will prove stronger than other more diffusion and community-centric messages.

Marketers have used this "real-life experience" strategy to market products for years. This is why infomercials urge you to try their product out for free with no commitment. This strategy is built on the premise that your real-life experience during the trial period will provide you with positive schemata of reference, and to return the product would create great dissonance. Once users have a pleasant experience with a product, it is difficult to turn away. Research shows how simply allowing consumers to experience touching a product significantly increases their likelihood to purchase (Citrin *et al.*, 2003).

Of course, this creates challenges for social media marketers. It is impossible to allow Internet users to have a real-life lived experience online. Therefore, marketers should stop using the medium to tell users how wonderful their product is, and should instead make it as easy as possible to promote users to sign offline and try the product out for themselves.

Heilman *et al.* (2011) investigated the power of in-store free samples on food products and their influence on subsequent purchasing behavior. Results of this study demonstrate how providing free real-life samples of food significantly increases the likelihood of shoppers buying a product that they otherwise would not have purchased. There was an even greater likelihood of a customer purchasing the food if a person was interacting with consumers in addition to the free sample. This finding is consistent with the idea of an interpersonal network influencing behavior change. Marketers must use social media as a space for consumers to share their real-life experiences with their personal network through community techniques.

Consumers like to be in control of their own media consumption habits. Uses and gratifications research shows how audience characteristics and personal motivations influence exposure and consequent attitudes (Haridakis & Rubin, 2005). Users select media that gratify their needs, and the more motivated they are by that gratification, the stronger the experience. (We will discuss more about uses and gratifications research and active audience behavior in Chapter 5.) This includes a user's locus of control (Potter, 1988).

Locus of control is a trait personality that reflects one's conceptualization of who controls the events in one's own life (Haridakis & Hanson, 2009). Those who believe that they hold power over external circumstances are more internally controlled. Those who believe that things such as fate, luck, and other people act as controllers of their lives prove more externally controlled (Levenson, 1974). Locus of control has also been positively associated with the amount of media consumption and involvement in social activities (Levenson, 1974). It is an incredible tool for mobilization. Therefore, it makes sense to turn to locus of control when interested in a predictive variable for behavior change through media messages.

The goal of social media messages should be to make your community feel as though they have a strong locus of control. Singhal and Rogers (2003) explain how most communication interventions fail because technocrats design them based on their own personal view of reality. This is why audience analyses are such a critical part of marketing and public relations. Instead, we should allow for true participation, where users, individually and collectively, are able to reflect on their social situation and articulate their own discontent and action. One way to achieve this is through user-generated content (UGC).

Today, hundreds of millions of Internet users are self-publishing consumers (Cha *et al.*, 2007). As discussed in Chapter 2, UGC fulfills three requirements: (i) is published on a publicly accessible website or on a social networking site accessible to a selected group of people; (ii) shows a certain amount of creative effort; and (iii) needs to have been created outside of professional routines and practices (Kaplan & Haenlein, 2010). One of the largest and oldest UGC social media sites, YouTube, promotes users to "Remember that this is your community! Each and every user of YouTube makes the site what it is, so don't be afraid to dig in and get involved" (Van Dijck, 2009). It is no wonder that the site, built on the premise of user creation, has become the most successful Internet short video sharing service (Cheng *et al.*, 2008). Based on this information, the following mobilization action plan can be put into place.

Mobilization Action Plan

There are four steps towards maximizing an action in audiences through social media.

1 Ensure that your social media allows users to create their own user profiles, connect with friends, and provides tools of communication where users can communicate and organize themselves. This can either be done on an existing social media site (Twitter, Facebook) or a new application designed specifically for your organization and audiences.

2 Encourage participatory communication that allows users to define themselves, their needs, and the resources needed to get there. Communicate with them often, but don't control conversation. Really listen to what your audience is saying. Allow conversations to emerge naturally from your audience.

3   Treat your audience like an informed public, not a passive audience that is in need of information. Provide enough resources so that if they invest enough time or resources, they are able to make decisions on their own. This will create a stronger locus of control and will transform them into a stronger brand advocate. Ask their opinions often and treat them like the experts of your organization.

4   Prompt social participation, where you are combining social media content with interpersonal behaviors. This can be done through the use of user-generated technologies. Allow your audience to participate in "real-life" offline behaviors, such as creating a video, sharing pictures, or voting in a poll or product development.

Clearly, creating social media content becomes a much more powerful part of our schemata for interpretation. Once your audience invests their own time, energy, and sometimes even money, the stakes are higher. These efforts become a part of their life experience and personal identity, and play a critical role in brand advocacy.

Offline Advocacy

The purpose of any social media campaign should be to encourage message creation by audiences. As a social media marketing practitioner, you should constantly encourage users to comment, respond and interact with your content. In addition to this online participation, your audience may become so vested in this community that they become brand advocates offline as well.

One company that has been able to integrate their online and offline marketing is TOMS. TOMS is built on a *contributory consumption* business model, where if a consumer purchases a product, the organization donates something to a cause. TOMS calls this a "One for One" model, where a user purchases a pair of shoes and the company gives a pair of shoes to a person in need.

Beyond a great brand narrative (CEO Blake Mycoskie traveled to Argentina, where he saw children living without shoes and decided to do something about it), TOMS has been able to integrate the mission of philanthropy and strong audience locus of control in every piece of their marketing strategy. TOMS sends customers a flag of their logo with every shoe purchase and asks consumers to take a picture and share their personal story of giving, whether it has to do with TOMS shoes or not. Rather than focusing their marketing on the purchase of shoes, TOMS has centered their brand on a lifestyle and social movement. Their website states:

TOM is not a single person, it is the idea that the decisions we make today can echo into the future. If you believe in finding adventure while building a better tomorrow, you're TOM. If you shop consciously, volunteer with an organization that is changing lives, take part in creating a sustainable future or help raise awareness of issues affecting lives across the globe – you are TOM (http://www.toms.com/i-am-tom).

This brand strategy encourages consumers to do good things in real life, capture it on photo or video, and then share it on TOMS social media accounts with the hashtag #iamtom. Though this campaign is not directly selling shoes, it is making their consumers feel emotionally attached to the brand and creating a strong community among audiences that are taking control over the brand narrative.

[handwritten margin note: emotional attachment to a brand]

The importance of community cannot be understated in the mobilization process. TOMS consumers purchase shoes because they represent the way they construct their own identity and the role that they play in the world around them. They don't feel as though TOMS is just another shoe company that is trying to sell them an item for profit. They feel a strong locus of control about their purchase because TOMS is allowing them to control the product narrative. Wearing TOMS identifies a person as a philanthropist. The website is filled with strangers high-fiving each other because they are also wearing TOMS shoes. TOMS is not selling to consumers; consumers are TOMS because TOMS has given them the freedom and tools to share personal stories of how they have interpreted the mission into their own lives.

In terms of mobilization, TOMS shoes has certainly implemented an effective social media strategy. They have an annual "One Day Without Shoes" event where audiences are asked to go without shoes for one day and share their experiences online (Figure 4.3). Their website also asks users to take pictures and share where they have been wearing their TOMS. They take TOMS fans on international shoe drops with them and blog about their experiences. Their website is filled with images of the people whom they help, and prompts for customers to share! share! share! (TOMS, 2013). Each of these real-life experiences makes consumers feel more emotionally invested with the brand.

These real-life efforts all become a part of their consumers' life experiences. Rather than just thinking about a pair of shoes when consumers think about TOMS, they remember the emotional connection that they felt when they did something good for the world, or the sacrifice of going an entire day without shoes. This transforms the consumer process

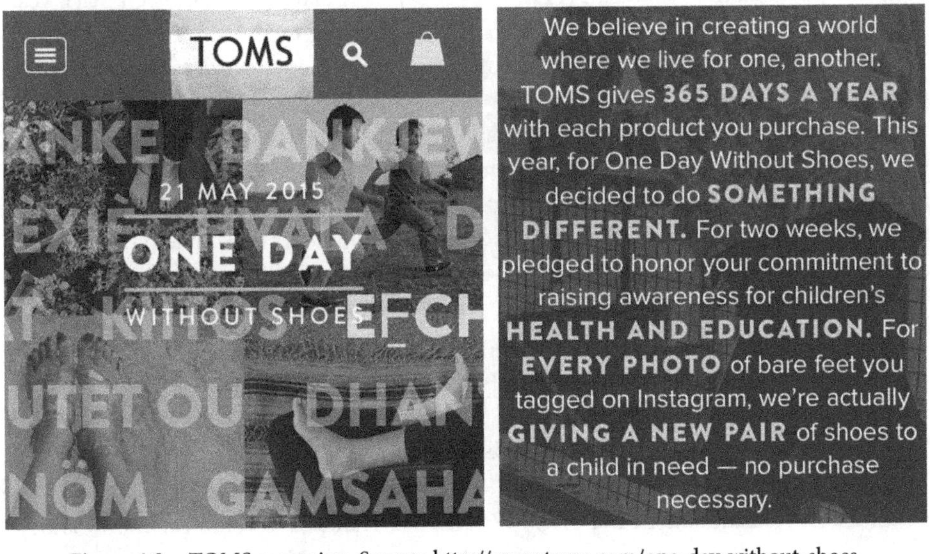

Figure 4.3 TOMS campaign. Source: http://www.toms.com/one-day-without-shoes.

Figure 4.4   Frito Lay's campaign. Source: www.dousaflavor.com.

into a much more emotional experience. Moreover, consumers can share their experience online through social media so that their personal network can witness the community movement. Undoubtedly, these images and videos hold great pathos and the community would want to join in.

Every social media campaign, regardless of the purpose, should urge users to do the same. You want your product to be a part of their everyday experiences. Mobilization extends beyond just clicking and interacting. It is about asking users to generate new content and to share it as part of their own message.

Another company that has been successful in integrating the power of participation in a social media marketing campaign is Frito Lay's "Do Us A Flavor™" campaign. Each year, Lay's potato chips company creates and distributes a new flavor to add to their lineup. In 2012, the company decided to allow consumers to participate in the process through online and mobile submissions.

Rather than just creating various flavors and allowing users to vote on their favorite, Frito Lay actually allowed users to take part in the creation process. Users were urged to submit any idea that they felt would make a tasty potato chip. By giving up control of the process, undoubtedly the company received many ideas that could never reach market. This is one disadvantage of a participatory marketing campaign. However, by giving up control of the message, they were able to find three possible flavors out of the 3.8 million fan submissions. These included Cheesey Garlic Bread, Sriracha, and Chicken and Waffles.

The social media campaign (Figure 4.4) took participation another level by creating each of the flavors and featured a biography for each of the submissions. This helped personalize the flavors and made it easier for users to identify with the contestants.

- Christina Abu-Judom, creator of Lay's Chicken & Waffles, is a volunteer coordinator at a nonprofit in Phoenix, Arizona. Her nephew encouraged her to enter the contest and his favorite dish has always been chicken and waffles.

- Karen Weber-Mendham submitted Lay's Cheesy Garlic Bread, and is a part-time children's librarian and mom of three in Land O'Lakes, Wisconsin. She loves going out for pizza with her family, and while waiting for the pizza to come to the table, she always orders a bowl of cheesy garlic bread for the family to enjoy.
- Tyler Raineri created Lay's Sriracha and is a student at Illinois State University. Tyler prefers to coat his chips, and pretty much everything else, in sriracha. It was a taste he inherited from his grandmother whose homemade chips were always seasoned with a dab of this red-hot sauce. And it's a tradition he now shares with his housemates at school (FritoLays, 2013).

Even if users did not have a strong preference for one flavor over another, they were able to see and read about each of the contestants and then vote on their favorite flavor through the Lay's Facebook page, text message or Twitter using the hashtag #SaveChickenWaffles, #SaveGarlicBread or #SaveSriracha.

This is a multi-layer participatory campaign. Audiences were involved in every stage of the campaign: inception, creation, and feedback. It is easier than ever to get users to share their experiences with your product in their "real" lives. Mobile media technologies are both wireless and portable, allowing individuals to share pictures, videos, and check-in "on the go" where they are (Wei, 2013). This campaign was able to transcend from just being about a potato chip, to an emotional story about how three lives were changed by Frito Lay.

The opportunity for mobilization is only possible if companies are willing to give up control of their brand narrative and allow users to not only participate but also design, create and produce media content. This requires a strong and trusted mission statement. For mobilization to be successful, users must understand the authenticity of your brand, identify with the lifestyle, and want to share it with their own network. With this type of strategy, a shoe becomes a social change movement, a potato chip becomes a vote to change someone's life, and an audience becomes a marketing executive who is able to control a brand narrative. This of course comes with great risk, as you are leaving your social media account open for audiences to say whatever they want. If they are unhappy with your product, this will come through in their messages. Social media shifts power to the consumers, which can be very powerful, or detrimental, to your brand.

Case Study: Breast Cancer Meme   *cyberactivism*

One of the most powerful forms of social media mobilization is cyberactivism. Here, individuals utilize the Internet to promote a particular cause or charity. Every person has their own cause that is close to their heart, and we often feel these things speak closely to our life experience and identity. Therefore, we are eager to share cyberactivism efforts with our own-networked community and ask them to join. These calls for awareness filled with empathetic emotional appeals spread quickly. One of the reasons these calls hold so much virality is because individuals like the idea of others associating them with charity or a good cause. Humans want to do the right thing, and if the call is to simply ask you to push a button to "like" a status, we don't mind obliging. Your own Facebook page may be filled with charities and organizations that your friends have sent to you, yet you have never actually participated with. Calls for cyberactivism can spread quickly, but make little difference in the world because they are not linked to any real-life mobilization. Social media practitioners want to be sure that their media messages encourage behavior change.

Each October, various individuals, businesses and organizations celebrate National Breast Cancer Awareness Month. Generally, this is a cause that most individuals don't mind participating in and sharing with their social network. Various forms of Internet memes circulate on Facebook to help spread awareness.

One of the most popular breast cancer Facebook memes was a private message request where females were asked to put a single color as their status update. The message asked females to choose a color that was the same as the bra that they were wearing. The status simply read: NAME, COLOR (i.e., "Melissa, black", "Rebecca, red"). The idea of the meme was that men would log onto Facebook, see that their female friends had these bizarre single-color statuses and become confused. This fun activity was designed to raise awareness for breast cancer (Albanesius, 2010).

Other forms of this viral meme have spread each year during Breast Cancer Awareness Month. One private message asked females to change their Facebook status to the location where they like to put their purse. These status updates would read "I like it on the floor" or "I like it behind the couch." This undoubtedly sexualized the meme further, and more and more women began to share. The meme's Facebook fanpage even read "Whether you are a full-fledged Breast Cancer supporter or a shameless, sexually-charged horndog, this page is for you" (Albanesius, 2010).

An additional call prompted females to:

> Put the number, followed by the word "inches," and how long it takes to do your hair... Remember last year so many people took part it made national news and, the constant updating of status reminded everyone why we're doing this and helped raise awareness!! Do NOT tell any males what the status' mean, keep them guessing!! And please copy and paste (in a message) this to all your female friends to see if we can make a bigger fuss this year than last year!!! I did my part...now YOUR turn! Go on ladies...and let's have all the men guessing!! (Trussell, 2012).

These memes are very successful at diffusing a message and getting individuals to participate. They are filled with fun personalization. Individuals who share the message feel good about doing their part to spread breast cancer awareness. However, they raise the question of whether cyberactivism is actually activism at all. Is a secret message really going to mobilize real-life action to help cure breast cancer?

The Susan G. Komen Foundation reported an increase in interest and contributions following the popular viral memes (Stein, 2010). However, it should be noted that these memes circulated during the opening days of Breast Cancer Awareness Month, and it is difficult to link the cause of donations. Many individuals found sexualizing of breast cancer problematic (Stein, 2010), others wished that they were linked to additional breast cancer prevention material or donation options, instead of a private message.

The problem with these types of diffusion-centric campaigns is that they are not linked to real-life action. These types of memes allow individuals who want to help spread breast cancer awareness to put their efforts into a vague Facebook status instead of something more useful to the cause. Additionally, lack of awareness is not always the biggest challenge of a cause or charity. The Centers for Disease Control states that one of the biggest misunderstandings about breast cancer is that women are the only ones who are susceptible. However, over 2000 men were diagnosed and over 400 men died from the disease in the United States in 2012 (Komen, 2012). It seems counterintuitive to brand awareness campaigns with the color pink or even to go as far as to purposefully keep awareness messages out of the hands of males.

Before creating a social media mobilization campaign, it is important to ask whether lack of awareness is the biggest challenge to the cause. Is your biggest challenge that individuals don't know that you exist, or are they just not interested in your services? In some cases, lack of awareness is a huge issue. Nonetheless, breast cancer campaigns do little to actually spread tangible information regarding the initiative's goals, even though these viral campaigns put great efforts into disseminating prevention and self-check information to the general public.

Most every organization would benefit more from messages that were tied to practical real-life mobilization efforts. These could include volunteering, donating money, signing a petition, or writing a letter. Often, these can be accomplished with just a simple click of a button as awareness-only techniques. Imagine spending an entire afternoon volunteering at a chemotherapy treatment center. How much more powerful would that experience shape your audience's behavior than stating the color of their bra on a Facebook status? This is especially true in causes that already have a strong, tightly knit community such as breast cancer survivors. Through more action-oriented mobilization approaches, your message will transform audiences into more interested, knowledgeable and vested advocates for your cause.

Discussion questions

1   What qualities of the Facebook breast cancer awareness meme make it so viral in nature? Why would thousands of social media users want to participate and share with their friends?
2   How did the social media meme fall short of user mobilization? What changes could be made to make more of a difference to breast cancer causes?
3   Creating emotional real-life experiences for users is one of the biggest indicators of mobilization success. How do cyberactivism and other prosocial movements have a natural advantage to social media mobilization strategies? How can this be incorporated into a brand authenticity and mission statement?

Summary

Think of the most influential moments in your life – the experiences that shaped you as a person, and the stories that you tell over and over. Chances are these are not scenes that you've watched play out on a television screen or a website that you visited online. We are not most influenced by the technologies in our lives, but by our experiences and the people closest to us.

If your goal as a social media marketing/communication practitioner is to have your product or message become an intricate part of others' lives, you must provide opportunities for them to experience it for themselves. Social media has many affordances that make this type of real-life mobilization easier than ever. The technologies aid better planning and easier execution and facilitation of action.

In addition to utilizing social media to prompt users to gain experience with your product, you must also use it as a space to create and share. UGC is critical to the transformation of users into message advocates. Message diffusion allows users to comply with a request. Community gives users a space to ask questions or post feedback. Mobilization is the only way for users to willingly and permanently have a voice in your campaign.

As discussed in previous chapters, using media to ignite behavior change exists on a tricky continuum. Strictly diffusing messages allows you to have tight control over what is being said about your product. However, it has a lousy return on investment in terms of sparking behavior change. Allowing others to experience your product and speak on your behalf through strict participation means a much stronger vehicle for behavior change. However, this provides you with little control over what is being said. It is important to find a balance.

Have you ever had a terrible experience with a product? Perhaps you went to a restaurant where the staff was rude, you had to wait forever for a table, and the food did not taste good. It does not matter what future reviews you read, or recommendations the restaurant receives, you will not go back. Before moving to a participatory strategy, you must be confident that the customer experience with your product will be positive.

This does not mean that your goal as a marketing practitioner is to please everyone. In fact, this is impossible in today's digital landscape. Consumers are going to give negative reviews. However, if you are finding that this negativity accounts for the majority of the feedback you are receiving, it is time to reign in the participatory features and start from the beginning. Reevaluate your brand's mission statement, authenticity and transparency. Companies should constantly be monitoring and evaluating their community and feedback (more on this evaluation process can be found in Chapter 12).

There are very few products where consumers will become brand advocates. These consumers already want to wear tee-shirts with the company's logo, and talk about the new products with their personal network. This small group of individuals strongly identify with these products and the lifestyle that they stand for (Table 4.1).

The best social media strategies are not those that only use participation and mobilization-centric techniques; there should be a three-pronged social media strategy in combination with diffusion, community, and mobilization approaches. There are millions of social media sites in existence today. While it is important and useful to learn how the most

Table 4.1   Mobilization: inducing individuals to participate with your social media campaign through real-life action. Source: Author.

Pros	Cons
Users highly identify with media message	Targets individuals, not mass audience
Transforms audience into brand advocates	Requires established brand recognition and trust
Strongest behavior change yield	Loses control over message

popular work, all of them offer options for these three functions: diffusion, community, and mobilization. It is up to you to determine which tools you are going to use to accomplish your goal.

Now that we understand the most important functions of social media (diffusion, community and mobilization), it is time to turn our attention to the users and messages involved. How has social media transformed audiences into active users for behavior change? How do social media structures influence user behavior? How does social media encourage more active engagement than traditional media? What tools help generate user participation? We will explore these questions and more in the next four chapters as we look at social media users and messages.

Key Takeaways

1   Social participation, a combination of mass dissemination and media engagement, provides users with real-life lived experiences and has proven the most efficient and effective way to spark behavior change.
2   Mobilization requires more than just interest. Marketers must use social media to make planning, execution and facilitation of action as easy as possible for users.
3   Give consumers a strong locus of control by allowing them to create and generate content and discussions in every step of the process, including product and message design. This will pull consumers in, not push messages out, and transform consumers into brand advocates.
4   Cyberactivism should go beyond awareness only. Be sure a tangible action is tied to your messages that correspond with your initiative's goals.

References

Albanesius, C. (2010) Why the color Facebook updates? Breast cancer awareness. Available at http://appscout. pcmag.com/social-networking/270867-why-the-color-facebook-updates-breast-cancer-awareness (accessed June 8, 2016).

Bandura, A. (2004) Health promotion by social cognitive means. *Health Education and Behavior*, 31, 143–164.

Boulos, K. & Wheeler, S. (2007) The emerging Web 2.0 social software: an enabling suite of sociable technologies in health and health care education. *Health Information and Libraries Journal*, 24, 2–23.

Boyd, D. (2011) Social network sites as networked publics: affordances, dynamics and implications. In: Z. Papacharissi (ed.) *A Networked Self. Identity, Community and Culture on Social Network Sites*, pp. 39–58. New York: Routledge.

Byrne, A. with Gray-Felder, D., Hunt, J. & Parks, W. (2005) Measuring change: a guide to participatory monitoring and evaluation of communication for social change. Available at http://www.communicationfor socialchange.org/pdf/measuring_change.pdf (accessed June 8, 2016).

Cha, M., Kwak, H., Rodriguez, P., Ahn, Y.Y. & Moon, S. (2007) I tube, you tube, everybody tubes: analyzing the world's largest user generated content video system. In: *Proceedings of the 7th ACM SIGCOMM Conference on Internet Measurement*. New York: ACM Press. Available at http://an.kaist.ac.kr/traces/papers/imc131-cha.pdf (accessed June 8, 2016).

Cheng, X., Dale, C. & Liu, J. (2008) Statistics and social network of YouTube videos. In: *16th International Workshop on Quality of Service*, pp. 229–238. Piscataway, NJ: IEEE.

Citrin, A.V., Stem Jr D.E., Spangenberg, E.R. & Clark, M.J. (2003) Consumer need for tactile input: an Internet retailing challenge. *Journal of Business Research*, 56(11), 915–922.

Crawford, K. (2009) Following you: disciplines of listening in social media. *Continuum: Journal of Media and Cultural Studies*, 23(4), 525–535.

Dutta, M. (2006) Theoretical approaches to entertainment education campaigns: a subaltern critique. *Health Communication*, 20(3), 221–231.

Eltantawy, N. & Wiest, J.B. (2011) Social media in the Egyptian revolution: reconsidering resource mobilization theory. *International Journal of Communication*, 5, 1207–1224.

Enjolras, B., Steen-Johnsen, K. & Wollebaek, D. (2013) How do social media change the conditions for civic and political mobilization? Available at http://www.academia.edu/1353639/How_do_social_media_change_the_conditions_for_civic_and_political_mobilization (accessed June 8, 2016).

FritoLays (2013) Lays do us a Flavor. http://www.fritolay.com/lays/ (accessed June 8, 2016).

Gladwell, M. (2010) Small change. Why the revolution will not be tweeted. Available at http://www.newyorker.com/magazine/2010/10/04/small-change-malcolm-gladwell (accessed June 8, 2016).

Gowers, T. & Nielsen, M. (2009) Massively collaborative mathematics. *Nature*, 461(7266), 879–881.

Gray-Felder, D. & Deane, J. (1999) Communication and social change: a position paper and conference report. New York: The Rockefeller Foundation. Available at http://www.communicationforsocialchange.org/publications-resources?itemid=14 (accessed June 8, 2016).

Haridakis, P. & Hanson, G. (2009) Social interaction and co-viewing with YouTube: blending mass communication reception and social connection. *Journal of Broadcasting and Electronic Media*, 3(2), 317–335.

Haridakis, P. & Rubin, A. (2005) Third-person effects in the aftermath of terrorism. *Mass Communication and Society*, 8(1), 39–59.

Heilman, C., Lakishyk, K. & Radas, S. (2011) An empirical investigation of in-store sampling promotions. *British Food Journal*, 113(10), 1252–1266.

Howard, P.N. (2011) *The Digital Origins of Dictatorship and Democracy: Information Technology and Political Islam*. Oxford: Oxford University Press.

Husain, S. & Shaikh, B. (2005) Stalling HIV through social marketing: prospects in Pakistan. *Journal of the Pakistan Medical Association*, 55(7), 294–298.

Jenkins, J.C. (1983) Resource mobilization theory and the study of social movements. *Annual Review of Sociology*, 9, 527–553.

Kaplan, A.M. & Haenlein, M. (2010) Users of the world, unite! The challenges and opportunities of social media. *Business Horizons*, 53(1), 59–68.

Khamis, S. & Vaughn, K. (2011) Cyberactivism in the Egyptian revolution: how civic engagement and citizen journalism tilted the balance. *Arab Media and Society*, 13, 1–36.

Komen (2012) Facts for life: breast cancer in men. Available at http://ww5.komen.org/uploadedfiles/content_binaries/806-320a.pdf (accessed June 8, 2016).

Levenson, H. (1974) Activism and powerful others: distinctions within the concepts of internal–external control. *Journal of Personality Assessment*, 38, 377–383.

McCarthy, J.D. & Zald, M.N. (1977) Resource mobilization and social movements: a partial theory. *American Journal of Sociology*, 82(6), 1212–1241.

Morris, N. (2003) A comparative analysis of the diffusion and participatory models in communication for development. *Communication Theory*, 13(2), 225–248.

Neuhauser, L. & Kreps, G. (2003) Rethinking communication in the e-health era. *Journal of Health Psychology*, 8, 7–22.

Potter, J. (1988) Perceived reality in television effects research. *Journal of Broadcast and Electronic Media*, 32(1), 23–41.

Raftery J. (1991) Faster access to modern treatments? Analysis of guidance on health technologies, *BMJ*, 323(7324), 1300–1303.

Rosenstone, S. & Hansen, J. (1993) *Mobilization, Participation, and Democracy in America*. New York: Macmillan.

Singhal, A. & Rogers, E. (2003) *Combating AIDS: Communication Strategies In action*. Thousand Oaks, CA: Sage Publications.

Stein, S. (2010) Breast cancer awareness just gets sexier every day. Available at http://jezebel.com/5657153/breast-cancer-awareness-just-gets-sexier-every-day (accessed June 8, 2016)

Sterne, J. (2010) *Social Media Metrics: How to Measure and Optimize Your Marketing Investment*. Hoboken, NJ: John Wiley & Sons, Inc.

Stone, S. (1993) Getting the message out: feminists, the press and violence against women. *Canadian Review of Sociology und Anthropology*, 30, 377–400.

Stratten, S. (2012) *UnMarketing: Stop Marketing. Start Engaging*. Hoboken, NJ: John Wiley & Sons, Inc.

TOMS (2013) TOMS: One for one. Available at http://www.toms.com/ (accessed June 8, 2016).

Trussell, D. (2012) Pinktober! Queue another stupid Facebook meme. Available at https://www.washingtonpost.com/blogs/she-the-people/wp/2012/10/02/pinktober-queue-another-stupid-facebook-meme/ (accessed June 8, 2016).

Van Dijck, J. (2009) Users like you? Theorizing agency in user-generated content. *Media, Culture, and Society*, 31(1), 41.

Waisbord, S. (2001) Family tree of theories, methodologies and strategies in communication for development. Prepared for the Rockefeller Foundation. Available at http://www.communicationforsocialchange.org/pdf/familytree.pdf (accessed June 8, 2016).

Wei, R. (2013) Mobile media: coming of age with a big splash. *Mobile Media and Communication*, 1(1), 50–56.

Weisbrod, B. (1991) The health care quadrilemma: an essay on technological change, insurance, quality of care, and cost containment. *Journal of Economic Literature*, 29(2), 523–552.

Part II

Social Media Users and Messages

5

Transforming Audiences into Users

Learning Objectives

After reading this chapter, you should be able to:

1 Explain active audience theories, such as uses and gratifications, social cognitive theory and selective exposure, and be able to identify opportunities and challenges when marketing to social media users.
2 Identify individual and cognitive factors that influence social media use.
3 Analyze social media user profiles and understand how to utilize them for effective social media marketing.

Introduction

Part I of this book introduced social media functions and three strategies for creating messages: diffusion, community, and mobilization. Regardless of which approach you are using in your social media strategy, all marketing should begin with a thorough audience analysis. This chapter will help in that process by explaining why audiences use social media, identify individual and cognitive factors that influence social media use, and pinpoint opportunities and challenges you may face when using social media to reach and influence an audience.

We have learned how social media transforms passive audiences into empowered users. Users are able to simultaneously receive a sales message from their Facebook page, share thoughts (positive or negative) about your company on Twitter, and provide suggestions for your next product line via your official website. They may also accidently encounter a pin board on Pinterest, make their purchase directly through the link, and re-pin it to make more people aware of their "likes." Social media has aided more user-centered communication, brought increased sense of community, and prompted more positive participatory behavior change. It has transformed passive audiences into active participants that endorse products directly in the marketplace.

Social media audiences today actively seek media content to gratify their needs, and have greater control over their media choices than ever before (Sundet & Ytreberg, 2009). As a social media marketer, you should encourage more direct communication with your consumers and build customized user content (Chan-Olmsted & Ha, 2003; Lin & Cho, 2010). Since many factors can impact people's social media use, you first must identify a range of factors that explain how marketing content is consumed on social media, as well as what motivates consumers to make a purchasing decision.

Transforming Passive Audiences to Empowered Users

In today's digital marketplace, social media audiences act as *prosumers*, or individuals who consume and produce content at the same time (Toffler, 1980; Ritzer & Jurgenson, 2010). The dynamic nature of social media makes audiences interact with the medium in a much more direct and personalized manner than traditional media. Thus, social media marketers should aim to provide consumers with a personalized experience, and seek to achieve a thorough understanding of why and how people use social media and how such a use would influence their purchasing decision. What works well to persuade one individual may not be successful on another. Each individual user consumes social media messages for reasons that are unique, yet specific to the context and life situation. It is important for you to consider your unique social media audience as an individual, rather than a macro unit of aggregated mass (Potter, 2009). *What* to disseminate to the audiences is just as crucial as *how* to get the information to them when designing a social media strategy.

Active audience theories provide an explanation of why people choose and use media. Scholars within this theoretical school believe that audiences are active and goal-directed, and they make a rational choice to use media content to satisfy their personal needs and desires. Essentially, these theories seek to answer the question what people do with media, not what media do to people (Katz *et al.*, 1974). This dramatically changes the traditional conceptualization that audiences are passive laid-back message receivers.

Active audience theories suggest that audience activity is prevalent in a new media environment as the experience lends itself to a convergence culture wherein individuals have more choices and control on what, when, where, and how they want to consume media content (Ruggiero, 2000; Sundet & Ytreberg, 2009). These theories adopt a psychological viewpoint and focus on how individual motivations, moods, personality, attitude, preferences, and demographics influence social media use (Akar & Topcu, 2011; Sweitzer, 2014). A few illustrations of active audience theories include uses and gratifications theory, social cognitive theory, mood management, and selective exposure theory.

Uses and gratifications theory

Uses and gratifications theory explains how audiences use media to satisfy their needs. The theory is based on five fundamental characteristics proposed by McLeod and Becker (1981), including:

> First, audiences are active. Second, media use is goal directed. Third, media use fulfills a wide variety of needs. Fourth, people can articulate their reasons for using the media. And fifth, the gratifications have their origins in media content, exposure, and the social context in which exposure takes place (Potter, 2009, p. 142).

Researchers suggest that the social and psychological origins of needs lead to different patterns of media exposure (Katz *et al.*, 1974).

Specifically, the uses and gratifications theory identifies two orientations that explain why audiences use media: instrumental media use and ritualistic use. According to Rubin (1984, p. 67), "*instrumental media use* reflects more active patterns of using media content to select information from realistically perceived messages. *Ritualized media use* reflects less active patterns of using the media to fill time and relieve boredom [emphasis added]." While academia has debated the active/passive role of audiences, it seems trivial for marketers to participate in this conversation. A more important question for social media marketers to answer is what motivates audiences to use what types of social media content. How can they develop effective social media messages to serve audiences who have different motivations and goals?

There are many examples of marketers achieving this in your own life. Let's imagine that you were watching the Oscars award show on television. During this activity, you were also actively tweeting your thoughts and predictions of who will take home an award. During the commercial break, you decided to fill the time by skimming through tweets. You see a post talking about Lady Gaga's elegant Versace gown. The dress captures your attention, and you immediately retweet the post, pin it on Pinterest, and begin to actively search for more information about Versace. This scenario indicates how both instrumental and ritualistic motivations influence our media use. People do use a medium both purposefully and out of habit (Cooper & Tang, 2009). We will talk more about the relationship between motivations and social media use in the section "Predicting social media use and audience behavior."

Social cognitive theory

Social cognitive theory has been widely applied to explain many stages of media choices, including the initial adoption, content selection, and habitual behavior. It suggests that outcome expectations, self-efficacy, and self-regulation are the conscious factors that determine audience behavior (LaRose & Eastin, 2004; LaRose, 2009). *Outcome expectations* refer to both positive outcomes and negative consequences that enact the behavior (LaRose, 2009), including novel, social, activity, monetary, self-reactive, and status outcomes (LaRose & Eastin, 2004). Novel outcomes refer to using media to find new information or features.

Social outcomes suggest that audiences use a medium for social support, sense of belonging, and relationship development. Activity outcomes are similar to entertainment motivations, while monetary outcomes indicate that using a medium can help people save time and money. Self-reactive outcomes refer to using media to pass the time, and status outcomes suggest that people use media to get respect and values (LaRose & Eastin, 2004).

Self-efficacy indicates the belief in one's capability to perform a task (LaRose & Eastin, 2004). Self-efficacy is different from actual skill level or previous experience, but simply indicates people's confidence level in their ability to use a media product/service. *Self-regulation* is a process that incorporates three stages: self-observation, judgmental process, and self-reaction (Bandura, 1991). Research suggests that audiences observe their behavior, compare the behavior with social norms, and then decide whether to repeat the behavior or change it (LaRose & Eastin, 2004).

Social media use is based on the mutual influence of outcome expectations, self-efficacy, and self-regulation. Let's imagine that your client is planning a wedding. You introduce her to Pinterest because you believe that Pinterest is able to meet her unique social and status expected outcomes. She can use Pinterest to follow your newest products, trending must-haves for a spring wedding, communicating with other brides-to-be, sharing with friends and family, and retelling her experience with thousands of people via the virtual community. These are all the possible benefits of following your Pinterest page.

Next, you aim to build your customer's self-efficacy, in particular those who have never used Pinterest before. Here, you help your customers connect with their friends and social networks, link them to the boards they would like, encourage them to join social groups with which share the same interests and passion, and reinforce the positive values they would get via your continuous conversations with them. As suggested by social cognitive theory, your clients' initial exposure to a new social media endeavor may be led by your recommendation or their previous experience with a similar site. However, it is the perception of their future use of the endeavor, rather than any objective technological features, that determine their adoption and continuous use.

Mood management theory

Mood management theory suggests that individual's media choices vary with their moods (Zillmann, 1988). There are many reasons why individuals turn to media during emotional situations. When people are excited, they are likely to select a more relaxing media outlet. Bored people, on the other hand, seek to find stimulating content. People who are stressed prefer to consume calming programs. Men tend to use media for distraction when they are in a bad mood, while women tend to watch sad movies to mediate their moods (Nolen-Hoeksema, 1987). In general, people like to consume media content with a positive tone, and tend to avoid any message that generates disagreeable feelings (Knobloch-Westerwick, 2007). Therefore, you should set up a positive and pleasant tone in your social media messages. Most of your audience simply wishes to use social media for fun.

It is also important for social media marketers to match their messages with a context and audiences' mood. This requires practitioners to stay up to date on important public sphere issues. For example, maybe your audience was very excited about the Netherlands–Spain game in the 2014 World Cup. If your audience is mostly from the Netherlands, they probably looked for a way to express their national pride. This provided a great opportunity to connect with your Netherlands consumers via social media. Before and during the game, you could have created engaging visualizations about the World Cup on Facebook and Twitter, kept up with the game in real time to show your support, and celebrated when the Netherlands scored a goal. These actions allow you to take part in the conversation that is already taking place, and will make you seem more like a human and less like a brand. Remember that identification is crucial to behavior change. It is important that your social media messages adapt to the real-life experiences and moods of your audiences. Social media should be a place to have fun with your audiences.

An example of a company that was able to have fun and match their audience personality is Just Eat, a leading takeaway ordering service. Just Eat connects more than 36,000 local restaurants and 5 million consumers in 13 countries (Carver, 2013). In fall 2012, the company launched a multimedia campaign titled "Don't Cook, JUST EAT" in the United Kingdom. The campaign began with a 90-second TV commercial that positioned Just Eat as an "anti-cooking rebel" who was out to get rid of home cooking. In the commercial, a group of takeaway chefs attempted to prevent amateur chefs from cooking at home, and kidnapped Antony Worrall Thompson, a well-known TV celebrity chef. The TV ad aimed to stimulate audiences' interests and the anti-cooking mood. To further engage the audiences, Just Eat used the hashtag #JUSTEATkidnap and encouraged audiences to share anti-cooking texts and images on social media. They also developed an online game that allowed audiences to "slap" Antony Worrall Thompson across the face with a catch-of-the-day fish. The campaign encouraged audiences to share the game on Facebook and Twitter with friends during the campaign period (Carver, 2013). As a result, in just one week audiences used #JUSTEATkidnap hashtag more than 1000 times, and "slapped" Antony Worrall Thompson 850,000 times (online). The campaign was successfully able to increase Just Eat's brand awareness through a diffusion message about their product, brought an increased sense of community through dialogue with participants, and demonstrated the importance of incorporating the mood and personality of your audience into your social media strategy.

Selective exposure theory

Selective exposure theory offers a similar approach to explain media use by suggesting that audiences tend to hold certain attitudes, values or opinions and that these predispositions make people choose media content that matches their beliefs, but avoid media that challenges them (Webster & Phalen, 1997; Prior, 2005). For example, if your company's "smiling face" logo appears on social media in the middle of sad disaster news, your audiences may feel very offended. As a social media marketer, you need to take your audiences' likes, beliefs and attitudes into consideration when developing the messages. Only after you reach consumers emotionally, can you impact their purchasing decisions (Sweeney *et al.*, 2014). Now that we understand the relationship between social media marketing and audience mood and emotions, let's turn our attention towards using this information to predict audience behavior.

Predicting Social Media Use and Audience Behavior

In November 2014, Sephora, a company that sells beauty products, launched a rare full-shop discount to loyal customers. However, the promotion quickly turned into a social media crisis when Sephora began blocking selected user accounts during the sale. Some customers with a registered Chinese email address (for example qq.com; 163.com) were having trouble purchasing products. Other users with an East Asian last name also had trouble (Northrup, 2014). Without an official online customer service department to vent to, Sephora's angry customers gathered on the company's Facebook page, shared their stories, supported each other, and sought further social and legal help via social media. Within a day, Sephora's Facebook was filled with hostile comments, racial discrimination accusation, as well as uncertainty and confusion from those whose account was not impacted. Customers demanded that Sephora speak up and fix the situation. Forty hours after the chaos, Sephora made an official statement on Facebook as quoted below (Sephora, 2014):

> A Message To Our Clients: Sephora is dedicated to providing an exciting and reliable shopping experience and we sincerely apologize to our loyal clients who were impacted by the website outage that occurred yesterday.
>
> Our website is incredibly robust and designed to withstand a tremendous amount of volume. What caused the disruption yesterday was a high level of bulk buys and automated accounts for reselling purposes from North America and multiple countries outside the US. The technical difficulties that impacted the site are actively being addressed and our desktop US website is now functioning normally. We are actively working to restore our Canadian, mobile website, and international shipping where applicable. There has been no impact on the security and privacy of our clients' data.
>
> The reality is that in taking steps to restore website functionality, some of our loyal North American and international clients got temporarily blocked. We understand how frustrating it is and are deeply sorry for the disruption to your shopping experience.
>
> However, in some instances we have, indeed, deactivated accounts due to reselling – a pervasive issue throughout the industry and the world. As part of our ongoing commitment to protecting our clients and our brands, we have identified certain entities who take advantage of promotional opportunities to purchase products in large volume on our website and re-sell them through other channels. After careful consideration, we have deactivated these accounts in order to optimize product availability for the majority of our clients, as well as ensure that consumers are not subject to increased prices or products that are not being handled or stored properly.
>
> We have established a VIB hotline to ensure that if we are able to verify that your account was erroneously deactivated, it is reactivated immediately. Please call 877-VIB-ONLY (1-877-842-6659).

This statement did not satisfy customers. Many of the social media users stated that if Sephora were able to release this announcement in a timelier manner, they would be more willing to accept this explanation and apology. However, a delay of 40 hours seems too long to address customers' concerns in today's digital landscape. This example illustrates how expectations of customer service and immediacy have changed because of social media.

Today's social media users have more power than ever before. Here, social media was utilized as a place for individual customers to vent about their problems, communicate with each other, and request an apology. As such, social media marketers and communication specialists must understand people's social media use patterns and factors that influence social media use before they develop a social media campaign, or respond to their social media crisis.

Individual factors influence social media use. Research has shown that genes influence human behavior (Bouchard, 2004; Freese & Shostak, 2009; Kirzinger *et al.*, 2012). Gender, age, income, ethnicity, and/or sexual preference make audiences use different media, and hence make various purchasing decisions (Sewell, 1992). Who we are directly influences what media we choose to use and which communication we seek to pursue. For example, Pinterest is considered a more female-oriented social media. Facebook is a universal social media that attracts audiences of different sex, age, and social economic status. For this reason, marketers and communication specialists have long conducted demographic analysis of their target audiences. Age, gender, education, social economic status, ethnicity, and occupation are all important data any marketer should obtain about their consumers before developing their marketing strategies. It is important for you to select an appropriate social media platform to best reach your target consumers.

Personality is also a predictor of media consumption (Zillmann, 1988). Researchers suggest that there are five personality traits: neuroticism (sensitive/nervous vs. secure/confident), extroversion (outgoing/energetic vs. solitary/reserved), openness (inventive/curious vs. consistent/cautious), agreeableness (friendly/compassionate vs. cold/unkind), and conscientiousness (efficient/organized vs. easy-going/careless). This is often abbreviated to *OCEAN* (*o*penness, *c*onscientiousness, *e*xtroversion, *a*greeableness, *n*euroticism). Media use can be explained by the personality continuum OCEAN (Rammstedt & John, 2007; Jenkins-Guarnieri *et al.*, 2012).

For example, extroverted people tend to choose activities that provide direct social contact (Argyle & Lu, 1990). Introverts like to use print media because print media can provide them a sense of control. People who are anxious and moody are likely to use media as a way to escape. Those who are curious and willing to try new ideas tend to spend more time doing pleasure reading, but less time watching TV. Audiences who are more neurotic choose news and information programs and prefer objective messages (Finn, 1997; Krcmar & Strizhakova, 2009). In terms of social media use, outgoing people and those who are open to new ideas tend to use social media frequently, while those with emotional stability rarely use social media (Krcmar & Strizhakova, 2009; Correa, Hinsley & Gil de Zuniga, 2010). Extroverted people like to tweet. Those who are less open and disclosing tend to use LinkedIn (Sweitzer, 2014).

As you can see, personality influences what media your audiences choose to use. When developing a social media campaign, you need to understand your audience's personality. In addition, give your brand campaign a personality, find the social media platforms that can best carry the personality, and reach audiences who share or appreciate the personality.

We are going to discuss how to give your campaign a personality in Chapter 11 when we talk more about social media marketing strategies.

In addition to demographics and personality traits, cognitive factors predict which media we choose to use (or not use). These cognitive factors include, for example, motivations, attitudes, self-efficacy, and preferences. Compared to individual factors (demographics, personality), cognitive factors are less fixed and can change from time to time. They set up internal boundaries for our media use and other social behavior. For example, your consumer may have a desire to visit your company's Vine account because they are outgoing and extroverted, but their attitude towards your Vine account will ultimately decide whether they will use it. If they do not like the constant pushy videos about your product on Vine, or if they hold a negative attitude towards the increasing amount of social media advertising in general, they will not visit your Vine account no matter how outgoing they are.

As mentioned earlier, attitude is a cognitive factor that predicts social media use. When consumers hold a negative attitude towards your page, they stop visiting it (Akar & Topcu, 2011; Sweitzer, 2014). Researchers suggest that attitudes towards online media are based on attitudes towards elements other than the media itself (Wang *et al.*, 2002). An advertisement, a picture, or a message on your social media page can affect your consumer's opinion about the entire page. Audiences have personal preferences and primarily consume media materials that fit their tastes. Therefore, it is important to carry out solid audience research to know your consumers' likes and dislikes. Many social media monitoring tools now allow you to assess your audiences' attitudes towards your company. We will talk more about these tools in Chapter 12.

Four motivations – intrinsic motivation, identified regulation, external regulation, and automotivation – can influence social media use (Ryan & Deci, 2000). *Intrinsic motivation* refers to the reason that simply comes from the satisfaction and pleasure of using the media itself. For example, your audiences may watch a YouTube video just for fun. *Identified regulation* indicates that people use media because they believe that the media can be beneficial to them in the long run (Ryan & Deci, 2000). They choose to use the media for the reward. For example, you may use Coursera to take an online social media marketing course, because you believe the course can put you ahead in the social media marketing field. Identified regulation thus explains why you use the media.

External regulation suggests that people use media to avoid a negative outcome or to seek external rewards (Ryan & Deci, 2000). The difference between identified regulation and external regulation is that when people use media for external regulation, they feel that they have no choice but use the media. Nonetheless, when people use media for identified regulation, they feel that they have free choices and they use the media because they want to. For example, you may participate in an online discussion board because your professor requires you to do so. People can also use a medium without a clear motive. They may use the medium simply because it is available. We call this type of behavior *automotivation* (Ryan & Deci, 2000).

Your social media messages must fit your audiences' motivations and be able to satisfy their wants. Motivations are not necessarily equal to the gratifications people obtained from using the media. The uses and gratifications theory defines gratifications sought and gratifications obtained. *Gratifications sought* are the reasons for using the media, whereas *gratifications obtained* are the results after using the media (Krcmar & Strizhakova, 2009). For example, your audience may seek out social media for social uses, but end up being lonelier after spending hours on Facebook. Thus, social is the "gratification sought" while passing time may become the "gratification obtained."

Mismatched campaigns can lead to negative outcomes that offer disincentives for social media use, and hurt product sales in the long run. Let's say you are now in charge of the Facebook page of Urban Fitness, a popular gym in the United States. Your audiences wanted to learn about weight loss tips and how to maintain a healthy lifestyle (i.e., basically to seek identified regulation) from Urban Fitness's Facebook page. If they successfully obtained this information after the initial exposure, they would be satisfied and would go back to your page. However, if they found that the Facebook page were full of funny videos, their identified regulation motivation would not be satisfied, which would discourage them to revisit the page, and ultimately influence their purchasing decision of gym membership. As a social media marketer, you want to use identified and/or external regulation as your communication strategy, or simply make using your social media site an automatic behavior of your audiences.

KIXEYE is an online gaming company with popular titles like War Commander, VEGA Conflict, and Battle Pirates. One unique feature of the company is that all of its games are made by gamers for gamers. One challenge that KIXEYE faces, however, is to attract high-quality gamers and keep them engaged at a low cost. In 2012, KIXEYE created a social media engagement campaign. The marketing team of KIXEYE used social media monitoring tools (which we are going to discuss in great detail in Chapter 12) to understand the audiences' motivations, likes and dislikes (Nucleus Research, 2013), and then recommended audiences to play a new game or try new features based on the games that they have already played and liked. As a result, the social media engagement campaign extended the life cycle of each KIXEYE game by 6 months, and increased user engagement by 7.5% (Nucleus Research, 2013).

Self-efficacy is another cognitive factor that influences social media use. As mentioned earlier in this chapter, self-efficacy is not equal to the actual technology skill, but rather about your audiences' personal belief of their ability to use the media. People with high self-efficacy generally are more willing to adopt and use new media, while those with low self-efficacy tend not to do the same. Positive previous experience generally enhances one's confidence in ability to repeat the behavior. However, it is the self-reflection, rather than the objective skill, that guides or constrains people's social media use (LaRose, 2009). Social media marketers thus need to positively affect their consumers' self-efficacy mechanism.

HubSpot is a leading company in the United States that provides marketing tools for businesses. The company has used a content creation plan that reflects what their clients want. When HubSpot writes articles on social media, they tag their articles based on their clients' experience level, and develop different materials to match their clients' interests and skill levels. HubSpot's interface is very easy to use. They make sure that the site prominently displays like, share, email, print, and comment widgets next to each article/message. These all help enhance HubSpot users' self-efficacy and make them continuously use the site.

In addition to creating user-friendly content display, making your content part of your audience's daily routine will lead to a successful social media marketing endeavor. Habit has a big impact on human behavior. Researchers suggest that over half of all media behaviors are habitual (LaRose, 2009; Wood *et al.*, 2002). Over time, morning browsing Twitter may become a habit, independent of the particular content posted on Twitter. Morning, being an environmental cue, leads audiences to Twitter. Twitter use is then no longer a conscious decision but an automatic behavior.

Understanding your audiences is the first step towards a successful social media campaign. Below is a step-by-step action plan to help you get to know your audience.

Know Your Audience Action Plan

1   Be certain to gather basic demographics information (e.g., age, gender, education, income, geographic location) about your audiences, and choose the social media platforms that can reach these people.
2   Conduct a more in-depth audience analysis to understand your audiences' interests, passions, personality and, more importantly, why they would use your social media messages. Then, develop your social media messages to match your audiences' interests and personality, and satisfy their desires.
3   Enhance your audiences' self-efficacy by guiding them to materials at their skill/knowledge level and making your campaign/messages easy to navigate.
4   Use social media monitoring tools to track audience attitudes towards your campaign.

Social Media User Profile

Before you start a social media campaign, you may want to answer the following question: Who are the social media users that I am likely to attract? According to Pew Research Center, more than 70% of online adults have used social media and 40% of them use multiple social media sites multiple times on any given day (Duggan *et al.*, 2013). Slightly more females than males use social media. About 90% of young adults, 78% of 30–49 year olds, 65% of 50–64 year olds, and half of 65 year olds or older are social media users. Simply put, social media is used by people with various occupations, education, and income today (Duggan *et al.*, 2015).

Different social media sites, though, attract different audiences. Facebook is the most popular social media platform, with more than 1 billion users worldwide (Facebook, 2014). It reaches more than 70% of online adults, and is thus a great mass (social) medium for you to send marketing messages with a general appeal. Facebook is also one of few social media sites that can reach older demographics, as more than half of the Internet users aged 65 years old or older use Facebook (Duggan *et al.*, 2015). In addition, Facebook users generally have more social support and are more politically engaged than nonusers (Pew Research Center, 2011). Overall, Facebook is a great platform for reaching the mass, developing trust, and building a community. Nonetheless, Facebook users create more than 2 billion pieces of content on any given day (Constine, 2012). Because of the large amount of information available on Facebook, your audiences could easily ignore your messages.

Twitter, a micro-blogging site, is another popular social media site. About 23% of Internet users have currently adopted Twitter (Duggan *et al.*, 2015). In particular, Twitter adoption is high among younger people. More than 30% of 18–29 year olds are Twitter users while only 5% of older people (i.e., 65 years old or older) have used Twitter (Duggan *et al.*, 2013). Overall, there are 560 million active Twitter users, and 5700 tweets are sent every second (Bennett, 2013). Therefore, social media marketers can use Twitter to provide quick updates and feedback. One of the biggest challenges of using Twitter to disseminate social media messages is the short shelf-life of tweets. Twitter is a great place to provide up-to-date information, but may not be the best place for permanent message diffusion.

Instagram is also a social media site used mainly by young adults. About 53% of those aged 18–29 years old currently use Instagram. And half of Instagram users visited the site on a daily basis (Duggan *et al.*, 2015). Instagram is a photo-heavy social media. Its photos are searchable through hashtags. Feeds are displayed in chronological order, so users tend to share photos that are happening now. Instagram has been believed to be an effective tool for carrying photo ads for marketers (Smith, 2014). The *Wall Street Journal* has identified Instagram expertise as one of the skills most desired by employers who look for social media marketers or social media communication specialists (Stone, 2013). While Instagram is a great tool for disseminating visual products, it does not allow you to organically connect with consumers. It is up to audiences who they follow in their feed.

LinkedIn is a social networking site that aims to help users build professional networks. Currently, 28% of all Internet users are LinkedIn users (Duggan *et al.*, 2015). It is one of the few social media sites used more by men than women. The platform also tends to attract people with a college degree or higher, and those with a household income of more than $US75,000. More interestingly, LinkedIn is the only major social media used more by older adults compared to young adults. While only 15% of 18–29 year olds use LinkedIn, 24% of 50–64 year olds are LinkedIn users (Duggan *et al.*, 2013). The platform also reaches people currently employed and those unemployed (27% vs. 12%). It is clear that LinkedIn is a unique social media platform, with users quite different from other social media sites, and thus could be an effective tool for marketers/organizations interested in B2B communication and/or targeting of professionals or people with relatively higher levels of education and income. LinkedIn also allows users to be in charge of their social media content. The content people post on LinkedIn tends to be more polished (and consequently less interesting). Users do not visit LinkedIn as often as the other social media platforms.

Pinterest is a social media platform designed for users to organize bookmarks on the interest. It tends to be a more female-oriented site. Among Pinterest users, 68% are female and 32% male (SEO, 2015). Pinterest users also skew towards people with relatively higher levels of education and social economic status. Most of the Pinterest users are loyal and active to the media. Pinterest is an effective social media platform that targets audiences based on "who they are" (e.g., their interests, passions). One of the biggest challenges of Pinterest is that it is difficult to track pins and users. It is not the best social media site for local small businesses to market their products.

In no way is this an exhaustive list of social media platforms. As a practitioner, it is important that you stay up to date on the greatest trends in technology. The most popular social media platforms are those with user-friendly interfaces. Therefore, it should not be too difficult to learn how to create and maintain any emerging social media platform. That is why this book focuses on social media function rather than platform-specific recommendations.

Additionally, the best social media practitioners use a cross-platform approach. According to Pew Research Center, more than half of Internet users use multiple social media today. Only 28% of people use just one social media site (Duggan *et al.*, 2015). Here, 93% of Instagram users also use Facebook; 53% of them are Twitter users. Twitter users tend to use LindedIn, while Instagram users are likely to use Pinterest (Duggan *et al.*, 2013). When audiences use social media today, they rarely choose just one space to share and receive content. It is important that you are not creating one message to share identically across all platforms. Instead, social media marketers need to be aware of the reciprocity relationships between different social media sites; think of all the social media tools available and develop an integrated social media campaign to deliver messages effectively and efficiently.

Case Study: Weixin

This chapter has discussed how different individual and cognitive factors influence your audience's social media use and how knowing your audiences will lead to a successful social media campaign/product. One such example is Weixin (pronounced "way-shin"), a popular Chinese social networking app. Weixin is a social media product, similar to WhatsApp in the United States or Line in Japan, which allows users to send messages, share news, and pictures via their mobile phone. It was first introduced to Chinese users in 2011. Three years later, in 2014, Weixin has already had more than 300 million active users in China, Southeast Asia, Europe, and America. Tencent, the Chinese social media company that owns Weixin, is now worth $100 billion on the Hong Kong exchange (Barboza, 2014).

Weixin's success is the result of the thorough approach that it takes to understand its audience. The platform targets on young, urban smartphone owners and aims to provide these audiences an "all-in-one-platform" app. It offers a wide range of functions from sending a baby photo to friends, getting news, text messaging, to finding a cab on the street. Weixin is more than a combination of Facebook, Instagram, Twitter, Snapchat, and eBay. Audiences can do almost anything via Weixin, which makes the platform particularly appealing. With unlimited media choices available to users today, audiences are doing whatever they can to reduce "search costs." If audiences can get all they want from one platform, why bother to find other options. This helps to explain the success of Weixin.

Weixin is also easy to use. Its interface (Figure 5.1) and all the functions are designed to be straightforward and convenient to users. For example, Weixin allows its users to record messages by simply holding on one button and talking, which saves the trouble of typing Chinese characters on the phone. When people read news items on Weixin, instead of sending them to the news organization's official website, Weixin links them to the news source's URL within its own in-app browser, which is more viewable and visually pleasing. Audiences rarely need to leave Weixin to open a mobile browser no matter if they want to read news or make a purchase, which is not only convenient to audiences but also helps Weixin keep the audience flow. Even when audiences want to open an online store on Weixin, it only takes a few clicks, as Weixin claims in its Beijing subway ad: "one minute is all you need to open a Weixin shop" (Li, 2014, p. 2). It seems that because Weixin makes everything so easy to do and significantly enhance its users' self-efficacy, it has gradually become the norm for Chinese people's media use.

Figure 5.1   Weixin interface.

Moreover, Weixin keeps introducing new functions/campaigns that attempt to satisfy audiences' new needs or to fit audiences' mood at a certain time or in a certain context. In January 2014, just before the Chinese New Year, Weixin introduced a "Qiang Hongbao" campaign (i.e., Red Envelope campaign), which allowed its users to link their bank account to Weixin account, send or receive red envelopes virtually. Red Envelope is a traditional Chinese culture that includes a monetary gift that Chinese people give to family and friends during holidays. To evoke an exciting and suspenseful mood, Weixin further allowed users to put a sum of cash in the Red Envelope and then distribute the money randomly among a group of recipients the user set up (Horwitz, 2014). For example, if you want to give a total of $50 to Sarah, Maxx,

Fiona, and Tracy, Weixin will assign this money randomly to these four people. Maxx may be the lucky one who will get $30, Fiona will have $10, Sarah $8, and Tracy will just get $2. The campaign definitely made audiences excited, and ultimately encouraged them to spend more time and money using the social networking tool. As a result, nearly 5 million people participated in the Red Envelope campaign, and sent out 20 million cash-filled red envelopes virtually (Horwitz, 2014).

Also in 2014, Weixin introduced a cab reservation function called "Didi Taxi." Working with 350,000 taxi drivers in more than 30 cities in China, Weixin allows its users to book a taxi via Weixin payment. More than 22 million users have used this service thus far, and half a million bookings are made via Weixin every day (Chen, 2014; Millward, 2014). This new feature not only satisfies a niche need of Weixin users, but also trains them to pay via Weixin, which will bring a financial benefit to Tencent in the long run.

One big takeaway from the success of Weixin is that you should make your social media product a part of your audiences' everyday routine and habit. Since Weixin targets mobile users, it is always with people no matter they are at work, waiting for their food in a restaurant, or taking the subway. When your social media product becomes a part of people's daily life, it will be easier for you to make a behavior change, whether this behavior is a purchasing decision or a positive social change, starting with an audience analysis.

Discussion questions

1   In this chapter, we have discussed how knowing your audience is the first step towards a successful social media campaign. What can you do as a practitioner to ensure that you know as much as you can about your audiences? How did Weixin achieve this goal?
2   How do Weixin's features fit into their audience's needs, tastes, and interests? Is it possible for audiences with different backgrounds to individualize the social media for their individual lives?
3   What elements of Weixin make it a part of Chinese people's daily life? How were they able to integrate the technology to accommodate every characteristic of their audiences? Do you think Weixin will be successful in other countries?

Summary

This chapter focuses on the active audiences of social media. Specifically, it explores factors that influence social media use and identifies marketing opportunities and strategies to reach your social media audiences. Active audience theories (uses and gratifications, social cognitive theory, mood management, and selective exposure) suggest that audiences are active and goal-directed and make a rational choice to use media content to satisfy their needs and wants. Facing an abundance of media options, your audiences have a greater control over their media choices than ever before. They can decide when, where, how, and what to consume. It is important for you to consider your audience as an individual, rather than an aggregated mass. You must provide your audience a personalized experience.

Both individual characteristics and cognitive factors influence social media use. Different types of audiences use different social media sites. Your audiences make their media choices based on "who they are." As a social media marketer, you want to use the social media platforms that your target audiences use, and give your social media campaigns a personality.

There are four motivations – intrinsic motivation, identified regulation, external regulation, and automotivation – that explain people's social media use. Audiences today do use various social media for various purposes. It is important for your social media messages to fit your audiences' motivations and be able to satisfy their wants. Please remember that motivations are not equal to gratifications obtained. Mismatched campaigns can lead to negative outcomes that offer disincentives for social media use.

Social media marketers also need to present audiences with materials based on their knowledge and experience levels, since self-efficacy can both guide and constrain audience behavior. In addition, this chapter has suggested that social media use can be a habitual behavior. Making your brand and/or social media product a part of people's daily life should be your terminal goal. Develop environmental cues, and encourage automatic use of your social media messages.

Knowing your audiences' tastes, interests, and motivations is the first step towards a successful social media endeavor. Nonetheless, social media use is not free of constraints. Many structural factors, such as availability, access to media technologies, and the infrastructures provided by the industry and society, can influence audience behavior. Now let's turn our attention to the role of structure in social media use in Chapter 6.

Key Takeaways

1 Audiences gain increasing power over their media use. Tailoring your social media marketing campaign to your audience's needs, mood, and interests is a must.

2 Conduct a thorough and accurate audience analysis before any social media endeavor. Both individual characteristics (i.e., demographics, personality) and cognitive factors (i.e., attitude, motivations, self-efficacy, habit) influence social media use.

3 Keep your social media messages/product simple and easy to use. Often, audiences choose to use a media simply because it is convenient. Guide your audiences to materials at their skill/knowledge levels. Training your audiences' self-efficacy mechanism is important for them to adopt and continuously use your product/service.

4 Use a special occasion/context to develop a social media campaign. Make your audiences excited about your campaign, and put them into a social mood. Most often, your audiences are using social media for fun. Only the marketers who

successfully engage audiences emotionally are able to influence their purchasing behavior.

5   In today's multimedia environment, marketers need to notice the reciprocity relationships between different social media platforms. Use all the social media tools available to you, and develop an integrated social media marketing campaign.

6   Ultimately, your goal is to make your social media product/your brand a part of your consumer's daily life. When it becomes a part of their everyday life rituals, you do not need to sell your product/service any more.

References

Akar, E. & Topcu, B. (2011) An examination of the factors influencing consumers' attitudes toward social media marketing. *Journal of Internet Commerce*, 10, 35–67.

Argyle, M. & Lu, L. (1990) The happiness of extraverts. *Personality and Individual Differences*, 11, 1011–1017.

Bandura, A. (1991) Social cognitive theory of self-regulation. *Organizational Behavior and Human Decision Process*, 50, 248–287.

Barboza, D. (2014) A popular Chinese social networking app blazes its own path. Available at http://www.nytimes.com/2014/01/21/technology/a-chinese-social-network-blazes-its-own-path.html (accessed June 8, 2016).

Bennett, S. (2013) Everything you ever wanted to know about Twitter. Amazing statistics, facts and figures. Available at http://www.adweek.com/socialtimes/amazing-twitter-stats/492284 (accessed June 8, 2016).

Bouchard, T. (2004) Genetic influence on human psychological traits: a survey. *Current Directions in Psychological Science*, 13, 148–151.

Carver, S. (2013) Just Eat: Using Social Content to Deliver a Stellar Anti-Cooking Marketing Campaign. Available at http://www.marketingcloud.com/blog/social-content-case-study (accessed June 22, 2016).

Chan-Olmsted, S.M. & Ha, L.S. (2003) Internet business models for broadcasters: how television stations perceive and integrate the Internet. *Journal of Broadcasting and Electronic Media*, 47(4), 597–616.

Chen, L. (2014) Tencent invests in China cab booking app to tap mobile users. Available at http://www.bloomberg.com/news/2014-01-08/tencent-invests-in-china-cab-booking-app-to-tap-mobile-web-users.html (accessed June 8, 2016).

Constine, J. (2012) How big is Facebook's data? 2.5 billion pieces of content and 500+ terabytes ingested every day. Available at http://techcrunch.com/2012/08/22/how-big-is-facebooks-data-2-5-billion-pieces-of-content-and-500-terabytes-ingested-every-day/ (accessed June 8, 2016).

Cooper, R. & Tang, T. (2009) Predicting audience exposure to television in today's media environment: an empirical integration of active-audience and structural theories. *Journal of Broadcasting and Electronic Media*, 53(3), 1–19.

Correa, T., Hinsley, A.W. & Gil de Zuniga, H. (2010) Who interacts on the web? The intersection of users' personality and social media use. *Computers in Human Behavior*, 26, 247–253.

Duggan, M., Ellison, N.B., Lampe, C., Lenhart, A. & Madden, M. (2013) Demographics of key social networking platforms. Available at http://www.pewinternet.org/2015/01/09/demographics-of-key-social-networking-platforms-2/ (accessed June 8, 2016).

Duggan, M., Ellison, N.B., Lampe, C., Lenhart, A. & Madden, M. (2015) Social media update 2014. Available at http://www.pewinternet.org/2015/01/09/social-media-update-2014/ (accessed June 8, 2016).

Facebook (2014) http://www.facebook.com (accessed October 23, 2014).

Finn, S. (1997) Origins of media exposure: linking personality traits to TV, radio, print, and film use. *Communication Research*, 24, 507–529.

Freese, J. & Shostak, S. (2009) Genetics and social inquiry. *Annual Review of Sociology*, 35, 107–128.

Horwitz, J. (2014) Chinese WeChat users sent out 20 million cash-filled red envelopes to friends and family within two days. Available at https://www.techinasia.com/wechats-money-gifting-scheme-lures-5-million-chinese-users-alibabas-jack-ma-calls-pearl-harbor-attack-company/ (accessed June 8, 2016).

Jenkins-Guarnieri, M.A., Wright, S. & Hudiburgh, L.M. (2012) The relationship among attachment style, personality traits, interpersonal competency, and Facebook use. *Journal of Applied Developmental Psychology*, 33, 294–301.

Katz, E., Blumler, J.G. & Gurevitch, M. (1974) Utilization of mass communication by the individual. In: J.G. Blumler & E. Katz (eds) *The Uses of Mass Communications: Current Perspectives on Gratifications Research*, pp. 19–32. Beverly Hills, CA: Sage.

Kirzinger, A.S., Weber, C. & Johnson, M. (2012) Genetic and environmental influences on media use and communication behaviors. *Human Communication Research*, 38, 133–171.

Knobloch-Westerwick, S. (2007) Gender differences in selective media use for mood management and mood adjustment. *Journal of Broadcasting and Electronic Media*, 51(1), 73–92.

Krcmar, M. & Strizhakova, Y. (2009) Uses and gratifications as media choice. In: T. Hartman (ed.) *Media Choice: A Theoretical and Empirical Overview*, pp. 53–69. New York: Routledge.

LaRose, R. (2009) Social cognitive theories of media selection. In: T. Hartman (ed.) *Media Choice: A Theoretical and Empirical Overview*, pp. 10–31. New York: Routledge.

LaRose, R. & Eastin, M.S. (2004) A social cognitive theory of internet uses and gratifications: toward a new model of media attendance. *Journal of Broadcasting and Electronic Media*, 48(3), 358–377.

Li, H. (2014) Will WeChat succeed in mobile commerce? Available at http://knowledge.ckgsb.edu.cn/2014/08/26/technology/will-wechat-succeed-in-mobile-commerce/ (accessed June 8, 2016).

Lin, J.S. & Cho, C.H. (2010) Antecedents and consequences of cross-media usage: a study of a TV program's official web site. *Journal of Broadcasting and Electronic Media*, 54(2), 316–336.

McLeod, D.M. & Becker, L.B. (1981) The uses and gratifications approach. In: D.D. Nimmo & K.R. Sanders (eds) *Handbook of Political Communication*, pp. 67–99. Beverly Hills, CA: Sage.

Millward, S. (2014) 21 million taxi rides have been booked on WeChat in the past month. Available at https://www.techinasia.com/wechat-21-million-taxi-rides-booked/ (accessed June 8, 2016).

Nolen-Hoeksema, S. (1987) Sex differences in unipolar depression: evidence and theory. *Psychological Bulletin*, 101, 259–282.

Northrup, L. (2014) Customers accuse Sephora of banning shoppers with Asian surnames. Available at http://consumerist.com/2014/11/07/customers-accuse-sephora-of-banning-shoppers-with-asian-surnames/ (accessed June 8, 2016).

Nucleus Research (2013) Benefit case study. Available at http://www.salesforcemarketingcloud.com/wp-content/uploads/2013/08/KIXEYE-Benefits-Study.pdf?03a0bd (accessed June 8, 2016).

Pew Research Center (2011) Social networking fact sheet. Available at http://www.pewinternet.org/fact-sheets/social-networking-fact-sheet/ (accessed June 8, 2016).

Potter, W.J. (2009) *Arguing for a General Framework for Mass Media Scholarship*. Thousand Oaks, CA: Sage.

Prior, M. (2005) News vs. entertainment: how increasing media choice widens gaps in political knowledge and turnout. *American Journal of Political Science*, 3, 577–592.

Rammstedt, B. & John, O.P. (2007) Measuring personality in one minute or less: a 10-item short version of the Big Five Inventory in English and German. *Journal of Research in Personality*, 41, 203–212.

Ritzer, G. & Jurgenson, N. (2010) Production, consumption, presumption. *Journal of Consumer Culture*, 10(1), 13–36.

Rubin, A. (1984) Ritualized and instrumental television viewing. *Journal of Communication*, 34(3), 67–77.

Ruggiero, T.E. (2000) Uses and gratifications theory in the 21st century. *Mass Communication and Society*, 3(1), 3–37.

Ryan, R.M. & Deci, E.L. (2000) Self-determination theory and the facilitation of intrinsic motivation, social development, and well-being. *American Psychologist*, 55(1), 68–78.

SEO (2015) Social media by the numbers. Available at http://www.seoinc.com/seo-blog/infographic-friday-social-media-by-the-numbers/ (accessed June 8, 2016).

Sephora (2014) https://www.facebook.com/Sephora/posts/10152536253844405?pnref=story (accessed June 8, 2016).

Sewell, W.H. (1992) A theory of structure: duality, agency, and transformation. *American Journal of Sociology*, 98(1), 1–29.

Smith, C. (2014) Here's why Instagram's demographics are so attractive to brands. Available at http://uk.business insider.com/instagram-demographics-2013-12?r=US&IR=T (accessed June 8, 2016).

Stone, Z. (2013) Social-media schooling is on the rise: but is it necessary? Available at http://blogs.wsj.com/digits/2013/07/29/social-media-schooling-is-on-the-rise-but-is-it-necessary/ (accessed June 8, 2016).

Sundet, V.S. & Ytreberg, E. (2009) Working notions of active audiences: further research on the active participant in convergent media industries. *International Journal of Research into New Media Technologies*, 15(4), 383–390.

Sweeney, J.C., Webb, D., Mazzarol, T. & Soutar, G.N. (2014) Self-determination theory and word of mouth about energy-saving behaviors: an online experiment. *Psychology and Marketing*, 31(9), 698–716.

Sweitzer, B. (2014) Structurational Twitter: an examination of individual and structural predictors of Twitter use. Paper presented at the Broadcast Education Association annual conference, Las Vegas, NV.

Toffler, A. (1980) *The Third Wave*. New York: Bantam Books.

Wang, C., Zhang, P., Choi, R. & D'Eredita, M. (2002) Understanding consumers' attitude toward advertising. Paper presented at the 2002 Annual Meeting of the Eighth America's Conference on Information Systems.

Webster, J.G. & Phalen, P.F. (1997) *The Mass Audience: Rediscovering the Dominant Model*. Mahwah, NJ: Lawrence Erlbaum.

Wood, W., Quinn, J.M. & Kashy, D. (2002) Habits in everyday life: thought, emotion and action. *Journal of Personality and Social Psychology*, 83, 1281–1297.

Zillmann, D. (1988) Mood management through communication choices. *American Behavioral Scientist*, 31, 327–340.

6

Active Within Structures

Learning Objectives

After reading this chapter, you should be able to:
1   Explain active within structures theory and determine constrained active use.
2   Define social media structures and explain the role of structure in social media use.
3   Understand how to utilize social media structures to create messages that influence social media users.

Introduction

Chapter 5 explored how social media has transformed audiences into more active media users and discussed how individual psychographic factors such as motivations, mood, preferences, and demographics influence your consumers' social media use. We learned that as a social media practitioner, you should design campaigns based on an audience analysis, create social media messages to feature interests, cultural values and life experiences of your target audience, and stimulate an appropriate emotional mood. However, we also learned that there is little you can do as a marketer to control consumers' personal preferences, life experience, mood, and other individual psychological factors. This chapter focuses on the structures of social media technology and discusses how you can use social media structures to guide audience behavior to better meet campaign objectives.

Strategic Social Media: From Marketing to Social Change, First Edition. L. Meghan Mahoney and Tang Tang.
© 2017 John Wiley & Sons, Inc. Published 2017 by John Wiley & Sons, Inc.

As social media users gain increasingly greater control over their media choices, they continue to function within structures of time, cost, and resources. With only 24 hours in a day, audiences simply cannot consume all the media content available to them. They must use infrastructures provided by the technology and by society to find the messages that satisfy their needs and desires. Structures now, more than ever, influence the amount and type of media use. Or, as Nobel laureate Herbert Simon (1971, p. 40) observed, "A wealth of information creates a poverty of attention, and a need to allocate the attention efficiently among the overabundance of information sources that might consume it."

As a social media practitioner, it is important for you to know how the interactions between individual psychological factors, structures and habits influence social media use. There are many opportunities for you to use structural strategies to guide audiences' navigation of social media messages. To begin, let's focus on Cooper and Tang's active within structures theory, one of the newest and most innovative approaches to systematically examining media audiences in today's dynamic environment.

Theory of Active Within Structures

Understanding how and why audiences use social media is crucial information for anyone interested in creating social media messages to influence behavior change. Researchers suggest that there are two primary though conflicting theoretical perspectives that can help explain audience media use: active audience and structural theories. As discussed in Chapter 5, active audience theories believe that your social media users are active and make media choices according to their preferences and needs (Reiss & Wiltz, 2004; Sherry, 2004). On the other hand, structural theories see audiences as passive in consuming media, and suggest that media use, including social media use, is influenced by structural features such as time availability, access to media technologies, and infrastructures provided by the technology and by society (Webster *et al.*, 2006; Webster, 2011).

Consider the various kinds of media users with differing levels of participation along this active–passive dichotomy. Let's assume for a moment that you are a heavy Internet user. You probably check your email every five minutes. From the active audience perspective, you are actively seeking communication with others in your life. You may like to reply to your customers' emails as soon as possible, worry that something may go wrong with family, or simply want to know when your recent Amazon.com purchase will be shipped to your office. However, the reality is that no one is actually emailing you every five minutes. Most of the time, you would check your email account and end up disappointed that there is no incoming email. So why do you still check so often? The answer is simple: structure and habit. Personal computers now have software that allows users to check email with just one click of a button. If it were more difficult to check email, and required answers to five security questions before access to email, you would probably change your behavior.

This example demonstrates how our media use is guided by both active and structural constraints. We purposefully select media, but our selection is constrained by awareness, time, cost, and resources. Today, your consumers seek to actively structure their preferences, and if the structure of your social media site/campaign makes it too difficult to participate, they will go elsewhere.

The *active within structures theory* integrates the active-audience approach with the structural approach, positing that individuals actively seek media content within internal and external structures. *Internal structures* refer to cognitive structures that guide or constrain media use, such as motivations, attitude, and habit strength, while *external structures* refer to the relatively hard constraints of environmental/contextual factors that influence media use, such as time availability, access to technologies, and infrastructures provided by the technology, industry and society. This perspective highlights the role of active choice in convergent media environments, while acknowledging the continuing influences of habit and structure. As Cooper and Tang (2009, p. 416) suggest:

> With hundreds of television channels and millions of websites currently available to many media users, individuals may even seek structure as a way to deal with the vast multitude of content and media options available. This may be manifest in decisions to pay for one type of content or delivery system over another, or to self-impose limits on media use. Thus, structure should not be viewed as a "passive" characteristic of media use, but rather as one of several valid influences on media use.

The active within structures approach suggests that individual characteristics (e.g., personality, demographics), internal structures (e.g., motivations, preferences, repertoire, habit), and external structures (e.g., availability, access, social media structures) interact with each other and influence media use. For example, your boss is in charge of many individuals and must be very organized so may prefer a technological device with easily synchronized calendar applications, while a social teenager down the street may be more interested in a technological device that has camera features that makes it easy to edit and send images to friends.

We have learned in Chapter 5 how individual factors and internal structures influence social media use. Now, let's focus on the external structures. Audience availability is one of the most powerful structural determinants of media use. Years of industry practice tell us that Thursday night generally has the highest rating because most people stay at home watching TV on Thursdays. More audiences watch TV in January and February than in the summer. The total television audience size varies predictably by hour of the day, day of the week, and week of the year because of audience availability (Cooper, 1996). TV programmers have applied this understanding to their scheduling practices by putting different types of programs into different parts of the day.

While social media is available to users on a 24/7 basis, Beyers (2004) suggests that day-parting still exists in the online world. For example, in the morning (6 a.m. to 8 a.m.), your audiences tend to check emails and have a quick read of news. From 8 a.m. to 5 p.m., they are likely to go online for fun. In the evening, your audiences may have more interests in looking for product information and doing online shopping. Thus, you should place different content at different times of the day. Creating a social media content calendar will be useful to guide what type of content you should display at a particular time of day, on a particular day of the week, and on a particular social media site. We will discuss a social media content calendar in detail in Chapter 11 when we discuss various social media marketing strategies.

In addition to audience time availability, the kinds of technologies and services owned by your audiences also impact their media use (Webster, 2006). For example, during the 2012 London Olympics, only subscribers to a cable, satellite or telco service could access the live broadcasts of the London Olympics online or via mobile. If you did not have cable, you were not able to watch the Olympics in real time on almost any device in the United States.

Access to technologies also guides specific media consumption where your audiences can choose to use certain media simply because one device is available over another (Tang & Cooper, 2012). Access to mobile devices, smartphones in particular, significantly predicts social media use. Mobile users spend more time using social networking sites than nonusers (Sweitzer, 2013). As a social media marketer, it is important for you to understand where and how audiences access your social media messages, and put mobile app development and mobile content design into consideration.

Habit/repertoire is another structural factor that is worth mentioning. Researchers suggest that more than half of media behaviors are habitual (Wood *et al.*, 2002; LaRose, 2010). You may notice from your own media use that it is largely driven by routine with little conscious thought. Each morning you probably habitually check a few websites. Maybe it is your email, a news site, and one or two social media platforms such as Facebook and Twitter. This is where you get all of the information that you feel is necessary before starting your day. It would be almost impossible to prompt you to check a sixth or seventh website and break your routine in the morning. Therefore, if someone wanted to reach you, they should not spend too much effort doing it through an alternative website, but should find a way for one of these four sources to include their content.

Despite the endless options online, your audiences tend to revisit the sites that they just accessed, and browse a small cluster of similar pages frequently to gratify their specific needs quickly and with little effort (Ferguson & Perse, 2000; Webster, 2008). Practitioners need to make sure that your social media messages are incorporated into your consumers' media use routine and becomes a part of their daily life. This is why having a social media presence on popular platforms is critical. Building habits for your consumers is more crucial for your business than ever before.

Furthermore, social media structures (search, links, recommendations, catalog of content) also impact social media use. For example, before 2009, there was no "like" button on Facebook. To express opinions about any posts, you had to leave comments, which required more effort. Now, you are able to simply press a button to say "like." Facebook provides a much easier and effortless structure for your consumers to interact and communicate with each other. We will discuss these social media structures in detail in the next section and explain how these features guide social media use and engage social media users.

When developing social media messages, it is important to consider the active within structures process. This should be completed through a four-step action plan.

Active Within Structures Action Plan

1   Be sure that your online content is easy to find and desirable for audiences. If initial audience interest is not there, there is nothing that a social media practitioner can do to augment structure and promote participation.

2 Encourage your audiences to provide personalized registration early in the social media process. This will help create a media routine where your consumers will not have to uniquely sign in each time to access their desired information.

3 Once habit is formed, media use will become automatic behavior rather than active decision. Be sure that content is updated with enough frequency so that there is new information each time your audience accesses the site.

4 Monitor and evaluate the media use of your target audiences frequently. Determine what device they are accessing content through and ensure that your social media product is created accordingly.

Let's imagine that a close friend of yours is diagnosed with a scary illness. You would most likely feel scared, anxious, and have little control over the situation. You will probably seek as much information about the illness as possible online. Community health forums such as Caringbridge, a social media site for ongoing information exchange about medical conditions, may help fulfill your immediate need to actively seek information about the diagnosis. Once registered on Caringbridge.com, you will be guided through the process of connecting with a group of people by the embedded site structure. Such a connection structure pushes you to keep coming back. After a while, visiting Caringbridge becomes a part of your daily morning routine. You may find yourself visiting the site when you have time available, even after your friend recovers.

This example mirrors the active within structures process. The media routine starts with an active choice. During the initial exposures, external structures and the content provided by the site encourage the use and gradually make the use a habit, forming the internal structure. When such an internal structure is formed, the use becomes an automatic behavior and the active drive fades. Individual, internal structures and external structures interact with each other, which influences social media use.

The Role of Structure

Structure is a crucial yet elusive concept in social science (Sewell, 1992). It has been defined as hard rules and resources that place constraints on individual action (Giddens, 1984; Sewell, 1992; Webster, 2009). Structure is active and multidimensional, and acts as a valid factor that constrains and also guides media use. With the overwhelming amount of information available today, your consumers are increasingly relying on the infrastructures provided by the technology and by society to find content that enacts their preferences (Cooper & Tang, 2009; Webster, 2009). This section introduces 10 *social media structures* that can guide your social media strategy to engage social media users, including search, profile, message/chat, comments, connection to group/people, like/ratings, share, links, advertising, and catalog of content.

Search

Search is one of the most commonly used social media structures. It allows your audiences to find preferred information quickly and easily by entering key words and choosing from a list of results (Pan *et al.*, 2007; Earnheardt *et al.*, 2008). Today, 92% of online adults use search engines, and almost 100% of the social networking sites provide a search feature (Purcell, 2011; Tang, 2013a). Since most of us only scroll through less than two pages of search engine results (Jansen *et al.*, 2000; Rainie & Mudd, 2004; Pan *et al.*, 2007). The ranking of the search results heavily influences whether your audiences can find your social media content. That's why you need to make good use of the search feature to ensure search engine optimization (discussed in greater detail in Chapter 9).

User profiles

User profiles are a unique structural character offered by most of the social media sites. More than 95% of social media sites allow users to create their personal profiles (Tang, 2013a). A profile includes personal information such as age, marital status, pictures, and interests. On Facebook (Figure 6.1), users are able to upload their pictures, share personal information (birthday, marital status, etc.), contact (phone number, email address, web page, IM ID,

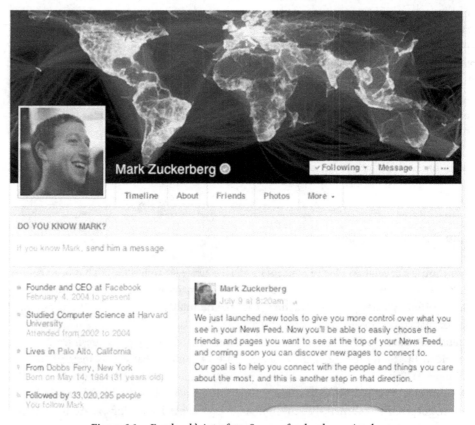

Figure 6.1   Facebook's interface. Source: facebook.com/zuck.

home address, etc.), interests (favorite books, movies, music, TV shows), as well as values and beliefs (political affiliation, favorite quotes). Twitter provides a much simpler profile that has users introduce themselves within 140 characters. Other niche social media sites, like Gaia, allow users the ability to customize profiles by creating avatars representing themselves in many different ways, including skin tone, hair style, race (e.g., human, vampire, elf), and outfits. Online personification is often the first step in social media use. Allowing your audiences to create unique profiles leads to more user-centered communication and can become an effective tool to make your site a part of your audience's daily routine.

Recommendation

There are two types of recommendation system: implicit recommendation and explicit recommendation. *Implicit recommendation* is based on observation, such as times viewed, the number of "likes", times shared, and the "favorites" list (e.g., Facebook, Twitter, Google+). *Explicit recommendation* is based on numerical ratings such as average ratings, "one to five stars," and scales ranging from 1 to 100 (e.g., Yelp) (Sundar & Nass, 2001; Knobloch-Westerwick *et al.*, 2005; Thorson, 2008).

Like/ratings and share   Within the social media context, like/ratings and share are the popular recommendation systems. Research found that 64% of social media sites include a like/ratings feature and 63% of them allow users to share their favorite content (Tang, 2013a). Using these structures can help your consumers to reduce search costs and find their preferred product information in an efficient manner when you provide a lot of information on your social media page. Your social media audiences tend to actively seek impersonal influence and trust each other's recommendation when selecting media message (Sundar & Nass, 2001; Knobloch-Westerwick *et al.*, 2005; Pan *et al.*, 2007; Thorson, 2008). That's why the participatory approach discussed in Chapter 3 is crucial to your social media strategy.

Content-based recommendation and collaborative filtering   Some social media sites use more advanced recommendation models, namely content-based recommendation and collaborative filtering, which can provide personalized recommendations (Adomavicius & Tuzhillin, 2005). *Content-based recommendation systems,* such as DailyLearner or Stumble Upon, offer audiences a list of items/content similar to those they have already seen, preferred, or purchased in the past. *Collaborative filtering systems* such as Amazon and Netflix provide recommendations based on what a person "like you" may prefer. These structures apply stereotyped web consumption to predict an individual's tastes and find matching peers for each social media user (Adomavicius & Tuzhillin, 2005; Webster, 2009, 2011). If you think these recommendation systems would work for your product/organization, you may consider adopting one.

Advertising   Advertising is a more traditional form of recommendation. Social media, like Facebook, Twitter, and Pinterest, have been characterized to provide excellent brand engagement and development opportunities. Researchers suggest that Web ads can potentially influence the amount of awareness that each message/product attracts (Hargittai, 2000).

Your consumers must learn about the existence of your product/social media messages before they can choose to use it. The awareness sets up the boundaries for your audience's media choice (Napoli, 1999; Hargittai, 2008; Webster, 2009). This helps explain why almost 90% of social media sites link to Facebook and Twitter to increase awareness. In the online environment, your audiences are purposefully or incidentally exposed to banner ads, pop-up ads, paid links, and other indirect ad messages such as sponsored content, promoted tweets, or Google pay-per-click links, something that should increase your audience aware-ness and guide consumer flow to your message/product. We will discuss social media ads in greater detail in Chapter 10 when we talk about social media business models.

Messaging/chat

Messaging/chat is an important social media structure that highlights the social, participa-tory and synchronous feature of social media. More than 90% of social media sites provide a chat function and allow individuals to send private messages and make public comments (Tang, 2013a). This structure gives you a great opportunity to develop one-on-one conversa-tions, incorporate a direct feedback mechanism, and allow your consumers to express their opinions freely.

Facebook is a great example of a social media platform with various messaging/chat struc-tures. Many heavy Facebook users may log onto Facebook every morning and stay on for the entire day, using the site as background noise. While there are appealing components to the Facebook design, most of the content is asynchronous in nature, allowing users to catch up at any point throughout the day. The more synchronous chat feature prompts users to stay tuned in nonstop in case someone needs to reach them. Such a structure makes Face-book a combination of mass communication and interpersonal communication, and creates a space for a synchronous sharing experience, and demonstrates the unique social perspec-tive provided by social media.

Hyperlink

Hyperlink is a basic structural component of all websites. It refers to the text or graphics on a site that, when clicked, directs people to other places online (Dimitrova *et al.*, 2003; Roman, 2008; Turow & Tsui, 2008). Links allow audiences to choose not only what content to expose, but also the order and pace of content delivery (Eveland & Dunwoody, 2000; Turow & Tsui, 2008). Your audiences may visit a website simply because they have been exposed to the lead-in hyperlink. While hyperlinks provide audiences with a convenient way to navigate online materials, they can also change how attention is distributed (e.g., guide their attention to various internal pages by providing most of the links to internal sources) (Zarcadoolas *et al.*, 2002; Earnheardt *et al.*, 2008; Turow & Tsui, 2008).

It is important to understand how influential hyperlinks are to the online browsing pro-cess. For example, you may plan to check Facebook quickly before dinner. However, as you start browsing through the general newsfeed page, you notice that one of your friends posted 20 wedding pictures. You click the link to see these photos. While looking at these pictures, you notice that one of the pictures tagged a great friend whom you haven't seen for a long time. Then, you click the link to see what she has been up to. On her Facebook page, you find not only her recent status/activities, but also a recipe for general tso chicken, so you click the link and download the recipe. At the end of the recipe, the website provides links to several other recipes and healthy lifestyle tips, which all sound really interesting. Before you know it, two hours of your day are gone. Hyperlinks are a great way to keep your audiences reading more, but can also distract them away from the initial content in which they were interested.

Catalog of content

Catalog of content is a similar structure to hyperlinks, but serves more as a roadmap in the online world and helps classify content on the Web. Many social media sites provide a catalog to organize their content and offer users a one-stop information-shopping destination. Catalog of content is particularly useful for your audiences with limited Internet skills and/or those who have little knowledge and experience with your site. Facing an overabundance of information on social media, your audiences are increasingly dependent on such a structure to start navigation (Hargittai, 2000, 2008). Catalog of content can be very effective in guiding user flow.

Connection to groups/people

Connection to groups/people is a unique feature and probably one of the most important structures leading to the success of your social media strategy. For many social media sites, one of the first steps is to ask users to identify their friends, groups and interests, and connect them to their personal social network. By asking audiences to connect to groups, friends, and those sharing the same interests or problems, social media optimize user engagement and help build a community.

As mentioned previously in this chapter, let's assume you are using Caringbridge, a social media site for patients, family and friends to exchange medical information. Because of the connection structure, you are able to read many touching stories, supportive comments and discussions about different treatments. Members in your group not only share information but also openly express their emotions, fears and frustrations. Connecting with such a group and getting to know the group members made Caringbridge an important part of your social networking experience.

In sum, social media structures – search, like/share, profile, message/chat, connections, advertising, links, and catalog of content – change how attention is distributed and thus have a tremendous impact on guiding social media use. As a social media practitioner, you should well use these features when developing your social media campaigns.

Recognizing Constrained Active Choices

Social media leads to increased social support, more user-centered communication, and increased user empowerment. It has even been dubbed the instrument of ultimate individualism, and it has been suggested that social media use is solely determined by needs, wants, and preferences (Jenkins, 2009; Kaplan & Haenlein, 2010; Litt, 2012). Nonetheless, we have learned in this chapter that social media use is a constrained active choice. Structures of time, access, and resources can all influence your consumers' media use. For example, the 140-character limit of Twitter is a structure that can constrain Twitter use. Your consumers may feel that 140 characters are not enough to express their opinions, amd may thus decide to communicate through Facebook or Instagram instead.

Constrained active choice also means that in today's ever-changing media environment, it is impossible for us to be fully aware of all the available social media platform choices. Our awareness sets the boundaries for our media choice. Most of us only have knowledge of a limited number of social media sites, and tend to browse a few popular ones frequently. As Chris Anderson (2006) suggests, findability is more crucial than availability in today's marketplace.

Constraints also include the social media structures provided by the technology and industry. As mentioned in the previous section, structures such as the search feature heavily influence Web use, since most people only pay attention to the top search results. Search is able to lead or mislead user attention to a handful of popular sites over many other possible choices. Even your most active audiences still purposefully use such structures to get quick and convenient information. While users can actively choose how and what they use in theory, exposure to niche content is constrained.

Constrained active choice further refers to individual's self-constraints and routine. Habits and repertoire play a significant role in influencing social media use. Your audiences become their own content managers when faced with endless choice. They actively decide their media use pattern, such as checking Facebook after every coffee break, and they purposefully choose to use or not to use certain content at certain times of the day, such as no computer before bed. While these decisions are active choices at first, over time it becomes cognitive structures that your audiences impose to manage and constrain their lives. Your audiences cannot use every media and all content in 24 hours. Whether consciously or unconsciously, they are structuring and constraining their media use.

Overall, this chapter suggests that social media use is a constrained active choice. Your audiences are always free to use social media messages according to their motivations and preferences. Nonetheless, the physical and virtual boundaries that exist within a media routine play an important role in determining social media use and should be considered when you develop your social media strategy.

Case Study: NBC's Social Olympics

This chapter has highlighted the role of structure in social media use, and how companies should achieve a comprehensive understanding of their consumers and the structures that they live with, and create social media messages accordingly. NBC Universal applied this active within structures conceptualization into its social media campaign during the 2012 London Olympics, thus making the London Games the "first social media Olympics."

The 2012 London Olympic Games represented a vast expansion of media coverage, content choices, and user interactivity, making it the most-consumed media event in world history (Tang & Cooper, 2013). NBC Universal offered more than 5500 hours of coverage of the London Games across TV, Web, social media, and mobile platforms. For the first time, NBC live streamed all 32 sports and 302 medal games online and via mobile (Rey, 2012; Winslow, 2012). In addition to the live streams, the digital coverage included live statistics, athlete profiles, and social media interactivity (NBCOlympics.com, 2012).

In collaboration with Facebook, Twitter, and YouTube, NBC created social buzz during the London Games. More than 150 million comments were made during the Olympics via social media, breaking the previous social media record for a single event, held by the 2012 Super Bowl. Nonetheless, the social media buzz appeared to increase viewership among younger people on traditional television (Winslow, 2012). Despite, or more likely due to, expanded availability and uses of social media content, the London Olympics was the most-watched TV event in US history, drawing in 219.4 million television viewers (Abrams, 2012; Tang & Cooper, 2013).

There is no doubt that NBC successfully implemented social media during the London Games. During its 17-day run, NBC Universal heavily promoted the London Olympics on social media (Tang & Cooper, 2013). From July 27 to August 12, 2012, NBC Olympics posted 1525 social media messages on its official Facebook and Twitter pages (Tang, 2013b).

NBC's social Olympics campaign addressed its audience's active needs by offering content related to a broad range of sports and events and developing opportunities for its audiences to express national pride. Providing information was the primary goal for most of NBC's social media messages during the London Games. More than 70% of the social media posts by NBC simply reported contest results, shared background information, and reminded about game schedules (Tang, 2013b). Only about 30% of the messages requested user interaction or encouraged opinion expression, such as "Wow! Such a great win!"

Nonetheless, structural characteristics were a main concern when NBC Universal created its social media campaign during the London Olympics. To surround audiences with social buzz, NBC used social media structures to encourage audiences to consume a disproportionate amount of Olympic content out of habit (Tang & Cooper, 2013). Almost all the NBC social Olympics messages included options to like, share, and comment. More than 80% of the posts used hashtags, 50% provided hyperlinks, and 45% employed tagging (Tang, 2013b). While audiences could still actively choose not to use the Olympics content, these structures certainly helped funnel people to the Games.

In addition, NBC's social Olympics campaign followed an important structural concern: content must fit the style and structure of the medium. As shown in Figure 6.2, NBC's Facebook used image promotion during the London Games, while Twitter simply diffused information. More than 80% of the posts on NBCOlympics

Rio 2016: South America plays Olympic host for first time

Figure 6.2   NBC's Olympics social media. Source: http://nbcolympics.com.

Facebook page included photos, while only 16% of its tweets linked to pictures (Tang, 2013b). Moreover, NBC used significantly more Facebook (than Twitter) posts to encourage user interactions and build brand loyalty, since Facebook is perceived to have a potential to build fan community, as discussed in Chapter 5.

For the social Olympics campaign, NBC used a push-and-pray approach (see Chapter 4) to create its Facebook messages, but employed a pull-and-stay model for its tweets. For example, while tweeting, NBC would spotlight Michael Phelp's last Olympic competition, while their Facebook message would say something such as "Tune in now! You don't want to miss Michael Phelps' last competition." One message simply provided information, and the other tended to push users to the program.

It is important to note that today's media users, digital natives in particular, increasingly use multiple screens for media consumption. Thus, organizations and marketers need to design social media campaigns that not only address audience's active needs, but also make their social media messages fit the structural constraints of the platform, funnel consumers to the content, and make their product a part of users' daily routine. To this end, NBC's social Olympics provided a successful example of a

Figure 6.2   (*Continued*)

multiplatform campaign that fully considered the interplay between active choice, habit, structure, and social media consumption.

Discussion questions

1   How did the producers of the NBC social Olympics campaign best utilize social media structures to funnel users to subsequent coverage of the London Olympic Games? Why do you think their approach proved successful?

2   If you were in charge of creating content for the London Olympics social media campaign, how would you best determine the internal/cognitive structures that influence audience behavior? How would this impact your content decisions?

3   Not every social media platform provides the same media structures. What decisions did the NBC social Olympics campaign producers have to make with regard to the differences in messages broadcast on Facebook and Twitter to reach goals? How can you relate these messages to lessons learned in previous chapters regarding diffusion, community, and mobilization?

Summary

This chapter highlights the crucial role that structure plays in the behaviors of social media users. Specifically, the active within structures approach explains how we actively use media content within internal and external structures. As a social media marketer, there is little you can do to control your consumers' personal preferences, life experience, mood, personalities, and other individual psychological factors. However, what you can do, through a solid understanding of structure theories and literature, is gain a better sense of how to utilize structures of the technology, such as recommendation, links, and catalog of content as well as environmental factors like time, cost, and resources to guide your audience preference and content consumption.

In addition, this chapter explains the role of social media structures. Search, recommendations, profile, connections, links, comments/messages, share, advertising, and catalog of content, provide important contextual cues that direct and constrain your audiences' social media consumption.

This chapter also suggests that social media users increasingly access multiple portals from the same organization/brand/company. Despite the hype and promise associated with social media marketing, you need to achieve more accurate understanding about how to effectively use social media messages to reach and influence consumers by fitting in with your existing marketing plan. This can be done by considering multiportal content management, rather than focusing on medium-specific strategies.

Knowing your audience is the first step to developing successful social media messages. Without a comprehensive understanding of your consumers and the infrastructures and constraints that they work within, messages can prove scattered, repetitive, and useless. Social media strategies must reflect an understanding of the interplay between active choice, habit, and structures. Chapters 5 and 6 have provided you with a complete picture of your social media users. Now let's turn our attention to how to create social messages that encourage user engagement and community building in Chapter 7.

Key Takeaways

1   Active within structures is a nuanced conceptualization of social media users. Achieving a comprehensive understanding of your audiences is the first step towards designing successful social media marketing strategies. Social media campaigns should reflect an understanding of the interplay between active choice, habit, and structure.
2   Social media structures – search, profile, message/chat, comments, connection to groups/people, like/ratings, share, links, advertising, and catalog of content – can all influence social media use. Making good use of these structures and creating social media messages that fit the style and structure of the medium are crucial.

3 Habits, self-constraints, and routine help determine social media use. Thus, you need to find and use contextual and structural cues to encourage habit formation and build brand loyalty.

4 Eventually, facing unlimited options, your audience makes choices based on personal identity. Both social media consumers and creators need to consider the question "Who am I?"

5 Facing convergence, you must consider multiportal content management, rather than isolating your social media strategy to a single medium.

References

Abrams, N. (2012) London Olympics becomes most-watched TV event in U.S. history. Available at http://www.tvguide.com/News/Ratings-London-Olympics-1051938/ (accessed June 22, 2016).

Adomavicius, G. & Tuzhilin, A. (2005) Toward the next generation of recommender systems: a survey of the state-of-the-art and possible extensions. *IEEE Transactions on Knowledge and Data Engineering*, 17, 734–749.

Anderson, C. (2006) *The Long Tail: Why the Future of Business is Selling Less of More.* New York: Hyperion.

Beyers, H. (2004) Dayparting online: living up to its potential?. *International Journal on Media Management*, 6(1–2), 67–73.

Cooper, R. (1996) The status and future of audience duplication research: an assessment of ratings-based theories of audience behavior. *Journal of Broadcasting and Electronic Media*, 40, 96–116.

Cooper, R. & Tang, T. (2009) Predicting audience exposure to television in today's media environment: an empirical integration of active-audience and structural theories. *Journal of Broadcasting and Electronic Media*, 53(3), 1–19.

Dimitrova, D.V., Connolly-Ahern, C., Williams, A.P., Kaid, L.L. & Reid, A. (2003) Hyperlinking as gatekeeping: online newspaper coverage of the execution of an American terrorist. *Journalism Studies*, 4(3), 401–414.

Earnheardt, A.C., Earnheardt, M.B. & Rubin, R.B. (2008) Development and test of an Internet search evaluation measure. *Ohio Communication Journal*, 46, 45–72.

Eveland, W.P. & Dunwoody, S. (2000) Examining information processing on the World Wide Web: using think aloud protocols. *Media Psychology*, 2, 219–244.

Ferguson, D.A. & Perse, E.M. (2000) The World Wide Web as a functional alternative to television. *Journal of Broadcasting and Electronic Media*, 44(2), 155–174.

Giddens, A. (1984) *The Constitution of Society: Outline of the Theory of Structuration.* Berkeley, CA: University of California Press.

Hargittai, E. (2000) Open portals or closed gates: channeling content on the World Wide Web. *Poetics*, 27(4), 233–254.

Hargittai, E. (2008) The role of expertise in navigating links of influence. In: J. Turow & L. Tsui (eds) *The Hyperlinked Society: Questioning Connections in the Digital Age*, pp. 85–103. Ann Arbor, MI: University of Michigan Press.

Jansen, B.J., Spink, A., Bateman, J. & Saracevic, T. (2000) Real life, real users, and real needs: a study and analysis of user queries on the Web. *Information Science and Technology*, 56(6), 559–570.

Jenkins, H. (2009) *Confronting the Challenges of Participatory Culture: Media Education for the 21st Century.* Cambridge, MA: MIT Press.

Kaplan, A. & Haenlein, M. (2010) Users of the world, unite! The challenges and opportunities of social media. *Business Horizons*, 53, 59–68.

Knobloch-Westerwick, S., Sharma, N., Hansen, D.L. & Alter, S. (2005) Impact of popularity indications on readers' selective exposure to online news. *Journal of Broadcasting and Electronic Media*, 49(3), 296–313.

LaRose, R. (2010) The problem of media habits. *Communication Theory*, 20, 194–222.

Litt, E. (2012) Knock, knock. Who's there? The imaged audience. *Journal of Broadcasting and Electronic Media*, 56(3), 330–345.

Napoli, P.M. (1999) Deconstructing the diversity principle. *Journal of Communication*, 49(4), 7–34.

NBCOlympics.com (2012) http://NBCOlympics.com (accessed September 23, 2012).

Pan, B., Hembrooke, H., Joachims, T., Lorigo, L., Gay, G. & Granka, L. (2007) In Google we trust: users' decisions on rank, position, and relevance. *Journal of Computer-Mediated Communication*, 12, 801–823.

Purcell, K. (2011) Search and email still top the list of most popular online activities. Available at http://www.pewinternet.org/2011/08/09/search-and-email-still-top-the-list-of-most-popular-online-activities/ (accessed June 8, 2016).

Rainie, L. & Mudd, G. (2004) The popularity and importance of search engines. Available at http://www.pewinternet.org/files/old-media//Files/Reports/2004/PIP_Data_Memo_Searchengines.pdf.pdf (accessed June 8, 2016).

Reiss, S. & Wiltz, J. (2004) Why people watch reality TV. *Media Psychology*, 6, 363–378.

Rey, J.D. (2012) NBC plans Olympic-size test of digital limits. *Advertising Age*, 83(19), 6.

Roman, G. (2008) *Mass Media in a Changing World: History, Industry, Controversy*, 2nd edn. Boston: McGraw-Hill.

Sewell, W.H. (1992) A theory of structure: duality, agency, and transformation. *American Journal of Sociology*, 98(1), 1–29.

Sherry, J.L. (2004) Flow and media enjoyment. *Communication Theory*, 14(4), 328–347.

Simon, H. (1971) Designing organizations for an information-rich world. In: M. Greenberger (ed.) *Computers, Communications and the Public Interest*, pp. 40–41. Baltimore, MD: The Johns Hopkins Press.

Sundar, S. & Nass, C. (2001) Conceptualizing sources in online news. *Journal of Communication*, 51(1), 52–72.

Sweitzer, B. (2013) Structurational Twitter: an examination of individual and structural predictors of Twitter use. Paper presented at the Broadcast Education Association annual conference, Las Vegas, NV.

Tang, T. (2013a) Is structure relevant any more: preliminary development of a new measure of social media structures. Paper presented at the Eastern Communication Association Annual Conference, Pittsburgh, PA.

Tang, T. (2013b) An exploration of NBC's social media promotion strategies during the London Olympics. Paper presented at the Broadcast Education Association Annual Conference, Las Vegas, NV.

Tang, T. & Cooper, R. (2012) Gender, sports, and new media: predictors of viewing during the 2008 Beijing Olympics. *Journal of Broadcasting and Electronic Media*, 56(1), 75–91.

Tang, T. & Cooper, R. (2013) Olympics everywhere: predictors of multiplatform media uses during the 2012 London Olympics. *Mass Communication and Society*, 16(6), 850–868.

Thorson, E. (2008) Changing patterns of news consumption and participation: news recommendation engines. *Information, Communication and Society*, 11, 473–489.

Turow, J. & Tsui, L. (eds) (2008) *The Hyperlinked Society: Questioning Connections in the Digital Age*. Ann Arbor, MI: University of Michigan Press.

Webster, J.G. (2006) Audience flow past and present: inheritance effects reconsidered. *Journal of Broadcasting and Electronic Media*, 50(2), 323–337.

Webster, J.G. (2008) Structuring a marketplace for attention. In: J. Turow & L. Tsui (eds) *The Hyperlinked Society: Questioning Connections in the Digital Age*, pp. 23–38. Ann Arbor, MI: University of Michigan Press.

Webster, J.G. (2009) The role of structure in media choice. In: T. Hartmann (ed.) *Media Choice: A Theoretical and Empirical Overview*, pp. 221–233. New York: Routledge.

Webster, J.G. (2011) The duality of media: a structurational theory of public attention. *Communication Theory*, 21, 43–66.

Webster, J.G., Phalen, P.F. & Lichty, L.W. (2006) *Ratings Analysis: The Theory and Practice of Audience Research*, 3rd edn. Mahwah, NJ: Lawrence Erlbaum Associates.

Winslow, G. (2012) An Olympic test for TV everywhere, not just NBCU. *Broadcasting and Cable*, 142(29), 31.

Wood, W., Quinn, J.M. & Kashy, D. (2002) Habits in everyday life: thought, emotion and action. *Journal of Personality and Social Psychology*, 83, 1281–1297.

Zarcadoolas, C., Blanco, M., Boyer, J.F. & Plesant, A. (2002) Unweaving the Web: an exploratory study of low-literate adults' navigation skills on the World Wide Web. *Journal of Health Communication*, 7, 309–324.

7

Best Practices for Social Media Engagement

Learning Objectives

After reading this chapter, you should be able to:

1 Understand the theory of dialogic communication and be able to apply it to a social media strategy.
2 Define online engagement and virtual communities and understand their benefits to marketers.
3 Manage and maintain a dialogic loop with audiences.

Introduction

Previous chapters have stressed the importance of encouraging audience participation with social media content in order to yield the most effective results for a desired behavior change. Chapter 6 explained how active audiences are limited, or guided by the structures provided by the social media sites that they visit. This chapter provides practical advice on which features work best for active audience dialogue and feedback, even when audiences are dissatisfied with their online user experience.

Audiences utilize social media to fulfill many different gratifications. They access information, share content, and communicate with various networks, both private and public in nature. Think about the last product that you purchased online. What was that process like? How did you find the website you purchased from? Did you read customer reviews before making a decision? What types of feedback, if any, did the website ask of you after you made

Strategic Social Media: From Marketing to Social Change, First Edition. L. Meghan Mahoney and Tang Tang.
© 2017 John Wiley & Sons, Inc. Published 2017 by John Wiley & Sons, Inc.

the purchase? These are all important considerations that your consumers take into account each and every time they make purchase decisions online.

Consumer expectations have changed dramatically over the past 25 years. Rapid technological convergence, greater connectivity, enhanced interactive capacity, and increased organizational capability are making the information economy visible for the ordinary consumer (Butler & Peppard, 1998). The one or two retailers available in their immediate proximity no longer bind audiences. Instead, they use technology to help make consumption decisions that work best in their lives, whether the focus is on price, fair trade, quality of product, or speed of delivery.

These purchasing decisions are complex and extend along a continuum of problem-solving decisions. These decisions include categories such as price, perceived risk, experience, involvement, and information content. For the smaller ticket items that have less influence on their day-to-day lives (e.g., picture frames or a new tee-shirt), people tend to seek less information, experience and involvement in the purchase process. However, if your consumers need to make big changes or a substantial investment in their lives, they tend to rely on a more purposeful and involved information-seeking process. Past brand experience becomes much more important for these decisions. That is why so many individuals stick with one brand of electronics or car that they know and trust.

Customers now have expectations for accessing and leaving feedback on the products they purchase and use. Search through this feedback and you may come to the same resolution as other marketing professions: customers are most likely to leave online feedback when they are incredibly satisfied or dissatisfied with a product. The everyday average user is less motivated to make an online review. This often leaves professionals feeling discouraged from providing participatory structural features. After all, why prompt users to engage if there is a greater chance that users will respond negatively?

This chapter explains how to encourage participatory dialogue on social media that will help facilitate positive and useful feedback from online audiences. It provides a theoretical understanding of how public dialogue is best for both marketers and consumers. Next, it demonstrates the importance of virtual communities in sustaining online engagement. Finally, it provides tips for responding to dissatisfied online consumers and maintaining an effective dialogic loop.

The Theory of Dialogic Communication

Part I of this book explains the importance of igniting a participatory audience in social media messages in order to prompt behavior change. However, Chapter 6 demonstrates how social media users are limited and guided through the structural features available. Encouraging participation requires more than just providing users with a functional Internet structure option for dialogue, but needs a shift in the way we view the role that audiences play in the communication process.

Habermas (1984) describes dialogue as the coordination in good faith of a plan for action. This suggests a very cooperative communication process where organizational leaders are not hyper-focused on disseminating messages and selling messages to media audiences as one would see in a top-down diffusion model. Today's audiences expect brands to value their business and feedback. After all, every consumer carries millions of retailer options in their pocket. Audience communication is essential to the success of any social media strategy in today's social media environment.

True participation means working with and by the people, not working on or working for the people (Servaes, 1996). Yes, social media practitioners are trying to reach an audience to sell a product or increase numbers, but what makes social media unique is its potential for users to access, participate, determine, sharpen, and manage content (Singhal, 2004). It is time that marketers stop selling to audiences and begin engaging them in a truly participatory manner.

Each year, companies spend a great deal of energy and money in marketing design and research efforts. This includes both qualitative measurements (e.g., focus groups, direct observation, interviews) and quantitative measurements (e.g., survey and controlled experiments). Each of these takes skilled trained researchers, which can cost a significant amount of money. An eight-person marketing focus group is estimated to cost about $6000 (Suttle, 2013). While these are necessary measures for creating and sustaining products, this methodology is not foolproof. Each comes with its own sets of challenges and drawbacks.

Just one of these methodologies – focus groups, which have a long history in marketing research – tends to rely heavily on the role of the moderator. Often they fail due to *groupthink*, the psychological phenomenon in which people strive for consensus within a group (Irving, 1972). Lack of leadership or control can also lead to problems with focus group research (Gibbs, 1997). A popular research method, survey research, could also be problematic because of low response rates and sample reliability of longer multiple question surveys (Reichheld, 2003). In addition, these research efforts can succumb to what is known as the *Hawthorne effect*, where research subject answers are influenced by the presence of the researcher. Most often, participants give answers that they feel are desired, not what they actually believe to be true. They may say that a product is more useful than it actually proves in their everyday lives. Clearly, audience and marketing research is a difficult, expensive and challenging task. More information about alternative research methods is discussed in Chapter 12.

Social media allows the opportunities to provide immediate feedback, without the presence of a researcher to influence responses. While companies would pay a great deal of money for this type of information in marketing research, they often try to mitigate and control responses as much as possible due to the public nature of social media. Freire's theory of dialogic communication and action explains why these ideas and opinions should be valued rather than feared.

The *theory of dialogic communication and action* explains the importance of transactional communication for sustaining relationships through social media. It is defined as a type of relational interaction, where ideas and opinions are negotiated through communication exchanges (Kent, 1998). In other words, though the two parties do not have to agree on an absolute truth, they must be willing to reach mutually satisfying opinions. Here, dialogic communication is a product, not the process. The facilitator of communication is vested in both sides of the communication process, rather than the self-serving interest of marketing.

Stoker and Tusinski (2006) explain how dialogic communication aims to persuade like-minded publics by transforming dialogue into two-way asymmetric communication. The goal is to facilitate interactivity between an organization and the public. Dialogic communication demonstrates how they can work together to build more innovative ideas and a longer sustaining relationship, and is often considered a more ethical way of conducting public dialogue and public relations.

Social media users expect dialogic communication functions when they engage online content. There are many structural functions that organizations can include to promote dialogic communication online, including dialogic loop, usefulness of information, generation of return visits, ease of interface, and the conservation of visitors (Russell, 2008). Often, these can be achieved by the media structure options presented in Chapter 6.

It is also important to search your product beyond your own social media platform and see what people are saying about your brand. Respond to these customers. Just because they did not communicate with you directly, it does not mean that they would not want to hear from you. If there is something wrong with the direction of the dialogue, it is likely that something is wrong with the product. While this type of feedback would have cost thousands of dollars in traditional marketing research, social media makes it available for free. Social media allows consumers to let you know that your product is unsatisfactory before you continue to produce more of the same. Moreover, there is a chance for you to respond to their dissatisfaction to show how much you care and value their feedback. Social media marketing is about building and maintaining relationships.

Focus on promoting dialogue where people contribute in ways that others will want to hear. Rather than providing feedback in silos or discussion forum threads, prompt innovative options for participation: have contests; ask for pictures; allow audiences to share user-generated videos. Organizations must provide much more than the product that the customer has paid for. Your social media strategy should be based on a positive experience for users, not just a place where they come to access a product.

As a social media marketer you should adopt the role of facilitator, promoting an environment of nonjudgmental dialogue and active listening (Griffin, 2009). Nonetheless, this cooperative, two-way, ethical communication practice requires neither side to attempt to control the communication process (Habermas, 1990). Do not try to change consumers. Instead, change your product until it meets and exceeds their expectation. If this is not your goal, then you are not engaging in the mindset that meets the values of true participation.

Online Engagement and Virtual Communities

True participation should be the goal of any social media campaign. We have discussed the importance of a change in assumptions regarding the perception of audiences. Communication with them is no longer, and never really should have been, a top-down diffusion process. This hurts your brand and disengages consumers from participating further. Audience feedback is a critical and valuable asset for any organization. It is important to take as many steps necessary to encourage engagement between consumers and organizations. This is how long-lasting relationships are formed.

As mentioned, there are many structural elements that an organization can add to their website in order to encourage dialogic communication, including dialogic loop, usefulness of information, generation of return visits, ease of interface, and the conservation of visitors (Russell, 2008). Each of these functions help users engage and feel as though they are an intricate part of a community.

A *dialogic loop* is one of the most important features that social media users are beginning to expect from organizations. This includes ways in which audiences are able to exchange messages with the source of an organization. If consumers have a question about your product, they should not have to leave the webpage in order to send a query. There should be more than one structural feature that allows asynchronous (e.g., email contact form) and synchronous (e.g., instant chat) answers on your site.

It is important that the information you provide about your organization and product proves useful to the audience. Use narrative structures to build brand authenticity and be transparent about every stage of the production, product and price. One great way to provide useful information to users is to allow other members in the community to share reviews and experiences with your product. Do not filter this feedback to only include positive comments. Otherwise you may come across looking nontransparent and lacking authenticity.

If you are selling a shirt that runs small in size, it is better to have other reviewers state this so that consumers are able to negotiate this information in their purchasing decision. Maybe this will prompt them to order a larger size, or maybe they will order a different shirt altogether. Regardless, you are keeping them on your website because they feel as though you are being authentic and transparent about your product information. In fact, you can gain from having poor reviewed products available on your website. This allows customers to make informed decisions about purchasing higher-rated products. Customers prefer having a greater amount of information about products, rather than dealing with returns or exchanges later on. Remember from Chapter 2 that the theory of social penetration explains how an increase in self-disclosure leads to an increase in trust. Trust is a critical ingredient for online engagement and community.

Prompting users to return to your website is a difficult task. Current satisfied customers are top of the buying hierarchy (Stratten, 2012). It is best to nurture relationships with the customers that you already have. If your product is strong and their experience is positive, they will spread the word to their personal network and continue coming back for future purchases.

One way to encourage return visitors is to turn your website into a community. Facilitate conversations so that consumers who are interested in your product will want to come back and participate, even if they are not interested in buying a new product. If you notice a regular user has not visited in a while, reach out and let them know they are missed. Use social media to ask questions, update often, and prompt users to share. Make your space a place where people are happy to associate their identity with. Think about the types of content that would excite users to participate in conversations.

Don't make users frustrated when they visit your website. The ease of interface has a lot to do with how satisfied customers feel when they visit your page and whether they come back. This does not mean that you need to have the most technologically advanced page on the Internet. In fact, it means quite the opposite. Keep your design simple, and make sure that it aligns with your brand authenticity. Apple's website is a simple white background with grey font. This matches the simple and minimalistic style of their products. UNICEF's website uses colors of the globe: blue, green and white. This is consistent with their logo and globalized development vision for children. Choose one or two fonts and colors and stay consistent throughout. Ensure that every page on your site has easy-to-find links where users can ask questions and get to the home page. Users should be able to get to the home page from any point on the website.

Be careful with *CAPTCHA* (completely *a*utomated *p*ublic *T*uring test to tell *c*omputers and *h*umans *a*part), an application where users are required to type the word or numbers shown on an image to advance to the next step (Cui *et al.*, 2010). While these forms are a great way to minimize spam messages for you, they can be difficult to read and users can become frustrated with the process.

All of these prove effective ways to ensure the conservation of visitors. It may be worthwhile to ask your audiences for some information about themselves while they are on your website. Many companies are beginning to do this by making users register their email address before being able to look at products.

The brand Joss and Main is a home décor members-only company. It requires users to register an email address and create a home portfolio before they are able to access web content. The daily deal pioneer Woot makes users register their email address and hometown before they can browse. Zulilly, a website that sells goods for mothers and children, requires a username, password and email address for membership. While these strategies may lose some audiences upfront, the ability to learn more information and follow up with audiences may lead to greater sales.

While this approach is a great way to establish the exclusivity of your products, research demonstrates how customers do not like having to register with websites, even when checking out, let alone checking in (Charlton, 2007). You want audiences to return to your website because they had a positive experience, not because you bounded them by follow-up emails. So, find a balance between this push and pull of media content.

Humans function through habit and marketers know this. Companies all over the world are trying to determine how to get users to make their business a part of their regular online routine. The Target Corporation is known for recruiting shoppers during the biggest transitional periods of their lives, such as graduation, marriage and, most importantly, parenthood. These are dynamic periods of life where consumers are already going through substantial changes, and so it is likely to change purchasing patterns as well. New parents may appreciate the convenience of purchasing groceries and clothing in one stop, even if it means buying different products than they did prior to baby. In fact, *The New York Times* reported one instance of Target figuring out that a teen girl was pregnant before her father did, and sent coupons to their home for baby materials (Duhigg, 2012). If practitioners are able to entice customers to visit their store during these transitional periods through coupons or promotions, they may come back for life out of convenience.

Great sales, products and promotions are excellent ways to tempt users into visiting your site. You can set up user-friendly interfaces that save preferences, purchases, and shipment and payment information. Audiences are much more likely to purchase a product if they only have to press one button than if they have to fill out fields each time. However, the key to transforming customers into lifelong brand advocates is to make them feel as though they belong to your community. You want consumers to form relationships and become emotionally invested with your community.

Online engagement is an essential ingredient to this process. *Online engagement* is a dynamic and sustained relationship from user to brand that communicates brand value (Mollen & Wilson, 2010). This is only possible if you have a clear sense of your product vision and lifestyle. If you are not certain of your brand authenticity, there is no way you can expect your audience to know. Go back to Chapter 2 and help determine what makes you unique from other products in the field.

There are many ways to encourage true participation from audiences in your social media strategy. Based on this information, the following action plan has been advanced.

True Participation Action Plan

1   Set up structural features to promote dialogic communication, including dialogic loop, usefulness of information, generation of return visits, ease of interface, and the conservation of visitors.
2   Provide a narrative that clearly outlines your brand authenticity. Be as transparent as possible about production, product and price.
3   Allow consumers to share reviews directly on your website. Respond quickly to unsatisfied customers, but don't filter or censor. Having a few negative reviews can actually benefit a brand, provided the majority is positive.
4   Use social media to facilitate conversations that are consistent with the lifestyle of your target audience. Don't use this space to sell products. Instead, ask questions, update often, and prompt users to share information that is useful and speaks to them.
5   Ensure that your product interface is easy to use. Only use CAPTCHA forms if necessary, and ask audiences questions on signing in to save their preferences, purchases, shipment and payment information. Use this information to follow up with audiences, especially during transitional periods in their lives.

There are many ways to engage users online. One of the best approaches may seem counterintuitive, and that is not to think of social media as a way for you, a brand, to communicate with your community members. Instead, think of your social media as a place for users to communicate with other users. Allow structural features that enable audiences to reach you if they would like, but allow a safe space where they are able to create material on their own, and communicate with other members of the community about issues of importance to them. Be sure that sources of engagement are authentic, relevant to the audience, provide emotional connection between members, and fulfill a narrative structure for and with audiences. This hands-off approach is difficult, especially since you lose some control over the conversation. In addition, it will not work for every product. This strategy requires a strong authenticity, with a trusted history and niche lifestyle brand. Nonetheless, it supports user objectives, promotes independent satisfaction, and helps build community (Krause & Coates, 2008).

Consider why your audience has chosen your social media platform and the types of things that they are likely to be interested in. It is possible that your product speaks to a certain aspect of their lifestyle and identity that is difficult to find in interpersonal settings. Play to these emotions. These are the types of conversations you should facilitate through social media because your audience will want to engage.

One example of a company that has done this well is the Swedish furniture company IKEA. They target an audience that is likely on a budget, but still interested in home design and do-it-yourself projects (most furniture purchased in IKEA requires some level of do-it-yourself assembly). In 2011, the company launched a blog, *IKEA Share Space*, a photo-sharing community where users are able to upload photos of their living spaces to "easily find and share inspiration with one another" (Boerner, 2011). The structure of the website included a simple interface for users to communicate with each other and share their own projects.

Consumers would be interested in visiting this site at many stages of the consumption process. They may want to visit before making purchasing decisions to see how other members are using IKEA furniture. They could visit the site once they have purchased the furniture and have put it together to see ideas for how it should be arranged in a room. They could also use the space to share their own completed projects. No matter how audiences prefer to use the site, IKEA has incorporated a structure where they are not telling users what to talk about. Instead, they offer an opportunity for audiences to check into the site and communicate with other members according to their own needs.

The *IKEA Share Space* community allows members to send "kudos" to rate or ask questions about the photos. This would also encourage members to come back, even after their room is complete, to see what other users think. These features keep the process fun and positive, especially since this user participation limits the amount of control IKEA has over conversations.

IKEA has also kept users engaged through the use of *gamification*, or the utilization of game thinking and mechanics in a non-game context to engage users and solve problems (Zichermann & Cunningham, 2011). Members who upload three or more pictures earn the badge of a "Space Sharer." Members who tag five IKEA products in their photo collection earn the badge of an "Ikea Fan." Members who tag 25 products become a "Super Fan." If five other users save an audience space, they earn the "Admired Space" badge. If 25 other users save the space, they earn the "Exceptional Space" badge. Gamification is a great way to hook audiences into coming back and staying engaged. The best uses of gamification are those that are authentic to the purpose and shared vision of the virtual community.

Virtual communities are groups of people with common interests and practices that communicate regularly and for some duration in an organized way over the Internet through a common location or mechanism (Ridings & Gefen, 2004). This allows users the chance to personalize their online experience even more through character identification. Virtual communities are one of the earliest functions of Internet users, and are one of the fastest growing categories of website, exceeding 25 million sites (Horowitz, 1997). Virtual communities allow discussions to evolve into the feelings and connections of personal relationships. They tend to be asynchronous in nature, but an emerging trend of synchronous communities has emerged where users meet in real time through cyber-face to cyber-face social interactions (Hill *et al.*, 1995).

Some asynchronous online discussion forums are just places for individuals to meet and talk without any sense of belonging or consistency among group members (Ridings & Gefen, 2004). These do not necessarily meet the requirements of a virtual community. Members should feel part of a larger social group, have ongoing exchanges with other members, and sense lasting relationships with others. It may take repeat positive experiences and periods of disengagement before members realize the value of community membership. There are only so many online communities that individuals are able to make a part of their regular routine. The more your community brand and your audience values align, the more invested they will feel towards your organization.

Creating a virtual community is an important step for any social media marketing strategy. This will help foster relationships between users and the organization. It will keep users vested in the connections that they have made, push innovation forward and keep your consumers coming back. Remember that virtual communities require much more than the technological capability for communication. Authenticity, audience assumptions, and sincere facilitation play a huge role in how invested users feel.

The Dialogic Loop

The goal of social media marketing is to form relationships with customers. The importance of customer loyalty in organizational sustainment cannot be understated. Loyal customers mean more than someone who routinely buys products from a company. These customers may only be doing this because it is the simplest option available or because there is no alternative available. However, in a business climate that is constantly evolving, marketers cannot rely on these motivations.

Many takeout and delivery restaurants have begun utilizing the Internet to allow users to order takeout food online without ever speaking with the customer. By signing up for an Internet account, users are able to store their address, payment information and past purchases for future use. This process is much easier for consumers because they are able to order food without remembering a phone number or menus or digging their credit card out of their wallet. Furthermore, it mitigates some level of human error in getting the order and address correct. When this technology first became available, consumers may have only had one or two options for ordering online. Perhaps every time they wanted to order food for delivery, they returned to your restaurant since you provide online ordering, not because they felt loyal or liked your food the best, but because the structural features made it the easiest process.

Sure enough, time has passed and more and more takeout and delivery restaurants have made this online feature available. This is where customer loyalty plays a larger role than ease of use. Customer loyalty is one of the most important drivers of economic growth for a company (Reichheld, 2003), as they strongly identify with the product, put their own reputation on the line by recommending your product to their own network, and tend to buy more over time.

One of the most critical features for ensuring customer loyalty is the dialogic loop. If done correctly, customers will feel as though they are valued within the community. If done poorly, you may have lost their service forever. A dialogic loop allows users to query organizations and offers organizations the opportunity to respond to questions, concerns and problems (Reber *et al.*, 2006).

There are many structural features that you can include in your website to ensure a dialogic with customers. These include easy to find contact information, contact forms, information for donor or media publics, telephone options, satisfaction surveys, email subscription options, interactive forms and blogs (Kent & Taylor, 1998). It is imperative that you make it as easy as possible for customers to communicate with the organization.

Allowing opportunities for visitors to send messages to the organization, vote on issues, request regular information updates, and fill out surveys identifying priorities and expressing opinions on issues helps users see how much the content creator cares (Taylor *et al.*, 2001). However, they should never be included unless someone is able to respond in a timely manner. There is nothing worse than taking the time to query an organization and never hearing back.

Be sure to have an expert available who knows the product and the brand well. Remember that users are able to communicate with one another, and so have a policy about how you are going to handle certain scenarios and stick to it. Do not give one user special treatment over another. Through prompt replies to concerns and questions, users will begin to feel a sense of relational trust and commitment to the brand. These relationships should not only serve the public relations goals of an organization, but should also incorporate the interests, values, and concerns of users (McAllister-Spooner & Kent, 2009). Many companies have begun using personalized names of employees to answer customer questions. Have a question while using Skype? Simply tweet @PeteratSkype and you will receive a prompt reply. This helps humanize the public relations process.

In the book *Unmarketing*, Scott Stratten (2012) explains a five-step process for dealing with angry customers through social media.

1   Have an existing strategy in place. While every query should be handled on a personal level, there should be consistency across organizational policies and mission statements. This information should be transparent and easily found in the company website.
2   Acknowledge the customer's dissatisfaction. Let them know that you received their complaint and that you understand their frustrations.
3   Clarify the company policy and why the user may have had the unsatisfactory experience that they encountered. This is not the time to place blame on the consumer, but to ensure that the negative experience will not happen again.
4   Present a resolution that satisfies both the customer and the organizational policy and mission statement.
5   Social media allows companies to check back with consumers after a resolution has been made to ensure they are satisfied with their customer service experience. This allows you to continue communication with the customer and let them know that their business and feedback are important to you.

Responsiveness does not simply mean getting back to individuals; messages should be personalized to the query, be timely in nature, and involve specially trained response personnel (Gustavsen & Tilley, 2003). No one expects every user who comes to your site to be completely satisfied. However, it is imperative that your organization has a customer service strategy to handle unsatisfied users.

Today, consumers play a critical role in the communication process and the success of your social media strategy. Increased effective dialogue is the key for making your audiences feel valued and engaged. If your values do not align with the values of the theory of dialogic communication, this will come across in your customer service practices. True participation through social media is imperative for organizational sustainment.

Case Study: Second Life

Social media provides alternative spaces for communication among and between diverse communities. Much scholarly research investigates potential uses of virtual communities regarding issues of identity and relationship building (Hegland & Nelson, 2002; Nisbett, 2006) With no proxemic physical space limitations, virtual communities make engagement easy and help build long-lasting relationships between members. One of the earliest and most successful examples of a synchronous virtual community, Second Life, speaks to these identity features.

Second Life emerged in 2003 as the most popular computer-based multimedia environment that allows users to interact through their own graphical self-representations known as avatars (Boulos *et al.*, 2007). On Second Life, users are able to create an avatar and spend time traveling to various virtual "islands" speaking to other avatars. Though its popularity has dropped in recent years, there are still over 1 million regular users.

Second Life has many features of real life. It has unique in-world weather systems where users can coordinate their outfit according to that day's forecast, regular day–night cycles, and 3-D functionality where people can collaboratively create and edit objects in the virtual world (Boulos *et al.*, 2007). While these features mirror the real world, Second Life also enables users to live out any fantasies they may have.

Users can explore castles, fly around the world, interact with dragons, or take on the role of a human-sized rabbit. Second Life was designed as a space for socialization among community members that extends beyond the real world. It was built on the premise that users could have the opportunity to live out some dreams or fantasies that are not possible in their real, or first, life.

Think of a person you know who has shy tendencies in their everyday life. Second Life could provide a space where she or he may feel more comfortable communicating with others through her or his avatar. Perhaps a person is wheelchair bound, but has always dreamt of becoming a professional basketball star. Second Life offers a space where she or he is able to join and play with the Virtual Basketball Association. Additional features include the ability to stream audio, video and television collections, browse information in virtual libraries, virtually experience the world, play multi-player games with other avatars, buy and sell real-life goods and services, develop relationships with other avatars, attend live events, and engage in realistic voice chat that includes nonverbal gestures (Boulos *et al.*, 2007).

Synchronous cyberspaces are very decentralized. For the most part, communities are built, developed and controlled by the users. For this reason, they hold great potential for new social movements and protests to naturally emerge (Neumayer & Raffl, 2008). One such example was a Second Life demonstration for peace and justice in Burma, where hundreds of Buddhist monks were being arrested after protesting against the military regime (SLLU, 2007). Avatars wore robes, went bald, wore tee-shirts or held hands forming a human chain to show support and raise awareness.

There are many criticisms of this type of awareness, as many wonder if they are making any difference at all. After all, the only people who were likely to see the demonstrations were those who were also on Second Life at that time. Research demonstrates how behaviors from virtual worlds will translate to the real world. This connection may be due to how highly users identify with their personal avatar and their success in forming real social relationships with other avatars. There are many instances where demonstrations on Second Life translate into real-life behavior.

For example, in 2007, Second Life users built an unofficial campaign headquarters in support of then-Presidential candidate Barack Obama. While you cannot actually vote for a candidate through Second Life, users were able to pick up free hats and tee-shirts for their avatars, thus becoming walking endorsements in the virtual world. They could read about Obama's political platform and watch videos of his appearance on the *Tonight Show* (Wheaton, 2007). Individuals who live in certain regions of America may not know a single person in their proxemic community who is voting for Obama, but they are able to find alternative communities and learn more about him through this virtual space.

Individuals are highly persuaded by these synchronous virtual communities because they highly identify with their virtual avatar, communication is entirely participatory among users, and the cyberspace mimics the real world much more so than other text- and image-based social media sites. Thus, many businesses and organizations have included Second Life as a part of their communication strategy, including the World Stock Exchange, Adidas, BBC Radio, Disney, Cleveland Clinic, and Toyota. Second Life is a great example of a social media platform that uses the assumption of the theory of dialogic communication to foster true participation among members of its online community.

Discussion questions

1   What interface features of Second Life allow users the opportunity for dialogic communication? How could marketers use this to engage audiences and create a stronger sense of community among users?

2   *Second Life* is a decentralized space, where users control most of the content. Based on this understanding, where would it fall on our diffusion–participation continuum? What opportunities and challenges does this extend to social media practitioners?

3   How would the virtual community Second Life change if it were asynchronous in nature? How would the expectations of engagement change for audiences?

Summary

This chapter focuses on ways to construct social messages to ensure online engagement between users. These messages are bound by the structure opportunities available and the mindset in which they were produced. The theory of dialogic communication teaches us the importance of audience feedback, and how true participation is critical for social media marketing success. Though this feedback will not always be positive, it is necessary to maintain a dialogic loop where users feel as though they are listened and valued. True participation and cooperation between users and the organization will prove mutually beneficial.

This chapter also discusses many asynchronous and synchronous options for online engagement. Many factors can help you decide whether to use synchronous or asynchronous approach for long-term behavior change. There are benefits and challenges for both synchronous and asynchronous communication features. It is best to have both options available for users to choose which they are most comfortable with. However, it is most important to ensure that you do not have the option for dialogic loop unless you are 100% confident that someone is going to respond to user queries. Determine what works best with your current schedule and staff and create the features accordingly.

With the advances in mobile smartphone technology, there is no question that synchronous communication is the future of social media marketing. However, please note the challenge associated with synchronous communication. First, it is easier to make mistakes through synchronous communication. Participants become so engrossed that conversations can quickly become heated. Organizations can get themselves into trouble fast if they are not carefully crafting their messages. Second, some queries take time to investigate and asynchronous communication allows this opportunity. It would be frustrating to engage in a synchronous communication feature, such as an instant message service, and be placed on hold while the person on the other end looks into the problem. Finally, not everyone is interested in communicating synchronously. In fact, many individuals have communication anxieties when it comes to real-time communication. They feel more comfortable when they are able to carefully craft a message and do not feel as though they are pressing the respondent to get back in a timely manner.

Engaging in mobile technologies is one way to mobilize audiences towards true participation. For the first time in history, users are able to interact with technology in any place, at any time in their lives. This creates many opportunities for social media marketers. We will explore these mobile techniques and how they can be beneficial for you and your audiences in Chapter 8.

Key Takeaways

1   True participation is more than just the structural ability for two-way communication, but includes a cooperative process working with and by the people.
2   Freire's theory of dialogic communication and action is a more ethical relational interaction, where ideas and opinions are negotiated through communication exchanges with the goal of reaching mutually satisfying opinions.
3   Structural functions that promote dialogic communication online include dialogic loop, usefulness of information, generation of return visits, ease of interface, and the conservation of visitors.
4   Virtual communities hold great potential for fostering dialogic communication, forming a dynamic and sustained relationship, and making consumers feel part of a larger social group.
5   Dialogic loop features allow unsatisfied users to query organizations and allow organizations the opportunity to respond. These features include easy to find contact information, contact forms, information for donor or media publics, telephone options, satisfaction surveys, email subscription options, interactive forms and blogs.

References

Boerner, K. (2011) IKEA announces new "Design by Ikea" blog and "Share Space" photo-sharing website. Available at http://www.ikea.com/us/en/about_ikea/newsitem/Blog_Share_Space_2011_release (accessed June 8, 2016).

Boulos, M., Hetherington, L. & Wheeler, S. (2007) Second Life: an overview of the potential of 3-D virtual worlds in medical and health education. *Health Information and Libraries Journal*, 24(4), 233–245.

Butler, P. & Peppard, J. (1998) Consumer purchasing on the Internet: processes and prospects. *European Management Journal*, 16(5), 600–610.

Charlton, G. (2007) Hidden charges and poor usability deter online shoppers. Available at http://econsultancy.com/us/blog/718-hidden-charges-and-poor-usability-deter-online-shoppers (accessed June 8, 2016).

Cui, J., Mei, J., Zhang, W., Wang, X. & Zhang, D. (2010) A Captcha implementation based on moving objects recognition problem. In: *2010 International Conference on E-Business and E-Government (ICEE)*, pp. 1277–1280. Piscataway, NJ: IEEE.

Duhigg, G. (2012) How companies learn your secrets. Available at http://www.nytimes.com/2012/02/19/magazine/shopping-habits.html?_r=3&pagewanted=all& (accessed June 8, 2016).

Gibbs, A. (1997) Focus groups. *Social Research Update*, Issue 19.

Griffin, E. (2009) *A First Look at Communication Theory*. New York: McGraw-Hill.

Gustavsen, P. & Tilley, E. (2003) Public relations communication through corporate websites: towards an understanding of the role of interactivity. *PRISM*, 1(1), 1–14.

Habermas, J. (1984) *The Theory of Communicative Action. Vol. 1. Reason and the Rationalization of Society*. Boston: Beacon Press.

Habermas, J. (1990) *Moral Consciousness and Communicative Action*. Cambridge, MA: MIT Press.

Hegland, J.E. & Nelson, N.J. (2002) Cross-dressers in cyberspace: exploring the Internet as a tool for expressing gendered identity. *International Journal of Sexuality and Gender Studies*, 7(2–3), 139–161.

Hill, W., Stead, L., Rosenstein, M. & Furnas, G. (1995) Recommending and evaluating choices in a virtual community of use. In: *Proceedings of the SIGCHI Conference on Human Factors in Computing Systems*, pp. 194–201. New York: ACM Press/Addison-Wesley.

Horowitz, D. (1997) Homeless can connect on own Web site. Available at http://www.sfgate.com/news/article/Homeless-can-connect-on-own-Web-site-3127210.php (accessed June 8, 2016).

Irving, J. (1972) *Victims of Groupthink: A Psychological Study of Foreign-policy Decisions and Fiascoes*. Boston: Houghton, Mifflin.

Kent, J. (1998) Building dialogic relationships through World Wide Web. *Public Relations Review*, 24(3), 321–334.

Kent, J. & Taylor, M. (1998) Building dialogic relationships through World Wide Web. *Public Relations Review*, 24(3), 321–334.

Krause, K. & Coates, H. (2008) Students' engagement in first-year university. *Assessment and Evaluation in Higher Education*, 33(5), 493–505.

McAllister-Spooner, S. & Kent, M. (2009) Dialogic public relations and resource dependency: New Jersey community colleges as models for Web Site effectiveness. *Atlantic Journal of Communication*, 17(4), 220–239.

Mollen, A. & Wilson, H. (2010) Engagement, telepresence and interactivity in online consumer experience: reconciling scholastic and managerial perspectives. *Journal of Business Research*, 63(9), 919–925.

Neumayer, C. & Raffl, C. (2008) Facebook for global protest: the potential and limits of social software for grassroots activism. In: *Proceedings of the 5th Prato Community Informatics and Development Informatics Conference*. Available at http://cirn.infotech.monash.edu/assets/docs/prato2008papers/raffl.pdf (accessed June 8, 2016).

Nisbett, N. (2006) The internet, cybercafés and the new social spaces of Bangalorean youth. In: S. Coleman & P. Collins (eds) *Locating the Field: Space, Place and Context in Anthropology*, p. 129. London: Bloomsbury Publishing.

Reber, B., Gower, K. & Robinson, J. (2006) The Internet and litigation public relations. *Journal of Public Relations Research*, 18(1), 23–44.

Reichheld, F. (2003) The one number you need to grow. *Harvard Business Review*, 81(12), 46–55.

Ridings, C. & Gefen, D. (2004) Virtual community attraction: why people hang out online. *Journal of Computer-Mediated Communication*, 10(1), doi: 10.1111/j.1083-6101.2004.tb00229.x.

Russell, A.E. (2008) An analysis of public relations and dialogic communication efforts of 501(C)(6) organizations. Doctoral dissertation, Ball State University, Muncie, IN.

Servaes, J. (1996) Participatory communication research from a Freirian perspective. *Africa Media Review*, 10, 73–91.

Singhal, A. (2004) Empowering the oppressed through participatory theater. *Investigación y desarrollo: revista del Centro de Investigaciones en Desarrollo Humano*, 12(1), 138–163.

SLLU (2007) Second Life activists solidarity across SIMS. Available at http://slleftunity.blogspot.com/2007/10/second-life-activists-solidarity-across.html (accessed June 8, 2016).

Stoker, K. & Tusinski, K. (2006) Reconsidering public relations' infatuation with dialogue: why engagement and reconciliation can be more ethical than symmetry and reciprocity. *Journal of Mass Media Ethics*, 21(2–3), 156–176.

Stratten, S. (2012) *Unmarketing. Stop Marketing. Start Engaging*. Hoboken, NJ: John Wiley & Sons, Inc.

Suttle, R. (2013) Key costs and benefits from market research. Available at http://smallbusiness.chron.com/key-costs-benefits-marketing-research-26311.html (accessed June 8, 2016).

Taylor, M., Kent, M. & White, W. (2001) How activist organizations are using the Internet to build relationships. *Public Relations Review*, 27(3), 263–284.

Wheaton, S. (2007) Obama is first in their Second Life. Available at http://thecaucus.blogs.nytimes.com/2007/03/31/obama-is-first-in-their-second-life/ (accessed June 8, 2016).

Zichermann, G. & Cunningham, C. (2011) *Gamification by Design: Implementing Game Mechanics in Web and Mobile Apps*. Sebastopol, CA: O'Reilly Media.

8

Mobile Marketing and Location-based Applications

Learning Objectives

After reading this chapter, you should be able to:
1 Encourage users to use mobile digital projections to bolster their online identity.
2 Understand the role of peer influence and the concept of a "third place" in mobile marketing.
3 Implement a social media mobile strategy that generates return visits from users.

Introduction

Everyday decision-making is influenced by a multitude of factors: personality, mood, life experience, social networks, internal noise, external noise, and media structure. The way we negotiate the world around us is unpredictable and one of the most difficult tasks of a social media marketer. Communication philosopher Marshall McLuhan (1964) famously wrote that the "medium is the message." The characteristics of the media that carry content prove just as, if not more, important than the content itself. Part II of this book has taught how media structure influences and limits the many ways in which users interact with content. The purpose of this chapter is to explore how mobile technology influences user behavior and interpretations of social media content.

Imagine arranging a lunch date with one of your friends with the message "We should grab lunch." How would this message be interpreted if delivered by personally stopping by

Strategic Social Media: From Marketing to Social Change, First Edition. L. Meghan Mahoney and Tang Tang.
© 2017 John Wiley & Sons, Inc. Published 2017 by John Wiley & Sons, Inc.

your friend's house unannounced? What if you emailed him or her the request? What if the message was sent through text message? The sense of urgency and timeline for carrying through the desired action would change depending on the media choice, even though the content of the message remains exactly the same. If the message was received through text message, the recipient may think that the lunch date should happen right away. If received through email, a longer planning timeline may occur. Though this is not exactly what McLuhan meant with his statement, media choice has never been more important than in today's digital landscape.

Mobile technology is spreading across the world and is undoubtedly changing the way we communicate with one another. Mobile phones are vastly popular due to their affordability, portability, easy personalization, and location-awareness capabilities (Kurkovsky & Harihar, 2006). Users are able to customize mobile phone features so that they are virtually unlike any other person's device. Chances are, if you lost your mobile phone, the person who finds it would not only be able to track it back to you through your personal contacts, but also be able to make a pretty accurate guess about who you are based on some of your customization decisions. We use our mobile devices to keep track of all our important, and unimportant, contacts in our life, and store our photos, music and videos. Even the brand of mobile device we choose to carry says a great deal about who we are.

Because of their lower cost and faster infrastructure, mobile technologies are spreading around the world at a faster pace than older technologies. Some of the most successful Internet applications are mobile-capable only. Users wishing to communicate on the photo-sharing application Instagram, the location-based check-in application FourSquare, the service review platform Path, or the short video sharing site Vine are unable to do so through personal computers. These applications require people to share content through mobile devices, encouraging users to synchronize their file sharing with real-life events. Though users have the ability to share older photos through Instagram (there is a popular hashtag #tbt, or throw back Thursday, for such occasions), this is not the intended purpose of the application. In fact, this is why users decide to alert other users that they are not following through with the synchronous norm (no one ever tags photos with #happeningrightnowthursday). Mobile technology is all about up-to-date synchronous communication. Traditional boundaries of time and space have been transformed with greater immediacy, and this could spark changing economic situations in certain regions.

Many debates exist about whether perpetual mobile contact holds positive or negative implications for society. No definitive conclusions will ever be reached, but it is certain that mobile technologies have dramatically changed the way we behave and communicate with one another. In fact, approximately 46% of smartphone owners identify the device as something that they "couldn't live without" (Smith, 2015). Mobile phone users tend to check their phones over 150 times per day (Meeker & Wu, 2013). Mobile technology is engrained in users daily activities today.

Getting together in a small group is easier than ever before (Grob *et al.*, 2009). Planning and changing plans takes less time, especially since mobile phones have GPS potential to alert friends where users are located. For this reason many fear that mobile communication is simultaneously replacing interpersonal contact because it is also easier than ever to keep in touch via mobile without meeting interpersonally.

Because of the unlimited features available through mobile technology, it is difficult to place it on the diffusion–participation scale. The low cost, ease of use, and unlimited availability make it an essential component of social media marketing. Because users have their mobile devices available for virtually every new experience, it also could be incorporated into a mobilization strategy. This chapter aims to explore mobile digital projections, the influence of peers in a shared social journey, and strategies for generating return visits.

Mobile Digital Projections

Computer-mediated communication (CMC) has been at the forefront of media research for decades. However, much changes when technology allows users to gain instant access to their network at any time and any place. *Mobile-mediated communication* (MMC) is a type of CMC that emphasizes mobility. As phones begin to converge with portable multimedia computers, and traditional media devices become more mobile, the distinction between these blur.

Mobile technology is increasing the level of participation through social media features such as sharing, search and filtering of relevant data with other connected users (Lugano, 2008). It is much easier to share what you are doing while you are in the moment than it is to remember hours later when you have returned home and are sitting in front of your personal computer. Mobile technology allows users to instantly share where they are, whom they are with, and whether they would like to invite others to join.

Users are able to use mobile devices on the go to publish content to a social media site, insert textual statements about what they are doing, subscribe to others' statements, view and comment on submissions, and rate, review or otherwise symbolically indicate approval of media content (Lewis *et al.*, 2010). With mobile technologies, it is a never-ending cycle of information interaction and sharing. Thus, social media sites are never in a final completed stage but are dynamic and grow with the user. They provide spaces for users to share their own stories with the public, or with a network of carefully screened individuals.

Individuals share their everyday lives through a processed dubbed *digital projections*. Whether they are sharing a status, photo or video update, these digital projections are a way for people to construct their own identity through technology and share it with their network. Perhaps more than ever before, users have a say in how other people make sense of their lives. Of course, one cannot account for the sense-making process entirely.

If a social media user wishes to be associated with traveling, he or she could choose to share news articles from various locations around the globe, luggage recommendations, future dream trips, or photos from personal travels. They may also ignore sharing other aspects of his or her life, such as sitting at home watching reruns of a favorite reality show. Social media allows us to choose to project the best of ourselves and keep other features private.

Though individuals are able to utilize mobile technology in a variety of ways, so long as they stay within the boundaries of the media structure provided, they still must work within many of the unwritten rules, expectations and customs of other types of communication. Research on digital projections demonstrates how increased sharing of photographs of oneself is correlated with a decreased feeling of intimacy from the audience (Grenoble, 2013). While individuals connect through social media to receive life updates, there is a balance that must be struck between what constitutes too much sharing, and how much of it should be centered on the self.

This is not so different from the various other marketing rules that we have discussed thus far. Remember that social media is an outlet to market according to your own goals. Even if you as a social media practitioner are not selling a product, you are still sharing a narrative. It is important to interact, engage, and participate with other users. Use the platform as a tool for dialogue surrounding issues that are important to you and your audience. Share some pictures, but ask for, and comment on others, more.

Research demonstrates that the more individuals engage in these participatory activities, the more they entice further connections and participatory action. Continuous feedback is the keystone of social media, as individuals are able to engage in identity management of their own profiles. Audiences create a sense of who they are and the role that they play in society through collective feedback from their online communities. While social media users are aware of their own reputation management, they also hold an awareness of what their social networks are sharing online.

Online social narratives are never true depictions of our own selves. We tend to post idealized versions of ourselves, or only share when things are exotic, special or highly edited. Consider the places where you or your friends have "checked-in" or shared the location of a real-life interpersonal event. Chances are, these are places that you don't mind being associated with. We hardly share ordinary run-of-the mill experiences through social media.

Though the technology potential exists for mobile group communication, most mobile users utilize the technology for individual networking. This is the appeal of one-to-one mobile applications such as Snapchat. Snapchat is a mobile phone messaging technology that allows one user the ability to send another user a video message that will "disappear" on opening in as many as 10 seconds. This mitigates the permanence and public nature of other types of online communication.

Smartmobs, or mobilization of the masses through mobile technologies, is one of the few many-to-many features of mobile technology (Rheingold, 2003; Grob *et al.*, 2009). This is where many users are able to coordinate themselves at a particular place and time for an event. Often, these events are lighthearted and fun in nature, though sometimes they are arranged with hopes of raising awareness or to protest an event. Online group communication tends to be initiated by one person who invites a set of contacts to participate. However, some social media users find this annoying and do not accept or remove themselves from group conversation. A better way to initiate cohesiveness among a group is through tagging features (Grob *et al.*, 2009).

Tagging features exist in many forms. In general, they link individuals to the purpose or event of the communication. Some tagging includes a text-based hashtag, or a character string proceeded by the # sign to signal topic organization, audience or meaning (Efron, 2010). For instance, if you were attending a conference presentation at the 2016 International Communication Association convention, you may include the hashtag #ICA16 with all conference-related posts. This allows individuals who are interested in the conference, whether attending or not, to follow along. Tagging also includes labeling faces on pictures or bookmarking sites or contact lists under specific categories. In general, tagging helps people understand why they are being included on a message by seeing what they have in common with other people or designated topics.

Online communication does not mean that users must know each other interpersonally. Users who find each other through interest-based sites may not know each other very well at first, but through increased online interactions and sharing they could become quite friendly and begin to consider each other an important member of their life. Some individuals choose to exchange their contact information and meet in real life. However, most mobile-specific social networks are designed specifically for the mobile community (Counts & Fisher, 2008). Just because users do not choose to meet in real life, it does not mean that real feelings and emotions do not develop. Often, individuals are able to communicate more frequently through social media sites than they do with interpersonal-based friends.

We tend to have perpetual contact with those we wish to see interpersonally in our everyday lives. While Facebook has check-in features and Google and Foursquare alert you when others in your network are close by, researchers found that few actually use the feature to meet up interpersonally. Using location-based settings helps users project the type of social person they are, and holds potential for marketers to know more about their customers' everyday experiences, but it is unlikely that someone in your network will see these notifications and consequently come and join you without an invitation.

Dodgeball was one of the first mobile social media designed as a location-based information distributor where users could meet up in-person with their friends. Users would broadcast their location through their mobile device by checking in, and their chosen social network would receive a text message regarding the location. Google purchased Dodgeball in May 2005, but has since rolled the technology into other platforms (Humphreys, 2007), none with great success. Mobile networking applications should be utilized to make organization and social experiences easier and more enjoyable. They alter social experiences, but rarely do they create them.

Because users are able to carry and use mobile technology virtually anywhere, more and more information is being shared about their daily lives. Location-based features allow users the ability to find and interact with nearby events, businesses and friends (Grob *et al.*, 2009). If you check in at a local coffee shop online, other stores on the same road have the ability to see this check-in and send a coupon asking you to try their coffee next time you're in the area. However, users are growing more and more concerned with privacy issues of location disclosure. Do we really want everyone to know where we are at all times?

Mobile applications allow users the ability to capture and upload text, photo, voice and video messages. Generally, users are able to alter settings to allow the public to view content or to restrict such content to permitted followers. It does take some level of media literacy and communication competency to navigate through these permissions. The longer individuals grow with social media, the more competent they become.

Just because mobile technology allows you to share, realize it is not always appropriate or safe. While social media is a place for you to share your digital projections, remember that social media is about relationship building and transactional communication. A good rule of thumb is the 2 : 1 standard. You should interact and engage other users twice as often as you share information about your brand. Nevertheless, every organization is different, and undoubtedly your social media use will grow and change with you.

Peer Influence and a Shared Social Journey

There are seven billion mobile phone subscribers worldwide today (International Telecommunication Union, 2014). Mobile networking technologies allow users to create, develop and strengthen ties wherever they are, to keep in touch with acquaintances easier than at any other time in history, and hold potential for strengthening relationships with close family and friends.

Some research points to a new phenomenon where the technology is actually hindering relationships. An increase in mobile technology is found to limit the creation of new relationships we make (Ling, 2000). A possible reason for this change may be due to the way we utilize the technology. Often, we fill empty time between events or while waiting in line with mobile games, text messages or social media. While this empty space may have previously been an opportunity to communicate interpersonally with others who are also waiting, we are now able to communicate with individuals already in our network through mobile technology. This is a much more comfortable communication situation for many than talking to strangers.

Look around next time you are in a group situation. Some individuals will be using mobile technology in isolation, making little eye contact and ignoring interpersonal communication with those around them physically. Others will be using mobile technology to create a shared social journey with those they are with. They tag each other together in the real-time event; take pictures and comment online about the fun that they are having. Your friends' mobile communication may say just as much about you and your social life as your own.

The term *"Third Place"* is a traditional designation for a public place that hosts regular, voluntary, informal and anticipated gatherings of individuals beyond the realm of home ("First Place") and work ("Second Place") (Oldenburg, 1989). These are often popular restaurants, bars or events. Here, social networks gather on a platform that is central to their sense of self and community. Individuals identify with the Third Place much more than they do other spaces where they may spend more physical time, such as work. Generally, the mood is upbeat and relaxed at the Third Place (Humphreys, 2007).

Mobile technology allows individuals to experience the Third Place with each other even if they are far away. Consider the "Third Space" posts that your own social network shares. You may be able to follow their experiences and get to know their new group of friends even though you have never met them. Despite not being physically present, you are able to share in your friends' journey and let them know that you care by commenting and sharing online.

Another phenomenon of mobile technology is called schedule softening (Ling, 2000). *Schedule softening* is where individuals engage in minimal pre-planning rituals because they know that they will be able to reach the other party by mobile phone when it is closer to the actual time of the event. Users are also rearranging their schedules with minimal notice at an increased rate than before. For example, you may not feel bad about stopping at a store on your way to meet someone because you will be able to call them and let them know if you are running late. While individuals used to be more schedule conscious due to the lack of communication on the go, today short-term changes in circumstances are becoming less of a faux pas (Geser, 2006).

Every individual and generation utilizes mobile technology differently from one another. Individual blogging has declined in popularity among younger generations. Rather than having a designated website to share life experiences with those who choose to follow their blog, younger generations are relying on social media to tell their story, intermitted between the rest of their friends' social network.

Different cultures and genders utilize mobile technology differently as well. African Americans are the most active group of mobile Internet users, and this group is growing at an increasing pace (Lenhart *et al.*, 2010). Females tend to form a larger group of contacts, communicate more emotionally, and interact more frequently with their mobile network than males (Igarashi *et al.*, 2005). Baby boomers are emerging as the newest market for increased mobile gaming (Beck, 2004). People utilize mobile technology for social purposes and so it makes sense that their journey would be similar to those within their race, gender and age cohort.

Collaborative projections enable joint and simultaneous creation by many users (Kaplan & Haenlein, 2010). This is a great way to prompt your consumers to create new real-life experiences and share online. Mobile technology allows marketers to incorporate time and space into social media projects. There are many effective examples of how organizations utilize the synchronous nature of mobile technology to incite real-life behavior change in audiences.

Actor Misha Collins created an annual worldwide scavenger hunt competition, GISH-WHES (Greatest International Scavenger Hunt the World Has Ever Seen). Here, participants register a team, follow a posted list of items to find or create, photograph them and upload on the GISHWHES website (www.GISHWHES.com). Scavenger hunt prompts range from "Create a video of you visiting a children's hospital and giving a puppet show," to "Make an Igloo for your dog." The community has broken three Guinness World Records (i.e., an international authority that catalogs and verifies record-breaking achievements), with 14,580 participants registered for the competition in 2012. Mobile scavenger hunts are a great way to create life experiences and get users to share how much fun they are having with their social network.

Harrods department store in London created a mobile contest where consumers were urged to explore the city in search of their trademark "Green Man" dancing. They were then prompted to upload a picture to Twitter including the hashtag #HarrodsSale to enter a chance to win $1500 to spend in store (Shea, 2011). The Batman movie *The Dark Knight Rises* prompted fans to help unlock previews of the movie trailer. They posted a list of various locations around the world and asked followers to go to spots, take pictures and share their findings (Yoder, 2012). When enough users participated, more previews of the movie were shared.

While these are all great ways of getting audiences involved in the digital projection process, the best thing about GISHWHES is the memories created among team members. Their website shares testimonials from participants who talk about the fun they had, new outlooks on life that the adventures gave them, and the surprising willingness of strangers to help with prompts. Even though mobile phones are an individualized technology that serves the specialized and customized needs of each user, think beyond individual participation when using it in marketing strategies. Urge users to share, create and make memories with their social networks. Consider the following action plan when creating a mobile strategy.

Mobile Strategy Action Plan

1 Develop an alternative social media strategy for mobile devices. Consider mobile-mediated communication features, such as localization, portable sharing, and synchronicity.
2 Allow users to tag friends and share posts with their own social network. This will create a stronger sense of community, and speak to users' own gratifications for your product.
3 Incorporate location-based check-in features so that users can share their experiences with your brand with their own social network. Ensure that this experience speaks to the notion of the Third Place and will actually be something that they would want their online identity to be associated with.
4 Create collaborative campaigns where users contribute to a synchronous prompt, such as a scavenger hunt. Encourage them to leave their houses, have out-of-the-box experiences, and share photos or videos.

Generating Return Visits

Mobile technology is a shared social space for individual networks. Individuals are highly influenced by their social network and make purchasing and behavior change decisions accordingly. While mobile technology allows marketers the ability to deliver promotional information to consumers based on their individualized preferences and location (Wang, 2007), it would be more beneficial if they were able to prompt users to share their experiences with their social network, creating memories associated with their brand.

Often, businesses try to prompt customers to visit stores by offering free products through mobile updates. However, research demonstrates that consumers are more persuaded, especially towards long-term behavior change, if they are involved in the information-seeking process, rather than just being given a coupon. Remember that emotion and engagement highly influence our everyday decisions. Commitment can be enhanced through building emotional value (Varnali & Toker, 2010). *Push text messages* are a mobile alert that applications send to update users with new content. While these are efficient and cost-effective, they tend to lack emotion and may not be as persuasive as marketers hope. In fact, many mobile users find them disruptive and annoying. By allowing consumers to search for information, businesses may actually gain more benefits. Free materials with no-strings-attached offers may even prompt consumers to devalue the products. Make customers work for coupons, even if it is through simple acts such as scanning QR codes or sharing offers with friends.

Most mobile advertisements are based on text messaging services, which is not a very emotionally engaging communication medium (Wang, 2007). Companies offer special deals if consumers "opt-in" to receiving text messages from the company. This is called permission marketing, and is different from spam because it requires the recipient to agree to receive the messages (Bauer *et al.*, 2005). What separates mobile marketing from other forms of new media is its ability to personalize and customize settings based on what works best for the user. Most companies are not utilizing mobile media to this potential and are sending impersonal messages that seem interruptive. Remember that customers will be interrupted much more by text-based messages because they will arrive by phone, not in an asynchronous platform such as email. Most individuals will see your message, but will find it bothersome and not appropriate for what they are doing at the time, and will associate the brand with this negative feeling.

One way to improve this marketing strategy is to personalize the types of messages that your consumers receive. Mobile marketing allows you the ability to learn a lot about consumer demographics, location and interests (Scharl *et al.*, 2005). Once you begin to gain a sense of what your audience enjoys, construct the message accordingly. The simplicity, affordability and speed of mobile delivery makes this type of target messaging possible. Address the recipient by name and ask them to participate in the process. Let them know that there is a human on the other end of the message.

Location-based messages also help alleviate some of the bothersome qualities of interruptive mobile marketing. Register your business with location-based applications such as RetailMeNot or FourSquare so that you know when customers are close by. Offer these promotions to users who are participating in activities where these deals would be appropriate, rather than bothersome. It is much more interesting to learn that a store is having a sale when the person is on the same street, rather than miles away. However, imagine how unappealing it will be to receive messages from every store that you walk by. There has to be some balance. Collaborate with other companies that have similar brands and audiences. Mobile marketing does not allow for the same richness of information as Internet marketing, so be sure to keep all information concise (Shankar & Balasubramanian, 2009).

The best way to ensure users continue engaging with your mobile campaign is to make it creative and entertaining (Bauer *et al.*, 2005). Research demonstrates how these two constructs are the highest correlating factors with intentional customer return visits. While there is a slightly more addictive tendency with mobile technology than other types of media, marketers cannot solely rely on habitual routine for repeat use (Ehrenberg *et al.*, 2008).

The medium is the message, and while it is easy to make traditional Internet content friendly for mobile devices, mobile marketing requires more than just an interface change. Content and features should change according to the platform that users engage and the goals of the company.

Overall, commercially oriented marketing messages are less appealing than social and entertainment-related strategies (Grant & O'Donohoe, 2007). Users want control over their mobile technology; after all, it is an incredibly important construction of self-identity. Do not be the company that takes that personalization away through interruptive messaging. Mobile marketing should encourage users to strengthen relationships with those in their networks by prompting new experiences, offering promotions when they are out together, and providing games to play when they are away.

Case Study: Renren

The process of engaging audiences through social media constantly evolves as more users log on through mobile technology. China is leading the way in social media marketing, and mobile technology is set to increase this gap further. More than 50% of Chinese users spend more than 12 hours a week online, and 58% use a smartphone to browse social media sites (Chiu *et al.*, 2012). The number of mobile Internet users has reached 277 million, accounting for 65.9% of the total number of Internet users. This trend will continue as mobile phones become more affordable and accessible than personal computers.

In China, social network recommendations tend to have a greater influence on purchasing decisions than anywhere else in the world. This is a culture where community input is highly prioritized. Collectivist cultures such as China are highly concerned with others in their network, well above their own individual needs. Individuals would be more likely to communicate with their personal networks about life experiences than they are to talk about individual preferences directly to the company. Moreover, they see themselves as part of a larger community. They strongly identify with other members of the group. Therefore, what is satisfying to them will most likely be satisfying to others. What works for their family and friends is likely to work for them as well.

Renren is one such social media site that puts culture and mobile strategy into its design and operation. It was launched in 2005 and evolved from a university-based social network called Xiaonei. Today, Renren has more than 150 million users and become one of the largest and oldest social networking sites in China. Users are able to manage their personal profile, upload pictures, share blog entries, and establish links with their friends on Renren. It is similar to Facebook in terms of the structure, layout and features except that all friendship links are public. Renren has a perpetually changing visitor clicker at the bottom of the page that shows how many individuals have viewed the profile as well as the names and links to the last nine visitors (Jiang *et al.*, 2010). This illustrates the value of network and community in Chinese culture. It is just as important to know information about the user as it is to know information about the user's personal network.

Renren is also a place for companies to disseminate information about their products and services. Renren users are able to subscribe to real-time updates from companies that they choose to follow and then make these recommendations to their personal social network (Liu *et al.*, 2012). Location-based marketing is also possible through Renren, as brands are able to market attractive deals to specific groups, or allow users to share where they are, what they're doing, and who they are with. This is a great way to give networks the sense that they are together, even if they are not sharing the same proxemic place. Renren makes consumption a much more social experience (Ye, 2012).

Gaming has proven itself as one of the biggest drivers of mobile growth for Renren (Chiu, 2013). The most engaging games are those in which users are able to compete and share experiences with their network. Mobile games make the social experience more enjoyable and interactive, and allow users to create new experiences when they cannot be together.

Clearly one of the benefits of social media platforms is the ability for users around the globe to communicate and interact with one another. For marketers, social media like Renren provides more individualized options for sharing and participation from fans. In addition, Renren shows us the importance of culture in how we share. In a culture where users turn to their community as an influence in all decisions, mobile marketing allows them to be together for all decisions. It is important that structure, content and culture all align in order to maximize satisfaction for everyone.

Discussion questions

1   How do the features of Renren speak to the Chinese culture, specifically the values of community and relationship building? What opportunities and challenges does this provide to social media practitioners?
2   How would individuals that network through Renren utilize the social media to communicate about their identity in a positive manner? Specifically, how could they use mobile technology to share information about their Third Place experiences?
3   How might information shared on Renren be different between users that access the site through a desktop computer versus through mobile technology?

Summary

Marketers were just beginning to understand best practices for communicating with online users through social media as mobile technology became popular. We know that the media that carries online content alters the human behavior change process, but it is impossible to know for sure which device users will utilize when they access online information. It is important for social media marketers to be aware of the technology available and ensure that users are not prevented from participating in the process because a website is not mobile friendly. Marketing strategies should be inclusive of every type of online user, as there are opportunities and challenges with each new device.

While mobile-mediated communication holds potential for increased participation and engagement between online users, it could also decrease the value of interpersonal communication. There has been much concern about a mobile world where everyone is looking down at their mobile devices and missing the world right in front of them. While it is important to keep mobile content exciting and engaging, the focus should really be on encouraging real-life experiences through mobilization.

Mobile marketing must focus on culture, personalization, interactivity, socialization, and localization (Bauer *et al.*, 2005). These are all opportunities that were incredibly difficult to establish through traditional technology. GPS capabilities make traveling in foreign places simple, and have provided independence to those directionally challenged people. Families are better able to coordinate schedules through simple phone calls or texts. People are able to share applications that synch calendars, grocery lists and games of Scrabble.

However, mobile technologies also bring many interruptions, as users are perpetually connected to family, friends and work. The notion of a 9 to 5 workday has almost vanished completely (Castells, 2007). Concerns with privacy have shifted, and one cannot help but wonder whether the picture a person is posting will be shared with the world moments later. These are all changes that we are only beginning to research and understand. Regardless, it is very clear that mobile technology is here to stay for a long time.

This chapter focuses on how mobile users utilize technology to share their life experiences with personal networks. Differences in social media users, content, structure, and platform influence this process. It is your job as a social media communication specialist to apply traditional theories to social media messages in order to build relationships and establish customer loyalty. The next section of this book will focus on how to take these loyal relationships and apply marketing business models to sustain growth. While making profit may not be your goal in social media marketing, it is still important to understand how social media has influenced the marketplace.

Part III of this book explores social media marketing and business models. It will explore how digital media allows businesses to target smaller audience segments and sell a wider range of products. Next, it will explain how to know when to develop business models according to organizational goals, audience and marketing strategy. Finally, it will explain market analysis and how to measure and evaluate social media success through online analytic programs. You have already learned how to brand your online presence and build relationships with followers. A strong business and marketing strategy will help you plan for future sustainment and growth.

Key Takeaways

1   The characteristics of the media that carry content highly influence the way consumers use and interpret the content itself. Therefore, marketing content should vary depending on the platform that consumers utilize.
2   Mobile-mediated communication is a type of computer-mediated communication that allows for unlimited mobility, faster infrastructure, and low-cost plans where users share, search and interact with others.
3   It is important to incorporate structure, content, and culture in mobile social networks.

> 4   Social media users create digital projections of their lives through status, photo and video updates. Mobile technology allows individuals to easily share experiences with each other in real time, even if they are far away.
> 5   Mobile marketing should encourage collaborative projects where users create and share real-life experiences with their personal network. Commercially oriented marketing messages are less appealing than social and entertainment-related strategies for your consumers.

References

Bauer, H.H., Barnes, S.J., Reichardt, T. & Neumann, M.M. (2005) Driving consumer acceptance of mobile marketing: a theoretical framework and empirical study. *Journal of Electronic Commerce Research*, 6(3), 181–192.

Beck, J.C. (2004) *Got Game: How a New Generation of Gamers is Reshaping Business Forever*. Boston: Harvard Business Press.

Castells, M. (2007) *Mobile Communication and Society*. Cambridge, MA: MIT Press.

Chiu, C., Lin, D. & Silverman, A. (2012) China's social media boom. Available at http://www.mckinsey.com/business-functions/marketing-and-sales/our-insights/chinas-social-media-boom (accessed June 8, 2016).

Chiu, N. (2013) Is Renren going anywhere? Available at http://www.chron.com/business/fool/article/Is-Renren-Going-Anywhere-4470504.php (accessed June 8, 2016).

Counts, S. & Fisher, K. (2008) Mobile social networking: an information grounds perspective. In: *Proceedings of the 41st Hawaii International Conference on System Sciences*. Piscataway, NJ: IEEE.

Efron, M. (2010) Hashtag retrieval in a microblogging environment. In: *Proceedings of the 33rd International ACM SIGIR Conference on Research and Development in Information Retrieval*, pp. 787–788. New York: ACM Press.

Ehrenberg, A., Juckes, S., White, K. & Walsh, S. (2008) Personality and self-esteem as predictors of young people's technology use. *CyberPsychology and Behavior*, 11(6), 739–741.

Geser, H. (2006) Is the cell phone undermining the social order? Understanding mobile technology from a sociological perspective. *Knowledge, Technology and Policy*, 19(1), 8–18.

Grant, I. & O'Donohoe, S. (2007) Why young consumers are not open to mobile marketing communication. *International Journal of Advertising*, 26(2), 223–246.

Grenoble, R. (2013) Posting too many Facebook "selfies" can hurt your real-world relationships, study says. Available at http://www.huffingtonpost.com/2013/08/13/too-many-facebook-photos-study_n_3749053.html?ncid=edlinkusaolp00000003&ir=College (accessed June 8, 2016).

Grob, R., Kuhn, M., Wattenhofer, R. & Wirz, M. (2009) Cluestr: mobile social networking for enhanced group communication. In: *Proceedings of the ACM 2009 International Conference on Supporting Group Work*, pp. 81–90. New York: ACM Press.

Humphreys, L. (2007) Mobile social networks and social practice: a case study of Dodgeball. *Journal of Computer-Mediated Communication*, 13(1), 341–360.

Igarashi, T., Takai, J. & Yoshida, T. (2005) Gender differences in social network development via mobile phone text messages: a longitudinal study. *Journal of Social and Personal Relationships*, 22(5), 691–713.

International Telecommunication Union (2014) Facts and figures. Available at http://www.itu.int/en/ITU-D/Statistics/Documents/facts/ICTFactsFigures2014-e.pdf (accessed June 8, 2016).

Jiang, J., Wilson, C., Wang, X. *et al.* (2010) Understanding latent interactions in online social networks. In: *Proceedings of the 10th ACM SIGCOMM Conference on Internet Measurement*, pp. 369–382. New York: ACM Press.

Kaplan, A. & Haenlein, M. (2010) Users of the world, unite! The challenges and opportunities of social media. *Business Horizons*, 53(1), 59–68.

Kurkovsky, S. & Harihar, K. (2006) Using ubiquitous computing in interactive mobile marketing. *Personal and Ubiquitous Computing*, 10(4), 227–240.

Lenhart, A., Purcell, K., Smith, A. & Zickuhr, K. (2010) Social media and mobile Internet use among teens and young adults. Pew Internet and American Life Project. Available at http://www.pewinternet.org/2010/02/03/social-media-and-young-adults/ (accessed June 8, 2016).

Lewis, S., Pea, R. & Rosen, J. (2010) Beyond participation to co-creation of meaning: mobile social media in generative learning communities. *Social Science Information*, 49(3), 351–369.

Ling, R. (2000) Direct and mediated interaction in the maintenance of social relationships. In: A. Sloane & F. Van Rijn (eds) *Home Informatics and Telematics: Information, Technology and Society*, pp. 61–86. Boston: Kluwer.

Liu, L., Zhu, F., Jiang, M., Han, J., Sun, L. & Yang, S. (2012) Mining diversity on social media networks. *Multimedia Tools and Applications*, 56(1), 179–205.

Lugano, G. (2008) Mobile social networking in theory and practice. *First Monday*, 13(11). Available at http://firstmonday.org/ojs/index.php/fm/article/view/2232/2050 (accessed June 8, 2016).

McLuhan, M. (1994) *Understanding Media: The Extensions of Man*. Cambridge, MA: MIT Press.

Meeker, M. & Wu, L. (2013) 2013 Internet trends. Available at http://www.kpcb.com/blog/2013-internet-trends (accessed June 8, 2016).

Oldenburg, R. (1989) *The Great Good Place*. New York: Paragon House.

Rheingold, H. (2003) *Smart Mobs: The Next Social Revolution*. Cambridge, MA: Perseus Books Group.

Scharl, A., Dickinger, A. & Murphy, J. (2005) Diffusion and success factors of mobile marketing. *Electronic Commerce Research and Applications*, 4(2), 159–173.

Shankar, V. & Balasubramanian, S. (2009) Mobile marketing: a synthesis and prognosis. *Journal of Interactive Marketing*, 23(2), 118–129.

Shea, E. (2011) Harrods targets London shoppers via mobile scavenger hunt. Available at https://www.luxurydaily.com/harrods-targets-london-shoppers-via-mobile-scavenger-hunt/ (accessed June 8, 2015).

Smith, A. (2015) U.S. smartphone use in 2015. Available at http://www.pewinternet.org/2015/04/01/us-smartphone-use-in-2015/ (accessed June 8, 2016).

Varnali, K. & Toker, A. (2010) Mobile marketing research: the state-of-the-art. *International Journal of Information Management*, 30(2), 144–151.

Wang, A. (2007) How consumers perceive free offers: implications for mobile marketing. *International Journal of Mobile Marketing*, 2(2), 35–41.

Ye, S. (2012) Renren to emphasize user generated content and mobile marketing in 2012. Available at http://www.seeisee.com/sam/2012/01/16/p3580 (accessed June 8, 2016).

Yoder, G. (2012) "The Dark Knight Rises" taps social media users to find Batman. Available at http://www.boston.com/ae/movies/blog/2012/05/the_dark_knight.html (accessed June 8, 2016).

Part III

Social Media Marketing and Business Models

9

Reconsidering the Long Tail

Learning Objectives

After reading this chapter, you should be able to:

1 Explain the theory of the long tail and be able to identify the opportunities and challenges of marketing towards a latent audience.
2 Understand how to transform audiences into a niche commodity through social media.
3 Utilize social media for inbound marketing in order to best meet marketing objectives.

Introduction

The creation and implementation of a marketing strategy help organizations examine specific objectives and identify ways to reach their audiences over a long-term period of time. This involves careful research of the brand, audience and product market. Part II of this book highlighted the importance of prioritizing social media users and messages in this process. While this is a necessary first step in the marketing process, it is important that practitioners identify, anticipate and satisfy audience expectations through a purposeful business model. Often, communication specialists are not as familiar with various business strategies as they are with communication persuasive appeal theories. A combination of both is crucial for the development of successful social media strategies.

Strategic Social Media: From Marketing to Social Change, First Edition. L. Meghan Mahoney and Tang Tang.
© 2017 John Wiley & Sons, Inc. Published 2017 by John Wiley & Sons, Inc.

Part III of this book focuses on how social media has changed existing business models, identifies emerging marketing strategies, and suggests ways in which you can evaluate and predict marketing outcomes through formative research. A strong understanding of these areas will put you ahead of other social media communication specialists in the field. This is crucial to the long-term development of any organization or brand.

It is also important for organizations to integrate the design, implementation, and evaluation of marketing strategy and business models into day-to-day operations. It is not wise to segment these tasks into various departments. Communication will not seem cohesive and may result in a public relations nightmare for a company. This is especially true in today's digital age when every employee, customer and audience have unlimited opportunity through social media as a mouthpiece for your organization.

The primary purpose of a business model is to help a company reach goals. Often, that goal is to increase revenue. As we learned in previous chapters, it is not enough in today's marketplace to simply have a strong product. Social media makes it necessary for companies to foster relationships with consumers. This chapter will help you prepare and further explain how social media technologies have changed the marketplace.

Power-Law Distribution

One of the most consistent elements of the traditional marketplace is the *power-law distribution*. A power law is a statistical relationship between two quantities, where one quantity varies proportionally based on the fixed power of the other. While the concept is quite complex, the main idea is that a small change in one quantity can give rise to a proportional change in the other quantity (Bar-Yam, 2011). The formula for a power-law distribution is shown in Figure 9.1.

This distribution is very important to strategists because it helps to explain some regularity in the properties of a complex system. Companies prefer regularities in audience purchasing behavior because it provides some control over predicting the future of products and revenues. It is not just businesses that follow power-law distributions. Many natural and human systems also follow the same patterns. For example, the frequency of earthquakes is inversely related to their intensity, and the proportion of income distribution in society is inversely related to the amount of income (Jones & Kim, 2012).

Economists have found a significant power-law distribution in e-commerce, where significant profit can be made from a small sales volume of a large number of less popular items (Fenner *et al.*, 2010). This is especially true for media products, such as books, music and movies. Traditionally, companies have been able to make a profit by only providing audiences the opportunity to purchase a small number of "hits" rather than a larger quantity of inventory.

$$p(x) = \frac{\alpha - 1}{Xmin} \left(\frac{x}{Xmin} \right)^{-\alpha}$$

Figure 9.1 Power-law distribution. Source: Author.

Mass hits are included at the front of the distribution tail, and reach a large and diverse audience. More niche products are at the narrow, back end of the tail, and appeal to a much smaller latent market. The tail gets longer and longer, and the ability for marketers to profit on this inventory is traditionally lower (Jenkins *et al.*, 2013).

Economists often refer to this as the *80/20 rule*, where businesses are able to appeal to 80% of the population by offering only 20% of the available products (Brynjolfsson *et al.*, 2011). Consider for a moment your choices when you shop at a grocery store (which only carries a limited amount of products available in the market). Chances are you walk through the grocery aisles and are able to purchase most of the products that you need. Moreover, there are enough selection options that you feel fairly informed about the decisions you make. The available inventory is able to keep customers relatively happy, while also maintaining a profit.

Based on the 80/20 rule, the grocery store is able to achieve this balance by only stocking a limited number of the possible products available in the market. These products are those items that are used most often by the masses. If you were attempting to find an ingredient for a recipe that is less appealing to the masses, you may have trouble finding it at the regular grocer. Items not offered are considered to be a part of the *latent market*. These are products that cannot be profitably sold in traditional stores because they are not popular enough to recoup the costs of stocking it on the shelves (Spencer & Woods, 2010). Shelf space is expensive, and there is only so much available. The result of markets being dominated by a small number of best-selling products has often made it difficult for minority niche products to break through.

While business models have been developed based around traditional notions of power-law distributions, new technologies have changed the marketplace. Digital media and e-commerce have transformed our notion of shelf space. It is important for future communication and marketing strategists to rethink traditional models to make their organization fit for the future (Zott & Amit, 2010). One of the biggest shifts in thinking has been the theory of the long tail.

Theory of the Long Tail

For decades, products have been bought and sold based on the power-law distribution model, where a business is able to make a large amount of profit by offering a small number of hits to audiences. By stocking a larger quantity of inventory, businesses would risk losing profit because these less popular items would not be as attractive to the common customers. Therefore, it did not make sense for businesses to offer these less appealing "niche" products for a latent audience. Businesses would actually lose money by doing so.

Today's digital world offers a lower cost of distribution, especially with the opportunities of online commerce. Products are no longer bound by the constraints of physical shelf space and other bottlenecks of distribution. Anderson (2006) explored this phenomenon and developed a new business model for today's market called the *theory of the long tail* (Figure 9.2), which explains how a larger portion of the population exists in the niche tail of the probability distribution. Therefore, businesses are able to profit from niche products with low demand by using alternative distribution channels.

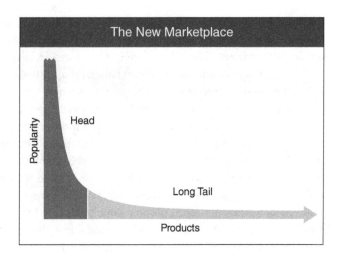

Figure 9.2   The long tail. Source: Reproduced with permission of Chris Anderson.

Not only are businesses able to profit from these niche sales, but the volume of latent commerce can collectively exceed the sale of a lower volume of hits. Marketers are actually able to make increased (or at least the same) revenue by selling to latent audiences than if they sold to the masses. Traditional businesses have only been able to stock the most appealing inventory because space is expensive. Online retailers, such as Amazon, are able to stock an unlimited selection of products. Given additional choice in products, consumers can gravitate towards these less popular niche products (Anderson, 2006). Therefore, it is important for social media practitioners to consider shifting their business model from targeting a mass market to a niche. Social media makes this more possible than ever before.

Let's consider the music industry for a moment. If you were in charge of determining the music inventory available in a traditional big box store, you likely be bound by the 80/20 rule. You would only have a limited amount of shelf space, so you would decide to stock the artists that prove most appealing to the masses, which would ensure the greatest number of sales.

An important transitional period in the media industry was in 2005, when Walmart was still America's largest music retailer and accounted for about one-fifth of music sales in the nation (Anderson, 2005). The most popular song in 2005 was Mariah Carey's *We Belong Together* (Billboard, 2005). Because of the song's mass appeal, Walmart personnel would certainly ensure that this album was available for purchase by giving it maximum shelf space.

Customers who purchased Mariah Carey's album from Walmart were likely satisfied with this stocking decision. They probably enjoyed the song when it played on their local radio station, so when they went to the store to make a music selection, it was an appealing purchasing decision. If they didn't like the song on the radio, they would likely choose to purchase a different available album from an artist that they preferred more. If they went home and ended up not liking their purchasing choice, Walmart also offered the opportunity to exchange the album for one of their other items in stock. Overall, customers felt fairly satisfied that they were able to make informed decisions about their music purchases.

While this traditional business model was working for customers and businesses alike, the digital media industry was about to change everything. The year 2005 was the first year that the number of legally downloaded digital singles outsold the physical products available in stores (Leeds, 2007). Customers were turning towards online music distributors, such as iTunes, to add songs to their personal music library rather than purchasing CDs from big box stores. They were no longer bound by the inventory of music selection that was decided by an outside agency. This shift provided a new opportunity for developing artists and independent labels.

Digital music changed the economics, players and speed in the music industry (Anderson, 2004). Suddenly, artists were not competing for a finite amount of shelf space, for example, of the estimated 30,000 new albums released each year, Walmart stocked an average of about 750. Through social media, rising artists were able to produce, collaborate, share and sell their music at a relatively low cost. They no longer needed to appeal to a mass audience, but were able to more authentically produce music that was individual to their own tastes, because hopefully, somewhere, there was a latent market that it satisfied.

The latent market shifted power from the label producers to the artists themselves. Not only did the digital music age provide opportunities for rising artists, but it changed the consumer experience. For the first time in history, consumers had unlimited access to every artist, genre and song available online. In fact, it is estimated that virtually every song ever made can be stored on just $400 worth of storage (Anderson, 2004). Imagine how much it would cost to store and distribute that amount of songs at a big box store!

This unlimited access to music made it easier for audiences to determine music styles that fit their own unique preferences and tastes. Maybe fans of Mariah Carey became aware of less popular artists through the recommendation structure of iTunes. E-commerce makes it just as easy to purchase a song produced and uploaded from someone's basement, as it is to purchase songs distributed from a major studio label.

The real potential of the long-tail business model resides in the emotional gratifications that customers receive after making a latent purchase. Remember that businesses are not just able to profit from these niche sales, but the volume of latent commerce can collectively exceed the sale of a lower volume of hits (Anderson, 2004). Why is it that consumers were spending more money collectively on latent music products than they were on mass hits (Anderson, 2006)? The answer is simple: consumers believe that their purchasing decisions are an extension of their individual identities.

Owning a Mariah Carey album does say something about a person's personal musical preferences. However, when there are only 750 available music options, the selection of Mariah Carey does not make a consumer that significantly different from another consumer. One would not get that excited to hear that a stranger also likes Mariah Carey, especially since her song was the most popular hit on the radio. Therefore, this lack of differentiation makes the purchasing experience far less satisfying than if a consumer feels their selection is unique, highly personalized, and tailored towards their individual preferences.

Consider a musical group or artist that you enjoy and follow, that no one in your own social network is aware of. Chances are you believe that your affinity for this music sets you apart from your friends. Your fandom for this artist becomes a large part of your identity. You may be more likely to follow that artist's social media updates, wear their tee-shirt, or stop a stranger on the street that you see also sharing in your niche musical preference.

Latent commodities are more exciting to consumers because they do not appeal to the masses; they set us apart from our social network. We do not like being seen as identical to other consumers. It is likely that your greatest passions and interests have transformed you into a niche commodity. Are you an avid runner? Regular athletic shoes sold at the local mall may not fulfill your unique needs. Niche stores sell specialized running products, such as attire, hydration packs and safety gear that are not necessary for the everyday consumer. Research demonstrates that consumers are willing to pay premium prices for niche products and subsequently make recommendations to others based on these latent purchases (Batte *et al.*, 2007; Dellarocas *et al.*, 2010). This gratifying experience transforms consumers into brand advocates for niche products. These are more than just products: they are an extension of ourselves.

Consumers prefer to be a part of something special and unique. While some social media sites have focused on growing broadly to appeal to a large mass audience, others have seen the benefits of targeting niche audiences. The social network ASmallWorld is a private international travel and social club with a capped membership of 250,000. It has been described as "The secret social network for the elite" (Yahoo News, 2013). BeautifulPeople is an online dating network for individuals where members vote on whether or not an individual is beautiful enough to join the community. It claims to be the "largest most exclusively beautiful community in the world." Both of these social media sites intentionally restrict access in order to appear selective and elite and are capitalizing on the idea of an audience as a niche commodity (Ellison, 2007). Even social media messaging applications such as Snapchat have grown in popularity because messages are not broadcast to the masses, but rather a preselected narrow niche of friends.

It is important to note that business models based on the concepts of the theory of the long tail are only successful if practitioners know how to best use social media to target the specific online audience that is interested in a latent product. Otherwise, the same limited audience binds organizations as traditional in-store retailers. A strong understanding of inbound marketing will help guide you in finding your latent audience.

Inbound Marketing

The theory of the long tail illustrates how businesses are no longer bound by offering only 20% of the available products in order to maximize profit. Instead, Internet marketers are able to capitalize on the collective sale of niche products. One way to explain this new profit possibility is by considering the active within structures theory from Chapter 6. You will remember that active within structures describes how audiences actively seek media content within internal and external structures. Consumers utilize media based on both an active choice for media content and by technological and social structures (Cooper & Tang, 2009).

Let's use the sport of rock climbing as an example. You are in need of a new pair of rock climbing shoes, but the local mall does not offer a lot of options. You make the active decision to go online and search for this product. Maybe you have a favorite rock climbing merchandise store, or maybe you ask a trusted rock climbing community for advice. Regardless, external structures, such as availability, access, and social media structures, all influence your ultimate purchasing decision.

One investigative study of the theory of the long tail examined what would happen to sales if the same frequency and price of product was available online and in-store. Results demonstrate that consumers still gravitated towards the niche products, regardless of the mode of transaction (Brynjolfsson *et al.*, 2011). This niche selection was aided through the structural features of Internet searches and website recommendations.

It is imperative for organizations to promote themselves through Internet structures to bring customers closer to the brand. This process is called *inbound marketing*, where customers are brought to the brand, rather than marketers having to go out and capture attention through traditional advertising such as cold calls or TV commercials.

Halligan and Shah (2009) explored how social media impacts inbound marketing in their book *Inbound Marketing: Get Found Using Google, Social Media, and Blogs*. This book suggests that consumers primarily make purchasing decisions after gathering information through search engines, trusted blogs or social media sites, such as Twitter or Facebook. Rather than relying on a business's own media platform, such as your organizational website or Facebook page, to distribute content, it is important to spread updates to new interested audiences more virally. In order to create a successful inbound marketing strategy, it is important to follow a four-step action plan.

Inbound Marketing Action Plan

1 Consider the "spreadability" of media content.
2 Blog about issues relevant to the industry, not the product.
3 Collaborate with trusted brands.
4 Invest in content marketing and search engine optimization.

Spreadability of media content

The ability to reach target audiences says just as much about the content of a media message as it does the channel of distribution. The digital media landscape has shifted mass distribution to individual participatory circulation, a function of a participatory culture. In this environment, content creators and consumers alike benefit from a centralized location for content. Social media marketing practitioners must begin to consider how well their content reaches new audience expectations by examining the spreadability of their media content.

Spreadability refers to the potential, both technological and cultural, for audiences to share content for their own purposes (Jenkins *et al.*, 2013). When material is produced for one-size-fits-all model, it imperfectly fits the needs of any given audience. Audiences will not feel as though your message is targeted towards them, and in a social media environment where personalization and customization are the norm, your message will be lost in the noise.

You must ensure that content is available when and where your audiences want it. Know your target audiences well, and stop thinking of them as a mass. Ensure that your product is portable, compatible with mobile devices, and easily reusable in a variety of ways. Use social media widgets and simple formatting for easier sharing. Finally, be sure that your updates are part of a steady stream of material. One way to establish this is through content blogging.

Content blogging

Content must be created to spread easily and quickly on social media sites that are already a part of your consumer's repertoire, such as Facebook, Twitter, or industry blogs. In fact, 75% of your marketing focus should be on creating and maintaining content that will be distributed in platforms external to your own website (Halligan & Shah, 2009). The focus of this content should be on your brand, the industry and your competitors.

Some types of content that work well for these external sources include how-to articles, industry trend reports, or noteworthy upcoming events. Blog content should focus on the industry and not on the individual product for sale, otherwise consumers will lose interest in following updates. Be sure to utilize both traditional long-form blogs and microblogs. There are some media structures that cater to niche audiences better than others. Text messaging, social networks and virtual worlds are better than email or website notifications (Eyrich *et al.*, 2008). The more you are able to personalize your message, the more excited your customers become about your content.

Brand collaboration

The Internet is designed as a collaborative platform. Rather than using the space to broadcast your message, create a place where like-minded people are able to connect with one another (Halligan & Shah, 2009). While previous marketing professionals thought of other businesses selling the same product as competitors, it is time to consider collaborating with them. While your audience is a small niche, it is important to remember that you are an authentic niche business as well. There is something that you uniquely offer that sets you apart from your competitors. Create content for others in the industry. This can include blog articles, industry trend reports, or video demonstrations. Be sure that all content is suitable for multiple platforms, and also links back to your home page. Additionally, try to highlight others in your own social media content. This will help establish you as a thought leader in the field and increase trust with customers. Hopefully, your competitors will choose to return the favor and promote your content on their social media spaces.

Search engine optimization

The importance of a strong search engine optimization (SEO) strategy cannot be understated. SEO helps to drive traffic to a website by increasing the ranking of the site in results returned by a search engine. The results of Google's first page capture over 89% of online traffic (Halligan & Shah, 2009). The first step in deciding your company's SEO strategy is to determine which niche keywords best fit your product and brand. These should include phrases that are broad enough to speak to your overall product, but specific enough to demonstrate what sets you apart from your competitors. Consider your product authenticity (discussed in Chapter 2).

Some basic recommendations for increasing SEO results include fine tuning your website's title tag, ensuring that search engines can easily index your website, conduct extensive keyword research to determine what people search for when interested in your product, include meta tags throughout the site content, and selecting a strong site title (Malaga, 2007). It is important to note that SEO is not a successful marketing strategy on its own, and must be integrated within a larger strategic marketing plan.

Targeting your latent audience through inbound marketing is an important shift for businesses in today's digital environment. However, there are many things to consider about the theory of the long tail before implementing a latent audience into your own business plan.

Questioning the long tail

The theory of the long tail is based on the idea that "niche media content is able to accrue value at a different pace, on a different scale, through a different infrastructure and on the basis of different appeals than the highest grossing commercial texts do" (Jenkins *et al.*, 2013, p. 238). While this has certainly resulted in audiences having more access to a diverse array of media texts than ever before, it is important that the societal impact of this phenomenon is not overstated.

One of the first caveats to consider is the type of media users most likely to purchase a niche product. Research demonstrates that heavy media users who engage in most of the media content are more likely to seek latent commodities than light and casual Internet users (Jenkins *et al.*, 2013). While finding niche products online does not require a high level of competency, it seems to be done most often by those with greater access, infrastructure and online experience. It is important to understand the online habits of your target audience before integrating the theory of the long tail into your business plan.

Second, the impact of the long-tail market on society can be overstated as very idealistic for producers and consumers alike. Virtually anyone is able to engage in e-commerce, transforming power from traditional media producers to everyday consumers. While digital media has certainly advanced opportunities for minority products, money still matters, especially when it comes to media institutions. For example, in the music industry, a very small share of artists (less than 1%) still account for 77% of all artist-recorded music income (MIDIA, 2014). While the potential for an independent latent market to break through exists, overtaking a well-established business with a large marketing budget still proves to be the exception.

Elberse (2008) offers four pieces of cautionary advice for those interested in profiting from the long-tail market.

1 Continue to include hits in your management strategy, as a few mass appeal items go a long way. Digital media has provided the opportunity for marketers to introduce the possibility of additional sales, but the common denominator products still matter.
2 Ensure that production cost of latent products is as low as possible. Distribution that appeals to only a small specific audience is risky. The more one is able to minimize the cost of this risk, including resources and time of production, the better.

3 Market your most popular products to a mass audience and use low-cost social media to target niche items. There is still a place for both traditional and new media advertising. Distribute messages according to the size of the potential audience.
4 While newer inventory will be available at a faster rate than ever before, do not forget to include old hits in your marketing strategy. Newer is not always better. Products can now virtually live forever and present a real opportunity for profit if the appropriate market is found.

These suggestions should help guide decisions about the business and marketing strategies of your organization in an ever-changing media landscape. Successful navigation of these changes requires practitioners to have a strong understanding of the present market conditions, be able to identify internal business processes, conduct external surveillance of competitors, and anticipate future impacting factors on long-term goals.

Case Study: Video on Demand

The video and film industry has historically been supplied by a very limited number of media producers, such as licensed broadcasters and production companies (Cha *et al.*, 2007). It proved difficult for emerging producers to break through the bottleneck of distribution. Consistent with the power-law distribution model, only a small number of hit films have been able to reach theaters and big box stores for mass-audience distribution. Just like every other media industry, new technologies and e-commerce changed the way producers, businesses and consumers were able to interact with and distribute video content.

The video on demand (VOD) industry allows consumers to use technology to select videos from a central server for viewing on a media device, such as television, computer or mobile phone. This alleviates the pressure for films to be broadcast in theater complexes or take up shelf space for in-store DVD sales. One of the largest and most popular players in the VOD industry is Netflix, Inc. Netflix is an American provider of on-demand Internet streaming media that licenses a large library of media content to subscribers. While a typical video store would be able to store about 3000 movies, Netflix is able to have over 40,000 (Anderson, 2009). In just four years, Netflix has gained 33.1 million US subscribers (Bloomberg News, 2014).

This is a really clear illustration of the theory of the long tail working for an industry. Consumers, producers and businesses have more options for customization and niche marketing. While VOD has certainly changed the way videos are distributed to audiences, research on Netflix audience behavior demonstrates how consumer-viewing habits have been altered as well.

VOD has caused audiences to move away from appointment viewing of television and movie releases. Instead, users expect to be able to access content when it is most convenient for their schedules. Audiences are also less willing to watch commercial interruptions, thus impacting traditional media business models (discussed in detail in Chapter 10). Users have also transitioned towards a "binge-viewing" model, where an entire television series is consumed in just a few sittings (Goodfellow, 2014). A Netflix report states that 73% of consumers define binge viewing as watching between two and six episodes of the same television show in one sitting (West, 2014).

Customers are also willing to spend more time on VOD sites locating appropriate niche products. These longer searches lead to additional consumption of niche products. The demand distribution becomes more evenly distributed, with a longer tail (Hinz *et al.*, 2011). Here you see the influence of the long tail on the VOD industry.

While it is important to understand how digital technologies are influencing media industries, it is even more critical to understand how traditional companies are adapting their business models to fit the new user experience. One of the first measurement studies of a large VOD system was deployed by China Telecom, which logged detailed accounts of 1.5 million unique users of the PowerInfo VOD system used by telecommunication companies across China (Yu *et al.*, 2006). This analysis includes 21 million video requests and over 317,000 minutes of video streamed.

This large-scale research study was designed to better understand how successful the company's business model was working in an emerging industry. The research examined three key variables of audience behavior – user accesses over time, user interest, and video popularity – to evaluate their current business model objective. By understanding how users accessed the VOD system, future resources were optimized to produce the best user experience possible.

Results of this formative VOD research study demonstrate that users followed a very clear pattern of behavior with regard to the amount of time spent searching for video content. The average user only scanned content, and session times proved very short. This was fairly consistent with what social media practitioners had envisioned in their strategy. Less popular videos were actually viewed longer than mass appeal videos, a finding consistent with the theory of the long tail.

One surprising finding of the study was in the user arrival rates. The study demonstrates that the heaviest user consumption was between 6 and 9 p.m. each day. While the current business model expected this heavy traffic, it was designed to under-compensate for less popular view times and over-compensate during larger arrival times.

Finally, this research illustrates how the popularity of a video over time is dramatically influenced by external media structures. Most notably, the recommendation system heavily influenced how many users accessed specific video content. External audience opinion highly influenced a user's choice in video selection, much more than practitioners would have liked.

The VOD industry is an emerging field where you can clearly see the principles of long tail marketing at play. Chinese telecommunication companies were able to capitalize on their business model by using formative audience behavior research. The American VOD provider Netflix is also putting resources into tracking audience behavior to best determine how their product fits to user expectations. Researching audience behavior is a great first step towards creating a successful business plan. However, careful research of the brand and product market is also necessary.

Discussion questions

1 How has VOD streaming influenced the amount and type of product available for audiences? Where does this increased product sit on the long tail graph?
2 One of the results of China Telecom's evaluation of the Powerinfo VOD service was the influence of structural features such as daypart, and recommendation systems. How do these structures help reach the latent market?
3 This formative research study examined the patters and behaviors of audiences to help develop business strategies. What other types of research should practitioners conduct when making both internal and external decisions about how to implement a long-tail strategy?

Summary

This chapter examines traditional notions of business models and how they have been impacted by new media technologies. A strong understanding of the industry's business trends should help guide future decisions about product revenue and audience relationships for social media practitioners.

Under the traditional notions of power-law distribution, businesses are able to make distribution judgments based on the idea that they could appeal to 80% of the population by offering only 20% of the available product (Brynjolfsson *et al.*, 2011). This strategy worked well for many decades, and was consistent with the business model of advertising to the masses. However, as digital media and e-commerce allowed for the cost of production and distribution to decrease, latent markets began emerging that provide new profit possibilities for organizations.

The theory of the long tail teaches us new possibilities for businesses to capitalize on the collective sale of niche products. While this latent market has less demand than bestselling hits, it can collectively make up a rivaling market share. The long-tail model has advanced many opportunities for minority products to compete in the marketplace, and has given consumers unlimited choices when it comes to product selection. This benefits the producer, consumer and retailer alike.

The real value of a niche commodity has more to do with the purchasing experience than it does with the potential revenue. We learned how consumers actually prefer to buy these niche commodities because they serve individual interests and passions. The purchasing experience becomes an extension of personal identity. Your consumers feel as though they are making an investment in themselves when they make latent purchases. This is how your consumers are transformed into brand advocates.

In order to best capitalize on this new market potential, you must identify these latent audiences and encourage them to engage the brand through inbound marketing. This requires marketers to engage in less selling and more relationship building with consumers. The focus of inbound marketing is getting consumers to willingly engage with your product by increasing the spreadability of media messages, investing in industry blogs, collaborating with trusted brands, and investing in SEO. It should be noted that the more latent the audiences, the more difficult it will be to find them online.

These industry trends should help guide decisions about your own business model development. It is even more important that formative research be conducted on the brand, audience, product market, and business strategies. This strategy will help you see connections between user expectations, the organization's long-term goals, and business model development.

Overall, this chapter explores the trends and impact of the long-tail marketplace. Chapter 10 will identify key components of a business model, and describe specific social media business models of various organizations and fields. It will provide you with steps for maximizing a strong return on investment that is appropriate for your market. This knowledge will help you create your own business model in order to reach your organizational goals.

Key Takeaways

1 The power-law distribution has dominated the conceptualization of traditional business models. However, as digital technologies have reduced the costs of production and distribution, latent markets began emerging.
2 The theory of the long tail identifies the possibility of increasing profit by focusing marketing efforts on a niche latent audience, rather than a mass appeal.
3 Consumers are willing to pay premium prices for niche products and are more likely to make niche recommendations to others. These latent purchasing experiences transform consumers into brand advocates, but are only possible if customers are able to find your product.
4 Inbound marketing helps bring customers to a brand, rather than you fighting for attention through traditional marketing approaches. You should consider the spreadability of media content, include an industry blog, collaborate with trusted brands, and invest in SEO.

References

Anderson, C. (2004) Technology's long tail. Available at http://www.ted.com/talks/chris_anderson_of_wired_on _tech_s_long_tail (accessed June 8, 2016).

Anderson, C. (2005) The long tail: Chris Anderson's blog. Available at http://www.longtail.com/the_long_tail/2005/ 07/americas_record.html (accessed June 8, 2016).

Anderson, C. (2006) *The Long Tail: Why the Future of Business is Selling Less of More.* New York: Hyperion.

Anderson, C. (2009) The long tail: Chris Anderson's blog. Available at http://www.longtail.com/the_long_tail (accessed June 8, 2016).

Bar-Yam, Y. (2011) Concepts: power law. Available at http://www.necsi.edu/guide/concepts/powerlaw.html (accessed June 8, 2016).

Batte, M.T., Hooker, N.H., Haab, T.C. & Beaverson, J. (2007) Putting their money where their mouths are: consumer willingness to pay for multi-ingredient, processed organic food products. *Food Policy*, 32(2), 145–159.

Billboard (2005) 2005 Billboard music award winners. Available at http://www.billboard.com/articles/news/ 60428/2005-billboard-music-awards-winners (accessed June 8, 2016).

Bloomberg News (2014) Netflix seen reporting Web users grew to 33.1 million. Available at http://www.newsmax. com/SciTech/netflix-reporting-web-grown/2014/01/22/ id/548377/ (accessed June 8, 2016).

Brynjolfsson, E., Hu, Y. & Simester, D. (2011) Goodbye pareto principle, hello long tail: the effect of search costs on the concentration of product sales. *Management Science*, 57(8), 1373–1386.

Cha, M., Kwak, H., Rodriguez, P., Ahn, Y.Y. & Moon, S. (2007) I tube, you tube, everybody tubes: analyzing the world's largest user generated content video system. In: *Proceedings of the 7th ACM SIGCOMM Conference on Internet Measurement*, pp. 1–14. New York: ACM Press.

Cooper, R. & Tang, T. (2009) Predicting audience exposure to television in today's media environment: an empirical integration of active-audience and structural theories. *Journal of Broadcasting and Electronic Media*, 53(3), 1–19.

Dellarocas, C., Gao, G. & Narayan, R. (2010) Are consumers more likely to contribute online reviews for hit or niche products. *Journal of Management Information Systems*, 27(2), 127–158.

Elberse, A. (2008) Should you invest in the long tail? *Harvard Business Review*, 86(7–8), 88.

Ellison, N.B. (2007) Social network sites: definition, history, and scholarship. *Journal of Computer-Mediated Communication*, 13(1), 210–230.

Eyrich, N., Padman, M.L. & Sweetser, K.D. (2008) PR practitioners' use of social media tools and communication technology. *Public Relations Review*, 34(4), 412–414.

Fenner, T., Levene, M. & Loizou, G. (2010) Predicting the long tail of book sales: unearthing the power-law exponent. *Physica A: Statistical Mechanics and its Applications*, 389(12), 2416–2421.

Goodfellow, C. (2014) Netflix's long tail is forcing the entertainment industry to evolve. Available at http://www. huffingtonpost.co.uk/christopher-goodfellow/netflixs-long-tail-is-for_b_4716228.html (accessed June 8, 2016).

Halligan, B. & Shah, D. (2009) *Inbound Marketing: Get Found Using Google, Social Media, and Blogs*. Hoboken, NJ: John Wiley & Sons, Inc.

Hinz, O., Eckert, J. & Skiera, S. (2011) Drivers of the long tail phenomenon: an empirical analysis. *Journal of Management Information Systems*, 27(4), 43–69.

Jenkins, H., Ford, S. & Green, J. (2013) *Spreadable Media: Creating Value and Meaning in a Networked Culture*. New York: New York University Press.

Jones, C.I. & Kim, J. (2012) Exploring the dynamics of top income inequality. Available at http://isites.harvard .edu/fs/docs/icb.topic1118825.files/Jones_Nov19.pdf (accessed June 8, 2016).

Leeds, J. (2007) Plunge in CD sales shakes up big labels. Available at http://www.nytimes.com/2007/05/28/arts/ music/28musi.html?_r=4&oref=slogin&oref=slogin& (accessed June 8, 2016).

Malaga, R. (2007) The value of search engine optimization: an action research project at a new e-commerce site. *Journal of Electronic Commerce in Organizations (JECO)*, 5(3), 68–82.

MIDIA (2014) The death of the long tail. Avaiable at http://musicindustryblog.wordpress.com/2014/03/04/ the-death-of-the-long-tail/ (accessed June 8, 2016).

Spencer, R.W. & Woods, T.J. (2010) The long tail of idea generation. *International Journal of Innovation Science*, 2(2), 53–63.

West, K. (2014) Unsurprising: Netflix survey indicates people like to binge-watch TV. Available at http://www. cinemablend.com/television/Unsurprising-Netflix-Survey-Indicates-People-Like-Binge-Watch-TV-61045.html (accessed June 8, 2016).

Yahoo News (2013) MySpace for millionaires: the secret social network for the elite. Available at https://uk.news. yahoo.com/myspace-for-millionaires–the-secret-social-network-for-the-elite-100113281.html (accessed June 8, 2016).

Yu, H., Zheng, D., Zhao, B.Y. & Zheng, W. (2006) Understanding user behavior in large-scale video-on-demand systems. In: *Proceedings of the 1st ACM SIGOPS/EuroSys European Conferenceon Computer Systems*, pp. 333–344. New York: ACM Press.

Zott, C. & Amit, R. (2010) Business model design: an activity system perspective. *Long Range Planning*, 43(2), 216–226

10

Social Media Business Models

Learning Objectives

After reading this chapter, you should be able to:
1   Define a business model and identify its key components.
2   Understand different social media business models, revenue streams, and values of social media that go beyond return on investment (ROI).
3   Determine factors that influence business model development, and explore business, entrepreneurship, and societal opportunities brought by social media.

Introduction

Chapter 9 introduced Chris Anderson's long tail theory and explained how social media marketing influenced traditional business models. We learned that social media has made it necessary for communication specialists and marketers to have an understanding of communication behavior change appeals, audience research and business models. This chapter will clearly define a business model, identify factors that determine your social media business model, as well as pinpoint the business and societal opportunities brought by social media.

As mentioned in previous chapters, social media has undoubtedly changed the way we work, play, think and connect. It has also become an important player in today's economy and marketplace. According to a recent research report, 90% of marketers want to engage

Strategic Social Media: From Marketing to Social Change, First Edition. L. Meghan Mahoney and Tang Tang.
© 2017 John Wiley & Sons, Inc. Published 2017 by John Wiley & Sons, Inc.

their consumers with social media, and believe social media plays an important role in their business and marketing strategies (Stelzner, 2014). Total social media advertising revenues in the United States is projected to reach $15 billion in 2018 (BIA/Kelsey, 2014). Facebook alone has attracted 1.35 billion users worldwide, brought 4.5 million job opportunities, and has had a $227 billion economic impact worldwide (O'Brien, 2015). Thus it is important to have a clear plan for how social media will impact your business strategy.

Despite the hype and promises associated with social media, relatively few marketers have a clear understanding of social media business strategies. Only 34% self-report being able to measure the return on investment (ROI) for their social media activities (Stelzner, 2014). Many seek to understand how to best maximize their social media endeavors towards a desired outcome, whether this outcome is maximizing profit or optimizing user engagement. Guiding your company towards a desired social media outcome requires a structured approach (Bennett, 2013). The first step is to develop a business model, use the model to guide your daily practice, and then be willing to revise your business model as you grow the business and social media plan. To begin, let's define a business model and identify its key component.

Developing a Business Model

In short, a *business model* explains how your organization works (Magretta, 2002). It serves as a foundation for managers and communication specialists to share their understanding of the business with different stakeholders, helps to maximize strengths and alleviate weaknesses of your company, and is extremely important to a business's long-term viability (Mahadevan, 2000; Hayes & Graybeal, 2011; Hu, 2011). You might think of the process of developing a business model similarly to how you would plan a party. You need to decide what's the occasion, who you would like to invite, how you could reach them, what you would provide in the party, what the desired outcome would be, and how much the party would cost (Bennett, 2013).

"Business model" is an often-misused term. Many have defined the term as a revenue model or a business statement about how a company can monetize consumers and make a profit (Stewart & Zhao, 2000; Cha, 2013). Here, the focus of the business model is on increasing revenue streams. However, business models should cover all matters of interest, including your business's value proposition, consumers, market position, distribution strategies, cost structure, and so on. Robert Picard (2000), a media economist, suggests that business models do more to examine the underlying characteristics that make commerce in the product or service possible. Business models should include various stages of a business, including conception, foundation and financial flow.

Osterwalder *et al.* (2005, p. 5) further define a business model as

> a conceptual tool that contains a set of elements and their relationships and allows expressing the business logic of a specific firm. It is a description of the value a company offers to one or several segments of customers and of the architecture of the firm and its network of partners for creating, marketing, and delivering this value and relationship capital, to generate profitable and sustainable revenue streams.

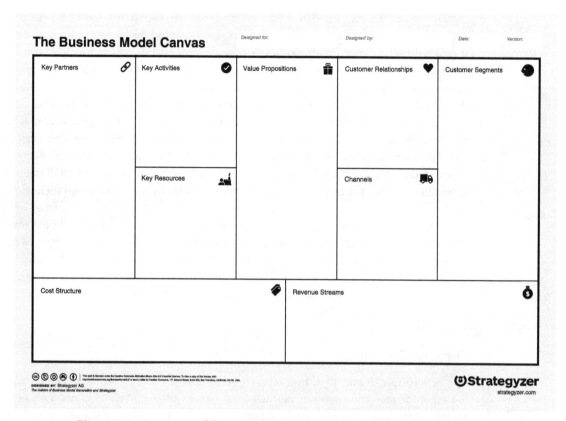

Figure 10.1 Business model canvas. Source: Reproduced with permission of Strategyzer.

Regardless of the theoretical conceptualization, a business model is a living document that decides your company's marketing, pricing, distribution, customer relationship, revenue, and product development strategies.

Based on all these understandings, there are seven components that you need to consider when developing your own business model: (i) your business/product's value proposition; (ii) customer segments; (iii) competitive strategy; (iv) marketing strategy; (v) revenue streams; (vi) cost structure; and (vii) organizational development (key partners, resources, activities) (Figure 10.1). Overall, your business model needs to answer two questions: What you can offer to your consumers and how you can do it?

Value proposition

Value proposition is one of the most crucial components of a business model. *Value proposition* defines the values that a business creates to fulfill the needs of customers. Think about what you can offer to your consumers. Know why your consumers need your product/message, and why they are willing to pay (Hayes & Graybeal, 2011; IMT, 2013). This construct, rather than revenue streams, is the heart of your business model. It is always important to know your key competencies and build your marketing strategies, revenue model, cost structure, and partnership upon this value proposition.

Many approaches can help define your company's value proposition. Generally, you will start the process with an educated guess. Your value proposition could rest on the scope of your business, key features of your product/service, the cost structure, pricing strategies, customization, service delivery, and so on (Cha, 2013; IMT, 2013). For example, Facebook's value proposition is to communicate with their audience's social network in a convenient way. Thus, Facebook's key features (e.g., wall post, event announcement, news, chat, private messages) are all built on this value proposition. LinkedIn's value proposition is to help users build professional networks. Groupon's value proposition is to provide lower prices to their customers for daily deals. TripAdvisor offers customer reviews and recommendations for traveling. Douguo, a Chinese recipe sharing site, received $10 million in funding because it shares 10,000 recipes online and via mobiles every month (Russell, 2012).

When identifying your own value proposition, consider the elements surrounding your brand authenticity (discussed in Chapter 3). Your value proposition does not need to be big, but instead should simply tell your audiences the benefits of using your business/social media product, and why they cannot get the same benefits from your competitors. The key is to think about your value proposition first, and revenue streams second. This will ensure a long-term commitment from your audience.

Customer segmentation

Another crucial component of a business model is customer segmentation. Customer segmentation defines your consumers, including demographics, psychographics, and geographic areas. *Demographics* refers to quantitative information on your audiences, such as age, gender, education, race, marital status, income, and occupation. *Psychographics* goes beyond numeric information to offer qualitative data on your customers, such as their attitudes, lifestyle, values, beliefs, needs, and wants. Both are crucial when identifying your consumers. *Geographic areas* indicate where customers can find your product/service (Cha, 2013). Though social media makes most organizations a global marketplace, it is still important to frame messages according to the cultural norms of your target audience. As discussed in Chapter 5, audience research is the first step for any social media endeavor. Before you start to develop marketing plans, revenue strategies and partnerships, you need to ask who your core consumers are, what problems they want you to solve for them, and what their dream social media product would be.

Each successful social media product serves unique customer segmentation, and differentiates their target consumers from existing businesses in the same market/category (Cha, 2013). For example, LinkedIn's customer segmentation is college students and professionals who seek professional development opportunities, as well as companies/organizations who would like to recruit talent. Pinterest focuses on reaching female audiences who would like to share their passion and interests with others. Groupon, a social media site focusing on collective buying, targets "hip, active singles who go out two or more times a week" (Gilman, 2011, p. 20). Xiaomi, a social mobile phone service, has decided its customer segmentation as young adults who like fashion and are open to new experiences, but cannot afford expensive products (Shih *et al.*, 2014).

Do as much as you can to step into the role of your customers during this phase. Try to go beyond stereotyping them, but conduct research to best understand their attitudes and behaviors. We have discussed factors that influence your consumers' social media use and purchase behavior in Chapters 5 and 6. Begin by making your own educated guesses, and then get out of your building, meet your customers, and take efforts to engage them in your business plan. This can include formative focus groups and survey research. In addition to identifying who your target consumers are, you also need to consider other issues related to your customers when developing a business model. For example, you need to develop your customer relationship strategies by asking a number of questions: How are you going to keep and build your customers? What types of relationships do you want to develop with them? What channels would you use to respond to their concerns both before and after sales? All are important to your business's long-term viability.

Competitive strategy

When developing a business model, you also need to specify your competitive strategies. The term *competitive strategy* refers to an analysis of your competitors who are doing similar business or selling the same type of products/services in the market. Knowing your competitive environment and competitive advantages is necessary before you start thinking about how to sell your business to consumers, partners and other stakeholders.

A number of marketing firms start their marketing efforts by conducting a *SWOT analysis*, i.e., an investigation of a product/service's strengths, weaknesses, opportunities, and threats. An effective business model should be able to maximize your strengths and lighten your weaknesses. Before you go out to reach your consumers (existing or potential), ensure that your product/service is superior to your competitors, and identify areas for improvement. Research to see if there are underserved segments in your market. What are possible threats? And be sure to consider the larger economic environment, policy change, technology innovation, and/or new players who may enter your market. Give attention to your major competitors and know the market share for each, including their value propositions and the price of each of their products. Use social media to track their customers' concerns, compliments and complaints, because your competitors' customers today could be your customers tomorrow (and vice versa).

Marketing strategy

The fourth component of your business model is your marketing strategy. A recent report from Nielsen reports that an average consumer only takes 13 seconds to purchase a brand in store, and 19 seconds online (Beard, 2015). How can you make the most of these 20 seconds? This period should be the highest priority to consider when developing your marketing strategies.

Marketing strategies explain how a business reaches its consumers and brands itself. Your marketing strategies should be simple, clear and vivid. Think about what you want your consumers to think about your brand in 20 seconds. Focus most of your research, marketing and evaluation efforts here.

Let's take 20 seconds to think about the company Disney. You are likely to immediately imagine Mickey Mouse, Disney movies, rollercoaster, and perhaps the happy experiences you had at the Disney theme parks/shops growing up. If you think about GEICO (i.e., an American insurance company), you may think about their green spokes lizard. When you think about Walmart, you may think about the yellow smiling face, low price, and one-stop shopping. There are limited details that your consumers will think about in 20 seconds. Your marketing strategies should focus on the elements of your brand that "easily come to mind" (Beard, 2015). Start with your value proposition, and then make it memorable. We will talk more about marketing strategy in Chapter 11.

Revenue stream

As business owners and marketers spend more money on social media, they become more concerned with monetizing social media products and endeavors. There is no doubt that revenue stream is a key component of a business model. The *revenue model* defines how a business makes revenue and monetizes its product/service (IMT, 2013). Revenue streams for social media businesses range from traditional advertising, subscription, sales, and transaction fees to the newer models, such as freemium model, affiliate revenue, crowdfunding, virtual goods, and micropayments. As we have learned, business models go well beyond identifying revenue streams; however, understanding how a business makes money and generates ROI is crucial. We therefore talk about different revenue streams for social media businesses in detail in the next section.

Cost structure

For many organizations, the ultimate goal is profit optimization. When considering profit, we must include both revenue and cost. Thus, cost structure is also a component of your business model. While most business owners spend a lot of time considering revenue streams, relatively less attention has been given to cost. Here it is important to think about the average cost to produce, deliver and sell a product. What would be your biggest cost to run the business? Which costs are fixed and which costs would be variable? Cost leadership is particularly crucial for social media businesses. As digital competition continues to saturate the marketplace, those who can produce the product that satisfies consumers' needs at the lowest cost will win audiences.

Cost leadership is important for traditional media as well. Let's take *Dancing with the Stars*, a popular American reality TV dancing competition as an example. The show has been airing since 2005 and still generates millions of advertising dollars in revenue. After airing for over a decade, *Dancing with the Stars* can still reach about a million audience members. However, it is a studio production, which has a much more limited cost than a scripted dramatic series. Even though the dramatic series may pull in a larger audience, the lower cost of production for reality television has more long-term viability.

Cost structure has often been ignored in social media business models. Many people believe that their cost for social media marketing/communication should be zero because we do not need to pay for using most of the social media sites. However, it is important to note that social media is not free. Effective social media endeavors require both financial and human resources. There are also opportunities to engage customers through giveaways and promotions. Thus, examine your budget and consider how much cost you can afford to improve and maintain your social media efforts.

Organizational development

Finally, your business model should address the plan for carrying out these concepts. *Organizational development* defines how a business organizes the tasks that will need to be done (IMT, 2013). It includes several major components, such as a business's key partners, resources and activities. After you know who your consumers are, what you can offer them, and how you can monetize them, it is time to think about how you will actually do the business. Who are your key partners? Suppliers? How can you locate them? What resources would you need to do your job? The resources could include physical, financial, and human resources. The finishing line of developing a business model is to decide what you would do yourself and what you would need others to do.

Developing a business model is both art and science. Start with your guesses, then test the model, and refine it constantly. Below is a step-by-step action plan to develop your business model.

Developing a Business Model Action Plan

1 Understand who you are (e.g., your unique strengths, weaknesses) and be specific about what unique problems you could help your customers to solve. Identify what customers' needs your product/service can fulfill that other similar businesses cannot.

2 Know your most important customers. Use the audience analysis methods discussed in Chapters 5 and 6 to gather information about your core consumers' interests, passions, personality and, more importantly, why they would use your social media product and what they want you to do for them.

3 Decide your revenue model. You may use more than one revenue stream, or simply decide to use your social media products to generate "social good" (rather than ROI). Nonetheless, determine and communicate how you can produce ROI.

4 Finally, find out how you can actually do your business. Identify the helps that you will need (e.g., key partners, resources, cost structure, suppliers).

The Return on Investment of Social Media

As more and more money is spent on social media, business owners and marketers want to know how they can get ROI on social media. In fact, 70% of businesses plan to increase their spending on social media marketing and engagement (Allen, 2015). Several revenue streams are believed to be applicable to social media businesses/endeavors, including advertising, subscription, freemium, transaction, affiliate, and commerce (Ha & Ganahl, 2009; Loayza, 2009; Hayes & Graybeal, 2011).

Advertising is the most-applied revenue model for both traditional and new media businesses (Perez-Pena, 2009). For broadcast radio and TV, audiences pay nothing to consume media content. Here, advertisers pay for the production cost in exchange for the audience's attention. For example, the popular US sporting event, the Super Bowl, charges $4 million for a 30-second television commercial spot. In China, a 30-second commercial spot during the evening news program on China Central TV (the largest TV station in China) costs ¥318,000 (approximately $US53,000), where the average household income is less than ¥70,000 (Baidu.com, 2015). There is no doubt that advertising dollars are a major revenue source for traditional media businesses. In the social media era, making revenues from advertising is still possible, but the online advertising price has dropped significantly (Anderson, 2010).

Social media advertising includes both direct and indirect ads. Similar to the ads displayed on traditional print media, some social media platforms still use direct ads. For example, Facebook offers businesses the ability to place domain ads, or banner ads displayed on the right-hand column of different Facebook pages (Qwaya, 2015). Facebook also works with large advertisers, such as Progressive, Subway, AT&T, and Ford Moto, to place their ads on Facebook's log-in page, where audiences first access the site via computer (Horn, 2011).

YouTube also uses direct ads, both display ads and in-stream video ads, to generate revenue. Under such a revenue model, audiences use YouTube to watch videos for free, but see display ads on the page, and watch a 15-second or 30-second in-stream video ad when they initially open a video clip (for the 30-second in-stream video ad, audiences can choose to skip the ad after 5 seconds). YouTube takes 45% of this advertising revenue and gives the other 55% to the video creators who generate the ad sale (Aguiar, 2014). Other major social media sites, such as LinkedIn and Google+, have also used display ads as a revenue stream. Still, social media advertising revenue comes mainly from indirect advertising.

One example of indirect advertising is a promoted tweet. Here, a company pays money to have Twitter promotes their tweets and make sure that it reaches a large target audience and achieves a set engagement rate (Kammerer, 2014). Through the years, promoted tweets have become a major revenue stream for Twitter. In just the third quarter of 2014 alone, Twitter generated $361 million revenue, and announced plans to collaborate with Yahoo Japan and Flipboard to expand its promoted tweet efforts (O'Malley, 2015).

Sponsored content and corporate/fan pages are also popular types of indirect ads. Many social media sites allow companies to set up their profile pages, show photos, and post information for free, but charge those who would like to promote their corporate/fan pages. In general, these sponsored posts/content target a specific group of audiences, and hold primary positioning so that audiences are more likely to see them. Many small companies choose to pay for these types of indirect advertising to increase brand awareness and overall reach. For example, LinkedIn uses sponsored posts and pay-per-click advertising as one of its revenue streams. Sponsored content has become a driver to increase a social media business's overall ad revenue (Sebastian, 2014).

More than 60% of Facebook's advertising revenue stems from small companies and indirect advertising (Cha, 2013). Facebook offers businesses 15 different advertising options (Yu, 2014). In addition to the domain ads mentioned previously, Facebook's ad options include page post ad, offer ad, event ad, page like ad, app ad, and sponsored stories (Facebook, 2014). As such, Facebook's advertising revenue was $3.59 billion in 2014 (Peterson, 2014). Its average advertising revenue per user (ARPR) has reached $1362 in the United States and Canada, $783 in Europe, and $469 in Asia. There is no doubt that advertising is a major revenue stream for Facebook and contributes to Facebook's business and financial success, as Facebook is now worth $14.25 billion in cash, cash equivalents, and other marketable equivalents (Constine, 2014).

While Facebook has succeeded in attracting advertising dollars, many other social media sites are struggling to attract advertising revenue (Duboff & Wilkerson, 2010) and must seek alternative revenue streams. Subscription is a revenue stream that has been used by both traditional and new media businesses. Cable companies charges customers for using their service. Half of the magazine industry's revenue comes from subscription. Circulation has always been a critical measure for evaluating a newspaper's success, and brought stable revenue to print media. Today, there are still digital media companies/services who charge audiences for quality niche content. For example, Netflix charges $7.99 to access its service. Label 2.0 asks musicians to pay $50 a month to use its online marketing tools. The *Wall Street Journal* also charges readers $28.99 to access financial/business news on its print and digital platforms.

Among social media businesses, the subscription model has gradually gained popularity. Recent industry reports indicate that paid service revenue will double and become a crucial revenue stream for social media businesses, even including those traditionally dependent on advertising income (eMarketer, 2009; Hayes & Graybeal, 2011). Nonetheless, social media businesses using the subscription model constantly face audiences who are not used to or willing to pay for online products/services. This is especially true for digital natives who are used to having many options for accessing online content for free. According to a recent report by the Boston Consulting Group (2009), Americans are willing to pay $3 for an online news subscription. As such, the freemium strategy was introduced for businesses that rely on digital subscription to make a living (Anderson, 2010).

The *Freemium model* is a revenue model introduced by Chris Anderson, creator of the long tail theory discussed in Chapter 9. The freemium model indicates that a company offers its basic service for free, but charges those who would like to access premium service/content. The hope is that after audiences try the basic/limited version for free, they would adopt the paid version if they like the basic one (Anderson, 2010). Businesses using the freemium model tend to employ two-tiered or multi-tiered price structures, with the basic free version and premium services for various prices. For example, Pandora, a popular online radio station in the United States, uses a two-tiered freemium strategy: the basic version offers users 40 hours of free music with commercials; the premium version charges $3.99 a month for unlimited commercial-free music. Hulu, a video streaming company, recently introduced Hulu plus, which provides 24/7 anytime anywhere video service to its premium members for $7.99 a month, while keeping its basic service free.

Recently, the popular social media site LinkedIn invited people to try its premium services. LinkedIn's premium services include $29.99 per month for premium job seekers; $59.99 per month for all-purpose business plus plan; $79.99 per month for sales people; and $119.99 per month for hiring specialists (Anders, 2015). While most LinkedIn users still pay nothing to connect with colleagues and professional networks, a portion of its customers choose to pay extra to generate better opportunities to find jobs or gain business leads. These premium subscriptions brought in $114 million to the company, accounting for 20% of LinkedIn's total revenue.

The key to implementing a freemium model in your organization is to decide the needs, services and prices for your free and paid consumers. Determine how much content/service you would like to offer for free, what kinds of service you would charge for a smaller fee, and gradually raise prices for advanced services. The success of using the freemium model not only depends on your ability to break the traditional "free" online culture (i.e., audiences consume online media content for free), but also requires you to understand the needs of your paying and free customers (Loayza, 2009; Lyons *et al.*, 2012).

It is also important to note that the freemium model is built on the low cost of actual production and distribution of digital media products/services (Anderson, 2010; Lyons *et al.*, 2012). As discussed in Chapter 9, it costs almost nothing to create and distribute one more copy of digital media content. Thus, even if a small portion of your users pays for your service, it would bring enough money to cover the cost.

You may have also noticed that even for popular social media sites like LinkedIn, subscription/paid service fee only accounts for 20% of the total revenue. Thus, it is important to consider using other revenue streams. E-commerce is another revenue source used by many e-businesses. Today, the virtual goods market is gaining in popularity. For example, the virtual community Second Life allows users the opportunity to buy almost anything "virtual" at the Second Life Marketplace, including clothing, pets, vehicles, and even virtual homes. These virtual goods have generated $100 million revenue for Second Life every year (Mitchell, 2011).

Facebook started to sell virtual goods in 2008. Consumers can buy and send virtual flowers and virtual balloons to their friends directly on Facebook, and this brought in more than $30 million to Facebook in just its first year of service (Social Times, 2008). iTunes also generated its fortune by selling virtual goods, such as rewards and supplies for mobile gamers. The popular Chinese social media site Weixin (see Chapter 5) allows users to send virtual goods, even virtual money to each other. Research indicates that selling virtual goods has generated $1 billion a year in the US market (Oreskovic & Lawsky, 2009) and has become an important revenue stream for social media businesses. Functional, status, and decorative items are the most popular virtual goods purchased on social media platforms (Loayza, 2009).

Because of the increasing demands of selling virtual goods, the industry developed a micropayment system to accommodate the needs. *Micropayment* is defined as a less than $5 content purchase (Smith, 2003). Media businesses such as the *Wall Street Journal* and *New York Times* have adopted this micropayment system (in addition to their traditional monthly subscription) to allow audiences to pay by stories (Musil, 2009; Hayes & Graybeal, 2011).

Micropayment may replace the traditional subscription to become an important player for social media businesses.

Alternative revenue streams that can be applied to social media businesses include transaction fees, affiliate fees, and fees for niche services. The *transaction model* refers to a model that allows social media businesses to make money from facilitating or executing transactions (Laudon & Traver, 2007; Enders *et al.*, 2008). Generally, this type of transaction is called an *exogenous transaction*, suggesting that social media platforms facilitate selling of third-party content/products/services to users and enable transactions between social media users (Enders *et al.*, 2008). Well-known businesses like eBay, Alibaba (China), qoo10.sg (Singapore), and snapdeal.coim (India) all rely on transaction fees for their operation.

Groupon, a popular collective buying site, also succeeds in using the transaction model. Within three years after Groupon's debut, it completed 20 million transactions, generated a profit of $850 million (Gilman, 2011), and attracted 42 million active users worldwide (Groupon, 2013). Using the transaction model, Groupon takes a small percentage of every transaction to cover the operation cost. Customers do not pay Groupon directly. There is no mandatory membership fee on the user end. In the meantime, there is no financial commitment on the businesses that sell products/services via Groupon either (Gilman, 2011).

Similar to the transaction model, the *affiliate model* suggests that businesses generate revenues by driving traffic to another company's website and/or providing leads for other businesses to sell products (Laudon & Traven, 2007; Loayza, 2009). Today, social media affiliates are important for media companies and other businesses. Google made its entire business based on driving traffic to other companies. Using this simple revenue model, Google makes $115,150 every minute with no original content (Hopewell, 2014). Even independent bloggers, such as Jonathan Mead for *Illuminated Mind*, can make a living from providing affiliate links on his blog (Loayza, 2009).

Offering niche services is another revenue stream used by social media businesses. LinkedIn made 40% of its total revenue by offering the niche service Hiring Solution (Noyes, 2011; Cha, 2013). Hiring Solution provides a headhunting type of service and charges a company as much as $8000 for using the program (Anders, 2015). More than 10,000 companies worldwide, including 82 of the Fortune 100 companies, have used the LinkedIn Recruiter service, which brought in $103 million revenue and became one of the most important revenue streams for LinkedIn (Luckerson, 2012).

While determining ROI is a growing concern for businesses' social media endeavors (Duboff & Wilkerson, 2010), the goal of some social media sites is to provide a free service to audiences. As we discussed in the previous chapters, social media opportunities rest in behavior change and the role it plays in community building and user engagement. If the entire premise of social media is the ability to hold a conversation online, would not a successful social media endeavor be to engage the intended audience through interactive dialogue rather than top-down diffusion? Thus, instead of generating revenues, many companies choose to use social media as a platform to enhance customer relationship, build a community, establish brand expertise, and/or aid a behavior change.

For example, American Express OPEN is a social media site that provides a free service to small business owners. OPEN consists of links to business/finance blogs and videos, and offers a platform for business people to network (Duboff & Wilkerson, 2010). The purpose of OPEN is not to generate additional revenue for American Express but build the company's brand image and expertise in business and finance. Popular TV shows such as *The Office* offer series of webisodes (i.e., short videos designed particularly for web use) for free, to hold fan interests during the off season, and bring more viewers to the regular TV shows (which generates advertising revenues). Research indicates that word-of-mouth recommendation via social media could decide 20–50% of the purchasing decisions (Duboff & Wilkerson, 2010). Social media can effectively reduce a company's cost in advertising, networking, and distribution and aid more effective target marketing (Vukanovic, 2011). In Part IV, we will further discuss social media's function in empowering users and aiding behavior changes for social good. Here we see how social media can go beyond direct ROI to change a company's entire structure.

One Business Model Doesn't Fit All

It is clear that social media businesses must integrate different revenue streams and adopt a hybrid revenue model (Enders *et al.*, 2008; Hayes & Graybeal, 2011). It is imperative that we move beyond this "either or" conceptualization, but think about "both and" and "all possible." An integrated approach can utilize the strengths and alleviate weaknesses of each traditional business plan, and find a path for your business in today's new media environment.

Almost all the popular social media businesses have used multiple revenue streams. For example, LinkedIn makes money via advertising, premium membership fees, and charging for hiring and recruiting services. Facebook generates its revenue via advertising (including both traditional banner ads, and newer forms of sponsored content), selling virtual goods, as well as charging license fees from search engine companies (Cha, 2013). As a practitioner, you will need to determine which revenue model(s) best suits your business.

Now, let's talk about factors that can influence your business model development. First, the type of your business largely determines your business model. If you work for a traditional business that provides professionally made products, you may rely on advertising, subscription and/or use social media as a marketing tool (rather than revenue generator) to reach target consumers, and build brand awareness and credibility. If your business is based on niche market and user-generated content, you may want to consider the freemium model, affiliate model, selling virtual goods, and charging for niche services. Research suggests that fun products and friendly services that require little research from the user end are the best fit for social media businesses (Duboff & Wilkerson, 2010). The value proposition is the fundamental factor that decides your business model.

As always, your first priority to consider is your target audience. Are you selling products/services to individual consumers or other businesses? Research suggests that B2B (i.e., business to business) companies tend to rely on social media to generate revenue and actively measure ROI, while B2C (i.e., business to consumer) marketers are more likely to use social media to build consumer trust and/or reduce marketing and distribution costs (Duboff & Wilkerson, 2010).

In addition to value propositions, *consumers' willingness to pay* influences your business model. Willingness to pay has been defined as the maximum price consumers would like to pay based on their perceived value of the product/service (Wertenbroch & Skiera, 2002). Willingness to pay is a constant challenge faced by social media business owners and marketers, since paying money is obviously inconsistent with the "free culture" of online media consumption. Nonetheless, willingness to pay is a precursor of many revenue models, including the subscription, freemium, and e-commerce models. Economists and marketers suggest that audiences only pay for "superior, timely, original content" (Clemons, 2009). Why would users pay for anything less? In addition, consumers prefer to use virtual currency (e.g., Linden Dollars in Second Life) and/or micropayment to pay for online transactions (Raghubir & Srivastava, 2002; Hsee *et al.*, 2003; Hayes & Graybeal, 2011).

Audience size is important to many media business models' success. Broadcast networks have charged advertisers millions of dollars because they can reach a mass audience (e.g., 90% of the US population). For years, reach has been used as a primary measurement for evaluating a marketing effort. In the social media era, customer size is particularly important for social media businesses that use the advertising, affiliate, and transaction models. Facebook became cash-flow positive in 2009 when it reached 300 million users (Carlson, 2009). Groupon started to make money when it owned more than 50 million buyers (Statista, 2014). Having the ability to generate a large amount of web traffic is vital to attracting advertising dollars, transaction fees, and other revenues. Companies targeted on niche audiences (e.g., hyperlocal news organizations) should not use advertising as their primary income source.

Moreover, consumer trust can drive revenues for social media sites. For example, the affiliate model rests solely on the level of consumer trust (Loayza, 2009; Hayes & Graybeal, 2011). Using such a model, your goal is to drive traffic to other companies' websites (and lead to sales). If audiences don't trust you, they will not visit the sites or buy the products that you recommend. Nonetheless, it is important to disclose the revenue source to your audiences. Remember from Chapter 2 that transparency is the first step to building trust.

In addition to consumer trust, perceived risk may also influence your business model. Whenever you ask customers to connect their financial information (i.e., bank/credit card information) to your website, perceived risk is involved. Products/services with higher prices and those that could be dangerous to use (e.g., health products) are generally associated with more perceived risks and require more consumer trust (Duboff & Wilkerson, 2010). Research suggests that audiences need to trust the product, company, and technology before they are ready to make an online transaction (Van Baalen *et al.*, 2005). Thus, only after you obtain consumer trust will e-commerce, virtual goods, and transaction models fit your business.

As you can see, many factors can influence your business model development. Ultimately, you need to choose the model based on your unique strengths and balance the different operations of your business (Berman *et al.*, 2006). More importantly, please remember that one model does not fit all, which indicates that you should use all revenue streams appropriate for your business. Do not limit your options. Maybe none of the existing business models that we have introduced here fit your business, but some of these concepts may work. That is why this book is not concerned with platform-specific approaches, but instead focuses on providing a strong understanding of how social media inspire human behavior change. The ability of social media to offer boundless choices has changed our traditional thinking of business models and the marketplace. Therefore, be innovative, test your ideas, prepare to shape your model, and embrace all the opportunities and challenges brought by the social media technology.

Case Study: Xing

This chapter discusses the many factors that influence business model development for social media companies, and examines how one business model/revenue stream doesn't fit all. Social media businesses should use all appropriate revenue streams, and build their business model based on their value propositions. Xing, a German-based professional social networking site, applied these principles when developing its business model, thus becoming one of the most popular social media among European professionals (Enders *et al.*, 2011).

Similar to LinkedIn in the United States, Xing provides a platform for its members to social, find jobs, build networks, recruit experts, and generate business ideas. It was first introduced to the public in 2006, and has since then recruited more than 15 million members worldwide (Xing, 2015). In 2014, Xing's total revenue reached €101.4 million, which represents a 20% increase compared to 2013.

Xing's financial growth is largely due to a successful business model that integrates multiple revenue streams from different stakeholders. Xing's primary revenue came from paid membership fees. It adopted the freemium model to provide a free service to its basic members, but asks the premium members to pay (€5.95 per month). More than 16% of Xing's members are paid members who brought in €61.3 million to the company in 2014 (Xing, 2015). The use of the freemium model not only generates a stable cash flow for Xing but also builds a large user base, something that is crucial for a business's continuous growth.

In addition to the premium membership subscription, Xing also generates revenues via traditional advertising, and offering niche services, such as e-recruiting and events (Gross-Selbeck *et al.*, 2011; Xing, 2015). As social media gradually gains recognition as a cost-effective recruitment and marketing tool, e-recruiting services and event strategies have become growing revenue generators, while traditional advertising only plays a small role in Xing's business model (Xing, 2015).

Xing's growth is also a result of the continuous development of its core value proposition. The business aims to build a connection between employers and job seekers, and offer users professional development opportunities. Thus, Xing's main features include managing personal information, finding and searching jobs/candidates/opportunities, and creating communities and events (Enders *et al.*, 2008). Its brand image is consistent: a serious, straight, business-only community. For years, Xing's development efforts all focused on its core competencies. For example, Xing developed unique search criteria for members to search jobs that better match their interests/matches, such as whether the company provides a family-friendly work environment and the social aspects of the company. It also emphasizes local integration to provide job seekers and employers offline networking opportunities (Gross-Selbeck *et al.*, 2011). Recently, Xing acquired jobborse.com, the largest job search engine in German-speaking countries, to further advance its core value proposition – job search (Xing, 2015).

One takeaway from Xing's case is the importance of building a business model around your unique strengths. It may not be apparent right away how social media can fit within your strategy, but by being authentic with your brand, opportunities will begin to emerge. As we have discussed throughout this chapter, one model doesn't fit all. Only after you find your product/service's unique value propositions will your business begin to make a profit.

Discussion questions

1   Your value proposition is the first step towards developing a successful business model. What is Xing's value proposition? If Xing decided to introduce new features, what suggestions would you offer?
2   The freemium model is a primary revenue model used by Xing. Currently, Xing uses a two-tiered pricing strategy (free for basic members; €5.95 for premium members). Should Xing add additional pricing tiers? If so, what could new membership types be?
3   For a period of time, Xing's leadership discussed whether Xing should get rid of displaying ads on its web (Enders *et al.*, 2008). What do you think? Should Xing keep advertising as one of the revenue streams? Or should it create an advertising-free environment?
4   Xing is a popular social networking site in German-speaking countries. Do you think Xing will be successful in English-speaking countries? Should Xing work on its global appeal in the future? Or should it focus on its local integration strategy?

Summary

This chapter focuses on social media business models. Specifically, it identifies key components of a business model, factors that influence business model development, various revenue streams, as well as business and societal opportunities for social media businesses. We have learned that the business model is not the same as the revenue model. A business model acts as a conceptual tool to guide your company's operation (Osterwalder *et al.*, 2005) and consists of seven components: value propositions, customer segments, competitive strategy, marketing strategy, revenue streams, cost structure, and organizational development. The business model should rest in your product/service's value proposition. Understanding your customers and knowing how to operate your business are as important as determining your business's revenue streams.

As business owners and marketers invest more in social media, they aim to monetize their social media audiences. Several revenue streams can be applied to social media businesses, including advertising, subscription, freemium, affiliate, transaction, and virtual goods. Facing today's competitive marketplace, it is important for a social media business to use multiple revenue sources, and discover new revenue generators.

In this chapter, we have also learned that no one existing business model fits all. You need to find one that works best for your business. Many factors can influence this decision, including the type of your business, user size, audiences' willingness to pay, and consumer trust. It is also important to note that social media's functions exceed ROI. As discussed throughout the book, social media's premise rests in its ability to empower and engage audiences via interactive conversation. Thus, instead of generating revenue, many businesses' social media efforts focus on building trust, creating a fan community, and providing "free" service. Social media can serve as a great marketing tool, and bring unforeseen opportunities to companies/organizations. Now, let's examine social media marketing strategies in Chapter 11.

Key Takeaways

1 The business model is not the same as the revenue model. Finding your unique value propositions and product–market match is the most important factor when developing a business model for your social media business.
2 Social media is not built for short-term sales. The advertising model may not be the best fit for all social media businesses. Find the niche revenue streams (e.g., freemium, virtual goods, affiliate) for your business.
3 A one-size-fits-all business model is not available for social media businesses. Social media businesses need to use multiple revenue streams and control cost to realize profit maximization.
4 Social media business model must fit a company's overall operation. Until now, investing in social media for revenue generation still requires careful consideration and examination.
5 Be innovative, embrace the conceptualization of "all possible," and welcome all the unforeseen opportunities brought by this new media technology.

References

Aguiar, R.J. (2014) The hidden costs of YouTube's controversial revenue split. Available at http://www.dailydot.com/opinion/youtube-content-creator-split/ (accessed June 8, 2016).

Allen, K. (2015) Survey: Most marketers will spend more on social media in 2015. Available at http://www.prdaily. com/marketing/Articles/17927.aspx (accessed on June 8, 2016).

Anders, G. (2015) LinkedIn reprices premium services, hoping users won't turn furious. Available at http://www. forbes.com/sites/georgeanders/2015/01/06/linkedin-reprices-premium-services-hoping-users-wont-turn-furious/#31c3df4c1106 (accessed on June 8, 2016).

Anderson, C. (2010) *Free: How Today's Smartest Businesses Profit by Giving Something for Nothing*. New York: Hyperion.

Baidu.com (2015) CCTV Commercial Price. Available at http://wenku.baidu.com/link?url=ROcfUkIYlxblpYVLvMBjmP1P3Ke1keTeJG04lLmiDAC45oeQ55Yfcigh-ZFjqBBAi0tqg-7WlmzcvuAC9jnp2HAXu_ubqNyaXm2MQjpow7y (accessed June 8, 2016).

Beard, R. (2015) Make the most of your brand's 20-second window. Available at http://www.nielsen.com/us/en/insights/news/2015/make-the-most-of-your-brands-20-second-window.html (accessed June 8, 2016).

Bennett, S. (2013) Paid, owned, earned: a strategic business model for effective social media marketing. Available at http://www.adweek.com/socialtimes/social-media-party/477660 (accessed June 8, 2016).

Berman, S., Abraham, S., Battino, B., Shipnuck, L. & Neus, A. (2006) Navigating the media divide: innovating and enabling new business models. Available at http://www-935.ibm.com/services/us/gbs/bus/pdf/g510-6551-02-mediadivide.pdf (accessed June 8, 2016).

BIA/Kelsey (2014) U.S. social media advertising revenues to reach $15B by 2018. Available at http://www.biakelsey.com/u-s-social-media-advertising-revenues-to-reach-15b-by-2018/ (accessed June 8, 2016).

Boston Consulting Group (2009) News for sale: charges for online news are set to become the norm as most consumers say they are willing to pay, according to the Boston Consulting Group. Available at http://www.marketwired.com/press-release/news-sale-charges-online-news-are-set-become-norm-as-most-consumers-say-they-are-willing-1175425.htm (accessed June 8, 2016).

Carlson, N. (2009) Facebook: cash-flow positive with 300 million users. Available at http://www.businessinsider.com/facebook-cash-flow-positive-with-300-million-users-2009-9 (accessed June 8, 2016).

Cha, J. (2013) Business models of most-visited U.S. social networking sites. In: A. Albarran (ed.) *The Social Media Industries*, pp. 60–85. New York: Routledge, Taylor & Francis.

Clemons, E. (2009) Business models for monetizing Internet applications and web sites experience, theory, and predictions. *Journal of Management Information Systems*, 26(2), 15–41.

Constine, J. (2014) Facebook beats in Q3 with $3.2B revenue, user growth up a slower 2.27% QOQ to 1.35B. Available at http://techcrunch.com/2014/10/28/facebook-q3-2014/ (accessed June 8, 2016).

Duboff, R. & Wilkerson, S. (2010) Social media ROI: marketers are seeking to answer the "greatest question." *Marketing Management*, Winter, 33–37.

eMarketer (2009) Paid social network opportunities alive and well. Available at http://www.emarketer.com/Article/Paid-Social-Network-Opportunitiesmdash-Alive-Well/1007350 (accessed June 8, 2016).

Enders, A., Hungenberg, H., Denker, H. & Mauch, S. (2008) The long tail of social networking: revenue models of social networking sites. *European Management Journal*, 26, 199–211.

Facebook (2014) http://www.facebook.com (accessed October 23, 2014).

Gilman, R. (2011) Groupon: marketing model. *American Agent and Broker*, 83(2), 20–22.

Gross-Selbeck, S., Chu, I. & Moeller, P. (2011) Xing: #1 European professional social network. Available at https://corporate.xing.com/fileadmin/user_upload/XING_AG_US_IR_Presentation_US_Roadshow_April2011.pdf (accessed June 8, 2016).

Groupon (2013) Groupon announces second quarter 2013 results. Available at http://investor.groupon.com/releasedetail.cfm?releaseid=783599 (accessed on June 8, 2016).

Ha, L. & Ganahl, R. (2009) Webcasting business models of clicks-and-bricks and pure-play media: a comparative study of leading webcasters in South Korea and the United States. *International Journal on Media Management*, 6, 74–87.

Hayes, J. & Graybeal G. (2011) Synergizing traditional media and the social web for monetization: a modified media micropayment model. *Journal of Media Business Studies*, 8(2), 19–44.

Hopewell, L. (2014) How much money do tech giants like Apple, Google, Microsoft and others make every minute. Available at http://www.gizmodo.com.au/2014/03/how-much-money-do-tech-giants-like-apple-google-microsoft-and-others-make-every-minute (accessed on June 8, 2016).

Horn, L. (2011) How Facebook earned $1.86 billion ad revenue in 2010. Available at http://www.pcmag.com/article2/0,2817,2375926,00.asp (accessed June 8, 2016).

Hsee, C.K., Yu, F., Zhang, J. & Zhang, Y. (2003) Medium maximization. *Journal of Consumer Research*, 30, 1–14.

Hu, X. (2011) Social media business model analysis: Case Tencent, Facebook, and MySpace. Masters thesis, Aalto University. Available at http://epub.lib.aalto.fi/en/ethesis/pdf/12544/hse_ethesis_12544.pdf (accessed June 8, 2016).

IMT (2013) 8 key elements of a business model. Available at http://imtebiz2013.blogspot.com/2013/10/8-key-elements-of-business-model.html (accessed June 8, 2016).

Kammerer, M. (2014) The social media advertising: beginner's guide for Twitter, Facebook and LinkedIn. Available at https://blog.bufferapp.com/social-media-advertising-twitter-facebook-linkedin (accessed on June 8, 2016).

Laudon, K.C. & Traver, C.G. (2007) *E-commerce: Business, Technology, Society*, 3rd edn. Upper Saddle River, NJ: Prentice Hall.

Loayza, J. (2009) 5 business models for social media startups. Available at http://mashable.com/2009/07/14/social-media-business-models/ (accessed June 8, 2016).

Luckerson, V. (2012) How LinkedIn makes money off your resume – and why that's good for you. Available at http://business.time.com/2012/07/20/how-linkedin-makes-money-off-your-resume-and-why-thats-good-for-you/ (accessed June 8, 2016).

Lyons, K., Messinger, P.R., Niu, R.H. & Stroulia, E. (2012) A tale of two pricing systems for services. *Information Systems and e-Business Management*, 10(1), 19–42.

Magretta, J. (2002) Why business models matter. Available at https://hbr.org/2002/05/why-business-models-matter (accessed June 8, 2016).

Mahadevan, B. (2000) Business models for Internet-based e-commerce: an anatomy. *California Management Review*, 42(4), 55–69.

Mitchell, J. (2011) Second Life makes $100M a year in revenue. Available at http://readwrite.com/2011/08/08/second_life_makes_100m_a_year_in_revenue (accessed June 8, 2016).

Musil, S. (2009) Wall Street Journal plans micropayments model. Available at http://www.cnet.com/news/wall-street-journal-plans-micropayments-model/#! (accessed June 8, 2016).

Noyes, J. (2011) Linkedin IPO reveals it's a job search powerhouse. Available at http://www.business2community.com/trends-news/linkedin-ipo-reveals-its-a-job-search-powerhouse-011881 (accessed June 8, 2016).

O'Brien, C. (2015) Facebook report says its 1.35 billion users have $227 billion global economic impact. Available at http://venturebeat.com/2015/01/20/facebook-report-says-its-1-35-billion-users-have-227-billion-global-economic-impact (accessed June 8, 2016).

O'Malley, G. (2015) Twitter to expand promoted tweets, pressured to up ROI. Available at http://www.mediapost.com/publications/article/243053/twitter-to-expand-promoted-tweets-pressured-to-up.html (accessed on June 8, 2016).

Oreskovic, A. & Lawsky, D. (2009) Virtual goods give web firms new revenue in ad slump. Available at http://www.reuters.com/article/2009/12/29/us-internet-virtual-goods-idUSTRE5BS2W420091229 (accessed June 8, 2016).

Osterwalder, A., Pigneur, Y. & Tucci, C.L. (2005) Clarifying business models: origins, present, and future of the concept. *Communications of the Association for Information Systems*, 16, Article 1. Available at http://aisel.aisnet.org/cais/vol16/iss1/1 (accessed June 8, 2016).

Perez-Pena, R. (2009) A.P. cracks down on unpaid use of articles on web. Available at http://www.nytimes.com/2009/07/24/business/media/24content.html?_r=0 (accessed June 8, 2016).

Peterson, T. (2014) Facebook now makes 62% of its ad money in mobile: what the new earning mean. Available at http://adage.com/article/digital/facebook-makes-62-ad-money-mobile/294295/ (accessed June 8, 2016).

Picard, R.G. (2000) Changing business models of online content services: their implications for multimedia and other content producers. *International Journal on Media Management*, 2(3), 60–68.

Qwaya (2015) A guide to Facebook ads. Available at http://www.qwaya.com/facebook-ads/guide-to-facebook-ads (accessed June 8, 2016).

Raghubir, P. & Srivastava, J. (2002) Effect of face value on monetary valuation in foreign currencies. *Journal of Consumer Research*, 29(3), 335–347.

Russell, J. (2012) Chinese recipe sharing service Douguo serves up $8 million in fresh funding. Available at http://thenextweb.com/asia/2012/11/27/chinese-recipe-sharing-service-douguo-serves-up-8-million-in-fresh-funding/ (accessed June 8, 2016).

Sebastian, M. (2014) LinkedIn ad revenue soars on strength of sponsored content. Available at http://adage.com/article/digital/linkedin-ad-revenue-soars-strength-sponsored-content/295664/ (accessed June 8, 2016).

Shih, C., Lin, T.M.Y. & Luarn, P. (2014) Fan-centric social media: the Xiaomi phenomenon in China. *Business Horizons*, 57, 349–358.

Smith, S. (2003) Paying for content and making content pay: online micropayment strategies and solutions. *EContent*, 26(4), 26.

Social Times (2008) Facebook selling virtual gifts at $30–40 million/year rate. Available at http://www.adweek.com/socialtimes/facebook-selling-virtual-gifts-at-30-40-millionyear-rate/213389 (accessed June 8, 2016).

Statista (2014) Number of Groupon's active customers from 2nd quarter 2009 to 4th quarter 2014. Available at http://www.statista.com/statistics/273245/cumulative-active-customers-of-groupon/ (accessed June 8, 2016).

Stelzner, M.A. (2014) 2014 social media marketing industry report: how marketers are using social media to grow their businesses. Available at http://www.socialmediaexaminer.com/SocialMediaMarketingIndustryReport2014.pdf (accessed June 8, 2016).

Stewart, D.W. & Zhao, Q. (2000) Internet marketing, business models, and public policy. *Journal of Public Policy and Marketing*, 19(2), 287–296.

Van Baalen, P., Bloemhof-Ruwaard, J. & van Heck, E. (2005) Knowledge sharing in an emerging network of practice. *European Management Journal*, 23, 300–314.

Vukanovic, Z. (2011) New media business models in social and web media. *Journal of Media Business Studies*, 8(3), 51–67.

Wertenbroch, K. & Skiera, B. (2002) Meauring consumer willingness to pay at the point of purchase. *Journal of Marketing Research*, 39(2), 228–241.

Xing (2015) Xing 2014: Quarterly revenue growth. Available at https://corporate.xing.com/no_cache/english/press/press-releases/details/article/press-release-br-xing-2014-quarterly-revenue-g/ (accessed June 8, 2016).

Yu, D. (2014) The smart marketer guide to Facebook's 15 ad types. Available at http://www.socialfresh.com/facebook-ad-types/ (accessed June 8, 2016).

11

Social Media Marketing Strategies

Learning Objectives

After reading this chapter, you should be able to:
1   Transition from a traditional marketing strategy to a more social approach.
2   Apply strategic theory to your organization's social media marketing campaign.
3   Include a branded social experience for your social media audience.

Introduction

Though social media offers new opportunities for businesses to market themselves to a larger global audience, the most successful companies are those able to utilize social media platforms to better communicate with individual users. Chapter 9 discussed how this process works through the theory of the long tail. Chapter 10 explored various business models and the importance of having a large full-scale model that puts different stakeholders into consideration. This chapter will help you design a marketing strategy that works best for your goals across multiple media landscapes.

We have discussed at length how today's social media market is controlled by consumers. The best practitioners are those who are comfortable giving up some control in order for consumers to mobilize experiences that transform them into lifelong brand advocates. This balance is complicated, and much of the behavior change theory that we have covered helps guide these decisions. While this knowledge will help you make decisions about individual

Strategic Social Media: From Marketing to Social Change, First Edition. L. Meghan Mahoney and Tang Tang.
© 2017 John Wiley & Sons, Inc. Published 2017 by John Wiley & Sons, Inc.

social media messages, it is important to always have a broader understanding of how the different social media platforms work together. Social media is a great resource for marketing practitioners, but it is just one piece of a larger campaign. Every successful social media campaign needs to be consistent with a company/organization's overall marketing strategy.

Therefore, this chapter provides tips for building an integrated marketing strategy for your business, explains how to use this strategy to create a branded experience for your audience, and presents best practices of existing industries. While consumers control today's market, practitioners are still able to make informed decisions about marketing strategy.

Transitioning from Traditional Marketing

The past two decades have changed the field of public relations and marketing drastically. There are many myths being perpetuated by marketing practitioners that are just no longer true in today's digital environment. According to Hanna *et al.* (2011), these myths include sentiments such as:

- brand managers own and orchestrate their brands;
- companies use marketing communications to control their message;
- consumers purchase products promoted by marketers;
- providing a forum for customers to talk is dangerous and risky.

Each of these myths illustrates the struggle of the industry to accept the new participatory role that consumers play in the marketing process. The role of a social media marketing practitioner should now focus on communication and relationships, rather than control and management. Marketing specialists have primarily adopted established and institutional tools, such as email and Internet, and top-down diffusion message structures, such as blogs and podcasts. There has been slower adoption of more technologically complicated tools that cater to a niche audience, such as text messaging, virtual worlds and gaming (Eyrich *et al.*, 2008). In fact, photo sharing and text messaging are only being used by about a quarter of practitioners.

It seems that marketing practitioners are picking and choosing social media tools that work within an outdated approach to marketing. They want to control media messages and disseminate them to a passive mass audience. More importantly, marketers are still ignoring many innovative social media opportunities that would actually improve their return on investment (ROI) and help them in reaching their marketing goals.

Alternatively, consumers have been quick to adopt social media tools to communicate about their brand experiences. We see consumers turn away from the traditional sources of advertising towards more immediate sources that they can access at their own convenience to make informed purchasing decisions. They perceive social media as a more trusted source of information regarding products and services (Mangold & Faulds, 2009). Thus, it is time for marketers to accept the reality that communication about their product is not primarily coming from their media distribution efforts. Consumers are talking to other consumers via social media about their experiences.

While social media provides new opportunities for marketers to talk at and with their consumer, one of the primary duties in today's marketing is to listen. *Listening* allows you to observe communication, feedback and insight about the customer experience from social media conversations (Solis & Breakenridge, 2009). There are two different types of observation that you can make: participant and unobtrusive listening.

Participant listening requires you to join a group and study it as an inside member. This can be done by directly asking your customers for feedback on social media about their experiences. You can also gain participant insights through feedback and comments that individuals make on your own social networking sites. Here, the customer is aware that their comments are reaching the company/brand.

Unobtrusive listening requires you to be detached and not take an active part in the situation. This requires the marketing practitioner to search for conversations that are happening about the brand and/or product through social media platforms external to the company's own platform. When individuals are dissatisfied with your product, they will not necessarily only discuss their dissatisfaction with the company. They may not include you in the conversation at all. Instead, they may discuss the product with their social network without tagging features. Fortunately, most social networking sites allow practitioners the ability to search conversations through keywords and phrases to find these conversations. This search may offer more natural insights into how individuals are reacting to your product. We will talk more about social media monitoring in Chapter 12.

It is important to keep track of how audiences use technology to communicate about their brand experiences. Mangold and Faulds (2009) developed a new communications paradigm to illustrate this communicative process (Figure 11.1). The diagram shows how several media platforms work together in a much larger process. This is why it is imperative

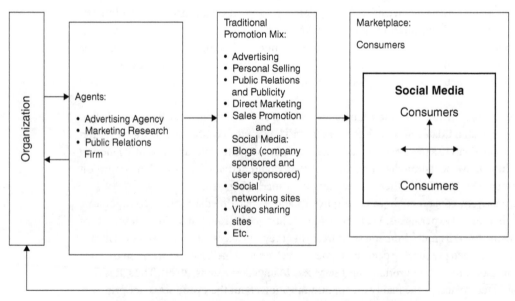

Figure 11.1   New communications paradigm. Source: Mangold and Faulds, 2009. Reproduced with permission of Elsevier.

to integrate social media into your existing traditional marketing efforts. One way to ensure that you are harnessing all the benefits of social media is through applied strategic theory.

Applied Strategic Theory

A social media strategy exists within a larger marketing campaign. It helps you make sense of all available communication tools for your marketing endeavors, and provides a predictable ROI that can be measured and improved upon in future years. When creating a social media strategy, it is important to consider a design framework that includes goals, target audience, social media choice, resources, policies, monitoring, and activity plan (Effing, 2013). This seven-step design framework action plan is outlined below and elaborated in more detail in the following sections.

Design Framework Action Plan

1 Goals
2 Target audience
3 Social media choice
4 Resources
5 Policies
6 Monitoring
7 Activity plan

Goals

Every company was created with some objective in mind. Hopefully, this objective extends beyond just creating an additional revenue stream. Perhaps you were working long hours at a job that you disliked. You decide to open your own Etsy shop with the hope of having more time at home to spend with family. This narrative helps set the tone for your company: you are a family-friendly company that values entrepreneurship and individual passions.

When determining the goals of your social media marketing campaign, consider your core business objectives and then link these objectives to desired outcomes and goals. These goals should be tangible and specific. Some could be monetary (e.g., make enough profit to pay the mortgage) but others should be on a larger scale (e.g., add "health and wellness" to the brand image). Consider what will make you most satisfied in the long term. Do you value mentorship/sustainability/health and wellness? Your brand authenticity can help you determine both short-term and long-term social media goals.

Once you have created your target goals, consider a practical action plan for how they can be actualized. It is likely that you will not be able to achieve all of the goals initially. Rank-order them according to urgency and affordability. Maybe you would love to utilize 100% sustainable packaging with your product, but it would simply cost too much at this stage in your business. Determine what is most practical at the current stage, and as your business grows, so can your efforts towards this goal.

Target audience

While traditional marketing strategies ask you to consider the audience that is most likely to use your product, a social media practitioner should consider which audience would likely be interested in each of your goals. You have already learned about how to conduct an audience analysis in Chapters 3 and 5. It is important that this analysis defines local priority populations, segmentation, and desired audience (Effing, 2013).

Chapter 9 discussed how smaller, more narrow latent targets may actually increase your ROI. Though this is one major difference between traditional and social media marketing campaigns, it is important to note that you will still be utilizing traditional media efforts to market your business. Therefore, you will want to determine who is your larger target audience. We will discuss how to utilize various platforms and benchmarks for each audience in a manageable manner below.

You will want to identify a larger target audience to reach through mass media messages (e.g., women, ages 25–54); a smaller niche audience to target through diffusion and community social media messages (e.g., mothers who enjoy yoga and live in southeastern Pennsylvania); and individual users (e.g., Kathy, who drives a Prius and composts her own food) to mobilize into lifelong brand advocates. For every goal, these three audience populations (target, niche, individual) should be identified.

Don't be frustrated if you cannot identify each of these three audiences for every goal right away. These should be informed decisions that come from research and experience. Chapter 15 will introduce the concept of the positive deviance audience that may help you identify these audience populations. This takes some knowledge of who is using your product on their own. Remember that the digital marketplace is guided by consumer behavior, and often you have to be patient and let actions happen organically in order to make the best strategic decisions.

Social media choice

Once you have identified the three audience populations (target, niche, individual) you will want to select appropriate social media channels and related content forms for each (Effing, 2013). Most platforms will provide statistical data about who is using their software. Other resources, such as Pew Research Center, provide third-party research results on Internet audience behavior. Don't just guess which social media your target audience is accessing. Research external sites and conduct focus groups or surveys to learn more about audience behaviors. This is one of the most important decisions that you can make as a social media practitioner. After all, how successful can you be if your messages appear on a social media site that your target audience never accesses?

A brief overview of social media user profiles is outlined in Chapter 5. This should be used as a guide, but remember that the market is always in flux. Likely, the landscape and patterns are perpetually changing and it is your job as a social media practitioner to stay up to date with trends.

Generally, Twitter is the best business tool for industries in need of multiple synchronous messages; Facebook is better for establishing dialogue between customers, but requires specific strategic management; blogs are an effective business tool if they enable readers to get to know and understand the blogger on a personal level; individuals within your organization should be listed on LinkedIn with some coordination to help build brand ethos; and a YouTube channel can present videos that help audiences get to know your product better (Bottles & Sherlock, 2011).

Consider whether your product would benefit through more visual, textual, or video messages. There are many benefits and challenges for utilizing each social media platform. Eventually you will want to exist across multiple channels. However, you do not want to disseminate the same message on every social media. What is posted on your Facebook page should be different from what is posted on Twitter. Remember that each social media serves a different function and has a different audience. You should also not open a social media account and then not update it regularly. Decide which platform makes sense initially, build and grow that audience, and then create additional spaces when you have the resources to do so effectively.

Resources

It is important to consider the requirements of running a successful campaign. This includes financial investments, the expertise of your employees, and quality control of messages for your organization (Effing, 2013). Here, you want to be honest about the skill-set that you can bring to help reach your target goals, and what is still lacking that may prevent you from reaching them.

The great news is that social media provides an opportunity for success with less resources than ever before. However, this also means that you could unexpectedly become an online viral sensation without adequate resources to deliver the product. Since the highest ROI comes from current satisfied customers (Stratten, 2012) you want to ensure that you are not making existing buyers frustrated with your product. Ensure that you are prepared for success.

Social media campaigns do not require a large budget. However, you still want to have some resources for marketing, whether that goes into giveaways, promoted posts, or evaluation efforts. A general rule of thumb is that 10% of your gross annual income should be reinvested into marketing (Entrepreneur, 2010). However, financial resources are not the only considerations you should make.

Many practitioners who try to navigate the digital landscape by themselves are experiencing fatigue that leads to their eventual demise. *Blogger burnout* is a phenomenon where first-generation successful bloggers are leaving the industry because they are overwhelmed by the task. There is great stress that comes when a passion transforms into a career. Many online professionals are unwilling to delegate tasks and feel as though that in order to be authentic, they must ensure that all social media messages come from the creator of the brand. Considering that the Internet never sleeps and constantly wants fresh content (Kurutz, 2014), this expectation is impossible. It is imperative that you surround yourself with individuals who share in your brand narrative and are able to help manage the social media load in order to prevent this fatigue.

Policies

Every organization must have guidelines for social media use, password policies, restrictions, and ethical considerations (Effing, 2013). Though these are not the most interesting or glamorous pieces of social media marketing, but they are essential to the success of any organization. It is important that these policies are established initially and not retroactively.

Social contract theory explains how members of society must give up some freedoms in order to reap the benefits of a functioning society. There are examples of this theory at play everywhere around us in our daily lives. For example, you follow traffic rules and regulations in order to prevent chaos on the roads. You enjoy the privilege of driving because you are willing to give up the freedom of doing whatever you want on the road. The same balance is true of social media.

You must set policies for how individuals within your company post social media messages, handle customer service complaints, and offer promotions to customers. You do not want the service to change according to which individual a customer is communicating with at any given time. Policies should be clear, specific and tangible. They should have a logical link to your mission statement. Employees and customers alike should be able to access these easily. A likely place for this distribution is on your product's homepage. Policies should be part of your transparency plan and diffusion strategy (discussed in Chapter 2).

Monitoring

Once messages are disseminated to your target audience, it is important to measure behavior and effects. Your strategy should include informed decisions about which effects will be measured by which metrics (Effing, 2013). We will discuss specifics about monitoring and evaluation in Chapter 12. It is important that each of these stages (goals, target audience, social media choice, resources, policies) is monitored periodically.

A social media marketing strategy is a dynamic process. You will never have a completed strategy that allows you to sit back and let it run on its own. It requires constant attention and research to determine whether current efforts are successful and what can be done to improve it. Otherwise, your campaign will become stale and a more innovative organization will capture your customers' attention.

Activity plan

Your social media strategy should identify a clear timeframe that governs when campaigns, projects and monitoring will take place (Effing, 2013). This includes individual social media posts, as well as broader strategic goals. The activity plan will help you to make mindful decisions about the roll-out of your campaign. It will also prevent you from feeling overwhelmed by all of the social media options available.

One way to manage social media posts is through a *social media content calendar*. This is a predetermined template that outlines all the necessary channels, resources and messages, and organizes them in a way that makes it easy to access information for dissemination when you need it (Sorokina, 2014). This is a day-to-day schedule that can be organized ahead of time about what messages are being published and promoted.

These postings can be organized through social media management software. *Hootsuite* is a social media dashboard that helps practitioners manage multiple social media channels through one platform (Hootsuite, 2015). Other available social media dashboards include Sprout Social, Sendible, and Cyfe. With social media management software, you do not have to sign into multiple social media channels.

You may choose to designate a specific day of the week for a certain kind of post. For example, each Monday you could highlight a loyal fan on Facebook; Tuesday you could have a live Twitter Q&A session with an expert; Wednesday you could share a video tutorial on YouTube; Thursday you could share a vintage picture of employees on Instagram using the Throwback Thursday hashtag #tbt; and Friday you could invite a guest to blog on your Tumblr account. Here, you have a managed and consistent plan across platforms that audiences can recognize and participate with. It is important to supplement each account with additional content as well. Otherwise, subscribers to your Instagram account will only see #tbt posts. Timely synchronous posts will help you have conversations with customers and make you seem on trend and relevant with current events.

Though a social media content calendar may help you stay organized, it is important not to enable functions that automatically post content. You can use these resources to set up media messages ahead of time, but a real-life practitioner should be the one to hit the button to publish. Remember that the goal of social media is to facilitate dialogue. This becomes impossible if there is not an actual person on one end of the conversation. It will also help ensure that your posts are not insensitive in the face of real-time tragedy, for example the company Epicurious posting Cranberry Scone Recipes after the April 2013 Boston Marathon bombing (Olenski, 2013).

Activity plans should highlight broader strategic goals as well. For example, you may decide to begin your social media campaign with a Facebook account before creating a Tumblr page. Having a longitudinal view of your social media activity will help you stay on track without getting lost in the day-to-day activity. This clear distribution timeline and benchmarks will help you determine when and where your marketing campaign will take place.

There are many moving parts to this activity plan. In particular, four aspects of this interactive process should be repeated over time in order to optimize your social media strategy. Effing (2013) illustrates this fluid process by the social media strategy design framework (Figure 11.2). This framework is most successful when senior-level sponsorship of the social media strategy is in place, organizations ensure a long-term social media commitment, and organizational behaviors are authentic to the real-life behaviors of personnel (Effing, 2013).

Now that we understand the strategy for creating, distributing and monitoring social media content, it is important to consider who should manage the strategy.

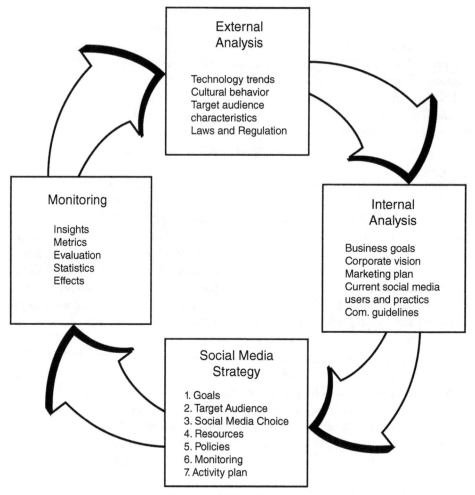

Figure 11.2   Social media strategy design. Source: Effing and Spil, 2016. Reproduced with permission of Elsevier.

A social media strategy is most successful when no single person is in control. Social media efforts should be an integrated portion of every employee position and should be managed by trained and qualified personnel (Bottles & Sherlock, 2011). By having individuals in every department who have been trained on company goals and policies, and how to use social media in a mindful manner, the task of posting often and authentically will seem less daunting.

It is essential that each employee listens to what is being said about your brand anywhere on the Internet, not just within your own social media platforms. Be sure that all employees are comfortable responding to and engaging with customers in a manner that is consistent with the authentic voice of the organization. This also means that you should hire individuals who present a clear and consistent voice on their own social media sites that align with your brand narrative. This is something that is too difficult to train.

In the digital age, every employee becomes a public relations/marketing recruit. You must train each employee how to establish relationships by showing audiences respect, honesty and enthusiasm, and then nurture those relationships by authentic personal interaction (Bottles & Sherlock, 2011). While you want to value audiences and pay attention to their insights and opinions, you must also negotiate between constructive feedback and trolls. You will not be able to please everyone, and this becomes especially true with a global audience on an open platform for dialogue. Find a balance of customer service with employees. While every employee should be able to utilize social media for the benefit of your organization, not everyone is trained in dealing with especially difficult service situations. Hire a designated person who handles these types of special circumstances.

Integrating social media into an existing marketing strategy is imperative in today's marketplace. Before doing so, ensure that you are able to address the needs of your target audience through social media. Understand how your target consumer utilizes social media technologies, and the costs, both financial and labor, associated with the process (Thackeray *et al.*, 2008). Finally, be prepared for the changes that an effective social media strategy will bring to your organization and audience.

Branded Social Experience

Once you have a social media strategy in motion, you may consider incorporating a branded experience into one or more of your goals. A *brand experience* is conceptualized as sensations, feelings, cognitions, and behavioral responses evoked by brand-related stimuli that are part of a brand's design and identity, packaging, communications, and environments. There are four dimensions to a brand experience: sensory, affective, intellectual, and behavioral (Brakus *et al.*, 2009). Social media provides opportunities to maximize each of these areas.

- *Sensory experiences* provide consumers with a real-life schema that they can reflect in the future. It gives them something to see, hear, taste, smell, and feel in association with your product. This is difficult to achieve online, but mobilization efforts discussed in Chapter 4 will help you create this brand dimension.
- *Affective experiences* allow customers to emotionally connect with your product. This requires a large amount of pathos, where you appeal to a part of your audiences' life where they are already invested. Creating a sense of community, as discussed in Chapter 3, may help achieve an affective experience for users.
- *Intellectual experiences* require audiences to put forth cognitive activity in order to carry out the call of your message. While you want your social media messages to be clear and concise, you also don't want to patronize your audience. The more thought and energy your customers place in your message, the more invested they will feel (provided there is a positive outcome). This is one area where a diffusion strategy, as discussed in Chapter 2, may ignite permanent adoption.

- *Behavioral experiences* change audiences' real-life action. This could be an adoption of a new ritual or the cessation of an existing one. Here, you are utilizing social media to prompt a real-life behavior change. This is consistent with the mobilization efforts of Chapter 4. However, rather than concentrating on a single sensory experience (e.g., taste test), you are combining multiple ones (e.g., create a video) to prompt a stronger frame of reference.

These four dimensions guide brand experiences. Your goal as a social media marketing practitioner is to speak to an existing set of social scripts that consist of expressions, actions and other behaviors that result from emotion (Morrison & Crane, 2007). Emotion highly influences how consumers select products and transform into loyal advocates to a brand. It is the goal of a practitioner to create and manage a positive emotional brand experience before, during and after the brand purchase.

Morrison and Crane (2007) suggest first creating a well-designed and attractive atmosphere. This can be done in person and online through font and interface design. Customer loyalty will stem from the emotional brand experience during the service consumption process as customers interact with this design. Practitioners should also continue communication after the point of purchase in order to establish trust and connection.

If customers positively associate emotions with your brand before, during and after purchase, it will result in brand advocacy. Brand advocacy leads to word-of-mouth marketing to outside social networks. This leads to the highest ROI pillar of the hierarchy of buying (Stratten, 2012). Brand strategy is much more about "emotion share" than it is market share (Morrison & Crane, 2007). Thus, practitioners should focus on innovation and customer-centric service to ensure the best possible customer experience.

Traditional marketing practitioners believe that they need to reach audience through an array of noise from other competitors. Marketers have long used the metaphor of a funnel to illustrate audience touch points: consumers start at the wide end of the funnel with many brands in mind and then narrow the brands down to a final choice (Edelman, 2010). There are many misconceptions regarding this customer decision-making process.

Most marketers prioritize brand awareness through advertising, in order to encourage purchase. This can be done through promotions, commercials, and diffusion techniques. However, new media make it easier for consumers to make informed decisions about products through self-seeking evaluation techniques. Therefore, it is not as important for brands to reach huge mass audiences. Audiences will find products and make informed decisions on their own, provided your search engine optimization is done well. It is more important for you to focus on the quality of your product and building a strong reputation. Once customers make an informed decision about a product, and have a positive service experience, they then spread positive word of mouth about the brand. Here is where the brand awareness process takes place. Rather than it coming from marketers, it comes from the social networks (Edelman, 2010). Thus, it is time that social media strategies focus on customer service and brand experience, rather than raising awareness about products.

This shift in marketing is perhaps most evident in changes to Facebook's Newsfeed algorithm. The goal of the Facebook Newsfeed is to organize a large amount of content and show Facebook users the things they want to see. When people see content that's relevant to them, they are more likely to stay engaged and continue being a user. This presents an interesting challenge to Facebook, as they also want brands to utilize the network and purchase promotional spots.

There are three different ways that let a marketer's content reach an audience through Facebook pages. The first is *organic reach*, where you write a post and individuals following your page will see the information, as long as it naturally shows up through their Newsfeed algorithm. The second is through *paid reach*, where a business will pay to have their post show up in a preselected audiences' Newsfeeds. The third is through *total reach*, which is the combination of both organic and paid.

Traditionally, the Facebook algorithm determined how worthy a page post was in a similar manner to most search engine algorithms (number of fans, likes, shares, source links). If a post had a high frequency of activity and fans, it would rank higher in the Newsfeed algorithm than a post with less. However, in 2015, businesses on Facebook that posted promotional materials began to see a decrease in their organic distribution. In fact, some reported having an organic reach rate as low as 1–2% (Eskensasi & Savio, 2014). Here, you see Facebook struggling to strike a balance, because if the Newsfeed becomes too heavy in promotional materials, users will disengage. However, if business posts quit, Facebook will lose money.

Facebook used research techniques to better understand this balance. They asked hundreds of thousands of users how they felt about the content in their Newsfeeds. The results of this research illustrated that users wanted to see more stories from friends and pages they care about, and less promotional content. These types of promotional posts include posts that solely push people to buy a product or install an app; posts that push people to enter promotions and sweepstakes with no real context; and posts that reuse the exact same content from ads (Facebook, 2014). Based on this information, Facebook redesigned their Newsfeed algorithm in January 2015.

The new algorithm prioritizes interactivity, trending topic discussions, longevity of posts, user shares, and audience engagement. Facebook's Newsfeed algorithm has begun prioritizing synchronous visual content that encourages audience interaction and engagement, rather than posts that solely push people towards a call to action (Facebook, 2015). Here, you see Facebook prioritizing brands that utilize pages to create a brand experience with customers rather than simply raising awareness about a product.

It is important to remember that social media serves as a function of the technology and culture, and that the actions and creations of consumers are also a function of the technology and culture (Berthon *et al.*, 2012). Technology and consumer behavior are intrinsically linked. Be sure to create a social media strategy that encourages a brand experience through sensory, affective, intellectual, and behavioral branding, rather than simply focusing on building awareness and a higher ROI. Let's explore one social networking service that capitalized on the relationship between technology and culture, Orkut.

Case Study: Orkut

Orkut is a social networking site (http://www.orkut.com) that was launched in 2004. It is owned and operated by Google and named after its creator, Orkut Büyükkökten, a Google employee (Geromel, 2011). Although it shut down in September 2014, it proved incredibly popular in the Brazilian market, with 90% of page views in Orkut accessed by users in Brazil (Feigenbaum, 2014).

Orkut is structured similarly to other social networking sites. The original purpose was for users to find communities through keyword search, including titles, description, and browsing through other users' memberships (Spertus *et al.*, 2005). Four months after its debut, Orkut had over 50,000 established communities. Within one year, this number rose to 1,500,000 communities (Spertus *et al.*, 2005). Most Orkut users are interested in finding classmates and friends, by joining online schools, workplaces and residential street groups (Kugel, 2006). In 2012, Orkut reached its peak popularity with 30 million users (Feigenbaum, 2014). It remained a market leader for 7 years and taught us a great deal about how to utilize social networking sites for marketing purposes.

Orkut was particularly popular among technology workers and students (Recuero, 2011). It allowed users to connect with not only people they knew interpersonally but people they admired. Early users were eager to try Orkut because of Google's strong reputation. Orkut also carried a high prestige factor due to its invite-only membership list. Being a member of the social networking site meant that you were well connected in the technology realm.

Orkut's interface was clean, simple and sophisticated, making it easy for users to navigate and join communities. Friends could rate other users based on how sexy, cool and trustworthy they found each other (Recuero, 2011). This competition element spread into the number of friends and the largest communities on the site. In addition, there were many reasons for its popularity, beyond the ability to connect. Orkut has put privacy concerns of users first and foremost (Recuero, 2011). Users were also able to make recommendations about products and services through community memberships (Spertus *et al.*, 2005).

We have discussed how the actions and creations of social media consumers are a function of technology and culture (Berthon *et al.*, 2012). Orkut is a great illustration of this connection. Brazil has emerged as one of the strongest markets for online retailers, ranking as the fifth largest online market in the world. In addition, the culture holds a high affinity for digital and social media, where cell phones outnumber people (Holmes, 2013). The nation also has a homegrown advertising market (Holmes, 2013). Outdoor advertising is banned in the country, which has led to a surge of online marketing. In fact, 77% of Brazilian social media users have a positive attitude towards online shopping; four-fifths of them use social networking sites to research products; and social media users trust recommendations from online contacts more than other sources (Holmes, 2013).

In order for brands to be successful in Brazil, they must allow users to blog, engage through social gaming, and incorporate online video into marketing campaigns (Translate Media, 2015). Brazilians are especially responsive to brand strategies that include online video, something that was difficult through Orkut. As such, the demise of Orkut seemed to deal with functionality problems with the website, including blockages, limiting the number of friends, and difficulties in loading and sharing photos (Translate Media, 2015). When Orkut stopped meeting the needs of the culture and audiences, they lost their consumers and were eventually replaced by other culturally appropriate cross-platform social media endeavors.

Discussion questions

1   How did Orkut successfully use the marketing action plan discussed in this chapter? In what areas did Orkut fall short?
2   How did the community structure of Orkut speak to the changing role of the digital consumer? Why would consumers be more interested in participating with these messages rather than a diffusion strategy?
3   How does the Brazilian culture speak to the brand experience of organizations and communities on Orkut? In a culture where brands must engage their fans on various digital platforms, what advice might you lend businesses about their future social media strategy?

Summary

This chapter discusses ways in which the changing digital landscape has influenced consumers, and how these changes should be incorporated into a social media marketing strategy. It is imperative that you understand how applied strategic theory fits into your overall marketing campaign and how to keep this up to date throughout the lifespan of your brand.

We have learned the importance of listening, both as a participant and as an unobtrusive entity. This must be done at every stage of the brand experience. Careful consideration must be made about goals, target audience, social media choice, resources, policies, monitoring, and activity plan of your overall social media strategy.

In fact, research measurements are one of the most vital factors in successful social media marketing. Now that we understand how to develop and implement social media business models and marketing strategy, let's turn our attention towards evaluation and research. Chapter 12 will focus on evaluating social media marketing. The ability to systematically monitor and evaluate marketing efforts will help you understand how and why individuals engage with your social media messages.

Key Takeaways

1   Social media practitioners should not just utilize technology to communicate with customers, but also to listen to what they say about your product. This can be done through participant or unobtrusive means.
2   Marketers must integrate a social media strategy into existing campaigns. The design framework should include goals, target audience, social media choice, resources, policies, monitoring, and activity plan.
3   Social media strategy should include a brand experience that highlights sensory, affective, intellectual, and behavioral dimensions of the consumer experience. This will shift strategy attention from increasing brand awareness to transforming customers into brand advocates.
4   The actions and creations of social media consumers are the function of technology and culture. Therefore, they should be fluid and change with society.

References

Berthon, P., Pitt, L., Plangger, K. & Shapiro, D. (2012) Marketing meets Web 2.0, social media, and creative consumers: implications for international marketing strategy. *Business Horizons*, 55(3), 261–271.

Bottles, K. & Sherlock, T. (2011) Who should manage your social media strategy. *Physician Executive*, 37(2), 68–72.

Brakus, J.J., Schmitt, B.H. & Zarantonello, L. (2009) Brand experience: what is it? How is it measured? Does it affect loyalty? *Journal of Marketing*, 73(3), 52–68.

Edelman, D.C. (2010) Branding in the digital age. *Harvard Business Review*, 88(12), 62–69.

Effing, R. (2013) Social media strategy design. In: Proceedings of the 2nd Scientific Conference Information Science in an Age of Change, Institute of Information and Book Studies, University of Warsaw, Poland, April 15–16, 2013.

Effing, R. & Spil, T. (2016) The social strategy cone: Towards a framework for evaluating social media strategies. *International Journal of Information Management*, 36(1), 1–8.

Entrepreneur (2010) Marketing. Available at http://www.entrepreneur.com/answer/222045 (accessed June 8, 2016).

Eskensasi, M. & Savio, C. (2014) What does the Facebook algorithm change mean for your brand? Available at http://www.mediapost.com/publications/article/225019/ what-does-the-facebook-algorithm-change-mean-for-y.html (accessed June 8, 2016).

Eyrich, N., Padman, M.L. & Sweetser, K.D. (2008) PR practitioners' use of social media tools and communication technology. *Public Relations Review*, 34(4), 412–414.

Facebook (2014) An update to News Feed: what it means for businesses. Available at http://www.facebook.com/ business/news/update-to-facebook-news-feed (accessed June 8, 2016).

Feigenbaum, G. (2014) Brazil to Google: please don't close our beloved Orkut. Available at http://www.vocativ.com/tech/internet/brazil-google-please-dont-close-beloved-orkut/ (accessed June 8, 2016).

Geromel, R. (2011) Facebook surpasses Orkut, owned by Google in numbers of users in Brazil. Available at http://www.forbes.com/sites/ricardogeromel/2011/09/14/facebook-surpasses-orkut-owned-by-google-in-numbers-of-users-in-brazil/#5ebe70dc4d5c (accessed June 8, 2016).

Hanna, R., Rohm, A. & Crittenden, V.L. (2011) We're all connected: the power of the social media ecosystem. *Business Horizons*, 54(3), 265–273.

Holmes, R. (2013) The future of social media? Forget about the U.S., look to Brazil. Available at http://www.forbes.com/sites/ciocentral/2013/09/12/the-future-of-social-

media-forget-about-the-u-s-look-to-brazil/#532f4c362
71c (accessed June 8, 2016).

Hootsuite (2015) Get serious about social. Available at
https://hootsuite.com/ (accessed June 8, 2016).

Kugel, S. (2006) A web site born in U.S. finds fans in
Brazil. Available at http://www.nytimes.com/2006/
04/10/technology/10orkut.html?pagewanted=all&_r=0
(accessed June 8, 2016).

Kurutz, S. (2014) When blogging becomes a slog. Available
at http://www.nytimes.com/2014/09/25/garden/when-
blogging-becomes-a-slog.html?_r=0 (accessed June 8,
2016).

Mangold, W. & Faulds, D. (2009) Social media: the new
hybrid element of the promotion mix. *Business Horizons*,
52(4), 357–365.

Morrison, S. & Crane, F. (2007) Building the service brand
by creating and managing an emotional brand experience. *Journal of Brand Management*, 14(5), 410–421.

Olenski, S. (2013) Epicurious uses the Boston Marathon
tragedy to cross that line. Available at http://www.forbes.
com/sites/marketshare/2013/04/18/epicurious-uses-
the-boston-marathon-tragedy-to-cross-that-line/
(accessed March 14, 2015).

Recuero, R. (2011) Understanding the rise of social networking in Brazil. Available at http://dmlcentral.net/

blog/raquel-recuero/understanding-rise-social-
networking-brazil (accessed June 8, 2016).

Solis, B. & Breakenridge, D.K. (2009) *Putting the Public
Back in Public Relations: How Social Media is Reinvent-
ing the Aging Business of PR*. Upper Saddle River, NJ: FT
Press.

Sorokina, O. (2014) 5 Reasons why a social media content
calendar is important for your business. Available
at http://blog.hootsuite.com/how-to-create-a-social-
media-content-calendar/ (accessed June 8, 2016).

Spertus, E., Sahami, M. & Büyükkökten, O. (2005) Evaluating similarity measures: a large-scale study in the Orkut
social network. In: *Proceedings of the 11th ACM SIGKDD
International Conference on Knowledge Discovery in Data
Mining*, pp. 678–684. New York: ACM Press.

Stratten, S. (2012) *UnMarketing. Stop Marketing. Start
Engaging*. Hoboken, NJ: John Wiley & Sons, Inc.

Thackeray, R., Neiger, B., Hanson, C. & McKenzie, J. (2008)
Enhancing promotional strategies within social marketing programs: use of Web 2.0 social media. *Health Promotion Practice*, 9(4), 338–343.

Translate Media (2015) Brazil social media. Available at
http://www.translatemedia.com/us/translation-service/
social-media/brazil-social-media/ (accessed June 8,
2016).

12

Evaluating Social Media Marketing

Learning Objectives

After reading this chapter, you should be able to:

1   Identify current social media marketing measures and trends.
2   Understand the importance of a hybrid approach to evaluation research.
3   Incorporate audience reception research methodologies into your social media marketing strategy.

Introduction

Part III of this book has discussed the many ways in which social media practitioners must alter traditional marketing strategies to best meet the needs of a digital era. Chapter 9 discussed how the theory of the long tail changes a mass audience to a more latent niche; Chapter 10 introduced various social media business models to increase a company's return on investment (ROI); and Chapter 11 illustrated how to incorporate strategic theory into marketing campaigns. Clearly, social media has dramatically changed the ways in which marketers produce and share media messages. In addition to this creation and dissemination process, the best marketers understand that research is the most critical indicator of success in strategy.

Research is vital at every stage of a marketing strategy: creation, production, dissemination, and evaluation. This chapter explains how current social media marketing measures

Strategic Social Media: From Marketing to Social Change, First Edition. L. Meghan Mahoney and Tang Tang.
© 2017 John Wiley & Sons, Inc. Published 2017 by John Wiley & Sons, Inc.

have evolved with new technologies, and explores how the changing social media users require a more hybrid approach to data analysis. We will identify how holistic measures are more possible than ever before through social media. A strong social media strategy is necessary for marketers to design, analyze, make sense, and apply data analytic techniques. Monitoring and evaluation efforts can only be aided, never replaced, by new media technologies. Let's explore the many ways in which the industry has changed how we evaluate audience behavior and the success of a marketing campaign in a social media era.

Current Social Media Marketing Measurements

Mass communication research is defined as the systematic study of media content, the forces that shape its creation, how and why people use media, and the impact of media content and media institutions on individuals and society (Folkerts & Lacy, 2003). Marketers are able to utilize mass communication research methodologies to better understand how their media messages are interpreted by and influence audiences. There are many different paradigms and approaches to mass communication research.

Three of the most basic distinctions between research methodologies have to do with the type of questions asked, and the ways in which data is collected. All research can be categorized as quantitative, qualitative, or hybrid approaches.

- *Quantitative research methodologies* emphasize objective measurements through the gathering of numerical data, and the generalization of findings across groups of people (Babbie, 2010). Quantitative data analysis is collected through various methods, including surveys, experimental studies, and secondary data or technology-enabled data analysis (e.g., Nielsen rating analysis).
- *Qualitative research methodologies* seek to understand the psychological operations by observing a broad interconnected pattern of variables, rather than the strength of the statistical relationship of variables (Graziano & Raulin, 2004). Qualitative data analysis is collected through participant observation, open-ended questionnaires, conversations, and textual analyses.
- *Hybrid research methodologies* are mixed-methods approaches that utilize both qualitative and quantitative data analysis by using the strengths of each and alleviating the weaknesses. Today, data fusion and data integration, two types of popular hybrid research methodologies, have become a trend for audience data analytics.

Some may believe that a more specialized understanding of research approaches is not necessary with today's technological landscape. There are numerous businesses, consultants and platforms available for companies to use in order to research their marketing strategy. Rather than learning the different methods and measurements themselves, companies believe that they can hire or use an outside technological service to tell them what they would like to know. This section argues that research should be the core of any marketing strategy. A thorough understanding of research measures and evaluation is important to any social media marketer.

Traditionally, the goal of mass media campaigns has been to reach the highest number of audience members possible. Since mass media institutions are so intrinsically linked to advertising, ensuring that the largest mass audience was reached by messages was always central to strategies. You may remember from Chapter 2 that this approach is called "push-and-pray" marketing. It is an outdated mindset to strategic goals in social media marketing. Instead, social media practitioners should have optimum audience engagement as the focus to their strategy.

This does not mean that large audience numbers do not matter. We have explored the endless options that audiences have for accessing media content. In this saturated environment, practitioners must ensure that their brand rises to the top of search engine listings. It is becoming more difficult for audiences to find brands as more and more brands emerge in the market. A strong search engine optimization (SEO) plan will help ensure that your company is found.

As we learned in Chapter 9, SEO is the art, craft and science of driving web traffic to websites (Davis, 2006). Understanding how various search engine software compiles a listings query is not as straightforward as it may sound. Very generally, search engines follow four basic mechanisms of Google: discovery of the meaning of websites, storage of links and page summaries, ranking of page importance, and return of results. This is often called DSRR (discover, storage, ranking and return). A complete understanding of how to optimize DSRR would require much more space than this book allows. Fortunately, if you are interested in learning more about SEO, there are many resources available, such as *The Art of SEO: Mastering Search Engine Optimization* by Enge *et al.* (2012) and *Search Engine Optimization Secrets* by Dover and Dafforn (2011). SEO concepts tend to stretch beyond the scope of a marketing practitioner. Thus, it may be wise to invest in an outside agency to meet the demands of SEO.

Nonetheless, Google's free Analytics Academy (https://analyticsacademy.withgoogle .com) is a quick guide for you to make sense of Google analytics data. It also helps you understand similar analytical programs, such as Facebook Page Insights (www.facebook.com/ insights) and Twitter Card (analytics.twitter.com). Google measurements are primarily interested in the number and type of click-through links posted to social media sites. In other words, these measurements can help you understand how many audience members your message is reaching. You can even break your audience down into segments according to age, race, gender, and geographical location. Since most websites and search engines model Google's design, it serves as a great starting place for understanding metrics.

Other popular social media measurement tools, like Radian6, a paid software developed by Salesforce, can monitor and measure live social media conversations occurring on thousands of social media platforms, including Facebook, Twitter, YouTube, blogs, and other online communities. Using such a data analytic tool, social media marketers can conduct both real-time and longitudinal social media data analyses that reflect attitudes, opinions, and trending topics. You can also obtain geo-targeting information for your campaign and identify top influencers.

All of these provide aggregate quantitative data of audience behavior on social media sites and are perfect for a beginner interested in designing an evaluation strategy. Though analytics may seem to be highly statistical in nature, there is no need to feel apprehensive about making sense of the data, as these programs do a nice job of presenting the information in layman's terms.

Quantitative methods have primarily led the measurement industry. FRY is a popular form of quantitative social media measurement (Blanchard, 2011). FRY refers to frequency (how often your target audience is reached by your social media campaign), reach (how many people your campaign can reach), and yield (average dollar value per transaction). Blanchard (2011, p. 241) suggests that FRY represents the three ways that consumer behavior could be changed:

> You could convince people already buying from you to do so more often, you could convince more people to buy from you, and you could convince people who were already buying from you, without doing business more often, to spend a little more than they already were per transaction.

Other quantitative measurements include search, traffic, retention, brand metrics leads, sales, and profit (Hudspeth, 2012). This is especially true when the number of visitors to a site is paying producers of social media content. Here, the brand strategy is to reach the largest number of a target audience engaging with a social media message as possible.

On Facebook, this focus on quantity means more views, likes, comments, and shares. On Twitter, marketers are interested in the number of retweets and favorites generated by each promotional tweet. Bloggers include social media platform widgets so that users can easily share every article with their social network. The "spreadability" of media becomes central to the success of social media content (Jenkins *et al.*, 2013).

However, these objectives are similar to those of traditional mass media marketing. For decades, advertisers have been producing television commercials and hoping that they are broadcast to the largest mass population possible. None of these measures account for the potential of the latent long tail market discussed in Chapter 9. Remember that there are various negotiations and levels to the consumer experience. If you are able to prompt behavior change through participatory means in your audience members, they are much more likely to be transformed into your brand advocates. These brand advocates hold a higher ROI than the "push-and-pray" model of mass media. A more sophisticated understanding of active audiences research design may help you personalize the research process.

As we learned in Chapter 10, social media business models are not as concerned with reaching the highest number of audience members as traditional media. Instead, social media marketers are increasingly interested in the manner in which their consumers interact with media messages, rather than only finding value in counting the number of followers or fans (DiStaso *et al.*, 2011). The quality of this interaction is key. This is consistent with everything we have learned about the value of participatory social media messages and mobilizing audiences.

Therefore, social media evaluation should mirror the assumptions of "pull-and-stay" marketing. Here, you use the medium to listen and engage conversation in order to increase trust and connect (Stratten, 2012). Evaluation and measurement efforts need to link to helping practitioners design, produce, disseminate, and evaluate social media strategy. In addition, it functions as a great way to *listen* to your consumers and tell them that you care about them. Quantitative data analytics is an important field, and necessary for the success of any business. However, social media marketing evaluation efforts should also employ audience reception research to measure relationship building with customers.

Building on the Focus Group

When designing a research strategy, it is important to know what methodologies help answer what types of questions. Qualitative research is great for examining a local or latent audience, while quantitative research provides insights into a larger mass community. Since social media audiences are generally seen as more individual than traditional mass research, it makes sense to turn to more qualitative measures. Qualitative research also helps to explain relationships, trends and patterns that emerge from quantitative measures (Garbarino & Holland, 2009). While quantitative research is great for identifying trends, until you know the reason behind them, there is little a practitioner can do to control change in behavior.

In the field of marketing, one of the most trusted and widely used research methods is focus group. *Focus group* is a controlled group interview of a target audience, usually consisting of 5–12 participants, that is led by a facilitator through a series of guided questions and topics (Entrepreneur, 2014). This is a great way for social media practitioners to capture audience opinions quickly, understand nuances between members, and gain a sense of sentiments towards a new product.

Perhaps you are interested in increasing the amount of female fans of your brand. You could bring in a group of 8–10 followers of your Instagram account to interview in a focus group setting. A focus group discussion with this small group of females will allow you to hear their attitudes towards your brand through a conversation with each other. This helps to explain some of the behavior that you see on social media analytic metrics via a particular focus lens.

While focus group research can be very valuable for social media marketers, there are other qualitative methodologies that you can utilize to better understand how audiences make sense of social media messages. These methodologies include, but are not limited to, in-depth interviews, participant observation, textual analysis, and anthropological studies. Qualitative research methodologies tend to be more time-consuming and costly. However, these efforts are worth it because the research can provide a unique view into audience behavior that you don't get with big data alone. Paired together, marketers are able to achieve both broad and deep insights into audience behavior.

There are many ways in which qualitative and quantitative research naturally work together. In fact, focus group interviews have become a favored methodology in recent years for researchers who are interested in combining qualitative and quantitative methods (Bernard, 2000). Focus groups complement surveys, rather than replace them, as they can help interpret results, especially when the meaning behind them is unclear. While survey research is able to tell you what your audiences think, focus groups are able to find out why your consumers feel as they do and how they arrive at these feelings.

A hybrid evaluation approach is useful for every stage of the product process – design, production, dissemination, and evaluation – to ensure best results. The Johns Hopkins Bloomberg School for Public Health Center for Communication Programs (2007) defined *monitoring and evaluation* as the process of collecting key data related to program objectives and operations, and analyzing these data to guide policy, programs and practices. Here, you see how this research must be done at every stage of the process, not just at the end when a product or message hits the market.

Furthermore, longitudinal, people-centered, qualitative methods can help researchers/ practitioners capture the social, cultural, economic, and political organizations of life (Singhal & Rogers, 2003). It is important that we now understand audiences' play in the interpretation process. Most evaluation research cannot reach comprehensive conclusions about audiences at all, because audiences constantly construct their reality and self-identity through media text negotiations (Fiske, 1987). Audiences are influenced by the text differently from one another depending on their consumption habits, motivations, and life experiences. Therefore, evaluations must move away from people as the objects of change and focus on more participatory methods, such as a focus on dialogue, cultural identity, and local decision-making processes (Byrne *et al.*, 2005). This can be done through more holistic evaluation research that also includes efforts aimed at understanding how audiences negotiate meanings (Petraglia, 2007). One of the best methodologies for capturing the complexities of an active audience is through audience reception research.

Audience Reception Approach

Often, marketers examine the media messages that have already been disseminated and wonder how they can shape them in order to trick audiences into following through with a desired behavior. Here, audiences are not seen as playing a very active role in the process. It is time to monitor audiences and evaluate social media marketing efforts through a more active process.

Audience reception research understands the active role that audiences play. It takes into account three areas of media reception: (i) individual qualities and life experiences of audience members; (ii) the meaning that audiences make at the moment of consumption; and (iii) subsequent decision-making processes. Audience reception research requires marketing practitioners to complete a strong audience analysis. By learning as much as possible about audience members, they will begin to feel more like individuals, rather than a homogeneous mass. You should focus on the daily life of the family, social temporality, and cultural competence (Tufte, 2002).

Understanding how individuals live in a natural environment requires complete and thorough media ethnography. *Media ethnography* explores everyday media practices and lived experiences, and is able to understand culturally specific ways of how individuals live in the world around them.

Consider how you access and use social media in your own life. It is likely that you don't often sit down at a computer and log in to a social media platform such as Twitter and access nothing but Twitter content for the entire duration. Today's social media users are on the go. They access an array of media content, simultaneously, across a wide range of platforms and devices. This convergent environment must be taken into account by social media evaluation research.

In addition, participants today no longer need to leave their natural environment in order to participate in research studies. This becomes increasingly true as wearable technology, such as Apple Watch, Go Pros, Google Glass, and other biometrics measurement tools, becomes popular. You are able to gather data about individuals as they live their lives. These are great technologies for capturing accurate audience data in a more natural setting rather than controlled experimental research.

Many technology-enabled measurement tools that attempt to account for cross-platform activity, including Google Analytics, Simply Measured, Rival IQ, BrandsEye, and Sysomos, provide a more nuanced understanding of how each of these platforms works with each other. Nonetheless, today's best practitioners are interested in identifying how users engage across different social media platforms (Rowe & Alani, 2014). This convergence of platforms is not going away, as more and more technologies are designed to easily interact with one another. You should examine entire media landscapes to best understand cultural trajectories that may influence interpretation through various dimensions of intertextuality. Though it is important that you create a separate social media strategy for each social media platform, your monitoring and evaluation efforts should take efforts to understand how these platforms work with one another.

Be careful that you are not just examining how users are accessing your content on cross-platform sites. It is also useful to see what other content is being accessed in combination with your brand. For instance, it may be useful to know that when consumers are looking at online information about Coca Cola, they are also looking at information about diabetes research. This will help you design a better product that serves the needs of your consumers.

Researchers have also identified media ethnography as a more useful evaluative methodology as it transcends the relationship between media audiences and media content to explore social and cultural transformations (Tufte, 2002). Your audiences' media environment very much influences how they interpret media messages. Even the experience of looking at social media content from a mobile phone is very different from a desktop computer.

Once you have a strong sense of who your audiences are, and how they are accessing media in their own lives, it is important to complete a genre analysis of media content. Here, you examine the media message landscape and identify where different layers of primary, secondary and tertiary media messages are distinguished from one another. This process provides a more holistic understanding of their relationship (Fiske, 1987; Tufte, 2002). While media ethnography examines how audience members access various technologies, genre analysis examines the many media messages to which audiences are exposed. Social media marketers need to identify pop culture media artifacts to see what audiences are finding the most pleasure in. They should also examine alternative media messages from organizations with similar objectives.

We have identified the processes for understanding the individual qualities and life experiences of your audience members. However, this is just one piece of the reception process. Next, you must try to understand the meaning that audiences make at the moment of consumption.

Social media marketers should ask questions about the dynamics between media messages and audiences and stop separating the audience from the message (Katz, 1988; Livingstone, 1991). It is also important for you to ask a number of questions. What key differences exist between audience members? How do audiences negotiate meaning from media messages differently from one another? Holistic audience reception research shifts the emphasis from an analysis of the audience consumption process to an analysis of the meaning audiences make of the media message. These can be understood through a textual analysis of your media message.

A *textual analysis* is a qualitative research methodology where researchers make an educated guess at some of the most likely interpretations that audiences may make of a media text. This is done in order to obtain a sense of the ways in which particular cultures live at particular times, how people make sense of the world around them, and the variety of ways in which it is possible to interpret reality (McKee, 2003). Here you see how audiences are seen as a much more active entity where they negotiate media messages differently from one another.

The focus of a textual analysis is to determine how audiences construct their reality and self-identity through media messages (Fiske, 1987). This methodology is not explicitly examining audience reception, but rather context about the themes and underlying messages in media content. The first step of a textual analysis is to identify themes and salient messages found within a media message (Bernard, 2000). Next, these themes and messages help determine narrative structure, symbolic arrangements, and ideological potential of media content (Fürsich, 2007). Here, what is of interest is not the text itself, but what the text signifies (Curtin, 1995). While a textual analysis is able to uncover many of the possible interpretations, a complex relationship exists between interpretation, expectations, and media genre. That is why a textual analysis should be paired with additional qualitative research that focuses on audience communication.

When doing social media monitoring and evaluation research, researchers also need to take into account the interaction between media messages and everyday life. Asking questions about what environment audiences consume messages in, and how that environment influences interpretation and subsequent behavior can do this. The most important part of this process is to get audiences talking and reflecting on their experiences.

Specifically, focus group discussions could be used when researchers are interested in gathering real-life data on issues that benefit from a group dynamic. Here, you are able to promote self-disclosure among focus group participants about what they really think and feel about a topic. Participants should be assembled with some common identifiable feature. This way, they identify with each other and are more open to reflect on that quality in their discussion.

In-depth interview discussions can be used when you are more interested in understanding what your audience means when they behave in a certain manner. Information gathered from multiple interviews allows practitioners to hear multiple perspectives on an event or issue. It is also a great tool to test emerging ideas about communicative action, such as a social media message. With this methodology, you define a purpose for such conversations to occur, select certain social actors to advance the conversational purpose, and draw out cultural logistics that audiences employ in their everyday experiences of communicating

(Lindlof, 1995). The most critical factor when conducting interview research is the ability of the researcher to perform a close reading of the transcript and draw conclusions once the interview is completed.

An added benefit of either of these methodologies is that your customers begin to feel valued by your brand. By allowing them to participate in the process, they feel more invested as a thought leader. This can easily be done through social media; just ensure that the process is personalized and allows for open-ended discussion. Predetermined questionnaires distributed by companies are impersonal and do not elicit the same fruitful results. Be open to what your audiences say and how they interpret your product. The following action plan can be used as a guide.

Audience Reception Action Plan

1   Research your audience through a thorough audience analysis.
2   Conduct media ethnography to examine the various platforms and technologies that your audience is accessing, and determine the many ways in which they work together.
3   Understand the various genres of media messages that your audience consumes.
4   Complete a textual analysis of your own media message to uncover possible interpretations and negotiations your audience will form.
5   Interview audience members to learn about their own sense-making and subsequent decision-making processes.

Very little audience reception research based on monitoring and evaluation efforts exists. One reason for this discrepancy could be the lack of trained researchers that are comfortable with hybrid methodologies. Most institutions focus on either qualitative or quantitative measures. It is important that we begin educating future professionals on both approaches to social media marketing research. Integrative methodologies are key to a successful social media marketing monitoring and evaluation strategy.

Case Study: @WalmartLabs

Hybrid research methodologies can prove time-consuming and costly, but may result in a strong ROI for an organization. This approach accounts for the active nature of media audiences. However, not all brands have the capacity or expertise to make sense of the big metric data that social media provides. Even if they have the resources, many companies do not have the training necessary to understand how and why they should pair metric information with deep qualitative research. One company that has focused a lot of attention and money on getting this balance is Walmart, an American retail giant.

In 2011, Walmart purchased Kosmix, a holistic categorization engine that aims to organize the Internet information in a more hybrid manner than traditional search (Clifford, 2012). This engine categorizes Internet content into topics and presents the information as magazine-style pages. These pages do not just include informative links, but also related videos, photos, news, commentary, opinion, communities, and links. One of the greatest advantages of Kosmix is the ability to analyze big metric data and monitor more qualitative social media conversations.

It may seem unconventional for a retail store to obtain a search engine, especially when you consider the high price tag. This transaction cost Walmart an estimated $300 million (Clifford, 2012). However, the return can be great, when competitors are only able to complete qualitative or quantitative analysis on a small scale. Walmart named the project @WalmartLabs (www.walmartlabs.com) and focused efforts on identifying trends in customer conversation on social media platforms.

@WalmartLabs claims to be an accelerator in evaluation efforts to meet the needs of their customers wherever they are. This includes a cross-platform approach, where they can see conversations of consumers shopping in a store, browsing websites, or using their mobile devices. They aim to use the software to integrate the online and in-store shopping experiences for millions of customers (Walmartlabs, 2015). In addition, they are able to see how consumers utilize various social media technologies to complete purchasing decisions and online transactions.

@WalmartLabs also emphasizes cross-media measurement. One example of a cross-platform feature of @WalmartLabs is Spark Studio. This function integrates popular Walmart.com pins from the social media platform Pinterest. Audiences are able to browse and share pins by category like brands, color, and top-pinned. These pins provide options to find out more information from the website, re-pin it to a personal page, rate or review it for others, or buy it from Walmart.com. Today's consumers are making consumption choices outside of retailers' websites. Walmart is able to use metric data to find potential customers in the online spaces where they already browse. This places less emphasis on reaching a homogeneous mass through "push-and-pray" marketing.

In addition to understanding how audiences use these cross-platform social media sites, @WalmartLabs also focuses on metric analytics. One segment of the software is called the Big Fast Data team, which allows the company to develop and operate the data feeds, analysis tools, and infrastructure to support hundreds of developers, data scientists, and analysts as an open-source tool. The company understands the power of data analytics, and has made it available so that outside agencies are able to expand on the product.

All this quantitative data is supported with a unique qualitative search feature. The trend function of @WalmartLabs helps the company see nuances in customer conversation, especially between geographical segments of population. This information is then used to expand reach into new audience segments by driving traffic into product areas through a visual browsing experience. The technology examines conversations on Twitter, Facebook, and search terms used by audiences. It is able to report the level of buzz and overall consumer sentiments about products (Clifford, 2012). As a result, Walmart uses this data to determine which products, and how much, to carry in which stores.

The software is also able to access the intricacies between American geographical cultures. One example of this information changing Walmart products is when the software identified that consumers in California and the Southwest were most excited about a new spicy chip called Takis. The retailer was then able to introduce a similar private-label product into that market (Clifford, 2012). Rather than taking up shelf space in stores that are less interested, Walmart is able to provide a different shopping experience for every population it serves.

Thus you can see how Walmart is able to use hybrid research approaches, cross-platform promotion, customer conversation, and cultural nuances to increase their ROI. @WalmartLabs is closing the gap between key marketing decision-makers who know audience behavior very well and data scientists (Ferguson, 2013).

Discussion questions

1   Why is it important for big retail stores like Walmart to have unique monitoring and evaluation software like @WalmartLabs? How might this put them ahead of their competitors?
2   One of the advantages of @WalmartLabs is the ability to categorize qualitative conversations on social media platforms, such as Facebook and Twitter. How might Walmart use these conversations to their advantage? How is this method of data collection different from predefined survey questionnaires delivered to customers after a purchase?
3   How is @WalmartLabs able to use the geographical feature of data to research their audience more critically than a homogenized mass? Why is this important in today's digital environment?

Summary

Social media technologies have changed much of the marketing experience for audiences. Your consumers use technology to make decisions about which products to buy, where to purchase them from, and share these experiences with their social network. Thus, as a social media marketer, you must stay on top of these digital opportunities in order to stay relevant. This includes incorporating an active audience into a monitoring and evaluation strategies.

Social media evaluation is transitioning from a quantitative metric-driven industry to a more audience-centered holistic approach. You should consider utilizing both quantitative and qualitative research methodologies to understand how audiences are making sense of social media messages. These hybrid strategies should be implemented at every stage of the product process, including the creation, production, dissemination, and evaluation of media messages.

Perhaps the most effective way to understand audience engagement is through an audience reception study. This is achieved through research centered on your consumers' real-life environment. Learn as much as you can about their individual attitudes, preferences, culture, and social networks. You should also conduct media ethnography to examine the various media that your audience is accessing, and how they are working together.

Consider how social media is being consumed in today's digital landscape. Users are engaging multiple social media platforms simultaneously. Monitoring and evaluation efforts should not just analyze what a consumer is doing on each platform, but also measure how these platforms are interacting with one another. Cross-platform measurements are vital for understanding the totality of consumer behavior.

Practitioners must also examine various genres of social media messages. Not only focus on technology and devices, but also examine the many different messages that audiences are exposed to each day. Be honest about how your product fits within this media landscape. This reflection should stem from a thorough textual analysis of your own media message. Identify the underlying themes and messages in your content. Consider possible interpretations from various populations. This illustrates the distinction between treating the audience as a large mass, and taking the time to consider the individual differences between them. Finally, allow audiences to retell their experience with social media content to explain why and how they experienced content. This dialogue will help you to connect with your audiences, uncover rich outside-the-box thinking, and empower them to be your lifetime brand advocates.

Part IV of this book will discuss ways in which social media practitioners are able to market their goods for social good. In this section, we learned new business theories, models, marketing strategies, and evaluation efforts. The next section will focus on incorporating this knowledge into health initiatives, civic engagement, and global development. The future social media opportunities exist within a globalized society. Let's explore these opportunities together.

Key Takeaways

1 Social media measurements are beginning to place more value on audience engagement and relationships than achieving a large mass following.
2 A hybrid approach to social media evaluation will provide the most complete view into consumer behavior.
3 Today's technological landscape requires a cross-platform analysis of social media use.
4 Audience reception research will help to explain how individuals make sense of media messages and nuances between audience members.

References

Babbie, E. (2010) *The Practice of Social Research*. Belmont, CA: Wadsworth.

Bernard, H. (2000) *Social Research Methods: Qualitative and Quantitative*. London: Sage Publications.

Blanchard, O. (2011) *Social Media ROI: Managing and Measuring Social Media Efforts in your Organization*. Boston: Pearson Education.

Byrne, A. with Gray-Felder, D., Hunt, J. & Parks, W. (2005) Measuring change: a guide to participatory monitoring and evaluation of communication for social change. Available at http://www.communicationforsocialchange.org/pdf/measuring_change.pdf (accessed June 8, 2016).

Clifford, S. (2012) Social media are giving a voice to taste buds. Available at http://www.nytimes.com/2012/07/31/technology/facebook-twitter-and-foursquare-as-corporate-focus-groups.html?_r=0 (accessed June 8, 2016).

Curtin, P. (1995) Textual analysis in mass communication studies: theory and methodology. Paper presented at the 78th Annual Meeting of the Association for Education in Journalism and Mass Communication, Washington, DC, August 9–12, 1995.

Davis, H. (2006) *Search Engine Optimization*. Sebastopol, CA: O'Reilly Media, Inc.

DiStaso, M., McCorkindale, T. & Wright, D. (2011) How public relations executives perceive and measure the impact of social media in their organizations. *Public Relations Review*, 37(3), 325–328.

Dover, D. & Dafforn, E. (2011) *Search Engine Optimization (SEO) Secrets*. Indianapolis, IN: Wiley Publishing, Inc.

Enge, E., Spencer, S., Stricchiola, J. & Fishkin, R. (2012) *The Art of SEO: Mastering Search Engine Optimization*. Sebastopol, CA: O'Reilly Media, Inc.

Entrepreneur (2014) Focus group. Available at http://www.entrepreneur.com/encyclopedia/focus-group (accessed June 8, 2016).

Ferguson, R. (2013) It's all about the platform: what Walmart and Google have in common. Available at http://sloanreview.mit.edu/article/its-all-about-the-platform-what-walmart-and-google-have-in-common/ (accessed June 8, 2016).

Fiske, J. (1987) *Television Culture*. London: Routledge.

Folkerts, J. & Lacy, S. (2003) *The Media in Your Life: An Introduction to Mass Communication*. Boston: Allyn & Bacon.

Fürsich, E. (2009) In defense of textual analysis: restoring a challenged method for journalism and media studies. *Journalism Studies*, 10(2), 238–252.

Garbarino, S. & Holland, J. (2009) Quantitative and qualitative methods in impact evaluation and measuring results. Available at http://www.gsdrc.org/docs/open/EIRS4.pdf (accessed June 8, 2016).

Graziano, A. & Raulin, M. (2004) *Research Methods: A Process of Inquiry*. Boston: Pearson.

Hudspeth, N. (2012) Building a brand socially. *Journal of Brand Strategy*, 1(1), 25–30.

Jenkins, H., Ford, S. & Green, J. (2013) *Spreadable Media: Creating Value and Meaning in a Networked Culture*. New York: New York University Press.

Johns Hopkins Bloomberg School for Public Health Center for Communication Programs (2007) What is monitoring and evaluation? Available at https://www.k4health.org/sites/default/files/guide-to-monitoring-and-evaluating-health-information.pdf (accessed June 8, 2016).

Katz, E. (1988) On conceptualizing media effects: another look. In: S. Oskamp (ed.) *Television as a Social Issue*. Newbury Park, CA: Sage Publications.

Lindlof, T. (1995) *Qualitative Communication Research Methods*. Thousand Oaks, CA: Sage Publications.

Livingstone, S. (1991) Audience reception: the role of the viewer in retelling romantic drama. Available at http://eprints.lse.ac.uk/999/1/AudiencereceptionPDFTODAY.pdf (accessed June 8, 2016).

McKee, A. (2003) *Textual Analysis: A Beginner's Guide*. London: Sage Publications.

Petraglia, J. (2007) Narrative intervention in behavior and public health. *Journal of Health Communication*, 21, 493–505.

Rowe, M. & Alani, H. (2014) Mining and comparing engagement dynamics across multiple social media platforms. In: *Proceedings of the 2014 ACM Conference on Web Science*, pp. 229–238. New York: ACM Press.

Singhal, A. & Rogers, E. (2003) *Combating AIDS: Communication Strategies in Action*. Thousand Oaks, CA: Sage Publications.

Stratten, S. (2012). *UnMarketing. Stop Marketing. Start Engaging*. Hoboken, NJ: John Wiley & Sons, Inc.

Tufte, T. (2002) Soap operas and sense-making: mediations and audience ethnography. In: A. Singhal, M.J. Cody, E.M. Rogers & M. Sabido (eds) *Entertainment-Education and Social Change: History, Research and Practice*, pp. 399–415. Mahwah, NJ: Lawrence Erlbaum Associates.

Walmartlabs (2015) About Walmart Labs. Available at http://www.walmartlabs.com/about/us/ (accessed April 23, 2016).

Part IV

Marketing for Social Good

13

Social Media and Health Campaigns

Learning Objectives

After reading this chapter, you should be able to:
1   Understand the activation theory of information exposure.
2   Apply concepts from the health belief model to your social media strategy.
3   Practice mobile reach in order to meet marketing goals.

Introduction

Together we have examined the influence of social media on behavior change literature, perceptions of the audience, business models, and various marketing strategies. While these all demonstrate the dynamic power of social media, perhaps nothing demonstrates as great a potential for global social change as the field of communication. The next four chapters will explore new media transformations in the public health sector, civic engagement, communication for development, and entertainment education for social change.

Throughout each of these chapters, more will be understood regarding social media's role in transferring considerable power from traditional authorities to everyday citizens. For the healthcare industry, this includes examining the powers of physicians, hospitals and insurance companies, and creating efforts that help empower patients, family and communities for positive action.

Today, the world is using the Internet to find, create and share information at a faster rate than ever before. One of the largest disciplines that has been revolutionized by these changes

Strategic Social Media: From Marketing to Social Change, First Edition. L. Meghan Mahoney and Tang Tang.
© 2017 John Wiley & Sons, Inc. Published 2017 by John Wiley & Sons, Inc.

is the field of public health. Health communication scholars have spent considerable efforts over the past decade determining the best way to disseminate and engage users interested in personal healthcare management. Many of the strategies discussed in this chapter are similar to the persuasive techniques outlined in Part I of this book. Ultimately, the strategy for establishing behavior change remains consistent regardless of the discipline or content that the message contains. However, it is important for emerging scholars in the field to understand these changes and the influence of access on the welfare of society.

The Pew Internet and American Life Project (2012) estimates that 80% of Internet users seek health information online. These health-centered websites are the number one resource for users interested in being more proactive with their personal healthcare management and cover everything from long-term illness, common colds, to weight loss or even skincare (McMillan & Macias, 2008). Many people are now using the Internet as the first stop when seeking health information. It is important to understand how these new trends impact the public health online information gathering and dissemination process.

New media technologies have sparked many positive changes in public health communication. Patients are now able to gather information from their home living room. Often, these searches are completed through fairly diffusion-centric portals, the most popular being WebMD, a public website that focuses on health information, including a symptom checker to help users self-diagnose individual ailments. This convenient information access increases the public's knowledge, awareness and empowerment regarding personal health issues. Moreover, it fuels a new expectation for patients to take action, reinforce knowledge, and refute incorrect health myths (National Cancer Institute, 2001).

In addition to seeking health information online, social media provides opportunities for individuals to video chat with physicians, find a community with similar diagnoses, or ask for support from a current social network. While these may not seem like huge influences when it comes to the treatment and prevention of certain illnesses, they have drastically changed the amount and type of health communication the average patient engages.

Increased health communication provides individuals with more choice, both in their own personal healthcare management (Collins *et al.*, 2002) as well as in healthcare provider decisions and treatment advice (Haean *et al.*, 2008). Health websites do more than just diagnose possible ailments, but also provide alternative treatment options and recommend various physicians in a patient's area of residency. All could lead to better health outcomes. Research demonstrates that patients who are more proactive in personal health management are more willing to follow treatment advice (Berry *et al.*, 2008). While it may be easy to dismiss what a physician has prescribed, it is less likely that an individual will ignore information sought through his or her own efforts.

It is possible that you have been using social media for health information without even realizing that you had crossed into the public health sector. Do you know someone in your own social network who hates going to the doctor? Hopefully, you or someone else in the network encourage them to get regular check-ups. If they are still unwilling, social media proves a resource for information that may make a case for seeking treatment. While online information should never replace the expertise of a physician, it does change the amount of top-down power physicians previously held.

With social media, individuals are no longer limited to the expertise of the one or two physicians in their hometown. The Internet is advancing more equal access to health communication across populations. Patients who may otherwise have limited access to healthcare providers are now using the technology for personal healthcare advice. Imagine that the closest physician's office was 60 miles away from your home. While that is a manageable distance for scheduled appointments or major health concerns, you may forgo the trip if you feel the risk is minimal. Social media allows the opportunity for many hard-to-reach patients to be seen by physicians through video messaging (Hawn, 2009), or simply allow an opportunity for patients to seek the information on their own through health communities and websites.

The same is true for other constraints, such as time, money or insurance. Online health communication has provided an opportunity for individuals to seek health advice without physically making a trip to the doctor. In fact, the number of people seeking health information online is currently higher than the number of people seeking medical care in person (Bastian, 2008). While there are many benefits to this phenomenon, it is presenting many challenges in the field of health communication as well.

This chapter explores the theoretical underpinnings of personal healthcare decision-making, as well as the advances of digital healthcare. Additionally, it explores the benefits of increased information access, and the challenges of misinformation and healthcare marketing.

Activation Theory of Information Exposure

Making decisions about personal healthcare management is complicated. Perhaps you have been lucky enough to go through life thus far without having the need to make decisions regarding your own health or, even more difficult, the healthcare of those close to you. Think of someone that you know in your own social circle who smokes cigarettes, whether the behavior is social or habitual in nature. Do you believe that they are unaware of the many adverse effects of smoking? Chances are, if they grew up in today's public health information age, they are well aware that smoking tobacco puts them at greater risk for cancer, respiratory disease, cardiovascular disease, and death (Centers for Disease Control, 2013). Why would someone still choose to smoke if they know it is bad for them? The same is true for individuals who binge drink, don't exercise, or consistently make poor diet decisions. When you think about how social media can help people to navigate these important health choices, it is necessary to understand the complicated cognitive processes that humans undergo when it comes to their personal healthcare decisions.

Chapter 2 discussed how difficult it is to achieve permanent behavior change in audiences through diffusion-centric media messages. It is not enough to spread knowledge and awareness about a certain health issue. Yes, cigarette smoking is an unhealthy habit. What type of message would it take for this knowledge to transform into a tangible decision not to smoke? The answer is different for everyone. What works for one individual may not work for someone else. Skilled health communication experts have been developing strategies for other impacting factors in the way we make decisions regarding personal health management. This strategy will increase the likelihood of an individual receiving a public health message and following through with the requested behavior change.

Health communication is defined as the art and technique of informing, influencing, and motivating individual, institutional, and public audiences about important health issues (Ratzan *et al.*, 1994). Scholars and health communication specialists have focused on topics such as disease prevention, health promotion, healthcare policy, the business of healthcare, and enhancement of the quality of life and health of individuals within a community (U.S. Department of Health and Human Services, 2000).

Effective health communication is essential to positive healthcare management (Collins *et al.*, 2002; Say *et al.*, 2006). Public health research states that lack of substance and vagueness of health communication may be linked to feelings of mistrust towards the source of messages (Collins *et al.*, 2002). If audiences do not understand what and why a message is being communicated with them, they are less likely to trust the motivations behind it. Have you ever received treatment advice from a physician that was too complicated to understand? Perhaps you have had the opposite problem, where a physician has used vague or oversimplified terminology. It is the duty of a health communication expert to ensure that health messages are constructed in an easy-to-understand manner. The way prescriptions are communicated is almost as important as the prescription itself.

Say *et al.* (2006) investigated factors that influenced patients' willingness to become involved in the health treatment process. The results of their study indicate that identification is vital to positive perceptions of health advice, as it makes patients feel as though they are a part of the decision-making process, igniting empowerment and a sense of control over their illness. This includes identification with the physician giving the advice, as well as the treatment prescribed. Individuals want to feel as though they have control over their own body.

Social media has the ability to increase the way patients identify with physicians. *Hello Health* is a Brooklyn-based primary care practice that utilizes a web-based social media in its communication with patients (Hawn, 2009). Included on the site are personal physician profiles, much like one would see on a standard social networking site such as Facebook, Instagram or Twitter. Listed on the site is Dr Devlyn Corrigan, an emergency medicine specialist who enjoys comedy improvisation and the movie *Cool Hand Luke*. These additional tidbits of information may seem unnecessary, but they could help patients see their physicians as less intimidating experts that they are unable to relate with. People are likely to seek out physicians with similar life experiences, which could increase the quality of information exchange and their willingness to open up about their personal healthcare.

This chapter demonstrates how decision-making regarding personal healthcare is not that different from other decisions that we make in our daily lives. Chapter 5 demonstrated how audiences are active users that interpret texts according to their own experiences and needs. Health communication specialists have utilized theoretical models with the same regard to the participatory audience. Therefore, it is important to learn the theoretical health communication models that explain how to incite behavior change in health audiences. This includes the activation model of information exposure and the health belief model. As you learn about both, consider how they relate to the earlier concepts of diffusion, community and mobilization approaches for behavior change in consumers.

Earlier we discussed how individuals growing up in today's society are probably aware that cigarette smoking is dangerous to their health. While diffusion-centric awareness campaigns are important for spreading information, they do little to prompt permanent behavior change, especially for those already engaging in the behavior. The *activation model of information exposure* (Table 13.1) is designed to explain how individual levels of need require both activation and arousal. If messages do not meet these levels, individuals will experience a negative state and will turn away from the given source of information. Smokers may feel turned off by messages that are too information-heavy or which portray users in a negative manner.

If adequate levels of activation and arousal are met, individuals will continue to expose themselves to the information (Donohew *et al.*, 1980). Today's health communication messages must not only fulfill individual need for information, but also to fulfill the need for stimulation or entertainment (Donohew *et al.*, 1998). Without understanding this second need for entertainment gratification, health information will be lost on audiences. The most skilled communication professionals will understand how to structure content so that it serves both needs, as well as create enticing messages that individuals will want to seek in their daily lives.

Table 13.1   Activation model of information exposure. Source: Donohew *et al.*, 1998. Reproduced with permission of John Wiley & Sons.

Characteristics

Cl	Individuals vary in their levels of need for stimulation as a function of their inherited drives and learned needs based on rewarded and nonrewarded experiences. High sensation seekers have higher needs for stimulation than low sensation seekers
C2	In messages, stimulation is provided by formal features, including (a) fast action, (b) novelty, (c) color, (d) stimulus intensity, (e) complexity, and others, and by the verbal content, including dramatic qualities and emotional intensity

Laws (theoretical statements)

L1	Individuals seek to achieve or maintain a level of activation at which they feel most comfortable
L2	Attention to a message is a function of (a) individual level of need for stimulation or cognition and (b) level of stimulation provided by a stimulus source (such as a message)

Deduced propositions

L3	Individuals will attend to messages that fulfill their needs for activation
L4	Individuals will turn away from messages that fail to generate enough arousal to meet their needs for activation to seek more exciting stimuli
L5	Individuals will turn away from messages that generate too much arousal to seek less exciting stimuli

Explanandum

E	Operational hypotheses, based on the propositions expressed in L3, L4, and L5, may concern exposure to information, attitude or behavior changes, or other variables

More recent research into the activation theory of information exposure suggests that individuals actually satisfy their need for stimulation and entertainment when attending to a message *before* they seek to fulfill their need for information alone (University of Kentucky, 2001). If given the choice, people would rather spend their time with content that is entertaining than informative. However, public health service announcements tend to be oversaturated with information and bore audiences. Thus, individuals tend to shift attention towards more entertaining commercial sites, rather than government or research-based sources.

One critical concern is the quality of health information consumed and diffused on the Web, especially as health communication and entertainment narratives begin to merge. We have discussed in Chapter 5 how audiences are more purposeful and selective when using the Internet. They would access the information that best gratifies their emotional needs. Because the Internet is unregulated and there are many sites with public health misinformation, some promoting products and others outright scams, the amount of misinformation is ever growing (Morahan-Martin & Anderson, 2000). Many healthcare professionals worry about the deadly consequences of spreading blatant misinformation online (Intlekofer *et al.*, 2012).

While it is impossible to examine how much influence this type of public health misinformation has on personal healthcare decisions, it is possible to change existing reputable health information sources so that they prove more appealing to users. Reputable health sources such as the Mayo Clinic have begun using storytelling techniques (e.g., Historias Mayo) to engage with niche communities regarding health issues (Hiatt, 2013). Historias Mayo is a global storytelling campaign that uses Twitter and Facebook to follow the stories of Hispanic patients and physicians. This is a great way for a reputable health source to diffuse effective communication in a way that is appealing to everyday users.

Hopefully you are seeing the application of the marketing strategies discussed in previous chapters to health communication campaigns. Chapter 2 discussed the importance of including brand stories in your diffusion marketing strategy. The importance of narratives in health communication is equally imperative to prompting behavior change.

Health Belief Model

The activation model of information exposure explained why individuals do not follow through with public health treatment advice, despite having the knowledge of the benefits of doing so. The *health belief model* (Figure 13.1) explains this process further, and demonstrates how healthy behavior is dependent on two variables: the value placed by an individual on a particular goal; and the individual's estimate of the likelihood that a given action will achieve that goal (Janz & Becker, 1984).

Before following through with a behavior change, individuals must actually have the desire to avoid illness or get well, and believe that the behavior change being asked of them will help them to avoid or treat illness. If a cigarette smoker does not prioritize health or feels that quitting smoking will have little effect because they are exposed to second-hand smoke

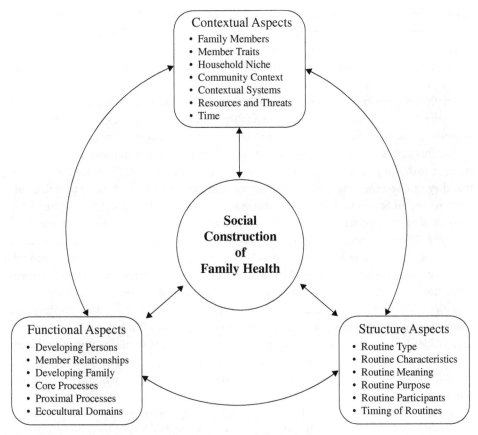

Figure 13.1   Health belief model. Source: http://www.diabetesfamily.net. Reproduced with permission of Ohio University.

all the time anyway, a public health message will have little influence. The health belief model outlines many dimensions social media practitioners must consider when creating health campaign messages (Janz & Becker, 1984).

First, you must consider the perceived susceptibility or the perceptions of personal vulnerability and risk to a condition. This proves difficult, especially in young adults, who may believe that they are invincible or that bad things will not happen to them. If they do not feel as though they will be impacted by the illness, they will not seek treatment.

You must also consider the perceived severity of contracting the illness. This happens when patients evaluate both medical and social consequences of contraction. Often, the effects of the condition on social interactions with friends and family mean more to a person than disability or pain. With sexually transmitted infections, patients often get them treated to avoid embarrassment in locker rooms or so that future partners will not raise questions, not because of the dangers if left untreated.

It is important to consider the perceived benefits of following through with the behavior. While individuals may accept that they are susceptible to a condition, the desired action may not be greater than the perceived risk. Consider the pharmaceutical commercials that you see on television. What do you think when you hear the long list of potential side effects? Why would someone take a medication to cure restless leg syndrome if the medication may cause heart failure or even death? It is important to ensure that the side effects from one treatment are less than the initial illness.

Finally, and perhaps most importantly, it is necessary to consider the perceived barriers of following through with a health recommendation. Individuals will engage in a cost–benefit analysis, where they weigh the behavior change effectiveness against the challenges of following through, such as cost, time or even social status. Many teen pregnancy initiatives struggle with the perceived barriers dimension, because even though young adults know that they can become pregnant through unprotected sex, are aware of the impact that this will have on the rest of their life, and know that wearing a condom is not that expensive or difficult, they feel embarrassed or uncomfortable asking their partner when it is time.

Hopefully you can see how the health belief model is contrary to a more diffusion-centric model that suggests a lack of information is the reason individuals do not follow through with a suggested behavior change. This model demonstrates the relationship and connection between health behaviors, practices and utilization of health services. It is easy to see how awareness-only campaigns are not very effective. If one was just to follow the diffusion of innovation strategy and raise awareness about the dangers and/or benefits of an action, it only tackles half of the health belief model. Instead, campaigns should motivate audiences through individual perceptions (evaluation of illness), modifying behaviors (demographic variables, perceived threat, and cues to action), and the likelihood of action (factors of recommendation) (Hochbaum *et al.*, 1952).

In addition, individuals should be able to easily pick out what behavior change is being asked of them. While there may be many steps a person could take, health campaigns should only choose one. Think of all the different possible ways an individual can stop smoking: immediate cessation, hypnosis, or the use of patch, gum or e-cigarettes. The message will be much stronger if a campaign is clear and provides specific advice for the audience.

It is also important that this solution presents a tangible course of action at acceptable cost. People should not feel as though they will lose a part of their individual or social selves by carrying out the desired behavior change. Finally, all campaigns should promote feelings of competency to take action while considering cultural factors, socioeconomic status, and previous experiences of individuals.

Social media provides a great platform to tackle some of these dimensions. It allows a networked community to create profiles based on their own individuality and interests and to network with others going through similar trials, and encourages dialogue that is supportive and encouraging. One example of a public health campaign that is utilizing social media for a very specific audience is Planned Parenthood.

Planned Parenthood created an online safe sex campaign (www.wheredidyouwearit.com) that distributed 55,000 condoms to college students. These condoms included barcodes that, if scanned, would connect them to mobile websites. These websites provided information about safe sex and condom use, and allowed individuals to anonymously "check-in" to the site's interactive map.

The campaign's tagline read "Be proud to wear protection" and tackled many of the social stigmas associated with condom use. Rather than telling college students that sex was something they should be ashamed of, they urged them to anonymously share their condom use with the world, because safe sex is something to take pride in. The map shows other condom users from 48 states in the United States and six continents (Johnson, 2012) that were also practicing safe sex.

Another online health campaign is 24/7 Townhall on the Public Internet Channel (PIC.tv). This social media intervention is a free website that offers short webisodes designed to help users live a better life. The webisodes on PIC.tv promote public health issues, including living healthy, managing diabetes, life as a single mother, and more. These videos are free and are designed to help users take action and improve their lives based on matters that are most important to their community.

The 24/7 website is designed to work in three phases. First, users share videos and articles with each other to raise awareness on various public health issues. Second, online communities are established to spark discussion forums based on local community events. Finally, individual profiles are created to allow users the ability to track their progress and create social networks with friends (24/7 Townhall, 2010). Unlike traditional mass media public health initiatives, no one is telling users what content to add to the site. Instead, users are able to define what issues are of most concern for them and network with others who may be interested in inspiring behavior change. It has recently won four Telly Awards (a primary award honoring groundbreaking media projects) for its participatory efforts in combating difficult public health issues.

Social media provides the ability for people to not just seek more information about the public health issues that are important to them, but to engage others who are dealing with similar illnesses. Public health practitioners can now use social media to diffuse their message, create a community of public dialogue, and mobilize audiences towards a specific desired action. The following action plan has been developed from the activation model of information exposure and the health belief model for creating a successful health campaign.

Health Campaign Action Plan

1 Conduct a strong audience analysis of your target, including demographics, cultural traditions, and socioeconomic status.
2 Ensure that the campaign contains an equal balance between entertainment and information through narrative techniques.
3 Create a site where users interested in finding information are clearly able to see the risks of the condition, the benefits of treatment, and solutions to perceived barriers for following through with the desired behavior change.
4 Provide incentives for audiences to take action.

Mobile Reach

We have discussed many ways in which social media technologies have transformed access, relationships and outcomes that users have with their personal health management. One of the biggest game changers in the health industry has been dubbed mHealth, or text-based health campaigns.

mHealth is defined as emerging mobile communications and network technologies for healthcare systems (Istepanian *et al.*, 2006) and is set to profoundly change the health industry (Delgreco, 2009). Mobile technologies have become an inexpensive and more efficient way for doctors and patients to communicate with one another. It is especially practical for patients who have limited access to traditional healthcare facilities.

The *short message service* (SMS) technology of mobile communication allows users to share written messages between handsets and has two main advantages over traditional phone calls or personal home computers: it is relatively inexpensive and it is asynchronous in nature. You may remember from Chapter 7 that synchronous communication requires individuals to be gathered at the same time in order to communicate. Text message users do not have to read the message immediately in order to effectively participate in the communication process (Ling, 2005). This technology is ideal for physicians who may have small pockets of time between patients to access "held messages" that patients may have sent earlier in the day.

Several health campaigns have already been developed and are successfully using mHealth technology with patients. For example, STOMP (Stop Smoking Over Mobile Phone) was created by Healthphone Solutions to reach members attempting to quit smoking. It sends a series of motivational text messages to users over the course of 26 weeks when a patient is trying to kick the habit. This extra communication prompted quit rates to jump from 13 to 28% (Bull, 2010).

The success of STOMP sparked a series of alternative mHealth initiatives. Ameratunga *et al.* (2012) modeled the STOMP program and developed an intervention to reduce problem drinking and injury among hard-to-reach trauma patients in New Zealand by sending them messages over a period of four weeks following hospital discharge. The weight loss program Sensei text messages subscribers health tips throughout the day to help them with their weight loss goals (Sensei, 2009). Intelecare Compliance Solutions Inc. provides women the opportunity to receive text message reminders about taking their birth control pills (Zimmerman, 2007).

Today, mobile technologies have become the most common form of electronically mediated communication worldwide (Boase & Ling, 2013) (Figure 13.2). In 2013, the number of mobile-cellular subscriptions reached 6.8 billion, representing a global penetration of 96% (ITU, 2013). Global mobile traffic represents 13% of all Internet traffic (Olson, 2012), which suggests that more and more users are getting smartphones with Internet capability. Health providers can virtually be with patients at all times.

While we cannot expect physicians to be on-call 24/7, nor would we want our physicians to oversee every decision we make in our lives, this increased connectivity is a game changer for the health industry. Mobile technology holds potential in increasing patient access to information, the type of personalized health information they receive, and the

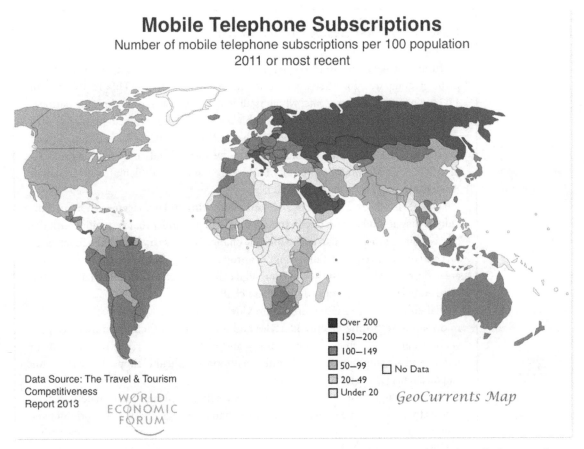

Figure 13.2   Mobile saturation map. Source: http://www.geocurrents.info/geonotes/mapping-the-cell-phone-revolution. Reproduced with permission of Martin Lewis.

amount of communication they are able to have with physicians (Deaton, 2004; Bar *et al.*, 2009). New media provide opportunities for individuals to have equal access to healthcare information and be able to communicate with physicians in ways that are not entirely disruptive to their lives.

Of course new media brings new sorts of concerns, such as increased misinformation, patient confidentiality, and liability concerns for physicians. While we continue to navigate through these opportunities and challenges, it is important to remember the principles of behavior change and communication theory. Regardless of the media platform that individuals utilize to communicate, their decision-making process remains complex. This chapter demonstrates the importance of incorporating communication theory into public health and behavior change initiatives. Beyond the need for information and awareness on public health issues, other factors, such as economic or sociostructural challenges, prevent individuals from carrying out a desired behavior change. The next generation will have better tools to access, engage and treat patients. Social media and mobile communication will play an intricate role in this process.

Case Study: Diabetes: A Family Matter

In rural Appalachian Ohio, residents are at especially high risk for obesity and diabetes compared to other populations in the United States. This region has an 11.3% diabetes prevalence rate, which is almost four points higher than the national average (Diabetes Family, 2013). Appalachia is a rural region, where families live very far apart from one another, and 20% live below the poverty line. In addition, 50% of the counties in Central Appalachia have only one hospital and one in five have no hospital at all (Appalachian Community Fund, 2008). It can be difficult for Appalachian residents to regularly see their physicians.

Diabetes is a disease that needs constant monitoring and management. Often, individuals diagnosed have no one in their immediate proximity that is familiar with the disease. Since most often an entire lifestyle change is necessary, especially in terms of diet and exercise regimen, family support proves critical. Sharon Denham, RN, DSN, created a culturally specific health campaign called Diabetes: A Family Matter for the rural Appalachian region to combat these challenges.

Diabetes: A Family Matter aims to provide people in the Appalachian region with information regarding healthy lifestyles and a toolkit that focuses on diabetes prevention and management from a family and community perspective. Immediate family and kinship have been identified as important health support networks for Appalachians (Diabetes Family, 2013).

This campaign also utilizes narrative storytelling in promotional materials, prescribes treatment to the entire family rather than to a single individual, and removes rhetoric that identifies physicians as the final expert decision-maker concerning health matters. Storytelling is incredibly powerful and valued in the Appalachian culture. Formative research was conducted to evaluate target populations as well as campaign materials to ensure that they were culturally sensitive and useful for reaching these rural populations (Figure 13.3).

Through online discussion forums, patients are able to share stories, ask questions, and provide recommendations to others struggling with diabetes. Though they may not know anyone in their immediate community with the disease, this type of network makes them feel as though they are not alone in their treatment efforts. It also provides family and community members a chance to ask questions that they may not feel comfortable asking their loved one.

Furthermore, this campaign encouraged individuals within the region to sign up to become "Sugar Helpers" and organize coalitions in smaller communities. These follow-up sessions and phone calls through these community groups help track the family's ability to stick with the medical treatment (Sherifali & Pinelli, 2007).

Overall, the social media health campaign Diabetes: A Family Matter allows for a networked approach in an otherwise hard-to-reach community, and facilitates stronger communication with patients through a holistic family approach by tracking both informational and cultural barriers. This is a strong example of how

Figure 13.3   Diabetes campaign materials. Source: www.diabetesfamily.net. Reproduced with permission of Sharon Denham.

experts must move beyond diffusing information onto individuals. Family, culture and information access are all critical factors in a successful behavior change initiative. It is necessary for health communication specialists to actually get inside the home of their target audience, and social media makes this more possible than ever before.

Discussion questions

1   Based on the activation model of information exposure, at what stage of a public health campaign like Diabetes: A Family Matter is best to hook the audience through a narrative technique? What role can social media play in this process?

2 Diabetes: A Family Matter hinges on cultural nuances to spread information about diabetes treatment and management. What are some possible ways that social media can be utilized in this process? How do conceptualizations of the mass audience change with this approach?

3 How does the media structure of Diabetes: A Family Matter encourage audience and community participation? What are some possible barriers for a physician's willingness to participate in the program?

4 When might it prove more beneficial to obtain public health information from a more diffusion-oriented website, rather than a community-oriented social networking community such as Diabetes: A Family Matter? What are possible benefits that the community provides that the diffusion website does not?

Summary

Traditional healthcare models require patients to recognize that something is wrong with their current health, seek a physician for answers, and adhere to their treatment recommendations. Today's patients are able to access health information, communities and alternative physicians at any point in this process, transforming them into more empowered, participating and active managers of personal healthcare (Couchman *et al.*, 2001; Roter & Hall, 2006).

The activation model of information exposure and the health belief model are just two of many health communication strategies that illustrate how complicated the process is for individuals who are trying to make decisions regarding their personal healthcare. Patients are using social media to seek second opinions, research their own symptoms, and discuss questions with online communities. Social media provides many of these participatory features that allow individuals to share stories and find community with others. While these technological advances hold great potential for positive change, they can just as easily be used in an ineffective or damaging manner. As the activation model of information exposure demonstrates, individuals are primarily concerned with the emotional dimensions of health messages. More efforts therefore need to be made to ensure that credible sources of health information are presented in ways that are understandable and entertaining to users. This is where storytelling and cultural narrative techniques should be utilized when implementing health campaigns.

Social media allows individuals the opportunity to participate in dialogue and form communities surrounding health issues. Whether you are a lifelong contributor or just stopping in to read other patient experiences, forums, discussion groups and topic blogs are a great way to feel less alone. Most cultures view health as a private sphere issue, something not openly discussed in public. Social media allows these conversations to happen anonymously, which is incredibly useful for taboo topics, such as sexual health, mental health issues, or addiction. It is also a great place to begin conversations, normalize health concerns, and shift public personas so that we feel more comfortable talking about these uncomfortable topics.

One of the greatest advances of social media is the ability to transcend virtual boundaries. Individuals do not live in isolation from one another. Social media allows communities to organize themselves and for individuals to find resources that they can use in their "real life." It is also a way to get families involved in the treatment of their loved ones. Finally, just as discussed in marketing, the goal of behavior change messaging is to turn everyday users into message advocates. Once individuals have successfully managed their own personal healthcare, social media provides an avenue for them to share their experiences with others who are just starting or struggling with their journey. These empowered users may be more meaningful to patients than physicians who simply prescribe, but have not had the personal experience in dealing with the illness.

The future of healthcare has a great deal to do with infrastructure, insurance and physician training. These have historically been the traditional powers in the healthcare industry. Hopefully, this chapter has highlighted the important role of social media and today's patients. For the first time, everyday patients are participating in their own treatment, and are able to aid in the treatment of others.

This book has hopefully highlighted the importance of diffusion, community and mobilization when constructing social media messages. While these are important constructs for social media marketing, they also play a role in the way we make and manage all decisions. It is important to consider how these elements fit into the public health arena as well. Public health is often defined as "What we as a society do to assure the condition in which people can be healthy," including the planning and implementation of health communication (Capper & Sands, 2006). Clearly, a healthy public extends well beyond adequate medical treatment when an individual makes a trip to the physician. The following chapters will explore the importance of healthy civic engagement in society, and how our personal well-being is connected to the world and cultures around us.

Key Takeaways

1 Social media has transferred power from traditional healthcare practitioners to everyday patients by raising knowledge levels, providing more choices, and empowering patients.
2 The activation model of information exposure illustrates how making decisions about personal healthcare management is a complicated process that involves the need for activation and arousal.
3 The health belief model prompts practitioners to consider the perceived susceptibility, perceived severity, perceived benefits, and perceived barriers of following through with a health recommendation when designing public health campaign messages.
4 mHealth, or mobile communications and network technologies for healthcare systems, is profoundly changing the health industry by providing an inexpensive and more efficient way for doctors and patients to communicate.
5 Social media can allow a networked approach to provide public health information in otherwise hard-to-reach communities.

References

24/7 Townhall (2010) Videos from 247Townhall.org. Available at https://www.youtube.com/user/247townhall (accessed June 8, 2016).

Ameratunga, S., Smith, E., Kool, B. & Raerino, K. (2012) Feasibility of a brief intervention delivered via mobile phone to reduce harmful drinking and injury among trauma patients in New Zealand. *Addiction Science and Clinical Practice*, 7(Suppl. 1), A92. Available at http://www.ascpjournal.org/content/7/S1/A92 (accessed June 8, 2016).

Appalachian Community Fund (2008) Available at http://www.appalachiancommunityfund.org/central-appalachia/ (accessed June 8, 2016).

Bar, F., Brough, M., Costanza-Chock, S., Gonzalez, C., Wallis, C. & Garces, A. (2009) Mobile voices: a mobile, open source, popular communication platform for first-generation immigrants in Los Angeles. Presented at the International Communication Association Conference in Chicago, Illinois. Available at http://www.lirneasia.net/wp-content/uploads/2009/05/final-paper_bar_et_al.pdf (accessed June 8, 2016).

Bastian, H. (2008) Health literacy and patient information: developing the methodology for a national evidence-based health website. *Patient, Education and Counseling*, 73(3), 551–561.

Berry, L., Parish, J., Janakiraman, R. *et al.* (2008) Patients' commitment to their primary physician and why it matters. *Annals of Family Medicine*, 6(1), 6–13.

Boase, J. & Ling, R. (2013) Measuring mobile phone use: self-report versus log data. *Journal of Computer-Mediated Communication*, 18(4), 508–519.

Bull, S. (2010) *Technology-Based Health Promotion*. Thousand Oaks, CA: Sage Publications.

Capper, S. & Sands, C. (2006) The vital relationship between public health and pharmacy. *International Journal of Pharmacy Education*, Fall, Issue 2, 1–3.

Centers for Disease Control (2013) Health effects of cigarette smoking. Available at http://www.cdc.gov/tobacco/data_statistics/fact_sheets/health_effects/effects_cig_smoking/ (accessed June 8, 2016).

Collins, T., Clark, J., Petersen, L. & Kressin, N. (2002) Racial differences in how patients perceive physician communication regarding cardiac testing. *Medical Care*, 40(1 Suppl.), 27–34.

Couchman G., Forjuoh S. & Rascoe T. (2001) E-mail communications in family practice: what do patients expect? *Journal of Family Practice*, 50, 414–418.

Deaton, A. (2004) Health in an age of globalization. Available at http://www.princeton.edu/rpds/papers/pdfs/deaton_healthglobalage.pdf (accessed June 9, 2016).

Delgreco, C. (2009) Wireless technology set to profoundly change the health industry. Available at http://www.businesswire.com/news/home/20090311006208/en/Wireless-Technology-Set-Profoundly-Change-Health-Industry (accessed June 8, 2016).

Diabetes Family (2013) Diabetes: a family matter. Available at http://www.diabetesfamily.net/ (accessed July 23, 2013).

Donohew, L., Palmgreen, P. & Duncan, J. (1980) An activation model of information exposure. *Communication Monographs*, 47(4), 295–303.

Donohew, L., Lorch, E.P. & Palmgreen, P. (1998) Applications of a theoretic model of information exposure to health interventions. *Human Communication Research*, 24(3), 454–468.

Haean, O., Ray, M. & Allegrante, J. (2008) Perceptions of health care provider communication activity among American cancer survivors and adults without cancer histories: an analysis of the 2003 health information trends survey (HINTS) data. *Journal of Health Communication*, 13(7), 637–653.

Hawn, C. (2009) Take two aspirin and tweet me in the morning: how Twitter, Facebook, and other social media are reshaping health care. *Health Affairs*, 28(2), 361–368.

Hiatt, E. (2013) Mayo Clinic announces video storytelling campaign with Hispanic patients and doctors. Available at http://www.diversityinc.com/diversity-press-releases/mayo-clinic-announces-video-storytelling-campaign-with-hispanic-patients-and-doctors/ (accessed June 8, 2016).

Hochbaum, G., Rosenstock, I. & Kegels, S. (1952) Health belief model. United States Public Health Service. Available at http://www.infosihat.gov.my/infosihat/artikelHP/bahanrujukan/HE_DAN_TEORI/DOC/Health%20Belief%20Model.doc (accessed June 8, 2016).

Intlekofer, K., Cunningham, M. & Caplan, A. (2012) The HPV vaccine controversy. *Medicine and Society*, 14(1), 39–49.

Istepanian, R.S.H., Laxminarayan, S. & Pattichis, C.S. (eds) (2006) *M-health: Emerging Mobile Health Systems*. Berlin: Springer.

ITU (2013) Global ICT developments. Available at http://www.itu.int/en/ITU-D/Statistics/Pages/stat/defa ult.aspx (accessed June 8, 2016).

Janz, N.K. & Becker, M.H. (1984) The health belief model: a decade later. *Health Education and Behavior*, 11(1), 1–47.

Johnson, T. (2012) Online-only: social media tools put condom use on the map. Available at http://thenationshealth .aphapublications.org/content/42/3/E14.full (accessed June 8, 2016).

Ling, R. (2005) The sociolinguistics of SMS: an analysis of SMS use by a random sample of Norwegians. In: R. Ling & P.E. Pedersen (eds) *Mobile Communications: Renegotiation of the Social Sphere*, pp. 335–349. London: Springer.

McMillan, S. & Macias, W. (2008) Strengthening the safety net for online seniors: factors influencing differences in health information seeking among older Internet users. *Journal of Health Communication*, 13(8), 778–792.

Morahan-Martin, J. & Anderson, C.D. (2000) Information and misinformation online: recommendations for facilitating accurate mental health information retrieval and evaluation. *CyberPsychology and Behavior*, 3(5), 731–746.

National Cancer Institute (2001) *Making Health Communication Programs Work*. Bethesda, MD: NCI.

Olson, P. (2012) 5 eye-opening stats that show the world is going mobile. Available at http://www.forbes.com/sites/ parmyolson/2012/12/04/5-eye-opening-stats-that-show -the-world-is-going-mobile/ (accessed June 8, 2016).

Pew Internet and American Life Project (2012) What Facebook and Twitter mean for news. Available at http://state ofthemedia.org/2012/mobile-devices-and-news-consu mption-some-good-signs-for-journalism/what-facebo ok-and-twitter-mean-for-news/ (accessed June 8, 2016).

Ratzan, S., Stearns, N., Payne, J., Amato, P., Liebergott, J. & Madoff, M. (1994). Education for the health communication professional: a collaborative curricular partnership. *American Behavioral Scientist*, 38(2), 361–380.

Roter, D. & Hall, J. (2006) *Doctors Talking With Patients/Patients Talking With Doctors: Improving Communication in Medical Visits*. Westport, CT: Praeger.

Say, R., Murtagh, M. & Thomson, R. (2006) Patients' preference for involvement in medical decision making: a narrative review. *Patient Education and Counseling*, 60(2), 102–114.

Sensei (2009) Sensei for weight loss. Available at http:// www.sensei.com (accessed June 8, 2016).

Sherifali, D. & Pinelli, J. (2007) Parent as proxy reporting implications and recommendations for quality of life research. *Journal of Family Nursing*, 13(1), 83–98.

University of Kentucky (2001) Communication capstone theory workbook. Available at http://www.uky.edu/~ drlane/capstone/health/act.html (accessed June 8, 2016).

U.S. Department of Health and Human Services (2000) Healthy people. Available at http://www.healthypeople .gov/2020/default.aspx (accessed June 8, 2016).

Zimmerman, R. (2007) Don't 4get ur pills: text messaging for health. Available at http://www.wsj .com/articles/SB119551720462598532 (accessed June 8, 2016).

14

Social Media and Civic Engagement

Learning Objectives

After reading this chapter, you should be able to:
1 Understand the historical shifts of civic engagement.
2 Apply civic engagement to the concept of the individual self.
3 Identify the influence of social media on political communication.

Introduction

Effective and regular communication with physicians is just one step towards a positive and healthy lifestyle. Chapter 13 explained how social media helps increase the frequency of health communication and aids positive personal health management. However, there is much more to happy citizens than achieving good health. Research demonstrates how an increase in civic engagement and volunteering leads to better physical and mental health (Lum and Lightfoot, 2005; Batista & Cruz-Ledón, 2013). *Civic engagement*, or membership in formal community groups and participation in social activities (Shah, 1998), is an easy way to bolster your own sense of belonging and accomplishment within a culture. Chapter 3 demonstrated the importance of communities in our lives. People feel better about themselves whenever they are making a positive impact on society. Social media technologies make it is easier than ever for individuals to get involved in organizations and join causes that they care about.

Strategic Social Media: From Marketing to Social Change, First Edition. L. Meghan Mahoney and Tang Tang.
© 2017 John Wiley & Sons, Inc. Published 2017 by John Wiley & Sons, Inc.

The benefits of civic engagement do not stop at individual needs. Social connectedness leads to better schools, faster economic development, lower crime rates, and more effective government in society (Putnam, 1995). The greatest advantage of becoming a civically engaged citizen is that you are able to help others while also helping yourself. Chapter 13 urged you to consider strengthening health communication between physicians and patients at the community level for better self-care. The remaining chapters in this section encourage you to consider individualized behavior change to positively influence the lives of a larger community. Small steps can make a big difference to others.

Remember from Chapter 3 our discussion of why community is so important to the behavior change process? Humans actively seek communities, whether they are based on proximity, mutual interests, health concerns, or family. These social networks play the strongest role in how we behave and construct the world around us. The building blocks of community – membership, shared emotional connection, influence, and needs fulfillment (McMillan & Chavis, 1986) – allow individuals to share in an identity and engage in dialogue with members (Campbell & Jovchelovitch, 2000). Many of these dimensions have now shifted, and are being fulfilled in the virtual realm. Social media provides resources for maximizing our own personal identity, as well as our collective identity.

Collective identity is a social psychological concept that helps to explain the human need to be part of a larger group, especially when tackling larger social issues. With a strong collective identity, movements are able to garner more support and power because individuals feel as though they are all working towards common goals. There is more power in larger groups. As long as the larger group has clearly defined objectives, opponents, and an integrated sense of being that is incorporated into the movement ideologies, they can become a strong force in society (McCaughey & Ayer, 2003). In a world with unlimited information at your fingertips, it has become nearly impossible to live in isolation from the world around you. It is only natural to find community with others who share in your vision.

Traditional top-down diffusion media made it easy to receive information and messages. Many utilized this opportunity to share crisis information from around the globe. You may remember hearing calls for individuals to send in money to help feed a child in a different part of the world. But what if you did not have any expendable income? Does that mean that you were unable to help the cause? Often, the solutions offered were based on predetermined objectives and targeted towards a mass audience. Social media allows individuals to seek out information, engage in dialogue, and come up with collective solutions and action plans that work best within their lifestyle. Perhaps a group of similarly minded individuals are able to put their resources together to help coordinate a fundraiser or event.

Social media makes it easier than ever to make a positive difference in the world. Technology has connected the world on a smaller, more tightly bound scale. Stiglitz (2002) explains how *globalization* has integrated the countries and people of the world through an increase in transportation and communication. This has resulted in a breakdown of barriers between the flow of goods, services and knowledge across borders. Think of your own social network: you have likely been able to stay in touch with individuals from many parts of your life that you otherwise would have lost touch with if not for social media. Maybe you have friends that you met from a summer camp, a study trip abroad, or even just a random night out with friends long ago. These connections are difficult to maintain without regular contact, and social media allows the opportunity with little effort from either party. Our sense of connection and network has completely transformed.

The purpose of this chapter is to explore the influence of social media on the nature and shape of civic engagement, and how it proves different from any other era. There is much ongoing debate in the field of communication about whether technologies are eroding our sense of civic responsibility (Stoll, 1995; Putnam, 2000; Dahlgren, 2009) or making it easier to get involved in our communities (Lévy, 1997; Rheingold, 2008). In order to better answer these questions, this chapter explores the historical trends of civic engagement, the influence of civic engagement on individuals, and the impact technology has on political communication and behavior change.

Historical Shifts of Civic Engagement

It would prove impossible to generalize levels of civic engagement across the world throughout history. While one country may experience record high levels, others may be in the process of disengaging. Civic engagement is a complex and dynamic process. While we often associate high levels of civic engagement as a positive phenomenon, spikes in levels may actually indicate problems within a culture, rather than a fluid functioning society.

In Chapter 4 we discussed one of the largest instances of collective action and civic engagement for social change, the Egyptian Revolution of 2011. Social media played an intricate role in connecting and organizing individuals beyond their own individual social networks to urge Mubarak to resign. We have discussed the many benefits of a civically engaged society, but lower levels of activism may actually indicate complacency with the status quo. How do you keep citizens from staying involved when they are happy with the way things are going?

In America alone there have been many changes over time in the extent and purpose for which individuals got involved in their community (Figure 14.1). In the 1950s, civic engagement was high, especially through union membership, volunteering at schools and religious organizations following World World II. In the 1960s this engagement shifted towards public demonstrations against oppression and gender rights, signifying an increase in citizens' sense of empowerment and dissatisfaction with government. This generation produced the National Organization of Women, Peace Corps, and Martin Luther King's "I Have a Dream" speech. The 1970s continued these fights, as well as protests against the Vietnam War and a greater awareness for environmental green initiatives. The 1980s were characterized as the "Me decade" due to low levels of individual volunteering at the community level. Parents were not as involved in local parent–teacher associations or the Red Cross. However, LGBT rights and healthcare reform were huge issues in the fight against the HIV/AIDS epidemic. In the 1990s, youth were seen as apathetic and irony-obsessed slackers. The 1992 Presidential election was the first time in twenty years that demonstrated an increase in youth voting, partly due to MTV's "Rock the Vote" campaign. There was also an increase in nonprofit organizations, anti-sweatshop labor movements, and peace building work. The millennium drastically changed how individuals communicate with one another through social media platforms. Social media has emerged as a primary tool for

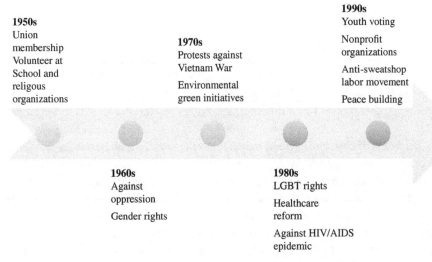

1950s
Union membership
Volunteer at School and religous organizations

1970s
Protests against Vietnam War
Environmental green initiatives

1990s
Youth voting
Nonprofit organizations
Anti-sweatshop labor movement
Peace building

1960s
Against oppression
Gender rights

1980s
LGBT rights
Healthcare reform
Against HIV/AIDS epidemic

Figure 14.1   Civic engagement timeline. Source: Author.

communicating with personal communities, political organizing, and aiding disaster relief efforts. Since 2010, young people are being seen as more socially, politically and civically engaged than ever before, especially with regard to human and LGBT rights in America (Koenig, 2013).

This timeline demonstrates just one country's flux in civic engagement levels. Here, you can see how complex and interconnected involvement is with issues of freedom, politics, public health, and technology. Every society, culture and subculture has their own dynamic process for when levels increase and decrease. There are also many different types of civic engagement, making it difficult to monitor and evaluate as a whole.

Researchers suggest that one of the most difficult problems facing Western democracy today is the decline in citizens' political engagement (Dahlgren, 2009; Shah, 1998). They worry is that the industrial and information revolution has led to the decline of community due to the weakening of private community, including contact with neighbors and friends; the decline of public community, such as voluntary organizations and civic concerns; and disengagement from community, including the willingness to contribute to the well-being of the community (Quan-Haase *et al.*, 2002). Many believe that technology is making individuals more and more individualistic and less concerned about how their behaviors impact the group.

There are many reasons for this decline in community, including increased television watching, more women in the workplace, increased mobility of families, and changing dynamics (Shah, 1998). People criticize technology for playing a role in this process because it takes people away from their in-person communities and replaces it with virtual ones (Stoll, 1995). However, these virtual communities could be utilized as public spaces to discuss cultural issues and mobilize civic action.

In Chapter 3, we discussed Putnam's (2000) book *Bowling Alone*. This text portrayed today's generation as having the lowest trends of civic engagement and social capital in history, illustrating how there are higher instances of bowling, but fewer leagues than ever in our nation's history. Putnam (2000) believes that electronic entertainment is the cause of decreased civic engagement due to its ability to transform people into a society of watchers rather than doers. Other researchers believe that the information era proves a positive and significant predictor of individual social capital and civic and political participatory behaviors, online and offline (Gil de Zúñiga *et al.*, 2012). They demonstrate how the Internet is being incorporated into the routine practices of everyday life, including social capital.

While our levels of civic engagement may not have changed significantly, they are definitely becoming augmented and more geographically dispersed (Quan-Haase *et al.*, 2002). The Internet is providing new ways of engaging in community and the finding of information (Lévy, 1997). This process is more genuine, because it allows us to interact with others without our voices, faces and bodies serving as a distraction to our message (McCaughey & Ayer, 2003). Here, audiences are active information-seekers and are driving the engagement process, rather than being forced to participate in something that is not as relevant to their gratifications and needs.

Quan-Haase *et al.* (2002) explain how individuals who spend more time online value the Internet for its positive social virtues and use it as a space for collective interactions. This purpose is a complementary and alternative way to find community in addition to those available offline. Our personal causes and interest in engagement are closely linked to personality and preferences. The Internet allows us the ability to seek out those activities that sound most appealing, even if they are not directly in our own community.

Regardless of the influence new technologies have on levels of civic engagement, it is safe to say that they are not going anywhere. Younger generations are increasingly using social media to express themselves, explore their identities and connect with peers as active creators and consumers of culture (Rheingold, 2008). New technologies are transforming civic engagement. Today, you are able to share information just as quickly with your next-door neighbor as you are with individuals across the globe. Social media makes civic participation easy and free and increases the types of advocacy efforts with which they are able to engage (McAllister, 2013).

The appeal of civic engagement through social media has much to do with the many benefits of participatory media discussed in Chapter 4. It allows users the ability to control conversation through blogs, wikis, RSS, tagging, social bookmarking, music/photo/video sharing, mashups, podcasts, digital storytelling, virtual communities, social network services, virtual environments, and videoblogs (Rheingold, 2008). Just as in the marketing realm, participatory media leads to more educated, empowered and motivated citizens (Boulos & Wheeler, 2006). There is something more inherently satisfying about deciding that you want to make a change and organizing action to do so than to be told what to do by someone in a position of higher power.

Technology is the future of civic engagement. While previous generations may have had to physically travel to Congress to march on the front lawn in order to protest, today's Internet users are able to voice concerns from their living room. The challenge becomes making their voice heard when everyone else is doing the same thing. Thus, let's now explore the potential of social media and the impact involvement has on voicing the individual self.

Civic Engagement and the Individual Self

Mass media has traditionally been used to voice public sphere issues. Chapter 3 discussed key differences between private and public sphere issues of communication. Private sphere involves issues such as family, relationship, goals, values, and health. Public sphere topics include issues of civic activity, news, politics, weather, and sports. Habermas (1992) imagined the public sphere as a place for citizens to engage the political process through critical and rational deliberation. This was the space for civic engagement. Media has traditionally been an outlet for the public sphere; a place to go when you are interested in consuming "water cooler talk." Think of television and radio as the replacement for individuals standing in the middle of crowded streets screaming to the masses on a soapbox. Today, social media has transformed this public space into a convergence of both private and public forms. The blurring sphere has interesting implications when it comes to civic engagement.

The importance of our personal social network cannot be understated. Putnam (1993) describes the function and social elements of network, norms and trust of our private sphere as our social capital. *Social capital* enables citizens to work together more effectively to resolve collective action problems. Social capital is also a public good because it benefits such a wider community than just the self. There is power in numbers and individuals are able to accomplish more if they are part of a larger group with tangible goals.

You may have heard the saying that "It is not what you know, but who you know." Perhaps you were encouraged to take more internship opportunities in college with hopes that the experience and relationships formed would lead to your first job out of college. We like to believe that we live in a society where with enough hard work anyone can achieve anything. However, the truth is that a larger social structure has much to do with who succeeds and who does not.

Your social capital of where you live and who you know helps to define who you are and thus to determine your fate (Putnam, 1993). For centuries, social groups were bound by proxemics to make connections and had to rely on local social capital. Many minority groups lack connections that allow them to get their feet in the door of the workforce. Nonetheless, social media today is able to minimize these inconsistencies, though not equalize them, by allowing individuals to connect through mutual causes, interests and collective actions. Social media is the new face of community engagement and allows anyone to communicate directly with decision-makers (McAllister, 2013).

Social capital is seen as one of the most vital ingredients to economic development around the world. Each individual must find his or her own voice, or unique style of personal expression that distinguishes one's communication from those of another (Rheingold, 2008). Once you are able to identify your voice, you are better able to engage with society as a citizen, moving from a private to a public voice. When aggregated with dialogue of the voices of other individuals, your voice becomes *public opinion*.

Remember from Chapter 3 the importance of authenticity, or recognizing and harnessing what you uniquely bring to the table. The same is true of your public voice. It should encompass your experiences, identity construction and confirmation. What if someone were to give you $100 to donate to any organization or cause of your choice? Where would you choose to donate? Perhaps you have received a scholarship that allowed you to attend college. You know how important this was in your own life, so you choose to donate your money to a similar scholarship fund. Maybe your family has a history of breast cancer and so you choose to donate the money towards a cancer research organization. Animal lovers may choose to donate the money to their local animal shelter or the World Wildlife Fund.

We decide what issues are important to us based on our own lived experiences. If someone were to give you that money 100 years ago, chances are you would not have donated to the same organization. Without new media, you may not have known about that scholarship or ever even heard of the World Wildlife Fund. You were bound by the experiences of your local community. Most likely, the money would have gone to a local church or nonprofit organization within your own community, within walking distance from your home.

Today, you receive millions of messages from all over the world about causes, concerns and organizations that need help. Some of these organizations are consistent with your own values and life experiences, but most of them are not. The only way to truly make a difference and find your authentic voice is to seek a community that shares in your values and passions. When utilizing social media to choose a civic engagement platform, it is important to have a strong action plan in place.

Civic Engagement Action Plan

1   Determine your own passions and values. What makes you excited about becoming civically engaged?
2   Seek out organizations that share in this vision. Don't become distracted by all of the other "virtual noise."
3   Research the authenticity and transparency of various organizations working towards this cause.
4   Determine whether you are able to make a tangible difference and mobilize for the organization, or whether you are just involved to improve your own virtual identity.
5   Spread awareness through your own social capital and network to recruit strong mobilized advocates with the same goals.

There is no reason to get involved with every organization or cause that asks you to connect through social media. We prefer that our online identity be associated with positive organizations and nonprofits. There is something appealing about having your social network see that you are connected with the local animal shelter. However, if you secretly have no interest in pets or animals, you should not feel pressured to connect with an organization just because it is a good cause. Their initiatives may be someone else's cause; you should only connect with those organizations that share in your voice and values.

When it comes to online activism, significant money and resources can be invested into social media with little return. Without a strong voice and little authenticity, efforts may result in "*slacktivism*" or half-hearted online activity that has no real effect on real-life outcomes (Morozov, 2009). One reason that this phenomenon may be so common is because social media makes it so easy to virtually connect. With just a click of a mouse an individual can say that they would like to receive more information and updates about an organization, even if they have no real interest in the mission. You may feel bad about turning down an organization that is trying to establish safe mining conditions and fair wages for diamond miners all over the world. It is okay to say no and be happy that someone else is interested in fighting for that cause. That person is just not you.

Research indicates that 57% of Facebook users connect with a charity on Facebook because they want to publicly display their support for the nonprofit (Mansfield, 2013). They want their friends to positively associate them with good causes. However, 43% of Facebook users "unlike" a charity on Facebook because they feel as though that charity posts messages too frequently. This means that individuals do not actually want to receive information and updates from the charity that they chose to connect with. Before agreeing to connect with a nonprofit organization, ask yourself if you really have the passion or energy to get involved. Otherwise, you are not really doing the nonprofit or yourself any favors.

What happens when you connect with a cause or organization that you feel as though shares in your voice and interests? Perhaps it is the same charity you decided would receive your $100 donation. You have decided that you want to increase your own life and the lives around you, and have actively sought out a connection with the charity of your choice. However, you may not actually have the expendable money to donate. Maybe the charity is too far away to actively volunteer and get involved with, or maybe you just do not have the time right now. Is connecting through social media really going to make a difference?

One problem with virtual civic engagement is that you may actually feel as though you are helping without doing anything for the cause. While this satisfies the natural human desire to help others, not much is done towards the mission objectives of the organization (Morozov, 2009), which is especially true with organizations that only ask social media users to connect or "like" them on social media.

Thus it is important for you to make an active effort to do more than just connect with the organization. Be a participatory user. Share your opinions and contribute your voice to the ongoing discussions. Even if there is little you can do financially or through volunteer work, you are contributing to the organization's public opinion and that is a huge step towards becoming a campaign advocate. Spread awareness through your own social capital and network. It's a great first step towards becoming actively involved, even if most of your tangible participation is in the future.

If you are in charge of communication for a nonprofit or charity organization, be sure that you are not spending all your efforts towards gaining social media numbers. While it is important to spread awareness about your organization's efforts, you do not want to be connected with hundreds of users who do not want to receive your messages and do not share in your voice. A few highly participatory and active connections will do more for your cause than if everyone on Facebook was passively connected. Also, remember to give those users who do want to participate clear and tangible direction. This should include monetary contributions, volunteering opportunities, and active dialogue centered around core issues in the area. Such tangible direction will allow everyone the ability to participate in areas that they feel comfortable with given their personal circumstances.

This section illustrates how to successfully connect causes with individual voice and passion. These recommendations will result in relationships that endure across a lifetime of advocacy. However, some acts of civic engagement require one-time real-life mobilization efforts. The field of political communication has explored how to prompt citizens to not only support a candidate's platform, but what it takes to transform that support into real-life votes on election day.

Technology and Political Communication

While civic participation includes activities such as volunteering for charities, attending political rallies, and forwarding online messages for social action, researchers generally equate participation with electoral activity (Gil de Zúñiga *et al.*, 2012). Everyone has her or his own feelings about democratic elections. Many are excited to participate in the privilege of voting. Others begrudgingly deal with the onslaught of political advertisement campaigns in the months leading in. Yet others remain apathetic to the entire process.

American rhetoric teaches children that voting is the duty of citizenry (Jones & Hudson, 2000). However, with over $6 billion spent on campaign advertisements, only 57.2% of eligible voters participated in the 2012 American Presidential election (Gans, 2012). Much research has been carried out into increasing these numbers and prompting voters, particularly first-time voters, to engage in the electoral process.

Voter turnout and decision-making over the past three decades has been a dynamic and complicated field of research study. Social media has drastically changed the way we receive and disseminate political news. Today's Americans are the first generation who grew into voting age with unlimited information (and misinformation) at their fingertips. It is their right and freedom to express their cultures, beliefs, views, and values. Social media provides a public sphere for everyday citizens to debate and engage dialogue with their own social network (Burgess *et al.*, 2006).

Political discussion is difficult, and some people feel as though there is no place for it on social media. Some may advise you that it is best not to discuss alcohol use, religion or politics on social networking sites. While there is some truth to these recommendations, especially with regard to alcohol use, this section argues that healthy public dialogue is essential to an informed citizenry.

Before engaging a political discussion on an online forum, be sure that you take extra efforts to demonstrate that you are contributing to the conversation in a respectful manner. Tell others when you agree with them, and if you do not, point out that you respect where they are coming from and then explain why your life experience has made you feel differently. Encourage them to share their opinion, because you should want to hear more. Even if you are not interested in changing your opinion, it helps to understand why other people feel differently from you. If you are not interested in hearing what others say, chances are you are not in a place to contribute to the discussion.

Social media has become the space where young adults go to read and share political information. The Internet has developed into a key political information source, as the percentage of Americans who obtained political information online between 1996 and 2008 rose from 4 to 40% (Kushin & Yamamoto, 2010). Just as television changed the election process by allowing voters to see candidates rather than simply hear them through radio, social media has been the most politically significant technological innovation of the twentieth century (Hong & Nadler, 2012), by providing candidates the opportunity to talk directly to voters and, more importantly, by granting voters access to talk directly with candidates. This holds great opportunity for creating a culture of openness, transparency and more egalitarian relationships.

President Barack Obama has been lauded for being one of the first politicians to successfully incorporate social media into his 2008 Presidential campaign. He successfully harnessed 13 million individuals on his email list, 3 million on his text messaging programs, and 5 million connections on more than 15 social networking sites. In addition, 8.5 million people visited his website (MyBarackObama.com) monthly, and 3 million personal phone calls were placed in the last four days of the campaign (Lutz, 2009). This multiplatform social media strategy mobilized people to utilize grassroots measures to spread campaign messages, campaigns and materials to their individual networks and transformed support into money and tangible votes.

While many candidates before Barack Obama also utilized social media in their campaigns, they were not as successful at transforming online connections into message advocacy. As we discussed with regard to social media marketing, sending messages on social media platforms does not mean that the information process is participatory.

Despite the success of Barack Obama's campaign, many politicians continue to use the social media outlets in the same top-down manner as traditional media platforms. Few politicians use their accounts to engage or answer voters. In fact, it was not until Father's Day 2011 that President Barack Obama (@BarackObama) actually sent a tweet himself (Thomson, 2012). In 2015, Obama opened his own Twitter account (@POTUS) and was able to directly communicate with Internet audiences, leading him to break social media records. He was the fastest user to reach 1 million followers, hitting the milestone in under five hours (Molina, 2015). While social media allows users to individually engage politicians, few are capitalizing on the opportunity. Instead, politicians are relying on users to engage their friends and social network about their support for individual candidates and platforms.

One reason politicians may not be eager to utilize social media in a participatory manner is due to the control–participation balance that we discussed in Chapter 3. In order to allow users to participate, a politician must give up some control over what appears on his or her social media site. It does not matter what President Barack Obama posts on his official Facebook account, users will respond in both positive and inflammatory ways. For instance, on Sunday, July 28, 2013, the President's Facebook page (Facebook.com/BarackObama) posted a picture of children petting their family Portugese Water Dog, Bo, stating that he is always a "Crowd pleaser." While this is not a very politically divisive message, users commented on the picture to express their dissatisfaction with high gas prices, Cambodian election results, immigration reform, and federal budget cuts. Politicians have the option of leaving the comment function open and allowing these comments to appear, or to turn off the comment function and have more control over what appears on their site. Most choose not to censor their audience completely, but do not respond to them either.

In addition to understanding how politicians are communicating with voters through social media, one of the most interesting takeaways of current voter research is the influence social media has on voter turnout. In one research study, a message was posted on various Facebook pages for users who were at least 18 years of age in the United States on Election Day, November 2, 2010. Users who received this message were shown a statement on top of their news feed that encouraged them to vote, providing a link to a local polling place and a clickable button where they could self-report that "I voted." This message would then be shared with their social network and displayed a counter of other users that had reported voting, including the names and faces of those that they know. Another group of Facebook users received the voting information, but were not shown the names and faces of friends. A third group received no message on their timeline.

Results from the study demonstrate that users who received the message with the names and faces of friends from their social network were significantly more likely to vote than users who received no message at all. Turnout among individuals who received the diffusion-only message, with no names or images from social network, proved identical to those with no message at all. This demonstrates the ineffectiveness of information-only appeals (Bond *et al.*, 2012). Community proved the significant game changer for voting behaviors.

Based on what we know about behavior change research, it makes sense that individuals would be influenced to follow through with a requested behavior change if they know that their social network is also participating. Humans model the behaviors of those who they identify with around them. Moreover, we seek community, and believe that issues that are important to our friends and family have importance to us as well.

Now we understand the importance that our private sphere relationships have on our political attitudes, a public sphere topic. Social media is the only media platform, thus far, that is able to converge these two spheres to encourage active voter participation. Each election cycle we learn more about what works and what does not. However, it is important that human behavior change theory is not forgotten as new technologies emerge. Humans want to participate and share with their network. It is important to investigate how other types of organizations encourage users to do so through social media.

This chapter has explored the process of civic engagement and the influence technology has had on individual willingness to participate, sense of self, and political engagement. Social media plays an increasingly critical role in how individuals find community and mobilize efforts into collective action. In this chapter, we discuss the importance of finding your personal voice and seeking causes and organizations that share in your passions and interests. However, some campaigns are hoping to raise awareness about issues that are invisible to the general public. The nongovernmental organization Invisible Children Inc. aimed to accomplish just that through the "Stop Kony" movement.

Case Study: *Kony 2012*

Kony 2012 is a 30-minute video that informs audiences about the horrific behavior of Joseph Kony, leader of the Ugandan group the Lord's Resistance Army that promotes guerilla warfare, including the use of abducted children as soldiers (Chatterjee, 2012). The video includes interviews with children who use personal narrative techniques to increase awareness about the terrible things that Kony was forcing them to do. Jason Russell, the film's director and overarching voice to the film's narrative, explains how he personally got involved in this campaign to capture Kony after meeting and becoming friends with Jacob, one of Kony's victims (Goodman & Preston, 2012). This story provided the film with much-needed authenticity, as it was clear to audiences that Russell was personally vested in and cared for the charity's mission.

Beyond a call to capture Kony, the film also asked for individuals to participate in a "Cover the Night" event on April 20, 2012. The event asked people to form teams with their interpersonal network and register on their campaign website, Kony2012.com. The video instantly went viral. It gained over 40 million views on YouTube and more than 13 million views on Vimeo. People were sharing the video on Twitter through the hashtag #kony2012. Celebrities tweeted their support of the campaign, including Oprah Winfrey, Ryan Seacrest, Kim Kardashian, and Justin Beiber (Goodman & Preston, 2012). Over 3.5 million pledges were registered on the "Cover the Night" website to participate in the event (Thomson, 2012). The campaign spread around the world, especially in North America, Europe, and Australia (Carroll, 2012).

One of the greatest successes of the viral spread of *Kony 2012* was its ability to connect individuals from around the world with the lives and citizens of Uganda. The video urged individuals to share the video's message with their social network, donate money, wear campaign paraphernalia, and attend the "Cover the Night" event, all in hope of raising awareness about the cause. It told a larger story of globalization and hope, urging younger generations to push back against the mainstream media and redefine culture (Thomson, 2012).

The social media campaign also urged audiences through the immediacy message "Nothing is more powerful than an idea whose time is now" (Kony, 2012). Individuals were able to brand themselves with the cause by selling action kits, which included shirts, wristbands and stickers. The purpose of these action kits was to use paraphernalia in spreading awareness with registered "Cover the Night" teams on April 20, 2012. On this day, cities were to be covered in event posters and stickers and rallies across the world.

However, weeks leading into the "Cover the Night" event, as the video became more and more popular, many media outlets began investigating Invisible Children Foundation, since the website had little transparency for the efforts and funds from the campaign. Criticisms and backlash began hitting social media outlets.

A 19-year-old college student from Nova Scotia created a blog on Tumblr called "Visible Children" and broke Invisible Children's charitable spending practices, citing that only 32% of campaign funds actually go towards the cause (Goodman & Preston,

2012). The government and citizens of Uganda made public statements resisting the video as well, stating that they felt that the video was over-dramatized and generalized the situation (Thomson, 2012). The oversimplified statement that Invisible Children used to appeal to everyone and get users engaged was the very same message that turned users away weeks later.

Additionally, Jason Russell, the director and voice of the campaign, was detained in San Diego after incoherently yelling and disrupting traffic in his underwear about a month before the "Cover the Night" event (Huffington Post, 2012). This prompted Invisible Children to post a public message on their website that reads:

> Jason Russell was unfortunately hospitalized yesterday suffering from exhaustion, dehydration, and malnutrition. He is now receiving medical care and is focused on getting better. The past two weeks have taken a severe emotional toll on all of us, Jason especially, and that toll manifested itself in an unfortunate incident yesterday. Jason's passion and his work have done so much to help so many, and we are devastated to see him dealing with this personal health issue. We will always love and support Jason, and we ask that you give his entire family privacy during this difficult time.

These events left Invisible Children in the midst of a public relations crisis. The movement's "Cover the Night" event, which urged registered teams around the world to blanket cities with *Kony 2012* paraphernalia fell short (Carroll, 2012). When the day arrived for registered teams to show their support and mobilize action in cities, the momentum of the movement had already passed.

There are many lessons we can learn from the *Kony 2012* campaign. The first is the potential global virality of a social media campaign with no formal advertising. If a campaign is able to tell a strong narrative, and emotionally appeal to users, the story will spread. The potential of spreading awareness through individual social networks is huge.

However, while the authenticity of Jason Russell's concern for the *Kony 2012* movement was evident, the campaign lacked tangible direction with its mobilization efforts. It is easy for users to go online and pledge to mobilize themselves, but in this case the mobilization being asked during the "Cover the Night" event was just additional awareness about the campaign. People were happy to spread and share the message with their personal networks, which led to a global awareness campaign unprecedented in history. Nonetheless, it led advocates to question how much awareness was enough. At some point, campaigns must move beyond awareness and demonstrate tangible outcomes from all of the supporters' efforts.

As discussed in Chapter 2, equally as important as message authenticity is clear transparency of campaign goals and monetary funds. Donors felt duped when they discovered that only 32% of campaign funds were going towards the cause. Information about where funds were going and the impact they were making should have been available on the Invisible Children website. This would have increased the amount of trust and loyalty advocates had with the campaign.

Finally, and perhaps most importantly, the Invisible Children campaign was tied to the voice of its director, Jason Russell. While this was essential to the initial awareness stages of the movement, it never moved on towards a participatory advocacy. Once Russell found himself in the middle of the public relations crisis, the movement was not able to rebrand itself away from his image or voice.

It would have been better if the campaign had asked smaller mobilization actions from users. It then could have used social media to allow others to contribute to the narrative and share their stories about the campaign. Russell's voice was powerful and made a huge impact on awareness. However, in order to translate into a successful mobilization campaign, others must also contribute to the dialogue and form a collective public opinion to help shape the movement.

Discussion questions

1   How did social media make it easier to spread the *Kony 2012* video? Why was the content of the message something that so many Internet users felt inclined to spread to their social network?
2   What are some possible reasons why the *Kony 2012* movement did not result in tangible social change outcomes? What could future social change campaigns do differently to mobilize audiences into action?
3   What role did narratives play in the spread of the *Kony 2012* movement? How could the movement have had less of Jason Russell's narrative, and more from its audiences?

Summary

This chapter illustrates the influence and impact of social media on civic engagement. While we are still not certain whether this change is inherently good or bad, we do know that it is here to stay and holds great potential for breaking some traditional power structures, such as the oppression of minority networks and the relationship between political candidates and citizens.

We have learned that levels of civic engagement are constantly in flux, and today's digital climate allows us the opportunity to find causes and goals that match our own voice, experiences and passions. The opportunity for connecting with individuals around the world is unprecedented, and it is important to capitalize on the many benefits of getting involved.

Social media has changed the way individuals make decisions about their community, the world, and the people in charge. The tools and function of social media make it possible to engage everyday citizens with political candidates. People's expectations of the political process have thus changed, as the community has grown beyond proximity boundaries and the issues and people we care about are bigger than ever before.

Social media is undoubtedly a game changer in the civic engagement arena. The technology is designed to allow society and groups within it to interact for their own needs and objectives. With enough virality, an invisible social media campaign can transform into public opinion. Nonetheless, while social media opportunity means great things for social change, it takes transparent and authentic voice as well as organized mobilization.

In order to maximize the amount of possible social change, people must feel as though they have control over their content. Social media brings opportunities for individuals to express their opinions, join causes, and interweave the private world of family and friends with their public interests (Valenzuela, 2013). The field of communication for development also believes that social media can be used for positive social change. Let's now explore this area in greater detail, and explain how to best incorporate media into development initiatives in Chapter 15.

Key Takeaways

1 Civic engagement allows individuals to meet in community groups and participate in social activities, leading to better health, sense of belonging, accomplishment, economic development, and more effective government within a
   society.
2 Globalization has integrated people around the world by breaking down many
   traditional barriers and transforming civic engagement to more augmented and
   geographically dispersed initiatives.
3 Groups with tangible goals and a clear voice are able to accomplish more than
   individuals alone. As individual voices become aggregated, they come together to
   form public opinion.
4 There is a danger that online activism has little authenticity and no real effect
   on real-life outcomes. It is important to seek out civic engagement that speaks to
   your experiences and passions, because half-hearted engagement may satisfy your
   desire to help others with little impact on society.
5 The Internet has become a key source for political information and significantly
   changed the election process by granting candidates and citizens the opportunity
   to communicate with greater openness and transparency, though few are using it
   to its full potential.
6 Social media campaigns should move beyond the awareness stage of advocacy,
   and encourage supporters to share in the narrative.

References

Batista, L.C. & Cruz-Ledón, A.M. (2013) The relationship between civic engagement and health among older adults. Available at http://digitalcommons.fiu.edu/cgi/viewcontent.cgi?article=1113&context=sferc (accessed June 8, 2016).

Bond, R., Fariss, C., Jones, J. *et al.* (2012) A 61-million-person experiment in social influence and political mobilization. *Nature*, 489 (7415), 295–298.

Boulos, K. & Wheeler, S. (2007) The emerging Web 2.0 social software: an enabling suite of sociable technologies in health and health care education. *Health Information and Libraries Journal*, 24, 2–23.

Burgess, J., Foth, M. & Klaebe, H. (2006) Everyday creativity as civic engagement: a cultural citizenship view of new media. Available at http://eprints.qut.edu.au/5056/ (accessed June 8, 2016).

Campbell, C. & Jovchelovitch, S. (2000) Health, community and development: towards a social psychology of participation. *Journal of Community and Applied Social Psychology*, 10(4), 255–270.

Carroll, R. (2012) Kony 2012 Cover the Night fails to move from the Internet to the streets. Available at http://www.theguardian.com/world/2012/apr/21/kony-2012-campaign-uganda-warlord (accessed June 8, 2016).

Chatterjee, S. (2012) Joseph Kony 30 minutes viral video shows power of social media. Available at http://www.ibtimes.com/joseph-kony-30-minutes-viral-video-shows-power-social-media-423830 (accessed June 8, 2016).

Dahlgren, P. (2009) *Media and Political Engagement*. New York: Cambridge University Press.

Gans, C. (2012) Bipartisan Policy Center. Available at http://bipartisanpolicy.org/sites/default/files/2012%20Voter%20Turnout%20Full%20Report.pdf (accessed June 8, 2016).

Gil de Zúñiga, H., Jung, N. & Valenzuela, S. (2012) Social media use for news and individuals' social capital, civic engagement and political participation. *Journal of Computer-Mediated Communication*, 17(3), 319–336.

Goodman, D. & Preston, J. (2012) How the Kony video went viral. Available at http://thelede.blogs.nytimes.com/2012/03/09/how-the-kony-video-went-viral/ (accessed June 8, 2016).

Habermas, J. (1992) *The Structural Transformation of the Public Sphere: An Inquiry into a Category of Bourgeois Society*. Cambridge, MA: Polity Press.

Hong, S. & Nadler, D. (2012) Which candidates do the public discuss online in an election campaign: the use of social media by 2012 Presidential candidates and its impact on candidate salience. *Government Information Quarterly*, 29(4), 455–461.

Huffington Post (2012) Jason Russell arrested? Co-Founder of Invisible Children "Kony 2012" creator, not charged in San Diego. Available at http://www.huffingtonpost.com/2012/03/16/jason-russell-arrested-invisible-children-kony_n_1354455.html (accessed June 8, 2016).

Jones, P. & Hudson, J. (2000) Civic duty and expressive voting: is virtue its own reward? *Kyklos*, 53(1), 3–16.

Koenig, L. (2013) Civic engagement: then and now. Available at http://werepair.org/civic-engagement-then-and-now/ (accessed June 8, 2016).

Kony (2012) http://www.youtube.com/watch?v=Y4MnpzG5Sqc (accessed June 8, 2016).

Kushin, M. & Yamamoto, M. (2010) Did social media really matter? College students' use of online media and political decision making in the 2008 election. *Mass Communication and Society*, 13(5), 608–630.

Lévy, P. (1997) *Collective Intelligence*. New York: Plenum.

Lum, T.Y. & Lightfoot, E. (2005) The effects of volunteering on the physical and mental health of older people. *Research on Aging*, 27(1), 31–55.

Lutz, M. (2009) The social pulpit: Barack Obama's social media toolkit. Available at http://cyber.law.harvard.edu/sites/cyber.law.harvard.edu/files/Social%20Pulpit%20-%20Barack%20Obamas%20Social%20Media%20Toolkit%201.09.pdf (accessed June 8, 2016).

Mansfield, H. (2013) 12 Must-Know Stats About Social Media, Fundraising, and Cause Awareness. Ad Council. Available from http://www.adlibbing.org/2013/04/24/12-must-know-stats/ (accessed June 23, 2016).

McAllister, A. (2013) New media and new voices. *The Philanthropist*, 25(2), 93–98.

McCaughey, M. & Ayer, M. (2003) *Cyberactivism: Online Activism in Theory and Practice*. New York: Routledge.

McMillan, D.W. & Chavis, D.M. (1986) Sense of community: a definition and theory. *Journal of Community Psychology*, 14(1), 6–23.

Molina, B. (2015). Obama's Twitter account breaks world record. Available at http://www.usatoday.com/story/tech/2015/05/20/obama-world-record/27640321/ (accessed June 8, 2016).

Morozov, E. (2009) The brave new world of slacktivism. Available at http://www.npr.org/templates/story/story.php?storyId=104302141 (accessed June 8, 2016).

Putnam, R. (1993) The prosperous community: social capital and public life. *The American Prospect*, (13), 35–42.

Putnam, R. (1995) Bowling alone: America's declining social capital. *Journal of Democracy*, 6(1), 65–78.

Putnam, R. (2000) *Bowling Alone: The Collapse and Revival of American Community*. New York: Simon & Schuster.

Quan-Haase, A., Wellman, B., Witte, J. & Hampton, K. (2002) Capitalizing on the net: social contact, civic engagement, and sense of community. In: B. Wellman &

C. Haythornthwaite (eds) *The Internet in Everyday Life*, pp. 289–324. Oxford: Blackwell Publishers Ltd.

Rheingold, H. (2008) Using participatory media and public voice to encourage civic engagement. In: W.L. Bennett (ed.) *Civic Life Online: Learning How Digital Media Can Engage Youth*, pp. 97–118. Cambridge, MA: MIT Press.

Shah, D. (1998) Civic engagement, interpersonal trust, and television use: an individual-level assessment of social capital. *Political Psychology*, 19(3), 469–496.

Stiglitz, J. (2002) *Globalization and Its Discontents*. New York: Norton & Company.

Stoll, C. (1995) *Silicon Snake Oil: Second Thoughts on the Information Highway*. New York: Doubleday.

Thomson, S. (2012) Political organizations and social media. Available at http://digitalcommons.olin.edu/cgi/viewcontent.cgi?article=1000&context=ahs_capstone_2012 (accessed June 8, 2016).

Valenzuela, S. (2013) Unpacking the use of social media for protest behavior: the roles of information, opinion expression, and activism. *American Behavioral Scientist*, 57(7), 920–942.

15

Communication for Development

Learning Objectives

After reading this chapter, you should be able to:
1   Understand and apply communication for development literature.
2   Examine the differences between modernization, dependency and participatory approaches to behavior changes.
3   Navigate the opportunities and challenges provided by communication for development approaches.

Introduction

Communication scholars have long been interested in the way popular culture is reflected in everyday life. Many believe that by looking at the media products that a society consumes, much can be understood about the society itself. With the advent of social media, it becomes more and more feasible to look at the media that everyday citizens produce. What does it say about our society that 133,518,980 Americans (Internet World Stats, 2011) currently subscribe to Facebook? Does this mean that we are a highly connected society? Or does it mean that we are a society of deep isolation? Drawing conclusions about a society based on media consumption habits is a difficult and careful process that should not be taken lightly.

Strategic Social Media: From Marketing to Social Change, First Edition. L. Meghan Mahoney and Tang Tang.
© 2017 John Wiley & Sons, Inc. Published 2017 by John Wiley & Sons, Inc.

In previous chapters, we discussed the complicated process of how media influences audience behavior. People negotiate media artifacts and engage in a sense-making process that contributes to the way in which they see the world. If nothing else, those 133,518,980 Americans are able to tell us who has access to the Internet in the United States and how willing those people are to use that technology to voice "What's on their mind." Clearly, media context influences the way cultures, ideologies and societies evolve. Thus, it naturally lends itself as a resource in positive social change and is often utilized in development contexts for social advancement. Oftentimes, these interventions are done through communication for development initiatives.

The past few years have made it very clear that social media is able to spark human organization (such as the 2011 Egyptian Revolution) in a way previously unheard of. If we look back at all the lessons learned from communication for development literature, it becomes much more clear why new media, specifically social media, have proven such an innovative tool for permanent human behavior change. This chapter aims to look at three strands of communication for development literature: modernization, dependency and participatory theories, and the opportunities and challenges of each. It then examines the positive deviance approach to behavior change and demonstrates how this approach can be applied to social media campaigns. This understanding will help you to better apply the concepts of diffusion, community and mobilization towards socially positive initiatives.

There have been many historical transformations that researchers interested in behavior change have studied over the past century. Despite these transformations, behavior change researchers suggest that media is a tool, and ultimately we should be interested in the way everyday citizens make decisions regarding their own lives. Through a theoretical understanding of human behavior, communication specialists are able to attract, persuade, and entice audiences with media messages. Your goal as a social media practitioner is to best understand these theories so that you are able to navigate audiences towards desired behavior change initiatives.

Introduction to Communication for Development

Communication for development refers to the application of communication strategies and principles in the developing world towards political democracy, rising levels of productivity and industrialization, high literacy rates, and longer life expectancy (Waisbord, 2001). Specifically, these initiatives promote political, economic and educational growth (Inkeles & Smith, 1974). While you personally may not be considering social media campaign messages in terms of these positive social change initiatives, Part V of this book will explain why these concerns are important for every global citizen, especially those interested in marketing. In today's globalized environment, every producer and consumer of online content must take into account how their own habits are influencing the world around them.

Initially, you may have different goals for your own social media audiences. In fact, you may only be asking them to "like" a Facebook page, or to simply try out a product. Even these small low-risk scenarios have difficulties enticing an online audience to carry through. While it is easier to reach audiences than ever before, this also means that the amount of media messages an individual is exposed to each day has increased. It is now estimated that your audiences see as many as 30,000 media advertisements per day (Malone, 2011). There is much to learn about message construction if you hope to break through this noise with your own social media messages.

The field of communication for development is not an obvious field to explore for those interested in social media campaigns. However, its roots as one of the historical strands of communication research interested in human behavior change has particular implications with regard to mass media interventions.

Communication for development scholars are interested in establishing a permanent behavior change among large audiences. *Behavior change* is defined as a research-based process for addressing knowledge, attitudes, and practices that are intrinsically linked to program goals (UNICEF, 2013). Here, participants are provided information through well-defined strategies, using an audience-appropriate mix of interpersonal, group and mass media channels and participatory methods. When interested in social change, UNICEF (2013) argues that one must be concerned with the way society is organized, including the distribution of power among institutions. For human behavior to change on a large scale, societal norms and structural inequalities have to be taken into consideration, and the focus is on the community as the unit of change. As such, strategists can no longer view their organization through a micro-lens. It is important to step back and look at the greater role decisions make on the broader environment. These communication for development approaches are complementary techniques and have transformed greatly over the past century.

Nevertheless, permanent behavior and social change is a lofty and near-impossible goal. Often, communication practitioners fight against centuries of habit and culture. How do you get a community to start living their everyday lives differently, especially if the message is counterintuitive to many of societies' most habitual practices? Some communication for development initiatives tackle enrollment, retention and completion of education by female children in cultures where parents refuse to send girls to school because they are needed for household work (KCCI, 2013). Other initiatives promote safe-sex communication between parents and children in cultures where sexual conversation is considered taboo (Guijarro *et al.*, 1999). One can see why the field of communication for development is interested in inspiring behavior change through more culturally appropriate methodologies.

Communication for development interventions take the perspective that mass media are best suited for organization and efficiency through staffing and funding (Hornik, 1993), which is a fundamentally different approach than using media to sell. If you are looking to organize individuals with a limited amount of finances and manpower, perhaps from your own living room, there is much to learn from the field of communication for development. This work has focused on effective message development, collaboration across various fields, and global implications. These are all imperative steps towards a successful marketing campaign. Therefore, it is important to study the trends and findings of communication for development and social change research.

Modernization, Dependency and Participatory Approaches to Behavior Change

Chapter 2 explained how Rogers' diffusion of innovations theory helps spread new ideas through media outlets over time among members of a targeted community (Haider & Kreps, 2004). Behavior change occurs as a result of this complicated process of diffusion, adoption and/or rejection of new ideas. This process involves four main interacting factors: an innovation, communication channels, social systems, and time (Haider & Kreps, 2004). However, we also learned that this process is difficult, is too top-down, and does not have a high return rate of permanent behavior change.

Think about how much you learn in a classroom where teachers only lecture at you, rather than allowing you to participate and engage in the process. It is probably not the most ideal learning environment. Without participation, individuals are much more likely to get sidetracked with their own thoughts or doodles or even fall asleep due to boredom. The same is true in behavior change initiatives.

The hope with diffusion-centric messages is that, over time, audience members will pass through various stages, and eventually adopt, implement and confirm recommended messages (Svenkerud & Singhal, 1998). If adoption is successful, individuals could initiate new desired behavior through commencement or end undesirable behaviors through cessation (Haider & Kreps, 2004). However, the diffusion process is difficult to account for, and there is not much message producers can do to guide audiences along the way to ensure completion.

This top-down approach to communication was apparent in every discipline, not just the field of development. We call this period the modernization era of communication. *Modernization theory* tends to be simple, ideal and mechanical. This perspective portrays development as an extremely linear process where a country must pass through five phases in order to become modern. Media transmits an idealized picture of the lifestyles that modernization theorists held as their ideal (Tufte, 2000). Here, the aim is the production of fully developed societies of mass consumption, much like the cultures of the Western World.

The assumption of modernization is that after an innovation is developed, widespread adoption will follow in a highly predictable and systematic process. This era of communication for development research lasted for many years, and the same assumption has been mirrored in the way we approach social media messages in marketing.

Consider the evolution of the modernization era as similar to the inception of Twitter. In 2006, Twitter co-founder Jack Dorsey (@Jack) developed an SMS-based communication platform so that individuals could update each other on their progress at work (MacArthur, 2013). At that time, text message plans were expensive, and Twitter allowed the opportunity for individuals to communicate without racking up their mobile phone bills. The goal of this social media was to increase production and efficiency, and essentially make money. However, during its debut, this technology provided users with no way of replying or engaging with one another. Users did not like this (and who could blame them; no one wants to keep up with constant updates intended for no particular audience) so they began including an @ symbol before their username to identify which user they were communicating with in their tweet. Eventually, the Twitter team added this function, as well as other interactive features such as hashtags and retweets.

We see this top-down, one-way communication messages all the time on social media: "Buy our product!"; "Check out our new line"; "Visit our store." The dissatisfaction with these top-down modernization approaches was apparent. Users find constant selling, with limited engagement, patronizing and annoying. Our society is filled with this type of noise, through billboards, television commercials, and flyers on our car windshields. This type of marketing tells consumers that you don't care who they are or what they have to say. You are telling them that you find yourself more knowledgeable than they are. In essence, you are giving audiences information that is important to you, but not them. This one-way communication process, where opinion leaders mediate the impact of mass media communications, is not an effective way to mobilize audiences.

In the 1960s, a new approach to communication for development began to emerge, as communication for development practitioners found that the early adopters of desired behavioral goals tended to be those individuals who were more involved in local organizations, better educated, and held community leadership roles (Melkote, 2001; Glanz *et al.*, 2002). This approach, *dependency theory*, served as a critique of the modernization process. Researchers from this paradigm did not believe that the problems of Third World countries would simply disappear as soon as development occurred in the form of economic growth and industrialization (Sood & Rogers, 2000; Tufte, 2000). In fact, they argued that quite the opposite would occur and that international capitalism was the root of developmental problem, not the solution. This is because developed nations profit from commerce while peripheral nations suffer from unequal exchange processes. In this theory, media promotes cultural imperialism and strengthens dependency on consumerism.

This peripheral process can be a complicated and difficult process to understand. Influenced by Marxist and other critical theorists, dependency theorists believe that the problems of the Third World reflect unequal distribution of resources created by the global expansion of Western capitalism (Waisbord, 2001). These challenges are due to a larger social structure, rather than a lack of information.

Let's take one community's challenge of dirty drinking water as an example. Yes, you can go in and teach a community through mass media the importance of boiling water before drinking it, but dependency theorists suggest that this transfer of information does not actually solve the problem. This disparity of resources is due to a broader social structure and inequity. In fact, by turning to mass media as the single resource in fighting these problems, fundamental problems of media access and content are often ignored. You are able to reach millions through public service announcements on television. This can prove an effective and efficient way to spread information about boiling water before drinking. However, the uneducated and the poor often do not have access to the technology. Moreover, the most powerful and rich often own broadcast services. Thus, the cycle of haves and have-nots continues.

This cycle of economic disparity is strongly linked to media access. *Digital divide* explains the inequity between those who have access to the latest information technologies and those who do not (Compaine, 2001). If an individual has limited access to new media, it leads to economic and social handicap. Today, our concept of the digital divide is changing. Internet nonadoption is narrowing, with less than 15% of US adults citing that they never go online, a number that has significantly shrunk since 2000 (Pew Research Center, 2015). Though new media (specifically mobile technology) is allowing more diversity among users than other mass media technologies, access is still influenced by factors such as age, education, income, race, and ethnicity.

The dependency approach to communication for development explained why the modernization approach was not yielding high levels of behavior change. It suggested that audiences do not like being talked down to. Individuals learn most when they are able to participate and engage in the information process. Unfortunately, this dependency era did not offer a lot of solutions. At that time, diffusion messages were still the most cost-effective way to reach a mass audience in a short amount of time. For many years, communication for development practitioners had little solution.

In the 1980s, an era of participatory approaches began to emerge. *Participatory theory* criticizes many of the underlying assumptions of modernization theory. However, unlike dependency theorists, the focus of participatory theory not only critiqued media power structures and consumerism, but also shifted efforts towards more of a facilitation role. Here, the goal becomes individual and collective empowerment of the people through community participation.

The role of the audience is much different in this participatory approach. Similar to what we discussed in Chapter 5, participatory approaches view audiences as playing an active role, rather than serving as receivers of information. This approach can be seen as a form of cultural studies, as it looks at popular culture as an outlet of everyday life and popular sectors of society. It examines the needs, histories, trajectories, and distinct sociocultural profiles (Tufte, 2000). Through participatory measures, the goal of communication moves towards sparking interpersonal dialogue to promote cultural identity, trust and commitment (Waisbord, 2001). Rather than disseminating information from the top to the bottom, it is a process where everyone discusses possibilities together. This more human-centered approach believes that the role of media and technologies should be used to supplement, rather than dominate, interpersonal methods (Gray-Felder & Deane, 1999; Waisbord, 2001). Only through sharing and reconstructing experiences can communication provide a sense of ownership to community members.

Let's go back to our earlier classroom example. Think about how much more you learn in a classroom when you were able to exchange ideas, ask questions, and take part in the creation of lectures. The role of the "expert" in this model is simply one of facilitation and moderator. Communities do not need to be injected with expert knowledge. Rather, communication technologies should be used as a resource in facilitating ideas that are already within the community. Even though the solutions of one culture may be different from those of another (or even from Western ideals), they still hold value. In fact, new media technology allows a space for every culture to have a voice.

Indeed, participatory theory is based on one of the concepts widely used by social media: collective intelligence. *Collective intelligence* is defined as the ability of a group to solve more problems than its individual members (Heylighen, 1999). There is wisdom in crowds, and everyone is essentially an expert in something. This phenomenon has been dubbed crowd-sourcing, peer production, and Wikinomics, and is based very broadly on the premise that groups of individuals do things collectively that seem intelligent (Malone *et al.*, 2009).

Wikipedia is a great example of how contributors from all over the world have collectively created a space for high-quality information with no centralized control; anyone can contribute and change anything at any time. Social media has provided a space where organizing and sharing is easier than ever, while traditional mass media technologies do not allow for this type of participation.

Today, most communication for development interventions fall along two conceptual continuums: diffusion and participation. The *diffusion model* is based on Rogers' diffusion of innovations theory and is central to the modernization approach of the 1950s and 1960s (Morris, 2003). Here, behavior change is achieved by educating individuals. By providing knowledge, individuals begin to experience a shift in attitudes, which then influences how they practice. These types of campaigns are generally completed through mass media.

The *participation model* is more grounded, by assuming that behavior change is a horizontal not vertical process (Gray-Felder & Deane, 1999; Morris, 2003). It stresses the importance of community dialogue for empowerment (Gray-Felder & Deane, 1999). By using participatory approaches to media design, one is better able to include and reach the voices of the targeted and hard-to-reach audience populations (Pant *et al.*, 2002).

Paulo Freire, an influential thinker in the field, suggests that the individual is able to intervene actively in his or her own process of becoming aware and conscious of his or her own reality. The dialogue of the social commitment and the constant dialectic among action–reflection–action are core elements in what has become to be known as the *Paulo Freire method* (Freire, 1969; Tufte, 2000). This methodology is based on horizontal dialogue between persons, something that traditional media does not provide.

Researchers further found that most communication interventions fail because technocrats design them based on their own personal view of reality (Singhal & Rogers, 2003). They demonstrate that true participation does not involve a subject–object relationship, only a subject–subject relationship. The audience does not need to be provided with expert knowledge:

> Once the oppressed, both individually and collectively, begin to critically reflect on their social situation, possibilities arise for them to break the "culture of silence" through the articulation of discontent and action (Singhal & Rogers, 2003, p. 232).

This diffusion–participation continuum (Figure 15.1) is something that behavior change theorists still struggle with today. Mass media tends to lend itself more towards diffusion approaches. It is a great way to get your message across to the masses. However, we know the benefits of allowing audiences more participation in the behavior change process. Social media has been able to bridge this gap by making it easier for thousands of individuals to engage and participate with media messages in a more egalitarian landscape. It is not always in your best interest to give the masses control and participation over your messages. However, a strict diffusion strategy will not get you far in today's digital climate. As a social media practitioner, it is important that you know the opportunities and challenges for each approach.

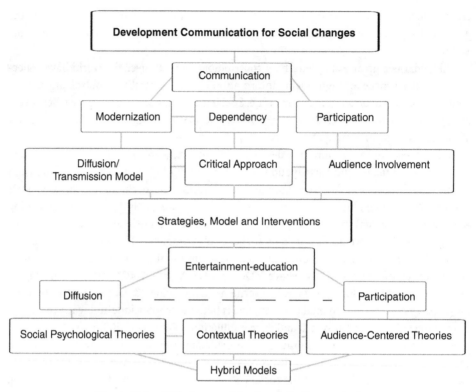

Figure 15.1   Diffusion–participation scale. Source: Author.

Opportunities and Challenges of Communication for Development Approaches

All three communication for development approaches continue to help guide various strategies, models and interventions for social and behavior change in the field today. It is important to note that all types of communication for development interventions fall along the diffusion–participation continuum based on the objective and type of resources available. There has yet to be a magical formula developed where individuals interested in behavior change can plug into any initiative regardless of the circumstances. Each approach has its own strengths and weaknesses (Figure 15.2).

We have already discussed the many challenges of a diffusion-centric model. Audiences are approached as masses, which is not very effective in terms of behavior change. The likelihood of actually achieving permanent behavior change in a large number of audiences is small. The process is also complicated and top-down in nature, which many users may find patronizing and annoying. It is also important to understand that the most problematic behaviors are cultural and habitual, not the result of a lack of information. Diffusion-centric strategies are not the best at prompting permanent behavior change.

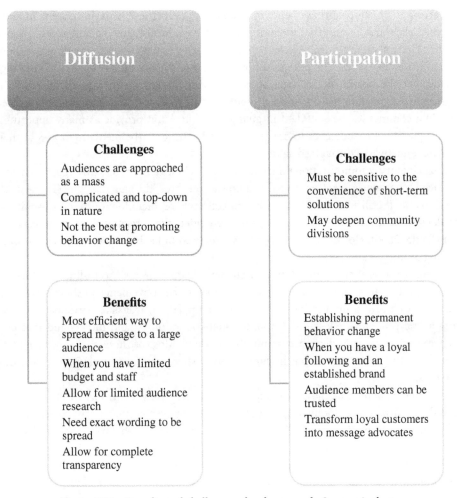

Figure 15.2   Benefits and challenges of each approach. Source: Author.

However, it is important not to forget the many benefits of a diffusion approach. This approach is the most efficient way to spread your message to a large audience. If you have a limited budget and staff, this approach may make the most sense. It allows you to reach a large number of individuals and gain a mass following with limited audience research. Also, diffusion allows you to have strict control over your message. This may be the best strategy if you have very clear, tangible objectives and it is important that the exact wording (such as event times or dates) is spread to your audience. Diffusion also allows complete transparency for your product and/or organization. Though we often talk about strict diffusion as a negative marketing tool, every product needs one place for strict diffusion. Often, this is your company's website where consumers seeking more information about your product are likely to go on their own.

Participatory campaigns are better at establishing permanent behavior change in audiences. They should be utilized once companies have a loyal following and an established brand. These audience members can be more trusted when it comes to handing over control of media messages. The release of power will transform loyal customers into message advocates. The power of this type of peer-to-peer marketing through social media is unmatched by traditional diffusion. If your organization and messages are well trusted within a community, be confident in giving up control and provide as many opportunities as possible for audiences to create, share and transform the media messages to their individual networks through social media.

Participatory communication for social change includes any process through which people define themselves what they need and how to get there, through dialogue (Byrne *et al.*, 2005, p. 3): "It utilizes dialogue that leads to collective problem identification of solutions to development issues." Participation makes provider–client relationships more egalitarian (Dutta, 2006). However, not everyone is interested in having more equal relationships among producers and users.

There are several criticisms of an entirely participatory model. According to Waisbord (2001), participatory approaches must be sensitive to the convenience of short-term solutions, recognize the implications of outside manipulation, translate participatory ideas into actual programs, take note of uninterested communities, and understand that participation may actually deepen community divisions. Most of these challenges could be avoided if they were carried out in communities where participants already hold strong linkages.

It should be noted that these two models are not completely antagonistic to one another. You should draw on components from both concepts, as even participatory projects require some sort of information transfer (Morris, 2003). It is imperative that you consistently monitor and evaluate how audiences are responding to your products. It is impossible for a company to always need diffusion or participatory messages. Your job as a social media practitioner is to know when to utilize each approach.

The following action plan can be used as a guide when you design your own media messages.

Diffusion/Participation Action Plan

1 Use more diffusion-centric techniques if tight control over your media message is needed, you have a limited budget, or are attempting to build a large mass media audience.
2 Use more participatory techniques if you know your audience well, are more interested in transforming existing audiences into loyal advocates, and hold trust within the target community.
3 Complete frequent monitoring and evaluation of your media strategy to determine where on the diffusion–participation continuum your message should fall.

Though many of these theories have incredible points of difference along the communication for development continuum, there are many points of convergence that have been achieved in the past few years. These include the need for political will and empowerment, a "toolkit" conception of strategies that provide different diagnoses for different contexts, an integration of "top-down" and "bottom-up" approaches, a combination of multimedia and interpersonal communication, and an inclusion of both personal and environmental approaches (Waisbord, 2001). You may want to use mass media for the diffusion portion of a campaign, but then send interpersonal community reinforcement to promote the participatory portions of the campaign.

One such example of a mixed methods "toolkit" strategy is a social media initiative in India dubbed VideoVolunteers. The purpose of VideoVolunteers is to train and foster community leaders as citizen journalists in their own communities (Rodrigues, 2010). This intervention integrates diffusion and participatory approaches by utilizing mass media and interpersonal communication. Individuals are provided with communication technologies and asked to make short films on local issues that they feel are important to prompting positive social change in their everyday lives. These videos are then broadcast within the community, as well as uploaded to YouTube and previewed at film festivals. The initiative has created over 15 community video units, trained 150 producers from local communities, and produced 50 other films. These films have been screened 1100 times to about 200,000 people in 350 villages (www.videovolunteers.org/impact). This intervention includes a community-based interpersonal communication component. Such an "on-the-ground" community approach is a great way to get specific audiences involved in a culturally specific manner towards an overall campaign goal or message. As mentioned before, the goal of communication for development is to promote political, economic and educational growth through the application of communication strategies. These strategies range on a continuum of diffusion and participatory approaches to behavior change. Regardless of where you stand on this continuum in your own approach to creating social media messages, most likely the goal is the same – to pass information to a target audience. Some messages are more successful than others (often, the most successful messages are those that have conducted the best audience research prior to content creation). Sometimes, a communication strategist can follow every theoretical rule for prompting behavior change and audiences still don't react.

A new trend in communication for development interventions that are faced with this challenge is beginning to look at this relationship differently through the positive deviance approach to behavior change. Rather than focusing on the best way to promote behavior change in a target audience, positive deviance "enables communities to discover the wisdom they already have and then to act on it" (Singhal, 2010, p. 2). This approach changes the role of the audience from passive receiver of information to a more empowered and participatory role. Audiences are actually problem-solvers that play an intricate role in message design and campaign goals.

In one famous positive deviance case study in Vietnam, childhood malnutrition across a village was reduced by 75% (Bradley *et al.*, 2009). Here, researchers examined community children that were thriving despite high rates of malnutrition and stunting in their rural village, and found that these mothers were feeding their children shrimp and crabs that they found on rice paddies. These fish were not traditionally used by the masses because they were thought to be inappropriate for young children. However, once this information was disseminated across the rural village, nutrition rates dramatically increased. Rather than an expert arriving and informing the population of solutions that work in an outside culture, communication for development practitioners identified deviants within the culture to find viable solutions.

This positive deviance approach demonstrates our changing perception of power and audience. Rather than viewing your audience as a passive receiver of information, consider how valuable their experiences and contributions would make to message design and product creation. After all, they know their lifestyle better than anyone.

While most social media practitioners do preliminary research to determine who is most likely to be interested in their organization and then construct a message according to their ideals and values, the positive deviance approach challenges you to think differently. Rather than focusing on what is wrong with a community (e.g., "Why isn't anyone donating to my cause?"), the positive deviance approach seeks out those few key community members who are in less than ideal situations but who, despite their circumstances, are engaging the desired behavior anyway. Instead of focusing on the most likely mass, it encourages you to give attention to outliers. Gladwell's (2008) best-selling book *Outliers* explains how outliers play a part in our intelligence and decision-making processes. It makes sense to examine these outliers, who have taken purposeful steps towards individual decision-making when interested in behavior change.

As a social media practitioner, you would examine your network to see who is most likely *not* in a life situation to participate in the campaign, but has gone ahead and done so anyway. This analysis allows you to highlight secondary communities that are likely to follow through with your projected goal, but which are not always apparent in a traditional audience analysis.

It should be noted that it takes time to learn how and why these individuals follow through with the behavior change, and then mirror their suggestions with other members of the community. The positive deviance approach is a behavior change strategy that requires message creators to give up a lot of control. It takes time to begin thinking about your audience differently and consider how much there is to learn from them.

In summary, communication development research has gone beyond individual-level behavioral change to looking at interventions and processes at the community level. The most important takeaway from this theoretical research is that behavior change interventions based on theory hold a better chance of success than those that are not (King, 1999). Theory makes it easier to understand why or why not an intervention proves successful. This is one area that will set you apart from other individuals on the social media job market. Having a clear understanding of theoretical approaches to behavior changes makes you much more valuable than a professional who is only familiar with the various tools of social media technology. Let's examine how one communication for development project, WITNESS, shifted its approach to include more hybrid features for audiences to ignite social change.

Case Study: WITNESS

The mission of the WITNESS project is to train and support individuals fighting for human rights through the use of technology, specifically video. Their slogan – "See it. Film it. Change it" – refers to their efforts to teach individuals the basics of video production so that they are better able to rise above critical at-risk situations (WITNESS, 2015). Musician Peter Gabriel founded the organization in 1991. He believed in many principles of the digital divide. Specifically, he thought that if individuals had access to the then new technology of hand-held video cameras, they could show the world instances of human rights abuse (McAnany, 2012). Over the past two decades, the organization has gone through many changes that speak to the diffusion, community and participation continuum of communication for development literature.

Initially, the mission of the WITNESS project was to hand out video equipment to individuals in high-risk situations. Once these individuals were "taught" how to use equipment, they could tell their story to gain attention to the human rights violations. This top-down approach to change suggests that the missing element for social change was a lack of knowledge. Individuals simply needed to learn how to tell their story through video equipment.

WITNESS realized the need to use a more community approach, through a people-to-people strategy (McAnany, 2012). Here, various organizations that already worked within high-risk communities were given the equipment to help train individuals they were serving. The training took place on an interpersonal face-to-face level. It is much easier to communicate with populations without a large proxemics gap between the nonprofit organization and the communities being served.

Over the years, the WITNESS project has grown. However, they have achieved success by actually lessening the number of organizations they work with, so that they are partnered with more trustworthy groups that can engage in years of training (McAnany, 2012). The training no longer focuses on simply the use of technology, or the predetermined diffusion solution. Instead, it focuses on all the principles of the popular participation movement. Media is used simply as a resource, and *people* are the change makers and storytellers of the movement. Organizations do whatever they can to ensure that individuals are able to tell the story that they choose. They are used as a resource to facilitate technology, law, or policy challenges. However, they strive to make the actual stories as participatory and bottom-up as possible.

The WITNESS methodology ensures that the voices of those directly affected by human rights violations are heard by audiences who can enact change (Gregory, 2006). This shift from an agent of change to a facilitator of change has proven highly effective. Today, WITNESS (2015) has partnered 360 organizations, trained over 6000 individuals, worked in 97 countries, and reached over 260 million people with their videos.

Discussion questions

1   How is technology being used as a solution in the WITNESS project? Apply principles of the digital divide.
2   What advantages did WITNESS gain when they started using a more community approach to reaching audiences? What challenges still remained?
3   What role does WITNESS play today in the way audiences create their stories through video? How is this different from the initial conception of the WITNESS project?

Summary

The field of communication for development has clearly evolved toward two very different positions. The first position argues that development problems stem from a lack of information among populations. The second position believes that power inequality proves the underlying problems of development challenges (Waisbord, 2001). These dyadic paradigms have informed diagnoses, recommendations and intervention implementations differently at every level. Arguably, the aim of both camps is to remove constraints for a more equal and participatory society (Waisbord, 2001). However, how each paradigm attempts to achieve such change is very different.

There is no right or wrong way to create behavior change messages. The goal of this chapter is to provide you with the knowledge and theory behind when to use each approach. If you are marketing a new product that needs tight control over your message and you are interested in short-term minimal behavior change across a wide audience, a primarily diffusion-centric approach may be right for you. If you have a strong understanding and faith in your audience and are ready to ask them for bigger, more permanent changes, a participatory approach is necessary. However, regardless of where you sit on this continuum, you must have some elements of both paradigms.

In fact, many communication for development interventions combine elements of both diffusion and participation. A hybrid model proves the most effective. In addition, communication for behavior change efforts also stress the need for monitoring and evaluating efforts through community dialogue and feedback at all stages (Waisbord, 2001), not just at the production level. Ultimately, behavior change is a process of public and private dialogue through which people define who they are, what they want, and how they can get it (Gray-Felder & Deane, 1999). Hopefully, this chapter has demonstrated the need for including theory in your social media campaign strategy. One might even argue that this theoretical understanding of human behavior is more important to social media marketers than mastering business models and technological tools. We now know how audiences negotiate media messages in accordance with their own experiences and lived reality. Just as media contexts influence the way cultures, ideologies and societies evolve, they also change these perceptions.

Chapter 16 will focus on a particular communication for development intervention, entertainment-education (E-E). This mass media strategy illustrates our need for oral storytelling and culture as we make decisions about our daily lives. As the world around us becomes more and more globalized, it is easy to ignore the nuances from one culture to the next. We begin to make consumer decisions based on these conceptualizations. E-E research demonstrates how imperative narrative constructions become in how we identify ourselves with the world around us. Through a thorough understanding of E-E, more can be done to ensure that audiences are not only interested in receiving your brand narrative, but will also want to contribute and share it with their own personal network. Let's talk more in the next chapter.

Key Takeaways

1 Communication for development is the application of communication strategies to promote political, economic and educational growth around the world.

2 In a globalized society, no content is produced or consumed in isolation, and it is imperative that you consider how your own online habits and practices influence the world.

3 Communication for development interventions have transitioned through three eras of approaches to behavior change: modernization, dependency and participation. There are challenges and opportunities with each approach, and good communication professionals will know where and why their message falls on the diffusion–participation continuum.

4 The positive deviance approach to behavior change does not focus on the best way to establish behavior change in a target audience, but instead enables communities to discover the wisdom they already have and then to act on it. This makes it a great strategy for gaining potential secondary audiences.

5 Theory makes it easier to understand why or why not an intervention proves successful. This is one area that will set you apart from other individuals on the social media job market. Having a clear understanding of theoretical approaches to behavior change makes you much more valuable than a professional who is only familiar with the various tools of social media technology.

References

Bradley, E.H., Curry, L.A., Ramanadhan, S., Rowe, L., Nembhard, I.M. & Krumholz, H.M. (2009) Research in action: using positive deviance to improve quality of health care. *Implementation Science*, 4(1), 25.

Byrne, A. with Gray-Felder, D., Hunt, J. & Parks, W. (2005) Measuring change: a guide to participatory monitoring and evaluation of communication for social change. Available at http://www.communicationforsocialcha

nge.org/pdf/measuring_change.pdf (accessed June 8, 2016).

Compaine, B. (2001) *The Digital Divide: Facing a Crisis or Creating a Myth?* Cambridge, MA: MIT Press.

Dutta, M. (2006) Theoretical approaches to entertainment education campaigns: a subaltern critique. *Health Communication*, 20(3), 221–231.

Freire, P. (1969) *Education for Critical Consciousness*. New York: Continuum.

Gladwell, M. (2008) *Outliers: The Story of Success*. New York: Little, Brown and Co.

Glanz, K., Lewis, M. & Rimer, B. (1997) *Health Behavior and Health Education: Theory, Research, and Practice*. San Francisco, CA: Jossey-Bass.

Gray-Felder, D. & Deane, J. (1999) Communication and social change: a position paper and conference report. New York: The Rockefeller Foundation. Available at http://www.communicationforsocialchange.org/publica tions-resources?itemid=14 (accessed June 8, 2016).

Gregory, S. (2006) Transnational storytelling: human rights, WITNESS, and video advocacy. *American Anthropologist*, 108(1), 195–204.

Guijarro, S., Naranjo, J., Padilla, M., Gutiérez, R., Lammers, C. & Blum, R.W. (1999) Family risk factors associated with adolescent pregnancy: study of a group of adolescent girls and their families in Ecuador. *Journal of Adolescent Health*, 25(2), 166–172.

Haider, M. & Kreps, G. (2004) Forty years of Diffusion of Innovations: utility and value in public health. *Journal of Health Communication*, 9, 3–11.

Heylighen, F. (1999) Collective intelligence and its implementation on the Web: algorithms to develop a collective mental map. *Computational and Mathematical Organization Theory*, 5(3), 253–280.

Hornik, R.C. (1993) *Development Communication: Information, Agriculture, and Nutrition in the Third World*. Lanham, MD: University Press of America.

Inkeles A. & Smith D. (1974) *Becoming Modern*. Cambridge, MA: Harvard University Press.

Internet World Stats (2011) American Facebook users. Available at http://www.internetworldstats.com/stats26. htm (accessed June 8, 2016).

KCCI (2013) Meena ki Duniya: an entertainment–education radio programme. Available at http://www. kcci.org.in/Document%20Repository/13.%20Meena% 20Radio.pdf (accessed June 8, 2016).

King, R. (1999) *Sexual behavioral change for HIV: where have theories taken us?* Geneva: UNAIDS. Available at http://www.who.int/hiv/strategic/surveillance/en/ unaids_99_27.pdf (accessed June 8, 2016).

McAnany, E.G. (2012) Social entrepreneurship and communication for development and social change. *Nordicom Review*, 33(Special Issue), 205–217.

MacArthur, A. (2013) The real history of Twitter, in brief. Available at http://twitter.about.com/od/Twitter-Basics /a/The-Real-History-Of-Twitter-In-Brief.htm (accessed June 8, 2016).

Malone, C. (2011) Can you hear me now? Web-enabled brand experiences that cut through the clutter. Available at http://www.forbes.com/sites/onmarketing/ 2011/11/03/can-you-hear-me-now-web-enabled-brand -experiences-that-cut-through-the-clutter/#563d12b82 14f (accessed June 8, 2016).

Malone, T., Laubacher, R. & Dellarocas, C. (2009) Harnessing crowds: mapping the genome of collective intelligence. MIT Center for Collective Intelligence, Working Paper No. 2009-001. Available at http://cci. mit.edu/publications/CCIwp2009-01.pdf (accessed June 8, 2016).

Melkote, S.R. (2001) Theories of communication for development. In: W.B. Gudykunst & B. Mody (eds) *Handbook of International and Intercultural Communication*, 2nd edn, p. 419. Newbury Park, CA: Sage Publications.

Morris, N. (2003) A comparative analysis of the diffusion and participatory models in communication for development. *Communication Theory*, 13(2), 225–248.

Pant, S., Singhal, E. & Bhasin, U. (2002) Using radio drama to entertain and education: India's experience with the production, reception and transcreation of "Dehleez." *Journal of Communication for Development*, 13(2), 52–66.

Pew Research Center (2015) Who's not online? Available at http://www.pewresearch.org/fact-tank/2015/07/28/15- of-americans-dont-use-the-internet-who-are-they/ft_ 15-07-23_notonline_200px/ (accessed June 8, 2016).

Rodrigues, U. (2010) The promise of a new media and development agenda. *Media International Australia*, Issue 137, 36.

Singhal, A. (2010) Positive deviance and social change. Available at http://www.communicationforsocialchan ge.org/pdfs/singhal_arvind_positive%20deviance%20 and%20social%20change_mazi%20june%202010.pdf (accessed June 8, 2016).

Singhal, A. & Rogers, E. (2003) *Combating AIDS: Communication Strategies in Action*. Thousand Oaks, CA: Sage Publications.

Sood, S. & Rogers, E. (2000) Dimensions of parasocial interaction by letter-writers to a popular entertainment-education soap in India. *Journal of Broadcasting and Electronic Media*, 44, 386–414.

Svenkerud, P. & Singhal, A. (1998) Enhancing the effectiveness of HIV/AIDS prevention programs targeted to unique population groups in Thailand: lessons learned from applying concepts of diffusion of innovation and social marketing. *Journal of Health Communication*, 3, 193–216.

Tufte, T. (2000) *Living with the Rubbish Queen: Telenovelas, Culture and Modernity in Brazil*. Bedfordshire, UK: University of Luton Press.

UNICEF (2013) Communication for development. Available at http://www.unicef.org/cbsc/index_42352.html (accessed June 8, 2016).

Waisbord, S. (2001) Family tree of theories, methodologies and strategies in communication for development. Available at http://www.communicationforsocialchange.org/pdf/familytree.pdf (accessed June 8, 2016).

WITNESS (2015) See it. Available at http://witness.org/about/ (accessed June 8, 2016).

16

Social Media and Entertainment-Education

Learning Objectives

After reading this chapter, you should be able to:
1 Understand the theoretical underpinnings of entertainment-education.
2 Apply entertainment-education for social initiatives.
3 Examine the role of culturally appropriate narratives in behavior change models.

Introduction

Stories are an important part of any culture. We teach children lessons, entertain ourselves, and share experiences through narratives. How many stories have you been exposed to in just this week alone? Do you have a favorite sitcom that you just can't miss? Maybe you shared a heartwarming story that you found online with your social network. Though storytelling has roots as an oral tradition, most of the stories that you have encountered have been broadcast through mass media. Media provides opportunities to disseminate stories to the masses and incorporate more visual appeals in our media content.

As discussed in Chapter 15, it is a very complicated process for media messages to spark behavior change in individuals. The field of development communication has long been interested in applying communication strategies in the developing world towards political democracy, rising levels of productivity, industrialization, high literacy rates, and longer life expectancy (Waisbord, 2001). This has been done through various interventions along the

Strategic Social Media: From Marketing to Social Change, First Edition. L. Meghan Mahoney and Tang Tang.
© 2017 John Wiley & Sons, Inc. Published 2017 by John Wiley & Sons, Inc.

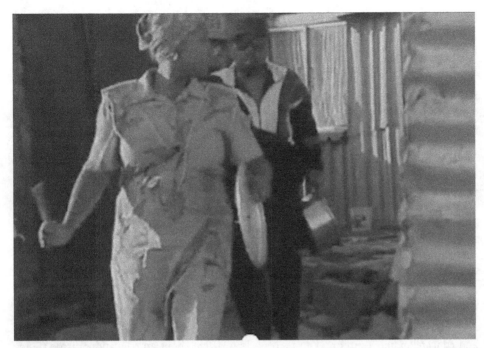

Figure 16.1 Scene from *Soul City*. Source: Soul City Institute. Reproduced with permission of Leah Marais.

diffusion–participation continuum. The behavior change intervention most often associated with mass media is entertainment-education (E-E).

One of the most successful and well-known examples of an E-E campaign sparking social and behavior change in a community is *Soul City*. This South African television series broadcast characters engaging in a new collective behavior to demonstrate how neighbors could intervene in a domestic violence situation, as domestic abuse is a substantial problem in South Africa that most citizens do not wish to discuss.

The *Soul City* television series (Figure 16.1) aimed to intervene with this crisis by developing a storyline in which its characters gathered around an abuser's residence, banging pots and pans to bring awareness and stop the violence (Singhal & Rogers, 2003). This storyline showed viewers that domestic violence is unacceptable, and it is a citizen's duty to bring attention to abuse going on in their neighborhood. Furthermore, this action lets abusers know that it is not okay and will not be tolerated within the community. This entertainment program sparked subsequent real-life action in its audience. Numerous media reports showed instances where the audience of *Soul City* intervened in domestic abuse situations in their own personal communities. Here, you see how a mass media intervention is able to spark real-life behavior change.

In this context, it is important to understand how E-E, though formally believed to be a diffusion-centric development tool, has transformed over time towards a more communication for social change approach (Waisbord, 2001). This chapter explores the theoretical underpinnings of E-E interventions, and how to apply E-E to many social change initiatives, including domestic abuse, HIV, and everyday practices such as proper hand washing campaigns. Indeed, this approach can be applied to any social media message hoping to inspire behavior change. Finally, we will take a deeper look into a specific E-E model, the MARCH model, to gain a better understanding of how to combine diffusion approaches with more participatory community-based reinforcement.

Theoretical Underpinnings of Entertainment-Education

Have you ever been influenced to change behavior because of something you have watched on television? Most often, people talk about the negative effects of television. There are fears of excessive television viewing causing violence, promiscuous behavior, and obesity. This chapter suggests that storytelling media, such as television, can actually teach people to be more socially responsible citizens through E-E.

Many communication theories provide the foundation for the E-E strategy, as it is one of the most interdisciplinary approaches to behavior change. *Entertainment-education* "seeks to capitalize on the popular appeal of entertainment media in order to show individuals how they can live safer, healthier and happier lives" (Pant *et al.*, 2002, p. 53). It involves a process of purposely designing and implementing a media message to both entertain and educate audiences in order to increase knowledge about an educational issue (Singhal *et al.*, 2004). E-E programs are able to hit on audience emotions and retell narratives until the stories become popular narratives of a culture. It is important to note that E-E is not a theory of communication, but rather a communication strategy that is informed by several theories in order to bring about behavioral and social change (Singhal *et al.*, 2004).

E-E programs generally have two central components: a multidisciplinary theoretical framework and a developed media production system (Singhal *et al.*, 2004). Many communication theories have been applied to E-E interventions. These include social learning theory, Shannon and Weaver's communication model, dramatic theory, theory of archetypes and stereotypes, elaboration likelihood model, audience involvement, dramatic theories, social constructivism, uses and gratifications, agenda-setting, knowledge-gap, cultivation analysis, diffusion of innovations, and Habermas' theory of communicative action (Sood, 2006; Singhal *et al.*, 2004; Barker, 2007). One of the reasons that E-E is such a powerful behavior change strategy is due to its multidisciplinary approach.

The purpose of this chapter is not to explain each of these theories in great detail but rather to provide a more conceptual understanding of how to best entice audiences through media narratives (Sood *et al.*, 2003). Chapter 3 explains how powerful narratives prove in the human decision-making process. Humans think in narrative patterns by nature. That is what makes E-E one of the most powerful ways to prompt behavior change in audiences. Fiske (1987) explains how audiences of media narratives go through a constant and subtle negotiation and renegotiation of the relationships between the text and the social to make pertinent and pleasurable meanings from a story. Stories are part of a long trajectory of history and culture historical process (Degh, 1994).

Most children's programming is built on the principles of E-E. One of the most popular preschool programs around the world is *Sesame Street*. The purpose of the program is to utilize colorful Muppets, music and celebrity visits to increase cognitive learning skills. It teaches young children letters, numbers, geometric forms, and prosocial qualities such as kindness and cooperation in audiences (Singhal & Rogers, 1999). Findings from research across all countries and cultures where *Sesame Street* is broadcast demonstrate its effectiveness in preparing preschool children for primary education (Fisch *et al.*, 1999). One reason that the program is such a great success is that the production is grounded in traditional behavior change E-E literature.

Two organizations drove the beginnings of E-E projects worldwide: Population Communications International (PCI), a nongovernmental organization from New York City, and Johns Hopkins University's Center for Communication Programs (JHU/CCP). By 2003, E-E had spread to over 100 projects in 50 countries (Singhal & Rogers, 2003).

The Sabido Dramas, named after the Vice President for Research and Scriptwriter at Televisa in Mexico, Miguel Sabido, were the pioneers of E-E in the 1970s (Refera, 2004). Audiences of these programs are able to enjoy conflict-filled suspense dramas while simultaneously receiving education. The success of these dramas led to the formulation of the *Sabido methodology*, which is based on character development and plot lines that provide audiences with positive, negative and transitional characters that impart messages and values.

Programs that represent similar structure and content of human behavior become a very telling depiction of the way a culture lives. These archetype stories are even more meaningful today because there are so many opportunities for media broadcast. At almost every level, individuals are able to share stories of their lived reality. Through a complex identification process, audiences are able to negotiate these stories and understand the role that they play in society. This has huge implications for everyday decision-making and long-term behavior change.

Conceptualizations of E-E argue that it contributes to behavior change in different ways. First, it influences members' awareness, attitudes and behavior towards a socially desirable end. It influences the audience's external environment to help create the necessary conditions for change at a system level (Singhal *et al.*, 2004). In addition, it triggers and facilitates public debate and discussion about difficult issues and helps mobilize social groups towards individual, community and policy action (Usdin *et al.*, 2003; Tufte, 2005). You can see from this description how diffusion, community and mobilization are all essential to a successful E-E strategy.

One of the earliest examples of E-E is the world's longest-running radio soap opera, *The Archers* (Singhal *et al.*, 2004). This British soap has long been regarded as representing realistic depictions of working class individuals and their problems. It also demonstrates a formula of drama, humor and education that was a balance of 40% education and 60% entertainment.

The success of this program paved the way for future British soaps, such as *EastEnders*, which produced self-defined "slice of life" stories that focused on issues of homosexuality, rape, unemployment, racial prejudice, single-parent families, teenage pregnancy, prostitution, arranged marriages, attempted suicide, drug dissolution, sexism, urban deprivation, problems with pregnancies, breast-feeding, domestic abuse, safety hazards, and mental health (Singhal *et al.*, 2004). Clearly, E-E strategies are able to incite behavior change in audiences older than preschool-aged children.

Now that we have a better sense of the theoretical underpinning of E-E, it is important to turn our attention towards the modern complexities of designing and implementing an E-E strategy to promote behavior change. One of the greatest attributes of social media is that audiences no longer take the role of passive receiver of narrative content. While there is great success in traditional E-E transmission broadcasting, such as *Sesame Street* and *East-Enders*, we are finding even greater advancements when individuals are able to participate and produce the content on their own.

Entertainment-Education and Public Health

As we know, people negotiate media messages in different ways from one another. What prompts behavior change in one person may turn someone else off altogether. Regardless of how much effort producers put into content creation, message reception is an incredibly critical component to the E-E strategy. Producers can never be certain how audiences will decode a message. Your job as a communication professional is to understand the best ways to ensure individuals identify with your product narrative.

One of the best-known examples of audiences resisting an E-E initiative has been dubbed the *Archie Bunker effect*. Vidmar and Rokeach (1974) explain how the main character of *All in the Family*, Archie Bunker, was produced as a negative role model that perpetuated sentiments of bigotry, racism and prejudice. Producers were hoping that audiences would dislike this antagonist and the way he behaved. However, rather than seeing this character as a negative role model, audience members identified with him and subsequently emulated his behavior (Singhal *et al.*, 2004). This case demonstrates the challenge in the use of media narratives to educate and promote behavior change: producers can never account for how individuals will identify with a story. A stronger understanding of what makes a successful E-E intervention is needed.

A 25-year meta-analysis shows that the most successful E-E campaigns are those in which cultural values hold a strong foundation in national and cultural artifacts. Because individuals within a cultural group may be at different stages of readiness, media messages must be modified to incorporate cultural settings (King & Howard-Hamilton, 2003). The best way to ensure this is to have members of the actual culture where the program will be consumed assist with production.

Let's take the public health crisis of HIV/AIDS as an example. This initiative comes with four distinct challenges for communication professionals to overcome: transmission challenges, behavioral challenges, response challenges, and targeting challenges (Singhal & Rogers, 2003). Transmission challenges are due to the nature of HIV/AIDS as an invisible, yet infectious disease. Behavioral challenges deals with human behaviors that involve interaction between unequal parties, as in a patriarchal society. Response challenges exist because efficacious response to the disease involves adoption of behaviors that depend on the compliance of more than one party. For example, if a husband is being secretly unfaithful to his wife with someone who is HIV positive, then she may still be at risk without engaging in any risky behaviors herself. Targeting challenges deal with populations that are often hard to reach by means of conventional media channels. Some of the most infected regions are rural and exclusive in nature, especially in countries such as Botswana, Namibia, Swaziland, and

Zimbabwe, where many urban dwellers and migrant laborers return to their village of origin when they fall ill (FAO, 2011). While your own campaign may not have challenges quite this complex, it is important to see how utilizing E-E strategies help tackle such a complicated public health crisis through culturally integrated means.

At first glance, it seems reasonable to utilize media to promote individual behavior change requests: "Go get tested!" "Use a condom!" "Don't share needles!" These are solutions to the HIV/AIDS crisis for any culture. However, it also is a very top-down message that asks individuals to change their behavior to reach a goal. Narratives must go beyond this individual behavior change initiative and portray stories of how to participate in advocacy, policy change and facilitate public dialogue. This dialogue has been identified as critical, particularly through UNAIDS, the Joint United Nations program on HIV/AIDS (UNAIDS, 1999).

In addition, rather than searching for a universal approach to E-E, it is more important to individualize each campaign based on cultural context (Airhihenbuwa & Obregon, 2000). Media messages should never be identical, as culture is one of the most important components in production (Singhal & Rogers, 2003). While Western practitioners may feel as though an individual approach to HIV/AIDS messages is appropriate, other cultures, such as those in Africa, Asia and Latin America, are more influenced by collective sentiments and stories (Airhihenbuwa & Obregon, 2000).

South Africa's Sesame Street program, *Takalani Sesame*, utilized this individualized E-E approach in 2002 when they introduced an HIV-infected muppet, Kami, into the program. The purpose of the narrative was to teach kids how to interact with an infected playmate, stressing positive attitudes and inclusion. This was the result of the AIDS epidemic, with over 250,000 South African children infected with HIV under the age of 15 facing isolation, rejection and grief from their community (Lim, 2002). While *Sesame Street* storylines produced in other cultures may have also taught positive prosocial behaviors, this narrative was unique to a specific localized crisis.

This is one of the biggest strengths of utilizing new media in E-E initiatives. Social media is inexpensive, fast and easy to produce. There is no reason why in today's media landscape, one narrative should be pushed out over and over again across different audiences. Conduct strong audience analyses and bring cultural social norms and policies into your narratives. Ensure that audiences are able to see their lived reality through your media messages. The easiest way to do this is to allow others to tell their story for you.

E-E interventions only begin to demonstrate the complexities of initiating a media strategy for positive social change. However, despite these complications, research suggests that because of the powerful nature of storytelling, E-E has evolved into one of the most commonly utilized components of public health campaigns in developing countries. Let's now turn our attention towards an E-E strategy that focuses on moving beyond transmission narratives to prompt audiences to make a positive behavior change.

MARCH Model of Behavior Change

Many food documentaries have been produced that focus on the meat industry crisis. They often contain horrific images of animal torture and unsanitary packaging practices. For some, these images are powerful enough to change the type of meals eaten in their everyday life permanently. They forswear meat altogether and become vegetarians. These individuals have followed the diffusion process by becoming aware of the problem (knowledge), agreeing with the documentary's concerns (approval), and deciding that they are no longer going to participate as a carnivore (intention to act practice).

Traditional E-E initiatives define success as an individual's willingness and ability to take appropriate preventive measures and adhere to recommended treatment regimens (Centers for Disease Control, 2009). It can be difficult to transition into a vegetarian diet, especially for individuals who use meat products as the staple of all their favorite meals. To permanently change behavior is hard, no matter how powerful the documentary proves. However, the ability to connect with other vegetarians helps to make this transition less likely to fail. Social media allows a space to connect with networks of like-minded individuals that makes the process less scary and isolating. Eventually, this new diet became second nature and they become the advice-giver, rather than receiver. Perhaps most importantly, social media provides information about how this community is able to help change laws and regulations of the meat industry, beyond just their own individual lifestyle.

In Chapter 2, we learned that the five steps towards effective behavioral change from a diffusion-centric message include knowledge, approval, intention to act, practice, and advocacy (De Fossard, 1996). The component of advocacy is incredibly important to establishing permanent behavior change in audiences, as people must engage with the message and take a participatory role in a larger movement. Participation cements their decision to act in a particular way and change their own personal behavior forever.

It must be noted that not everyone who watches the food documentary will be influenced to become a vegetarian. Maybe an audience member does not recognize his or her everyday life in what is being portrayed on screen. This is often the case when characters in a film only represent one niche demographic. Behavior change interventions must understand contextual differences, including social and cultural context, that are incorporated into E-E narratives (Airhihenbuwa & Obregon, 2000; Dutta-Bergman, 2004). Maybe the audience member grew up in a culture where animals are not as highly valued as they are in the first viewer's life. Perhaps the individual just enjoys the taste of meat too much to ever become a vegetarian. E-E programs must understand their audiences' willingness to engage, and speak to their cultural norms in order to influence.

It may be easier to change the behavior through interpersonal reinforcement than it is through mass media. If personal vegetarian friends forward emails, ask to sign petitions, and actually cook tasty meatless meals, the result may be stronger. This type of community-level reinforcement may eventually be able to change a meat-lover's perception of the industry.

But wait! How can you reach large numbers of individuals and get them to agree with your cause if it must be done on an interpersonal community level? You cannot possibly go door to door around the world and find everyone who would be interested in your message. This is where the principles of true audience participation begin to take shape.

The E-E approach demonstrates the need for you to take the issue away from yourself and turn attention towards relevant cultures, characters and situations that your target audiences are able to identify with. Let's pretend you are dedicated to the cause of stopping the consumption of plastic water bottles. You feel as though they are wasteful, unnecessary and harmful to the environment. Rather than explaining to your social network why the plastic water bottle crisis is important to you, bring the issue to a community level.

BantheBottle.net is a social media campaign designed to advocate bans on one-time-use plastic water bottles. Their approach to this social change is to ask individuals to organize screenings of the documentary *Tapped* in their own local neighborhoods and communities. This documentary focuses on the commodification of the water bottle industry and its impact on the environment. The campaign stresses the need for these screenings to be subsidized with support from community leaders, including office and school administrators. The website includes an interactive map where you can see the progress that each individual community initiative has made. Dozens of communities around the world have effectively banned the sale of water bottles through this initiative.

One of the reasons that this campaign has proved successful is that it subsidizes a mass media intervention with community reinforcement. In addition to the documentary screening the campaign asks clear tangible actions from audiences. Their social media links directly to a declaration page, where individuals can commit their efforts, and a page where individuals can find local government addresses to send letters and emails asking for regulatory legislation.

You could use these communication strategies in your own social media campaign efforts. Rather than just using social media to rant about how much you dislike plastic water bottles (diffusion), you could use the space to network with other environmentalists with the same goal (community). Through these efforts you could start a mobilization campaign initiative asking users to create videos of all the plastic water bottles they use in a week and upload it on YouTube. That lived experience is much more powerful than anything that happens in a virtual setting. It empowers the users and gives them complete control of the message. You have just transformed everyday social media users into empowered advocates for your cause.

True participation would take this campaign one step further. If you are truly looking for meaningful mass behavior change through a participatory process, you have to discard your message's predetermined objectives. Though *you* may be interested in decreasing the amount of plastic water bottle use, that cause may not be relevant to your audience. Facilitate discussion through social media of what is really important (in this case, the environment), participate in the discussion by mentioning how you have cut back on plastic water bottle purchases, and ask for others to come up with their own solutions. This is how you achieve true participation. Such a campaign allows you to prompt interaction and dialogue, gives users ownership of their own ideas, and diminishes power differentials.

In 2009, Ford sent 100 influential bloggers their new Ford Fiesta and a video camera and asked them to blog about their experiences, resulting in 6.2 million YouTube views, 750,000 Flickr views, and 40 million Twitter adds (Stott, 2013). This self-proclaimed user-generated content campaign allowed bloggers to experience the product and tell their own stories. Each of these bloggers has their own personalities, writing styles and brand. Their audiences voluntarily follow their blogs because they identify or, at the very least, are interested in what these bloggers have to say. This marketing strategy enabled Ford Fiesta the opportunity for 100 different authentic narratives. Moreover, they were distributed through the hands of bloggers with loyal audiences who already hold trust in what they have to say.

The power of interpersonal community measures has been applied to behavior change initiatives. Most notably, behavioral scientists from the Centers for Disease Control and the International Partnership Against AIDS in Africa launched the Leadership and Investment in Fighting an Epidemic (LIFE) and developed a new E-E strategy called the MARCH model initiative (Galavotti *et al.*, 2001). This strategy sets to influence audience behavior through a combination of mass media transmission, as well as community reinforcement and participation.

There are four key elements of the *MARCH model*: progression of change over time, the use of E-E as a vehicle of modeling, use of modeling in program content, and the creation of character models similar to the target audience (Pappas-DeLuca *et al.*, 2008). These interventions are not intended to result in quick behavior changes, but are designed for setting up long-term models lasting for months.

Perhaps most importantly, behavior change in the MARCH model is built on two principles: modeling and reinforcement. Modeling shows people how to change and reinforcement supports them in these efforts (Centers for Disease Control, 2009). The strategy also utilizes two main components: broadcast media and interpersonal community mobilization.

The broadcast media is used in line with early approaches of the Sabido methodology for E-E and is established through a positive, negative, and transitional character development strategy. MARCH narratives always include a positive role model who consistently makes responsible decisions, and a negative character that consistently engages in risky behavior.

Think of *Takalani Sesame*, the South Africa's Sesame Street program that we discussed earlier. Kami is the positive role model for children based on the narrative centered around inclusion of HIV-infected community members. She is the center protagonist for most stories and behaves in a positive, identifiable manner. Storylines also includes negative characters that tease and exclude Kami from games. These are antagonists in the story that audience members are not to identify with.

Transitional characters who may start by making negative decisions, but evolve over the series into an empowered, knowledgeable, and positive character are also included in MARCH narratives. For *Takalani Sesame*, these characters may start the program by having negative preconceptions regarding HIV-infected individuals. However, through the storyline, they learn to include Kami in the fun. These dynamic transitional characters serve as the most identifiable role models for audience members, as they are neither consistently positive nor consistently negative.

Then, through the reinforcement state, audiences are encouraged and given the necessary skills to achieve behavior change. Ideally these reinforcements support the messages verbatim that the modeling characters are facing. Audiences are able to internalize these challenges, apply them to their own lives, and come up with solutions through interpersonal interactions.

Still, this three-pronged approach to storytelling narratives may not be enough to prompt permanent behavior change. Remember that audience members are influenced differently from one another. *Sesame Street* tries to move beyond a one-way transmission model broadcast by having the Muppets look directly into the camera and ask questions to the audience throughout the storyline (i.e., "Our letter of the day is Z. Can you think of an animal that begins with the letter Z?"). These questions are followed by a brief silence where viewers at home are able to interact with what is going on in the program. The Muppet will then congratulate audience members for participating. For many years, this is as interactive as traditional media allowed for E-E programs. However, today there are many more opportunities for participation through social media.

A unique feature of the MARCH model is an interpersonal community mobilization component. The idea of interpersonal reinforcement is that programs train key leaders in the target community about the initiative. This could be a preschool teacher using the storyline of Kami and *Takalani Sesame* in their own lessons. Generally, the MARCH model provides subsequent media materials to use as well, such as workbooks, brief videos, or magazines. Reinforcement activities may also include holding listening and discussion groups, as well as community activities such as meetings or road shows. Some of the most effective community reinforcement activities are those in which individuals are asked to produce theater or stories that carry out these educational messages. This gives audience members a chance to ask questions and receive immediate feedback. It also provides a takeaway for audiences to bring home.

Consider how much more fun it is to watch favorite characters in person than it is on television. Children become so excited when they see characters walking around in amusement parks and parents pay large amounts of money to go to live events. Interpersonal experiences are much more powerful and provide a much greater catalyst for behavior change than transmission media messages. Nevertheless, E-E research demonstrates that a combination of both can be very successful.

Social media provides a great opportunity to bridge the gap between transmission E-E models and interpersonal reinforcement. *Sesame Street* has many online resources where children can talk to characters through smartphone applications, download educational games, and even create their own versions of Muppet characters (SesameStreet.org, 2014). This type of user-generated content is a great way to incorporate the principles of the MARCH model into positive behavior change.

When creating an E-E intervention that models the MARCH strategy, it is important to follow the reinforcement action plan below.

Reinforcement Action Plan

1 Conduct an audience analysis to determine the cultural norms of your target audience.
2 Create positive characters that make decisions in accordance with the desired behavior change.
3 Create negative characters that make decisions antagonistic to the desired behavior change.
4 Include transitional characters that start out as either a positive or negative character, but transform over time.
5 Create an interpersonal community-based mobilization effort to reinforce the message.

It is clear that there is still much to learn regarding behavior change through social media messages. Practitioners and researchers are now beginning to understand that the most critical factor of behavior change has nothing to do with using an appropriate communication strategy or model, but does allow for the culture and traditions of the intended campaign audience to be integrated within the narrative. It is impossible for a campaign that proved successful in South Africa to be mirrored in India and work in the same capacity. Each and every culture requires its own adaptation of these recommendations. Furthermore, it is important that E-E campaigns have community support that reinforces their messages. Community members should be involved in the inception, production, distribution, and evaluation of the messages. This in-house participation is key to a successful intervention and is most often left out of traditional marketing strategies.

This chapter has discussed the importance of including culturally appropriate narratives and community reinforcement in behavior change strategies. One such example is Botswana's *Makgabaneng*.

Case Study: *Makgabaneng*

Makgabaneng is an E-E radio serial drama in Botswana that was designed using the MARCH model. The name means "Rocky Road" as its motto is "Life is a journey on a rocky path. The hope is, with every fall, there is a rise" (Peirce, 2011). It first aired on August 20, 2001, in an effort to address critical HIV/AIDS awareness messages among citizens aged 10–49 years old across Botswana (Republic of Botswana Popular Report, 2005).

The *Makgabaneng* drama is the only Botswana-produced serial drama of its kind. Therefore, it is one of the only forms of media entertainment that citizens can turn to and see their culture played out in narratives. Many culturally specific issues are tackled, including infidelity, intergenerational relationships, and alcohol abuse. The program began as a radio drama that broadcast the same 15-minute episode twice weekly, on two different national broadcast stations.

It is important to note that *Makgabaneng* is more than a transmission media; it is an interactive, holistic, behavior change initiative. The program incorporates both the broadcast and interpersonal community mobilization components of the MARCH model. One of the elements that make this E-E initiative successful is that is written, acted, and produced by local talents within the urban center of the country, Gaborone.

The efforts for culturally specific content go beyond this in-house production. Producers of *Makgabaneng* recognize how various communities across Botswana have very distinct ideologies, values, and even language from one another. A separate department has been created to monitor and evaluate the reinforcement initiatives. The reinforcement department engages in many activities such as organizing health fairs and disseminating promotional materials, writing a teen magazine, overseeing field partners who host rallies at schools, overseeing and transcribing guides for field partners, and contracting special projects coordinators who develop campaign materials with similar messages for other stakeholders. These efforts ensure that audience members are able to engage with the characters and storylines long after the program is over.

Moreover, trained officers within local communities began to host interpersonal listener discussion groups (LDGs) to reinforce the messages of the drama in 2002. LDGs serve as one of the greatest reinforcement activities aimed to encourage safer HIV-related behaviors. In addition to the newly launched television series, producers have also begun utilizing social media in their strategy. At the end of every episode, fans respond and interact on the show's Facebook page (Facebook.com/Makgabaneng). There, they are encouraged to ask questions and share their own stories. Pictures from various road shows and discussion groups are uploaded on the *Makgabaneng* website for participants to check out. There is also a Twitter feed (@Makgabanen) that reinforces key messages from the program, as well as promoting casting and production announcements. Hashtags centered on the program are encouraged for users to promote live feedback as the series airs. These are all ways in which *Makgabaneng* is bridging the gap between one-way transmission broadcasting and interpersonal community reinforcement.

Because of these, *Makgabaneng* is successful in reaching and sustaining listenership among demographics aged 15–24. Audiences of *Makgabaneng* have higher levels of HIV knowledge and less stigmatizing attitudes towards those affected by HIV. Listeners also report increased intentions to get tested for HIV, and greater preventive behaviors such as continued discussion with partners about HIV testing, and HIV testing during pregnancy (Republic of Botswana Popular Report, 2005). Because of high positive reaction, *Makgabaneng* became an official NGO in 2006. In addition, producers launched a television version of the series in 2013 due to its popularity.

This E-E initiative encourages audiences to acquire the necessary skills and attitudes to achieve behavioral change. Through community reinforcement and use of social media, *Makgabaneng* is able to engage with audiences to stimulate applicable, individualized, relevant health conversation. As Byrne *et al.* (2005) suggests, evaluations of behavior change initiatives must move away from people as the objects of change, and focus on more participatory methods, such as community dialogue, local decision-making processes, and cultural identity. *Makgabaneng* proves a successful case for this type of participatory behavior change initiative.

Discussion questions

1   What are the greatest advantages to utilizing an E-E approach to behavior change, like the production of *Makgabaneng*? How does the likelihood for behavior change transition when media is not produced for simply profit's sake?

2   What steps can be taken to ensure that the cultural norms of your target audience are included within the narrative?

3   *Makgabaneng* combines a broadcast narrative and community reinforcement in a behavior change initiative. How is social media able to speak to both of these needs better than traditional media?

Summary

This chapter focuses on the importance of utilizing culturally specific narratives and community reinforcement in behavior change initiatives. This method has been applied to E-E interventions across the world and has yielded great results.

Fiske (1987) explains how individuals are likely to use media for their own purposes, rather than the goals of others. We know that audiences are very different from one another. They have unique emotions, relationships, passions, goals and stressors. They do not even need to misunderstand or disagree with a message in order to disregard it. Clearly, sparking behavior change through media messages is hard. One way to overcome these challenges is through narrative structures and community reinforcement strategies found in E-E interventions.

There are many different ways to apply the lessons learned from communication for development and E-E research to develop your own social media messages. The most important lesson is that your social media is not all about you and your product. Resist the temptation to use the media for your own purposes, rather than the goals of others. Listen to your audiences and allow them to participate with your campaign at all levels. The goal of social media marketing should shift from selling products towards empowering users to contribute to positive behavior change. Part IV of this book has discussed ways in which social media can be used for social good. Part V will explore the future social media landscape and how to incorporate old with the new.

Key Takeaways

1   Development communication interventions take advantage of strong storytelling to inspire behavior change in audiences. Entertainment-education is one approach.

2   The MARCH model is an E-E approach that uses the media intervention in a more participatory manner through community-centered initiatives. The interpersonal component has proven a more successful way to promote behavior change.

3   Social media holds great potential in bridging the gap between diffusion-centric mass media approaches and more participatory interventions for behavior change. E-E initiatives stress the importance of participatory components throughout all stages of the production process.

4   It is important that members of the culture that you are trying to reach assist with the production of media content. This will ensure that it is influential and appropriate for their lived reality.

References

Airhihenbuwa, C. & Obregon, R. (2000) A critical assessment of theories/models used in health communication for HIV/AIDS. *Journal of Health Communication*, 5, 5–15.

Barker, K. (2007) Sex, soap and social change: the Sabido methodology. Population Media Center. Available at https://www.populationmedia.org/2007/08/09/sex-soap-social-change-the-sabido-methodology/ (accessed June 8, 2016).

Byrne, A. with Gray-Felder, D., Hunt, J. & Parks, W. (2005) Measuring change: a guide to participatory monitoring and evaluation of communication for social change. Available at http://www.communicationforsocialchange.org/pdf/measuring_change.pdf (accessed June 8, 2016).

Centers for Disease Control (2009) Global reproductive health: modeling and reinforcement to combat HIV/AIDS (MARCH). Available at http://www.cdc.gov/globalhealth/programs/reproductive.htm (accessed June 8, 2016).

De Fossard, E. (1996) *How to Write a Radio Serial Drama for Social Development: A Program Manager's Guide*. Baltimore, MD: Johns Hopkins School of Public Health, Center for Communication Programs.

Degh, L. (1994) *American Folklore and the Mass Media*. Bloomington, IN: Indiana University Press.

Dutta-Bergman, M.J. (2004) Health attitudes, health cognitions, and health behaviors among Internet health information seekers: population-based survey. *Journal of Medical Internet Research*, 6(2), e15.

FAO (2011) HIV/AIDS: a rural issue. Available at http://www.fao.org/FOCUS/E/aids/aids1-e.htm (accessed June 8, 2016).

Fisch, S., Truglio, R. & Cole, C. (1999) The impact of *Sesame Street* on preschool children: a review and synthesis of 30 years' research. *Media Psychology*, 1(2), 165–190.

Fiske, J. (1987) *Television Culture*. London: Routledge.

Galavotti, C., Pappas-DeLuca, M. & Lansky, A. (2001) Modeling and reinforcement to combat HIV: the MARCH approach to behavior change. *American Journal of Public Health*, 91(10), 1602–1607.

King, P. & Howard-Hamilton, M. (2003) An assessment of multicultural competence. *Journal of Student Affairs Research and Practice*, 40(2), 119–133.

Lim, M. (2002) A-B-C, 1-2-3, H-I-V: *Sesame Street* tackles AIDS. *Virtual Mentor*, 4(9), ii.

Pant, S., Singhal, A. & Bhasin, U. (2002) Using radio drama to entertain and educate: India's experience with the production, reception, and transcreation of "Dehleez". *Journal of Development Communication*, 13(2), 52–66.

Pappas-DeLuca, K., Kraft, J., Galavotti, C. *et al.* (2008) Entertainment-education radio serial drama and outcomes related to HIV testing in Botswana. *Global Health Sciences Literature Digest*, 20(6), 486–503.

Peirce, L.M. (2011) *Botswana's Makgabaneng: an audience reception study of an edutainment drama*. Doctoral dissertation, Ohio University.

Refera, T. (2004) The role of Sabido entertainment-education radio serial dramas in the struggle for the prevention of HIV/AIDS: with specific reference to "Yeken Kingit" and "Dhimbiba". Available at http://www.comminit.com/hiv-aids/content/role-sabido-entertainment-education-radio-serial-dramas-struggle-prevention-hivaids-spec (accessed June 8, 2016).

Republic of Botswana Popular Report (2005) *Botswana AIDS Impact Survey III*. NACA in Collaboration with CSO and Other Development Partners.

SesameStreet.org (2014) Available at http://www.sesamestreet.org (accessed June 8, 2016).

Singhal, A. & Rogers, E. (1999) *Entertainment-Education: A Communication Strategy for Social Change*. London: Routledge.

Singhal, A. & Rogers, E. (2003) *Combating AIDS: Communication Strategies in Action*. Thousand Oaks, CA: Sage Publications.

Singhal, A., Cody, M., Rogers, E. & Sabido, M. (2004) *Entertainment-Education and Social Change*. Mahwah, NJ: Lawrence Erlbaum Associates.

Sood, S. (2006) Audience involvement and entertainment-education. *Communication Theory*, 12(2), 153–172.

Sood, S., Witte, K. & Menard, T. (2003) The theory behind entertainment education. In: M.J. Cody, A. Singhal, M. Sabido & E.M. Rogers (eds) *Entertainment-Education Worldwide: History, Research, and Practice*, pp. 117–149. Mahwah, NJ: Lawrence Erlbaum.

Stott, J. (2013) Inspire powerful content from your brand fans: 5 examples and ideas. Available at http://contentmarketinginstitute.com/2013/04/powerful-content-brand-fans-examples-ideas/ (accessed June 8, 2016).

Tufte, T. (2005) Entertainment-education in develop-ment communication: between marketing behaviors and empowering people. In: O. Hemer & T. Tufte (eds) *Media and Glocal Change: Rethinking Communication for Development*, pp. 159–174. Buenos Aires: CLACSO.

UNAIDS (1999) Communications framework for HIV/ AIDS. Available at http://www.unaids.org/sites/default/ files/media_asset/jc335-commframew_en_1.pdf (accessed June 8, 2016).

Usdin, S., Scheepers, E., Goldstein, S. & Japhet, G. (2003) Achieving social change on gender-based violence: a report on the impact evaluation of *Soul City's* fourth series. *Social Science and Medicine*, 61(11), 2434–2445.

Vidmar, N. & Rokeach, M. (1974) Archie Bunker's bigotry: a study in selective perception and exposure. *Journal of Communication*, 24(1), 36–47.

Waisbord, S. (2001) Family tree of theories, methodolo-gies and strategies in communication for development. Prepared for The Rockefeller Foundation. Available at http://www.communicationforsocialchange.org/pdf/ familytree.pdf (accessed June 8, 2016).

Part V

Social Media for Social and Behavior Change

17

Integrating Old with New

Learning Objectives

After reading this chapter, you should be able to:
1 Identify the impact of convergence culture on society.
2 Explain remediation theory and apply it to a social media marketing strategy.
3 Be able to integrate social media into a traditional media campaign in a post-convergence era.

Introduction

One of the greatest advances in society brought by social media is our ability to connect easily with individuals around the world. This insight into how other people live creates a greater sense of empathy towards others, a characteristic that allows us to emotionally participate, understand, relate and value the core elements that make us all members of the human race (Frenk & Gómez-Dantés, 2002). Hopefully, you have learned how creating social media messages for positive social change are not so different from creating messages for marketing and business goals.

This book has taken you through foundational principles of behavior change theory, the role of users and messages in the communication exchange process, and models and strategies for marketing, business and social good. These are all important elements in creating social media messages for your own objectives and goals. We will now turn

Strategic Social Media: From Marketing to Social Change, First Edition. L. Meghan Mahoney and Tang Tang.
© 2017 John Wiley & Sons, Inc. Published 2017 by John Wiley & Sons, Inc.

attention towards the future social media landscape to explain why today's globalized world requires that all social media messages are broadcast in a context that accounts for each of these areas, with special attention paid to social sustainability.

This chapter explores how to ensure that your social media strategy stays relevant in an ever-changing and unpredictable media landscape. This book is unable to teach you everything about the future of social media practices. We can advise how to integrate new technological advancements, whatever they may be, into an existing marketing strategy. Chapter 18 will introduce a *We First* approach to marketing for social behavior change that is consistent with the principles of diffusion and participation. Next, we will argue for a general framework for social media scholarship. Finally, Chapter 20 will provide general conclusions and recommendations for creating social media strategies for increased social participation.

Though once thought of as a fad that would disappear, most organizations now view social media marketing as a mandatory element of their marketing strategy (Hanna *et al.*, 2011). It is difficult to ignore social media's potential in reaching and communicating with customers. However, too many view social media platforms as stand-alone elements, rather than an "ecosystem whereby all elements work together toward a common objective – whether to launch and promote a new product or service; to communicate a new company initiative; or to simply further engage customers in a rich, meaningful, and interactive dialogue" (Hanna *et al.*, 2011, p. 273). These principles of integration are critical to success and require a long-term view of media marketing. Getting the correct balance of traditional and new media elements is important.

You do not want to set the technological bar so high that customers find it overly different and demanding from what they are used to. You also do not want your brand to seem too outdated from the technology that your competition is embracing. Today's marketing and communication professionals must be able to purposefully integrate traditional technologies with the new, and have a sense of what advances are ahead.

In order to better understand how to synthesize a social media strategy, let's first examine the transition from Web 1.0 to a convergence culture, a time in society where companies were forced to create strategy for an unimaginable media landscape that was changing at a rapid pace. We will then turn our attention towards the many challenges that we must consider in a post-convergence era. This knowledge will help you create your own marketing strategy for any media environment.

The Culture of Convergence

If you were interested in listening to music, which media device would you turn to? Perhaps you would turn on the radio and listen to your favorite local show. Maybe you would open iTunes and listen to your personal music collection. Or, if you wanted to be surprised by the playlist, maybe you would open the Pandora application on your mobile device and let the software determine your playlist. It is difficult to remember a time when we didn't have so many choices in media devices and content. Your choice of media device is dependent on a number of factors, including access, competence and connection. It could also depend on what other tasks you are attempting to accomplish simultaneously. Maybe you are working on a term paper and so your personal computer is open anyway. Though you may not have purchased your personal computer with the intention of using it as a music player, it is a convenient function of the device. The ways in which distinct tools or technologies combine from several different products is called *convergence* (DeVoss & Webb, 2008; Griffiths & Light, 2008).

Convergence

The term *media convergence* extends beyond just the merging of technological devices. It includes the flow of content across multiple media platforms, the cooperation between multiple media industries, and the migratory behavior of media audiences who will go almost anywhere in search of the kinds of entertainment experiences they want (Jenkins, 2006). In this definition, you can see the impacts that convergence has on audience behavior and expectations. Convergence is a process of industry changes that combine markets and products to meet various consumer needs (Thielmann & Dowling, 1999). It is likely that your expectations of music choice have changed over the course of your lifetime. You may expect that you should be able to hear any song, anywhere, at any time. This expectation could only be fulfilled if various industries work together.

media convergence

For example, Apple Computer, Inc. never began as a company interested in developing a music player. Their focus was on computers, software and servers. However, in 2000 they purchased the digital encoding program, SoundJam MP, and used it to create iTunes version 1.0 (McNulty, 2006). This is a great example of what can happen when two media platforms/companies work together. The cultural impact surely extends beyond device convergence. This media convergence changed the music industry forever, as consumers could now purchase individual songs, rather than complete artist albums, and they could also hear any given song at any given time with the click of a button from their own personal library. This also changed musical expectations forever. Everyday audiences were now able to become producers of music, as the software integrated well with home recording platforms such as Garage Band, and made it easy for anyone to upload their own music into the iTunes store. The existing digital music business model also changed, as audiences who previously downloaded free music from Napster were now willing to pay for their musical collection again (Blau, 2011).

Media convergence creates many technological, industrial, cultural, and social changes. Media devices are becoming increasingly less expensive and easier to use. More audiences have access and are able to accomplish their own goals and gratifications when they wish. This puts pressure on businesses to push towards stronger customer relationships, especially in a culture that privileges an active audience (Deuze, 2007). The effect of multiple entry points into the consumption process enables audiences to participate in a prolonged relationship with a brand's narrative, encouraging businesses to be more attentive to audience interests and directly solicit feedback to their products (Jenkins, 2003). Here, you can see the shift in power from top-down corporate control to one where audiences are able to actively engage the process.

Media convergence is heavily dependent on consumers' active participation (Jenkins, 2006). iTunes was only successful because customers were willing to engage the consumption and production process. Rather than thinking of convergence as simply a merging of technological devices and media content, it should be seen as a cultural shift that alters the relationship between existing technologies, industries, markets, genres, and audiences (Jenkins, 2004). This has created a new culture of expectations.

Convergence culture

Convergence culture emphasizes the changing patterns in the way narrative, informational, and visual content circulates, resulting in a cultural shift where consumers are encouraged to seek out new information and make connections among dispersed media content (Trigg, 2008). This process has merged the role of the producer and consumer in an interactive environment, representing an entirely new way of seeing the media audience, as it can be difficult to tell who is producing content for whom (Bird, 2011). The shift towards multimedia integration of customer inclusion in the production and product-innovation process of media companies has resulted in many changes in society (Deuze, 2008). As Jenkins (2004, p. 37) suggested:

> Consumers are learning how to use these different media technologies to bring the flow of media more fully under their control and to interact with other users. They are fighting for the right to participate more fully in their culture, to control the flow of media in their lives and to talk back to mass market content. Sometimes, these two forces reinforce each other, creating closer, more rewarding, relations between media producers and consumers.

As such, it is important to consider the action plan below when a practitioner is struggling to see the benefits of embracing the opportunities of a convergence culture. The action plan consists of seven steps: communication, commitment, cooperation, compensation, culture, competition, and customer (Appelgren, 2004).

Convergence Culture Action Plan

1 *Communication*: Social media is defined by the ability to facilitate dialogue between users. Media convergence makes it easier than ever for businesses to facilitate dialogue between the consumers and producers of content. However, it is important for businesses to understand the types of communication that works best with their individual company goals. Part I of this book discusses how the amount of participation users are given influences the amount of control producers have over content. Decisions regarding communication should be made carefully with long-term strategy in mind.

2 *Commitment*: Media convergence provides opportunities for customers to take part in the narrative of your brand. Therefore, it is important to consider how every individual associated with your product, both internal employees and external customers, are familiar with and committed to your goals. The importance of audience research may help you determine the level of commitment from each sector.

3 *Cooperation*: Convergence requires multiple industries to work together in order to fulfill new audience expectations. There are many available options for content delivery, and it is imperative that your business is willing to take risks and cooperate with other organizations that have similar goals. This requires a heightened sense of a product's brand and authenticity, as different sectors must share stories and ideas in a unified fashion that meets the goals of the organization.

4 *Compensation*: Though not a factor that many communication strategists consider immediately, compensation is a growing concern for individuals in a convergence culture. Access, devices and production costs are all decreasing, yet social media brings greater transparency than ever before regarding compensation and profit margins. Consider both employee wages and the gap between the top and the bottom. Would you be comfortable if this information became public? Compensation considerations should also take into account the external benefits to customers and society.

5 *Culture* involves the language, methods, and environment of an organization (Appelgren, 2004). Because convergence culture changes patterns in the way narrative, informational, and visual content circulates, your brand message can easily change or become diluted through multiple channels of distribution. Great care must be taken in fostering a unique culture for your product. Transforming your brand into a lifestyle is one way to ensure cohesiveness.

6 *Competition*: The Internet has made virtually everyone with a connection your competitor, as every market now has national and global competition. This can either be seen as a disadvantage or motivator for success. Companies that excel are those that have a strong sense of their authenticity, brand name, and credibility. If you are your authentic self, you have no competition (Stratten, 2012). Thus, find your niche in the marketplace and foster an engaged and like-minded community.

7 *Customer*: Finally, customers are central to the principles of convergence. Be sure that you are not considering them as passive viewers of your content, but rather active users that play a central role in your narrative. The more power that they have, the more invested they will feel in your brand. Remember that in a convergence culture it is better to have a few invested brand advocates than it is to have high numbers of passive message receivers. Empower the customers and keep them at the center of every decision that you make.

This action plan should help you as you consider the many ways in which media convergence could impact your organization's business and marketing strategies. These overall considerations illustrate the shift in power from producers of media messages to consumers. There are also more practical rules that can help guide you in the strategic process.

Remember that consumers need to see, hear and/or interact with your message three to five times before they start to believe what you are saying (Brito, 2013). Use converged media to distribute messages where your consumers are most likely already visiting in their daily media routine, such as social networking sites like Facebook or Pinterest. Be sure to integrate

[handwritten marginal note: interaction 3-5 times needed before they believe about you're saying]

traditional paid media with free social media platforms in your brand strategy. Converged media allows a space where users are not being sold to in a manner that is as obvious as a pop-up banner, but has more structure than all the information available on the Internet. By taking advantage of paid media in your marketing strategy, your content can reach high numbers of people who are likely interested in your community based on filters that you set. Your marketing strategy should not end there though. Integrate status updates on social networks as well. Whenever you post a status update on a business Facebook page, it only reaches between 8 and 10% of your current fan base (Brito, 2013). Constantly seek out other organizations or blogs with like-audiences so that you can reach a higher percentage of your community.

Hopefully, these suggestions will help guide you as you develop social media content and strategy. Remember that media landscapes are constantly changing, and some of the principles of media convergence may not remain true across your career as a practitioner. You will never be certain of what technological advances lie ahead. Instead, be sure that communication, media, and behavior change theories guide your strategy, especially when the media environment is uncertain. One such theory that explores the integration of traditional and new media content is Bolter and Grusin's (2002) remediation theory.

Remediation Theory

Media convergence is often turned to when individuals are interested in how new media has impacted traditional media marketing and business models (Picard, 2000; Chan-Olmsted, 2004; Cooper & Tang, 2009). In this chapter, we have learned how media convergence impacts the flow of content across platforms, the cooperation between industries, and the migratory behavior of media audiences (Jenkins, 2006). The implication is that media convergence is better for audiences, producers and content managers alike. Remediation theory attempts to provide further guidelines to developing and understanding convergent media products.

Remediation theory is the idea that new visual media are best able to achieve their cultural significance by integrating and refashioning more traditional media forms (Bolter & Grusin, 2002). This theory refers to the blending of traditional and new media, and was one of the first to explain why incorporating new media structure is not always the best decision as a media practitioner. Traditional media is able to refashion new media just as well as new media changes existing forms. Rather than drastically changing the existing media landscape, media convergence simply alters traditional forms.

Remediation theory suggests that media can be divided into two principal styles: hypermediacy and transparent immediacy (Bolter & Grusin, 2002). *Hypermediacy* privileges fragmentation, indeterminacy, and heterogeneity, emphasizing process and performance, much like a windowed style of World Wide Web pages, rather than the finished product (Bolter & Grusin, 2002). It offers random access, with no physical beginning, middle or end, serving much less as a story and more as immediate clips of information.

Hypermediacy requires audience interactivity as an "immutable law" of the medium (Ries & Ries, 2000; Bolter & Grusin, 2002; Ha & Chan-Olmsted, 2004; Lin & Cho, 2010). This is key to practitioners, as interactivity creates brand identity, enables greater control over media choice, and encourages direct communication between content producers and consumers (Chan-Olmsted & Ha, 2003; McMillan *et al.*, 2008; Lin & Cho, 2010). Hypermediation calls attention to the medium that it is deploying by encouraging audienes to look at it (McKain, 2005). These are all functions of media convergence as well.

Transparent immediacy does not rely on interactivity. Instead it includes two- and three-dimensional images projected onto traditional computer, film, or television screens (Bolter & Grusin, 2002). Audiences of transparent immediacy have an immediate relationship with the content of what they are viewing, as it is produced with a clear fourth wall. Content is more linear in nature, with a finished narrative structure, complete with a beginning, middle and end (Bolter & Grusin, 2002). Transparent immediacy encourages audiences to look through the device in order to view content (McKain, 2005).

When a form of new media comes along, as a marketing practitioner you will be forced to make a decision about how to refashion your existing marketing strategy. While the inclination may be that newer is always better, remediation theory cautions against this. It is better to include elements of both hypermediacy and transparent immediacy in products (Bolter & Grusin, 2002; Peirce, 2011). Adapting new media forms too quickly will turn audiences away. They may not feel competent enough to engage your strategy, or the end result may seem too unfamiliar. However, the inability to incorporate new media elements will make your brand seem outdated.

Remediation theory is especially important in a convergence culture, as no media event exists in isolation from other media, or from other social and economic forces (Rajewsky, 2005). It is important to make purposeful decisions about which technologies to embrace into your strategy. Many organizations are still transitioning towards a convergence culture under the assumption that new media is always better. The smartest practitioners are those that are looking forward to find a balance as we enter a post-convergence era.

Integrating Social Media in a Post-Convergence Era

The convergence era brought many exciting changes to society. As we step towards a time when these advances are the expected norm for audiences, there are questions about the future of marketing. Some believe that the concept of convergence has been stretched beyond what is meaningful (Fagerjord, 2010), and many of the same industry concerns and power structures that existed prior to the convergence culture are surfacing again.

Convergence culture is often talked about in very ideal terms where media producers are catering to audiences. While this era certainly marks a shift in thinking about the relationship between audiences and media producers, the impact should not overshadow the need to consider the process of sociocultural stratification (Apperley, 2007). For example, convergence has created a shared space where different genres in different media may be combined in new ways. Individuals are able to produce, add to, or change media texts. This has resulted in a remix of culture. *Remix* is the process of creating an alternative version of a media text by altering or introducing new elements to the existing form (Fagerjord, 2010).

Remix is a great way for individuals from different cultures to work together and collaborate on projects and even create new cultural forms of media. However, this blending of cultures can have other implications as well. Often, the dominant culture will take over smaller subcultures. Today, we can see how people live around the world, and many adopt the cultural depiction of those with whom they identify most, rather than those they live. While this has many benefits to individuals who may feel out of place in their immediate community, it can also erode cultural borders and small nuances between regions. One must consider the importance of culture preservation in a post-convergence era.

Media convergence also raises many questions about communication policy. In a world where everyone is contributing to the production process, it is difficult to determine who owns and has rights to what content. In a globalized era, it is also difficult to determine who is able to regulate or govern virtual spaces. Each device could potentially require a different rule or government agency (Bar & Sandvig, 2008). These policy and ownership issues are just starting to surface, and the implications are unclear.

Furthermore, much rhetoric surrounding media convergence examines the new opportunities for everyday consumers, especially with regard to media production. Anyone is able to become the next viral hit in a converged media environment. However, it is important to note that media structure still plays a role in how audiences access online information. While audiences do have unlimited access to information on the Internet, most of their uses are filtered by the results of a search engine. These search engines utilize algorithms that take into account the source of production and the number of individuals already linking to content. Unconventional and less mainstream sources are not easy to find (Nettleton *et al.*, 2005). Some of the same power differentials remain.

These concerns show us that in an environment where everything seems new, there are still many of the same challenges of media production that the industry has faced since the beginning of time. Overall, a strong audience analysis, coupled with a formative audience research strategy, is the foundation of any convergence marketing strategy. Specifically, there are eight items that practitioners should consider when creating content in a post-convergence world: transmedia, environments, narratives, rituals, community, audiences, identity, and devices (Laurel, 2000).

1 *Transmedia* is the ability to create media texts across multiple media platforms. Rather than producing text for one particular medium, it is time to start thinking about how it will be distributed across multiple platforms from the beginning. This new authoring places the emphasis on developing materials that can be selected and arranged to produce many different forms (Laurel, 2000). It also gives audiences more control, and ensures that the same message produced for one social media platform is not identical to a message produced for another.

2 *Environment*: Every product needs a strong narrative. This narrative exists within an overarching brand environment. Rather than retelling the same story over and over, focusing on a brand environment allows your product to support many stories, characters, and play patterns. This will help your social media messages focus on a lifestyle, rather than a product.

3 *Narratives*: Once you have established your product environment, you can begin considering its narrative. The importance of product narratives was discussed in Chapter 3, but this advice focused on the brand's authentic story. In a post-convergence world, it is imperative to allow a space where users are able to share their narratives in a structure that can fit in with the overall brand story.

4 *Ritual* is a kind of social form in which a designed narrative can unfold harmoniously (and simultaneously) within the larger context of an interactive environment in which most action is improvisational (Laurel, 2000). These unique patterns of behavior, such as an inside joke between you and your audience, help audiences feel a deeper connection to the community, as it is something that they are unable to share on other online forums.

5 *Community*: Media structures must promote dialogue and interaction among members. While this communication can be facilitated, you want to ensure that your audience feels as though the space is shared. This requires a high level of trust, where consumers feel confident that their input matters, and you feel confident that they will stay true to the product brand. A strong balance between control and participation must be maintained.

6 *Audiences* are central to marketers in a post-convergence era. Without them, your message does not spread. Therefore, audience engagement and audience research must be the priority of any social media marketing strategy. Audience contributions must be supported and integrated into your product's foundational narrative, not just an evaluation once the marketing strategy has been deployed.

7 *Identity*: It can be difficult to transition from your product to your audience being central to your brand narrative, but participation is essential to success. Remember that individuals are more likely to engage in a process that speaks to their own lived identity. Focus on an idealized lifestyle, allow collaboration with professional actors, or create characters with functional identities (Laurel, 2000). You can even enable technologies where audiences are able to create virtual identities on their own, even if they are different from their real-life personas. The more audiences are able to customize their experience, the better.

8 *Devices*: Media will take many different forms in a post-convergence world. Be sure to test content in different situations across various devices to ensure that it is working properly. Pay specific attention to the technologies that your audience is most likely utilizing, not what is most convenient or critical for you to produce. Remember that not everyone has the most up-to-date device or software. Ensure that you are not losing audiences because your content is not compatible.

These recommendations should help you determine how well your marketing strategy fits in a post-convergence world. In the era of social media, it can be difficult for marketers to determine the content, timing, and frequency of social media information about their product (Mangold & Faulds, 2009). Rather than adapting a business strategy around social media, it is better to let social media integrate into your business (Bond, 2011). After all, conversations about your product are happening whether you facilitate them or not.

To guide strategic decisions regarding monitoring, understanding and responding to different social media activities, it is recommended that four Cs are followed (Kietzmann *et al.*,

[handwritten margin note: 4 c's of monitoring]

[handwritten margin note: 90% listening 10% action]

2011): (i) *cognize*, where practitioners have a strong understanding of the social media landscape and the unique functions of various platforms; (ii) *congruity*, which determines how social media functions fit the goals of your organization; (iii) *curate*, where practitioners determine who, how often and when they engage into conversation on a social media platform; and (iv) *chase*, where practitioners scan the Internet to find information that influences the company's current or future position on the market.

As consumers turn away from traditional sources of advertising, such as radio, television, magazines, and newspapers, they turn towards social media as a trustworthy source of information (Mangold & Faulds, 2009). Consumers trust information that they find on social media more than they do traditional forms. It is equally important that you put the same trust in the information that you find about your product on social media platforms. Social media provides brands with one of the most personal, trusted and direct points of access to their consumers (Drury, 2008). Take time to read these online conversations and get to know your competitors, customers, prospects, peers, critics, influencers, and supporters (Bond, 2011).

Remember that the best social media strategies consist of 90% listening and 10% activation (Bond, 2011). Most of your marketing strategy should consist of not saying anything at all. Rather, stay up to date on what the public sphere has to say about your product. Information about products and services is now based on the experiences of audiences, rather than a predetermined and carefully planned marketing strategy developed by producers. The focus of social media specialists should not always be on the creation of online content. A strong practitioner will spend most of his or her time gathering and reading online content.

While the focus of a convergence culture was in the opportunities brought by increased audience dialogue, it is interesting that the focus of a post-convergence era is on not saying anything at all. Integrating social media into a marketing strategy requires a long view of an entire ecosystem, where all elements of traditional and new media work together (Hanna *et al.*, 2011). The focus of this type of strategy must remain on the audience. Perhaps no industry has struggled with the principles of integration of traditional and new media elements as much as the television industry. One reason may be its considerable lack of knowledge on its latent audiences, as the television industry has historically treated its audiences as an aggregate. Let's now turn our attention towards a case study to see how audiences react to an alternative form of a reality television show, *Rising Star*.

Case Study: ABC's *Rising Star*

Media convergence has substantially changed the ways in which individuals engage content. Often, traditional forms are remixed, remediated or refashioned to meet audience expectations. As users continue to adapt to convergence and gain more control over their content choices, it is clear that the television industry must also alter content in order to suit audience expectations.

One way that the television industries have attempted to meet this demand is through reality television programming. The reality television genre is built on the principles of a more factual and authentic viewing experience, where what the audience views on screen represents real-life individuals and behaviors (Hill, 2005). Viewers are attracted to reality-based programming because it represents real-life drama reflecting the complexities of the human condition (Orbe, 2008). Because of audience appeal and low production cost, the reality genre has now evolved into a $100 billion media industry (Rose, 2013). Almost every television network across the world has its own brand of reality-based television. In particular, reality musical competition programs have peaked in popularity over the past decade.

Some of the most popular musical competition reality shows include *American Idol* in the United States, *Popstars* in Australia, and *Pop Idol* in the United Kingdom. The formula for these reality shows is fairly similar, as everyday ordinary citizens hoping to become stars compete with one another each week. Television audiences are asked to call in and vote on which participant they feel had the best performance. Votes are tallied over a period of time, usually a week's worth of broadcasting, and on the next show performers with the highest number of viewer votes get to move. The final winner of the program usually gets a musical contract to become a star.

Here you can see many of the elements of a convergence culture at play. Not only is there a merging of two media devices – television and telephones – but there are cultural equalizers as well. Audiences are given more power in deciding who deserves fame and who doesn't, what musical genres and tastes should be rewarded, and the final resolution for a television narrative (Holmes, 2004).

The formula for the successors of reality musical competitions has not changed too much since its debut in 2000. However, the opportunities for integrating more synchronous and user-generated media elements into a television program have. One show that has attempted to redefine traditional television musical competitions is ABC's *Rising Star*.

Rising Star is a singing competition that is broadcast live and considered a "game-changer" for the television industry. Audiences are asked to download an application on their mobile devices, upload a personal picture, and vote in "real time" as they watch the program. If the voting reaches a certain threshold (70% of votes), the performer will move on to the next round of competition (ABC, 2014).

Some of the hypermediacy elements that make it more interactive than traditional musical competition reality shows include the synchronous nature of voting. The broadcast and voting are done live, which requires traditional appointment television viewing. Additionally, audiences include a picture of themselves with their vote, and so as they participate, they are able to see themselves on screen behind the performers. This personalizes the television viewing experience. Audiences are also encouraged to follow along and interact with other viewers on social media through hashtags. Moreover, the competition participants are able to see audience reactions while they are performing. This provides immediate feedback, which undoubtedly influences their final product.

The television series first aired on ABC on June 22, 2014. Just like all products of media convergence, it hinged on audience participation for success. Audiences needed to have already downloaded and registered the voting application on their mobile devices before the program began. Therefore, producers decided it would interrupt another reality program, *The Bachelorette*, earlier in the week to prompt audiences to download the application and test the voting system. If enough members participated and they reached the voting threshold of 70%, *Bachelorette* fans were rewarded with an exclusive premiere.

Nonetheless, online responses to the prompt were not well received. Online bloggers called it "super awkward," "a trainwreck" and "uncomfortable" (Dries, 2014; Snetiker, 2014). Others identified "the logistical nightmare of creating a show in which the producers do not know what will happen" (Kessler, 2014). This was especially apparent given that one of the show's musical hosts, Ludacris, was unable to make the live premiere due to being stuck in a helicopter (Yahr, 2014). It was a very strange situation, where the hosts of *Rising Star* felt inclined to apologize to television audiences for interrupting their broadcast and begging them to take action immediately (Dehnart, 2014).

Rising Star undoubtedly changes the traditional model of television viewing. It incorporates both traditional and new media elements into its content in a post-convergence media landscape. On the surface, it appears to be doing all the right things. However, it premiered at 1.5 rating among adults aged 18–49 years (Hibberd, 2014), which indicates the difficulty in predicting how audiences will react to hypermediacy elements on a traditionally transparent screen. The Internet will continue to bring many interactive features to the traditional television industry, including more interactive structural advantages, greater audience participation, and more flexibility in creating content. However, it is just unclear how willing audiences will be to adapt to these changes.

Discussion questions

1   How did reality television musical competitions change many of the transparent immediacy norms of traditional television broadcasting?

2   One of the great advantages of *Rising Star* over other reality competition shows is the increased interactivity from audiences. How does the process of audience identification change as the voting shifts from a pre-recorded broadcast to real-time results?

3   Audiences did not immediately react positively to the hypermediacy format of *Rising Star*. How can this reaction be explained based on the principles of remediation theory? What would you advise if you were in charge of future strategy for ABC?

Summary

This chapter discusses the many ways in which media convergence has influenced society. Beyond just the blending of traditional media devices, convergence has changed assumptions and powers associated with an online audience. Many media practitioners have approached the convergence era as an opportunity to reach multiple audiences across various media platforms. This still designates a push strategy, where strategies are developed based on predetermined marketing objectives. Instead, the convergence culture should focus on bringing audiences to the center of your production and post-innovation process.

Still, it can be confusing to navigate marketing strategies when new media landscapes are constantly changing. You must purposefully incorporate new technologies into existing business models. The principles of remediation theory should help guide your decisions. Remediation tells us that audiences adapt gradually to change, and therefore it is best to slowly introduce elements of hypermediacy, rather than revamping all existing media content at once. Rather than focusing on how existing models can be reformatted to fit within the media landscape, let audience behaviors and feedback guide these decisions. Remember that as a social media practitioner, it is almost always better to listen rather than speak.

There are many unknowns for the future of social media marketing. As we reach a post-convergence era, it is important to look ahead at many of the challenges future practitioners will face. The move towards user-generated content has certainly brought many great opportunities for everyday consumers. However, many of the promises of a more democratic industry promised by media convergence have fallen short. Issues of culture, policy and agenda-setting have yet to be sorted out, and without a careful watch we may lose the opportunity for substantial social change. It is important not to get lost in individual company goals. Take a long-term approach, as every decision impacts your future.

Overall, this chapter introduces principles that should help guide strategic social media marketing decisions in a changing media landscape. All decisions should be made with a focus on audience expectations and brand authenticity. This becomes even more important as audiences expect an increased amount of transparency from your company. In fact, these new expectations will be the center of future industry changes.

Let's now turn attention to the merging of these concepts: behavior change, marketing, social change, and future strategy development. Chapter 18 will examine social media for social behavior change. This explains how the future of social media must account for each of these areas in order to survive. The future of marketing is sustainability, and this requires a strong *We First* centered campaign.

Key Takeaways

1   Media convergence is a process of industry changes that combine markets and products to meet various consumer needs. Specifically, it is noted that media convergence goes beyond just the merging of technological devices, but includes the flow of content across multiple media platforms, the cooperation between multiple media industries, and the migratory behavior of media audiences.

2   In a convergent media environment, audiences should be at the center of the production and product-innovation process, and be given more control over the flow of media content, especially through social media platforms.

3   Decisions about how to integrate new and traditional media forms into a marketing strategy should be guided by remediation theory. Strategies should include elements that favor both hypermediacy and transparent immediacy to ensure the best reception from audiences. Integrating new media elements too quickly or slowly could be detrimental to an organization.
4   While the convergence culture brought many positive opportunities to society, many important concerns are surfacing again in a post-convergence era, including issues of culture, policy and structure. While these concerns have not yet been resolved, they should be considered as future marketing strategies are developed.

References

ABC (2014) *Rising Star*. Available at http://abc.go.com/shows/rising-star (accessed June 8, 2016).

Appelgren, E. (2004) Convergence and divergence in media: different perspectives. Available at http://elpub.scix.net/data/works/att/237elpub2004.content.pdf (accessed June 8, 2016).

Apperley, T. (2007) Citizenship and consumption: convergence culture, transmedia narratives and the digital divide. In: *Proceedings of the 4th Australasian Conference on Interactive Entertainment*, article no. 2. Melbourne, Australia: RMIT University.

Bar, F. & Sandvig, C. (2008) US Communication policy after conference. *Media, Culture, & Society*, 30(4), 531–550.

Bird, S.E. (2011) Are we all produsers now? Convergence and media audience practices. *Cultural Studies*, 25(4–5), 502–516.

Blau, M. (2011) 4 ways Steve Jobs and Apple changed the music industry. Available at http://mashable.com/2011/10/11/apple-changed-music/ (accessed June 8, 2016).

Bolter, J. & Grusin, R. (2002) *Remediation: Understanding New Media*. Cambridge, MA: MIT Press.

Bond, M. (2011) Demystifying social media. Available at http://www.coastdigital.co.uk/files/publications/coast_digital/social-media-guide.pdf (accessed June 8, 2016).

Brito, M. (2013) Converged media is imperative to your content strategy. Available at http://blog.hootsuite.com/converged-media-brito-part-2/ (accessed June 8, 2016).

Chan-Olmsted, S.M. (2004) Traditional media and the Internet: the search for viable business models. *International Journal on Media Management*, 6(1–2), 2–3.

Chan-Olmsted, S.M. & Ha, L.S. (2003) Internet business models for broadcasters: how television stations perceive and integrate the Internet. *Journal of Broadcasting and Electronic Media*, 47(4), 597–617.

Cooper, R. & Tang, T. (2009) Predicting audience exposure to television in today's media environment: an empirical integration of active-audience and structural theories. *Journal of Broadcasting and Electronic Media*, 53(3), 400–418.

Dehnart, A. (2014) ABC bribed Bachelor Nation to promote Rising Star and revealed a potential problem. Available at http://www.realityblurred.com/realitytv/archives/rising_star/2014_Jun_17_promo-app-chemistry (accessed June 8, 2016).

Deuze, M. (2007) Convergence culture in the creative industries. *International Journal of Cultural Studies*, 10(2), 243–263.

Deuze, M. (2008) The professional identity of journalists in the context of convergence culture. *Observatorio Journal*, 7, 103–117.

DeVoss, D.N. & Webb, S. (2008) Media convergence: *Grand Theft Audio*: Negotiating copyright as composers. *Computers and Composition*, 25(1), 79–103.

Dries, K. (2014) ABC tested the voting system for Rising Star and it was super awkward. Available at http://jezebel.com/abc-tested-the-voting-system-for-rising-star-and-it-was-1591897204 (accessed June 8, 2016).

Drury, G. (2008) Opinion piece: Social media: should marketers engage and how can it be done effectively? *Journal of Direct, Data and Digital Marketing Practice*, 9(3), 274–277.

Fagerjord, A. (2010) After convergence: YouTube and remix culture. In: J. Hunsinger, L. Klastrup & M. Allen (eds) *International Handbook of Internet Research*, pp. 187–200. Dordrecht, Netherlands: Springer.

Frenk, J. & Gómez-Dantés, O. (2002) Globalization and the challenges to health systems. *Health Affairs*, 21(3), 160–165.

Griffiths, M. & Light, B. (2008) Social networking and digital gaming media convergence: classification and its consequences for appropriation. *Information Systems Frontiers*, 10(4), 447–459.

Ha, L. & Chan-Olmsted, S.M. (2004) Cross-media use in electronic media: the role of cable television web sites in cable television network branding and viewership. *Journal of Broadcasting and Electronic Media*, 48(4), 620–648.

Hanna, R., Rohm, A. & Crittenden, V.L. (2011) We're all connected: the power of the social media ecosystem. *Business Horizons*, 54(3), 265–273.

Hibberd, J. (2014) ABC's "Rising Star" ratings: not so bright. Available at http://www.ew.com/article/2014/06/23/rising-star-ratings (accessed June 8, 2016).

Hill, A. (2005) *Reality TV: Audiences and Popular Factual Television*. Abingdon: Routledge.

Holmes, S. (2004) "Reality goes pop!" Reality TV, popular music, and narratives of stardom in Pop Idol. *Television and New Media*, 5(2), 147–172.

Jenkins, H. (2003) Quentin Tarantino's Star Wars? Digital cinema, media convergence, and participatory culture. In: D. Thorburn & H. Jenkins (eds) *Rethinking Media Change: The Aesthetics of Transition*, pp. 281–312. Cambridge, MA: MIT Press.

Jenkins, H. (2004) The cultural logic of media convergence. *International Journal of Cultural Studies*, 7(1), 33–43.

Jenkins, H. (2006) *Convergence Culture: Where Old and New Media Collide*. New York: New York University Press.

Kessler, S. (2014) ABC's "Rising Star" explores the app-driven future of TV. Available at http://www.fastcompany.com/3031870/most-creative-people/abcs-rising-star-explores-the-app-driven-future-of-tv (accessed June 8, 2016).

Kietzmann, J., Hermkens, K., McCarthy, I. & Silvestre, B. (2011) Social media? Get serious! Understanding the functional building blocks of social media. *Business Horizons*, 54(3), 241–251.

Laurel, B. (2000) Creating core content in a post-convergence world. Available at http://tauzero.com/Brenda_Laurel/Recent_Talks/ContentPostConvergence.html (accessed June 8, 2016).

Lin, J. & Cho, C. (2010) Antecedents and consequences of cross-media usage: a study of a TV program's official web site. *Journal of Broadcasting and Electronic Media*, 54(2), 316–336.

Mangold, W. & Faulds, D. (2009) Social media: the new hybrid element of the promotion mix. *Business Horizons*, 52(4), 357–365.

McKain, A. (2005) Not necessarily not the news: gatekeeping, remediation, and *The Daily Show*. *Journal of American Culture*, 28(4), 415–430.

McMillan, S., Hoy, M., Kim, J. & McMahan, C. (2008) A multifaceted tool for a complex phenomenon: coding web-based interactivity as technologies for interaction evolve. *Journal of Computer-Mediated Communication*, 13, 794–826.

McNulty, S. (2006) iTunes: From 0 to 7.0. Available at http://www.engadget.com/2006/09/14/itunes-from-0-0-to-7-0/ (accessed June 8, 2016).

Nettleton, S., Burrows, R. & O'Malley, L. (2005) The mundane realities of the everyday lay use of the internet for health, and their consequences for media convergence. *Sociology of Health and Illness*, 27(7), 972–992.

Orbe, M. (2008) Representations of race in reality TV: watch and discuss. *Critical Studies in Media Communication*, 25(4), 345–352.

Peirce, L.M. (2011) Remediation theory: analyzing what made *Quarterlife* successful as an online series and not a television series. *Television and New Media*, 12(4), 314–325.

Picard, R.G. (2000) Changing business models of online content services. *International Journal of Media Management*, 2(2), 60–68.

Rajewsky, I. (2005) Intermediality, intertextuality, and remediation: a literary perspective on intermediality. *Intermédialités*, 6, 43–64.

Ries, A. & Ries, L. (2000) *The 11 Immutable Laws of Internet Branding*. New York: HarperCollins.

Rose, M. (2013) The unreal rise of reality television. Available at http://www.huffingtonpost.com/michael-rose/

the-unreal-rise-of-realit_b_3976751.html   (accessed June 8, 2016).

Snetiker, M. (2014) "Rising Star" turns a clever voting gimmick into a reality trainwreck. Available at http://www.ew.com/article/2014/06/22/rising-star-review (accessed June 8, 2016).

Stratten, S. (2012) *UnMarketing. Stop Marketing. Start Engaging*. Hoboken, NJ: John Wiley & Sons, Inc.

Thielmann, B. & Dowling, M. (1999) Convergence and innovation strategy for service provision in emerging Web-TV markets. *International Journal on Media Management*, 1(1), 4–9.

Trigg, S. (2008) Medievalism and convergence culture: researching the Middle Ages for fiction and film. *Parergon*, 25(2), 99–118.

Yahr, E. (2014) Why are Brad Paisley, Ludacris and Kesha subjecting themselves to "Rising Star"? Available at   https://www.washingtonpost.com/news/arts-and-entertainment/wp/2014/06/18/why-are-brad-paisley-ludacris-and-kesha-subjecting-themselves-to-rising-star/ (accessed June 8, 2016).

18

Social Media for Social Behavior Change

Learning Objectives

After reading this chapter, you should be able to:

1 Apply *We First* marketing to a social media campaign.
2 Examine the role of identification in the behavior change process.
3 Understand how the creation of a socially conscious strategy may lead to an increased return on investment.

Introduction

Chapter 17 discussed many of the challenges of media convergence. This consolidation of traditionally separated communication has substantially changed the way organizations reach and interact with audiences. We also know that interface structure changes with media convergence. Media convergence requires you to incorporate structural elements from both transparent immediacy and hypermediacy into a new marketing strategy.

It is important to explore the many ways in which media content also converges with new media. Often, this is due to new participatory features available through digital media that encourages more transactional dialogue between users. We have discussed how users want more transparency and interactive opportunities from organizational websites. Understanding these new demands of convergent users is imperative for any organization trying to find a niche in today's marketplace.

Strategic Social Media: From Marketing to Social Change, First Edition. L. Meghan Mahoney and Tang Tang.
© 2017 John Wiley & Sons, Inc. Published 2017 by John Wiley & Sons, Inc.

Businesses face many challenges due to changes in user expectations. Consumers are now able to instantly compare prices with virtual marketplaces; they have unlimited buying options beyond their local retailers; and they are able to publicize negative anonymous feedback when customer service expectations are not met. Parts II and III of this book provided theoretical framework and advice for dealing with these issues. The purpose of this chapter is to explore how consumers are entering the marketplace with new globalized motivations to build a better world. Chapter 14 explored how social media influences civic engagement all around the world. While not everyone is interested in taking huge steps towards changing laws and social structure, there are many ways in which the marketplace is positively changing through small day-to-day consumer purchasing decisions. Marketers have new opportunities to target these socially conscious consumers in order to increase their return on investment, and make a positive change in society.

Socially conscious consumers are those who take into account the consequences of private purchasing decisions and choose products that minimize harmful effects and maximize long-run beneficial impact on society (Mohr *et al.*, 2001). New media have allowed users increased knowledge regarding the products that they consume. This information creates material expectations and values about social issues, such as the environment, and thereby encourages prosocial forms of consumption (Keum *et al.*, 2004).

This chapter begins with an introduction to the *We First* marketing movement and explains how it benefits companies, consumers, and the planet alike. Second, we explore ways in which users can better make purchasing decisions in their daily lives and the responsibility that comes with the privilege of unlimited information access. This chapter also explains why humans inherently identify stronger with prosocial consumption practices, which can be better for a business's bottom line. Finally, it explains the Global Reporting Initiative and how business stakeholders are developing transparent and sustainable guidelines for corporate social responsibility programs.

We First

We First is a book written by Simon Mainwaring (2011) that focuses on the role that social media plays in encouraging businesses and consumers to change practices to create a better world. The book is built on the premise that social media gives consumers the chance to demand increased transparency into how the products they buy influence the world they inhabit (www.wefirstbranding.com). While the normal buying and selling patterns of consumerism could remain the same, users are now empowered by online information about which products are best for the environment, global societies, and future generations.

In the opening pages of *We First* Mainwaring asks readers "Is this the world you want?" He references how free market capitalism is built on the idea of widespread and self-regulating wealth, but has transformed into a single-minded pursuit of profit for a small elite at the expense of the overall society (Mainwaring, 2011). The gap between rich and poor nations is growing, as well as the gap between rich and poor within these nations. There is a correlation between the information technology available in society and the increase in wealth for their economic future (Lucas & Sylla, 2003). Nations with better information access have growing economies, often at the expense of those who do not.

Remember from Chapter 15 that the theory of dependency suggests that the problems of the Third World would not disappear through economic development (Sood & Rogers, 2000), because the world is divided into three categories of societies: core, periphery, and semi-periphery. *Core societies* are wealthy, powerful, early-developing societies that maintain independent economic diversity. *Periphery societies* are relatively weak and poor nations that are subject to control by stronger societies. *Semi-periphery societies* are somewhere in between and are attempting to industrialize in order to gain more independence (Bollen, 1983).

Generally, as peripheral societies develop and gain economic markets, core societies also tend to benefit. This makes it more difficult for peripheral societies to minimize the economic gap, because as they get richer, so do the core societies. Developed nations profit from commerce while peripheral nations suffer from an unequal exchange process.

In some ways, the Internet is increasing this gap between the rich and the poor (Lucas & Sylla, 2003). Companies are now able to hire employees anywhere in the world, which may lead to lower wages and decreased employee regulations. While this does create greater job opportunities for some regions of the world, corporations also increase profits due to the lower cost of operation. Thus, the wide profit gap continues.

Many companies find that the least expensive option is to manufacture products at the expense of environmental concerns and poor labor practices in order to keep selling costs low and competitive. China is the world's largest manufacturer. This has severe consequences on the land, which is not designed to support such heavy usage. In China's northwest region, one-third of the country's grassland has now turned to desert. Dust storms carry pollutants to surrounding areas, so that China has 16 of the 20 most polluted cities in the world (Matisoff, 2013).

Consumers play an important role in the mounting pressure on businesses to keep costs low. Mainwaring (2011) warns that unless something is changed about the ways in which all societies consume products, we will only secure short-term profit for the few, at the expense of the environment and peripheral societies. Consequently, these changes will negatively impact the majority.

The shift from *Me First* thinking, where everyone is concerned with the single-minded pursuit of profit, to *We First* thinking, where all corporations, businesses, consumers, and citizens use capitalism as a driver of prosperity for the greater good, is more possible than ever before (Mainwaring, 2011). Social media provides the opportunity for individuals to connect around shared values and take action. Consumers are now sharing in brand narratives and sharing their experiences surrounding the products that they purchase. We have become more mindful about the products that we buy, and if we take the time to realize the influence that our purchasing decisions have on the world in production, distribution and profit stages, we can make small changes to fight against poverty, child mortality, clean water, renewable energy, climate change, and environment degradation (www.wefirstbranding.com).

There are many social media resources that consumers are able to turn to when making such a decision. Envimpact.org provides users with a composite environmental index that measures the life cycle of products and how much pollution is created to produce, use and dispose of the item. There is also a forum where users discuss other ways that they can get involved in local initiatives to help the environment. LocalHarvest.org is a website where users can go and look up local organic foods that are grown and produced in their neighborhood. The Local Harvest blog discusses the benefits of eating local and organic, and shares pictures from around the United States. LaborVoices.com provides workers the opportunity to anonymously report unfair working conditions, which helps guide employees to the best factories to work with and puts pressure on corporations to only supply their products through the most reputable manufacturers.

Users around the world are using social media to share concerns and inform themselves about consumption decisions. Mainwaring (2011) identifies globalization, interconnectedness, complexity of problems, population explosion, environmental threats, power shifts, and demographics of change as the reasons individuals are moving towards *We First* consumption.

Users receive information from all over the world each day, causing them to see themselves and the role they play in society as larger than just their everyday community. Younger generations see themselves as a member of a globalized society with less borders and increased cross-cultural communication. A stronger and more reliant interconnectedness between societies comes with globalization. In sum, we care more about the world we live in.

The theory of dependency illustrates how the actions of one society hold consequences for others. For example, simply throwing trash on the ground directly impacts the appearance of your own community, but it also has deeper consequences for wildlife, water sources, and vegetation. This helps to demonstrate the complexity of economic inequity around the world.

World populations are growing at an alarming rate and the planet cannot sustain the rapid growth. If the world continues to increase its population by 70 million people a year, the planet cannot sustain renewable energies, food production and clean water supplies and the effects of increased pollution (Ehrlich & Holdren, 1971). By visiting a developing nation with the intention to build stronger infrastructure and bigger buildings and increase consumerism, the larger problems of the Third World are not solved. Moreover, it could further widen the gap between wealthy and poor societies. To a certain extent, every single human is responsible for the destabilization of ecological systems and use of renewable and nonrenewable resources.

While it may be easy for businesses to ignore these environmental threats, the general public cannot. Public concerns for environmental issues have steadily increased over the years (Dunlap, 1991). Individuals are more mindful than ever on issues such as climate change and carbon emissions. New technology allows consumers the opportunity to find information and communicate with businesses about their growing concerns. There has been a shift in power where businesses are no longer able to make decisions behind closed doors and must answer to the demands of everyday consumers. Companies today are also concerned with a more diverse demographic of consumers than in previous decades. Previously muted minority cultures now have a voice through social media.

Part III of this book discussed how social media created business opportunities for every market segment and niche audience. While previous advertising efforts may have been focused on demographics with the most spending power, companies are now realizing the potential for marketing to all demographics. Based on all these changes, it has never been a better time to change our consumption and production habits. It is clear why *We First* consumption is the best approach for the environment, workers and consumers. One of the most interesting findings to emerge from the last decade of marketing research is the possibility for businesses to increase profit through socially conscious marketing.

Traditional marketing research demonstrates how companies that associate themselves with a prosocial cause for a variety of reasons, including the ability to gain national visibility, enhance corporate image, promote repeat purchases, increase brand awareness, broaden customer base, and reach new market segments (Varadarajan & Menon, 1988). It can actually be a good economic decision for a brand to identify itself with a cause; however, profit should not be the sole reason for doing so. Mainwaring (2011) calls for *profit with a purpose*, where businesses build their brand and prosocial movement through their authenticity and company's true values. There are many ways in which consumers are able to utilize social media in order to determine how authentic corporations are regarding their cause.

profit with a purpose

As we move forward with more conscious consumer purchasing decisions, much of the burden for change falls on everyday citizens. While large corporations are able to make more socially conscious decisions, they will not do so without pressure from consumers. The next section explores ways in which you can change your own daily purchasing habits to better align with the *We First* strategy.

Role of the User

One of the oldest ways in which businesses have aimed to improve the world around them is through corporate social responsibility programs. *Corporate social responsibility* (CSR) is the policy and practice of corporate social involvement to satisfy social needs through economic, legal, ethical, and philanthropic responsibilities (Lii, 2011). There are three types of philanthropic CSR: sponsorship, cause-related marketing, and philanthropy.

Corporate social responsibility

1   *Sponsorship* includes a strategic investment where resources (money, staffing or facility) are given to an activity with commercial gain. Companies may sponsor a local sports team, or help efforts for a charitable event. These are great ways to boost brand images. Sponsorships often work best if there is a clear link between the product and the charity. For example, Nike's sponsorship of the Livestrong Foundation makes sense, given both of their commitment to health and athleticism. Many felt as though Coca-Cola and McDonalds' sponsorship of the 2012 London Olympic Games was inappropriate because it led to increased junk food advertising towards children (Phillips, 2012).

2   *Cause-related marketing* is when a company promises to donate a certain amount of money to a social cause when consumers purchase products or services. The Gap's Product Red campaign donates 50% of all profits to the Global Fund to help eliminate HIV/AIDS in Africa. However, many online communities are critical of the company's enormous overlay, marketing costs, and lack of nonprofit collaboration (Frazier, 2007). The best way to build a cause-related marketing strategy is to increase transparency

to consumers with regard to how much of the profit actually is donated and the tangible results of the initiative. This is where you see the benefits of a strong diffusion strategy.

3   *Philanthropy* is when a business donates to a cause simply to be a good citizen, without expectations for commercial or economic gain. More businesses around the world are allowing employees to take paid volunteer days to volunteer at the charity of their choice. This has resulted in better turnover rates, higher job satisfaction, and stronger employee enthusiasm (Baxter, 2013). Philanthropy also helps bolster business image around the community, as employees would likely spread volunteering efforts across many initiatives, not just the one or two causes that the head of company chose.

There are many reasons why a company would choose to engage in CSR. Consumers who identify with a cause are likely to exhibit increased loyalty, repeat purchasing behaviors, spread positive word of mouth, and show increased resilience to negative information (Lii, 2011). While consumption often makes customers feel bad for spending money, especially if it is something they do not need, cause branding makes them feel satisfied because it appeals to the natural human impulse to help others. Moreover, consumers begin to associate the feeling of helping others with the brand, and identify strongly with the mutual desire to help others. Married mothers are the most likely consumers to spend more for prosocial products (Laroche *et al.*, 2001). This demographic has huge spending power and has always been the primary target for corporate advertising. Cause marketing is a great way to gain their long-term loyalty and trust.

More than 80% of the Fortune 500 companies market the CSR programs that they participate in, especially as cause marketing becomes more of a norm in business practices. Not all CSR programs are as altruistic as the brand surrounding makes them appear. Consumers must be wary of cause washing, green washing and local washing from corporate marketing. These three marketing challenges have increased greatly over the past decade as more brands navigate consumer expectations for sustainability.

Generally, *cause washing* is associated with events where the number of units sold is correlated with an associated donation to the cause. Often, these donation numbers are miniscule or have established donation limits set ahead of time. In this case, it does not make a difference how many units the customer buys, though consumers feel as though they are making a difference by contributing. The website Think Before You Pink (www.thinkbeforeyoupink.org) is a critical look into the feel-good cause marketing programs. They investigate how many proceeds of the pink breast cancer awareness products actually go towards cancer research. Often, the results are surprisingly low. The website also raises awareness about "pink" products that contain chemicals that may actually be linked to breast cancer.

Green marketing is very trendy right now, as businesses know that most consumers are willing to spend more for a product if they feel it is better for the environment than an alternative product. *Green washing* is when the environmental friendliness of a brand is overstated. Greenwashing.com has created an online index where users are able to post a product that they have seen being advertised as good for the environment, and other community members can rate it with a "thumbs up" or a "bogus thumbs down." Plastic water bottles that advertise being green for reducing carbon emissions are often at the top of the bogus list for making it appear that using plastic water bottles is a green thing to do.

Consumers are also willing to spend more money on products they feel are produced, manufactured or grown locally, rather than exported (Brown, 2003). There are many societal benefits to buying local. Local consumer spending keeps profits within the community where it is more evenly distributed than from large corporations. It also reduces environmental impacts due to a decrease in packaging and travel costs. Many companies are realizing that localness is becoming more important to today's informed consumers.

However, *local washing* is whenever a company makes a product appear more local than it actually is (Mainwaring, 2011). In Argentina, Lay's Potato Chips tested a vending machine where consumers drop a real potato into the traditional coin slot. The vending machine plays a video that creates an illusion that the potato is turned into a bag of potato chips right there in front of them, and even uses lights to warm up the bag before distribution, making it appear fresher and less packaged than it actually is (Wentz, 2011).

As a consumer with access to unlimited digital information, it is imperative to begin investigating the types of products that you buy and their impact on the environment. Generally, consumers look for a logical fit between a brand and a cause. They want to clearly be able to see why a product is choosing to invest resources in a social cause (Barone *et al.*, 2007). The alliance must make sense, and if it doesn't and the cause is "washed," users will turn to social media to voice their outrage.

Consumers also want to see that companies are making investments consistent with their own values (Gupta & Pirsch, 2006). Identification is one of the most critical assessments consumers will make when selecting a cause. It is impossible for you as a business to care about all causes, and so it is important to determine what is most important to you and find corporations that align with your values. Once you have found companies that share in your philanthropy goals, purchasing behaviors will turn into habitual routines and you will not even notice the change.

For example, perhaps you are interested in natural living, but have always found it difficult to navigate natural products in big box stores. Shopping in traditional stores for natural products can leave consumers with little choice and higher-priced items. With a few minutes of Internet research, you are likely able to find hundreds of online and in-store options for retailers that only sell natural products. For instance, Vine.com is an online retailer for thousands of natural and organic goods, including grocery, beauty, home décor, fitness and even pets. In order for a product to be available on Vine.com, the company must review the vendor ingredients to make sure that they are made from mostly sustainable materials and designed to remove toxins, taking most of the guesswork out for consumers. This retailer puts all natural options in one place and also offers free delivery, making it easier than ever to find natural products online that fit within your lifestyle and budget.

It would prove incredibly time-consuming to research every single product before purchasing. By choosing a small number of important causes that are unique to your life experiences, it will not take much effort to change your buying habits. Chances are there is a social media community that is dedicated to the same vision. Join, participate and share your experiences. Even if you just change one or two habits, it will make a difference. Do not worry about causes that you are not so enthusiastic about rallying behind. There is a social media community out there filled with people who strongly identify with their goals and values. It is their job to spread awareness and put pressure on companies in support of their initiatives. Focus on the prosocial causes that you already esteem and whose information and research you would actually enjoy receiving. Be a vocal and participatory member for the causes that you feel the most passionate towards.

It is your job as a consumer to spread the word if you see something that does not align with your prosocial vision. If you walk by a business that markets themselves as "green" yet has recyclable materials in their dumpster, put pressure on them to make a change. They may appreciate the suggestion, as they are hopefully invested in their green marketing strategy. Amazon has taken active steps to contact outside vendors that receive negative feedback from customers about excess product packaging. They send engineers to help companies build better designs. This initiative boosts customer satisfaction, lowers shipping costs, and appeals to environmentally conscious consumers (Edwards, 2011).

Research has found that 30% of people claim to be interested in the environmental and ethical integrity of products that they purchase, yet only 3% report translating this attitude into behavior change (Gordon, 2002). Changing consumption behavior is difficult, and often done with such mindlessness that you do not even realize that you could be making better choices. While individual users hold some responsibility in researching the products that they buy online, the more pressure we can put on businesses, the more they will voluntarily increase their standards for sustainability. It would be great to live in a world where individuals do not have to research every single product before purchasing because all businesses engage in ethical and long-term prosocial decision-making. Until then, it is our role and duty as consumers to be mindful about the products we buy.

We are all consumers of products. *We First* thinking encourages you to think about how your purchasing decisions influence the world around you. As a current or future social media practitioner, it is likely that you will have a say in future business strategies of the world. The next section explains the benefits of cause marketing, both on the world and on the company's bottom line.

Identification through Social Behavior

Mainwaring (2011) outlines a *consumer evolution process* to more responsible consumption habits, which includes individual commitment, community engagement, promotion of values, driving awareness, thought leadership, building a community, and connecting communities.

Individual commitment is the stage in which consumers change their own habits through more mindful shopping. They use the Internet to gain product information and investigate the ways in which their habits influence the world around them. Next they enter the community engagement stage. Here, they find online communities and participate in online conversations with like-minded individuals.

The third stage, *promotion of values*, is when consumers start to communicate with others in their network about their values, beyond those who already agree. They begin advocating through social media and taking real-life actions to push back on companies whose visions

[Handwritten margin notes:]

30% claim to care about environment
3% make actual behavior change

consumer evolution process
1. Individual Commitment
2. Community Engagement
3. Promotion of values
4. Become leaders + advocates for the cause — leadership process
5. Build a community
6. connect w/ other communities

do not align. This leads to the driving awareness stage. Others outside of the cause encounter these messages, which leads to an increased awareness. The activist's individual social network becomes more knowledgeable about the cause, as well as targeted organizations and businesses. In this stage, the single vision has turned into a more collaborative effort among a network.

Eventually, consumers become leaders and advocates for the cause. Next, they enter the thought leadership process, where they produce arguments that others need to persuade the public. These can take the form of books, articles, interviews, videos, webinars, blogs, and tweets (Mainwaring, 2011). This process leads to building a community, where consumers organize people to take collective action. This can occur online or offline. Finally, they connect with other communities to synchronize efforts, which results in a strong social change movement.

It is imperative for consumers to research and investigate the products that they buy in order to understand the impact it is making on society. It is also a smart business choice for corporations to brand themselves authentically through prosocial behaviors. Humans identify emotionally with cause marketing, which can lead towards more loyal and long-term behavior change practices. Communication professionals must take advantage of this opportunity and fulfill our natural desire to positively impact the world.

Advertising has always engaged in lifestyle marketing, where messages tell consumers the latest indicators of self-worth and social distinction and what makes "the good life." Consequently, consumers engage in status-conscious consumption where we desire to purchase goods that meet these ideals (Keum *et al.*, 2004).

We use consumption as a way to brand ourselves and the roles we play in society. *Social identity theory* demonstrates how humans perceive themselves through their interactions with others, the status of their network, and support from institutions (Ashforth & Mael, 1989). These distinctions are traditionally formed based on the community in which we live. If you were unable to find acceptance in your local proximity, your social identity consequently suffered. Social media has provided a space where individuals are able to find community outside the boundaries of where they live.

Nonetheless, shared identity is something that is difficult, if not impossible, to achieve with brands and corporations. After all, if humans perceive themselves based on interactions, status and support, there is a natural power difference in the consumption process. Consumers have always been at the bottom of the corporate relationship. Though a free market society is built on the premise that everyday consumers play a role in what is available and how much products cost, the process is complex. Consumers are unlikely to feel as though they have power as they hand their money over to corporations.

Social media has made great strides in transforming this relationship. We have discussed how consumers now have participatory relationships with brands through social media. They are now able to access, share and communicate with corporations. This helps us identify with businesses, as there is a real person responding (hopefully!) to social media messages.

Brands are also able to promote status in a way that members of our community are not. It feels very different receiving a message from a major corporation, especially one that you identify with, than receiving a message from your friend. We get excited. We share the experience with our network. This becomes a unique part of our life experience, and we feel valued by the brand. This is a brand's way of lending support, which increases identification even more.

Think of the prosocial cause that you strongly identify with. Is it cancer research? Environmental issues? Animal activism? There is a real-life experience that has made you passionate about that initiative. Maybe your mother was diagnosed with breast cancer, and you were able to talk to others going through the same scary experience. Online communities are formed based on these mutual experiences. Individuals who have never met in person are able to create and sustain relationships through these shared concerns Companies are now able to access these relationships and say "I care about that too." Every time you walk by a product that has "gone pink" in support of breast cancer research, maybe you will think of your mother. This makes shopping a much more emotional experience. Hopefully, this message is delivered with an authentic narrative that extends beyond increasing profits.

Humans have a natural desire to make a positive impact on the world. Volunteering increases individual happiness, life satisfaction, self-esteem, and sense of control over life, physical health and depression (Thoits & Hewitt, 2001). Consumers are able to experience some of the emotional benefits of giving that they normally would not receive through traditional consumption of goods. This purchase satisfaction is longer-lasting as you feel positive feelings about your cause each time it is used. These initiatives are also able to create a social experience, as you encounter others who have invested themselves in the same initiatives. This works best if a product is branded differently from traditional products, such as pink awareness ribbons or yellow Livestrong bracelets. Maybe every time you see someone wearing TOMS shoes you think more positively of them. They have branded themselves as someone who cares about a cause and is willing to make purchasing decisions to make a difference.

While there is much debate in the field about whether businesses are engaging in CSR activities solely for profit sake, the positive potential for social change is there. Humans want others to associate them as someone who cares about the world. This desire can translate into purchasing products that are better for social good.

Case Study: Global Reporting Initiative

This chapter highlights the many ways in which consumers are putting pressure on businesses to create a more mindful and sustainable marketplace. It is important to highlight many ways in which businesses are taking proactive initiatives by creating prosocial measures on their own. These businesses are paving the path towards good capitalism for the benefit of society.

TOMS shoes is one example of a business with an authentic desire for change. Their "One for One" contributory business strategy was one of the first of its kind: with every pair of shoes purchased at TOMS, a pair of shoes is given to a child in need. This business strategy results in more than 10 million shoes donated, and collaborations with other organizations with similar initiatives (TOMS, 2016). Accenture, an Ireland-based global management consulting technology service and outsourcing company, has been named one of the world's most ethical companies by Ethisphere consistently since 2006. Their website (Accenture.com) explains how the business is built on 58 action statements that include working with the best people, having respect for all individuals, and working with a vision for one global network.

While there is much individual companies can do in the pursuit of more conscious business practices, the most effective social movements are those done through collaboration efforts. Some of the biggest drivers for change include the United Nations Global Compact (unglobalcompact.org), the International Organization for Standardization (ISO.org), the International Labor Organization (ILO), World Resources Institute (WRI.org), and the Institute for Sustainable Communities (iscvt.org). One organization that is regulated and organized by businesses around the world, and which focuses on increased transparency and global social responsibility, is the Global Reporting Initiative.

The Global Reporting Initiative (GRI) is a leading coalition in the fight towards better guidelines for businesses to report economic, environmental, and social performance (Hedberg & von Malmborg, 2003). Founded in 1997 by organizations of the Coalition for Environmentally Responsible Economies, this nonprofit project aims to create guidelines for what voluntary CSR programs should include (Globalreporting.org).

The GRI sustainability reporting framework is based on a stakeholder network of thousands of experts, in dozens of countries worldwide (Global Reporting Initiative, 2009). These business leaders work together to determine how to best quantify sustainable measurements and share recommendations for better business practices. Sustainability reporting helps organizations recognize risk and opportunities. The hope is that the results of these reports will help shape policy, and future strategy and operations (Boulter, 2011).

The first step in the GRI process is for organizations to consider the sustainability of their core product. How long do products last? Are there any harmful side effects? How much waste is it contributing to society (Boulter, 2011)? Once these items are measured, more can be done to minimize negative impacts on the environment.

The hope is that as more businesses join GRI's efforts, sustainability report will become as routine as financial reporting (Global Reporting Initiative, 2009). It will be natural for organizations to consider environmental impact, just as they consider profit margins. Currently, a better balance must be met between individual and collective interests and GRI is one step towards doing so. This will benefit companies, civil society organizations, organized labor, and the financial sector (Brown *et al.*, 2009).

Nonetheless, the GRI struggles with mutually competing expectations, as many problems arise with increased transparency (Brown *et al.*, 2009). Businesses are likely to become competitive with the process, which can be a good thing for better regulations or lead towards inaccurate reporting (Levy *et al.*, 2010). Currently, there is little governance or oversight into how companies independently measure their efforts according to the standardizations put forth. These are understandable challenges, given the structure and innovative nature of the initiative. Each year these concerns are better addressed as the network continues to grow. The potential for future standards and regulations is hopeful.

The GRI's mission states that transparent and accountable disclosure will benefit consumers and businesses alike. A sustainable global economy should combine long-term profitability with social justice and environmental care. This allows companies the ability to better measure and report their sustainability performance in a more uniform manner. An increase in transparency will strengthen the trust that stakeholders and consumers have in one another. The more businesses that align with GRI, the less work consumers will have to put into investigating products before consumption.

Discussion questions

1 How does the Global Reporting Initiative align with the principles of *We First* marketing?
2 Why is it more important than ever for companies to consider increased transparency about the sustainability of their products in the age of social media?
3 What are the biggest opportunities for a uniform GRI process? What challenges will they have to overcome in the future?

Summary

This chapter further demonstrates how organizations looking to incorporate prosocial marketing into their business strategies should highlight diffusion, community and mobilization for consumers. There must be clear diffusion of information regarding the authenticity of prosocial initiatives. Companies should share their story about why they have chosen to get involved with the movement that they have selected. There are numerous examples of companies successfully providing this narrative for consumers online.

Brand narratives are very important to how audiences emotionally connect with your company. The McDonald's website shares the story of the first Ronald McDonald house opening in Philadelphia in 1974, and how it led to their mission to create, find and support programs that directly improve the health and well-being of children (RMHC, 2013). Apple's website includes an interactive section where users can see a visual timeline for how every product is produced and distributed, and why this transparency is important to them (Apple, 2013). Coca-Cola's website shares the personal experience of individual team members and their transformation from being hired, to their shared vision with the brand's commitment to partnership between business, government and civic society (Knoll, 2013).

These narratives help consumers identify more strongly with the cause. It is also important for companies to provide as much transparency as possible about the production, consumption and profit of products. Remember that consumer trust increases with the amount of information provided by the company. It should be made as easy as possible for consumers to identify what impact the company's efforts are making in the world.

Community is an crucial part of the *We First* business and consumer experience. It is the responsibility of each consumer to determine which social issue they identify strongest with and join online communities that share in that vision. By becoming more mindful in product choice, consumers advance on the customer evolution process, which helps spread awareness and puts pressure on organizations to make smarter production and distribution decisions. If we all used the power of collective community, it would take less research and mindfulness to make conscious consumer decisions.

Finally, mobilization is the third essential element of the behavior change process. It is not enough for users to care about certain prosocial issues, but this concern must translate into real-life action. Every small mindful purchasing decisions become a part of routine and habit. Eventually, these small changes evolve into personal advocates for change. Social media makes it easier than ever to investigate the impact your purchasing decisions make on the world. Investigate sustainability and environment indexes, and be willing to align your money with your value system. Mobilization allows consumers to join with other organizations and collaborate for change. These small real-life mobilization efforts will translate into substantial social changes.

When *We First* asked "Is this the world you want?" we likely all considered our own life experiences. There is something in all of our lives that we wish could be better: a family member not to be sick; education not to be so expensive; maybe more time to spend with friends. We have the ability to use social media to help change some of these scenarios. While it is always important to take a step back and look at what we can improve about our own lives, it is refreshing to see that future generations are taking the time to look at the lives and societies around them as well. It is probably the time to ask "Is this the world that *they* want? Is this the world that they *deserve*?" Your everyday actions hold potential in making things better for everyone.

This chapter discusses ways in which the *We First* movement changes the structure and power between companies and consumers. It introduces the small changes that individuals can make to be more mindful of our environment. It discusses the responsibility consumers now have in choosing and researching prosocial initiatives that are of interest them. Finally, it explains how humans identify stronger with cause marketing than they do with traditional marketing.

Social media has made a huge impact on the relationship between corporations and consumers. This book has highlighted ways in which it has influenced other areas of our lives as well, including the public health industry, civic engagement, and the products we buy. It is not just communication and marketing practitioners that prove interested in these changes. Nearly every field has been impacted by changes in audience communication and expectations through social media. Let's explore some of these areas and argue for a general framework for social media scholarship in Chapter 19.

> ## Key Takeaways
>
> 1 In an increasingly globalized society, it is difficult to ignore the way everyday purchasing decisions influence societies around us. This has caused consumers and business alike to start shifting decisions from what is in their best interests to what is best for society.
> 2 Social media is the key to *We First* thinking because it allows users to seek information, communicate with brands, and unite for collective action.
> 3 Brands are beginning to build prosocial programs in response to an increased consumer push. The most successful programs are those that are authentic, transparent and accountable.
> 4 Users have the ability to do more research on the brands that they purchase. This investigation can uncover cause washing, local washing, and green washing of products by businesses looking to make a profit without an authentic concern for the cause.
> 5 Consumers are willing to spend more money on products that align with their own social values. This helps companies make a profit while making more responsible decisions and helps consumers brand themselves as prosocial conscious consumers.

References

Apple (2013) Apple and the environment. Available at http://www.apple.com/environment/our-footprint/ (accessed June 8, 2016).

Ashforth, B. & Mael, F. (1989) Social identity theory and the organization. *Academy of Management Review*, 14(1), 20–39.

Barone, M., Norman, A. & Miyazaki, A. (2007) Consumer response to retailer use of cause-related marketing: is more fit better? *Journal of Retailing*, 83(4), 437–445.

Baxter, A. (2013) More companies encourage workers to volunteer, on the clock. Available at http://www.npr.org/2013/08/14/211961622/more-companies-encourage-workers-to-volunteer-on-the-clock (accessed June 8, 2016).

Bollen, K. (1983) World system position, dependency, and democracy: the cross-national evidence. *American Sociological Review*, 48(4), 468–479.

Boulter, J. (2011) Global Reporting Initiative: reporting sustainability sector by sector. *International Pharmacy Journal*, 27(1), 4–5.

Brown, C. (2003) Consumers' preferences for locally produced food: a study in southeast Missouri. *American Journal of Alternative Agriculture*, 18(4), 213–224.

Brown, H., De Jong, M. & Lessidrenska, T. (2009) The rise of the Global Reporting Initiative: a case of institutional entrepreneurship. *Environmental Politics*, 18(2), 182–200.

Dunlap, R.E. (1991) Trends in public opinion toward environmental issues: 1965–1990. *Society and Natural Resources*, 4(3), 285–312.

Edwards, C. (2011) Wal-Mart joining Amazon to promote rage-free packaging: Retail. Available at http://www.bloomberg.com/news/2011-11-29/wal-mart-joining-amazon-to-promote-rage-free-packaging-retail.html (accessed June 8, 2016).

Ehrlich, P. & Holdren, J. (1971) Impact of population growth. *Science*, 171(3977), 1212–1217.

Frazier, M. (2007) Costly red campaign reaps meager $18 million. Available at http://adage.com/article/news/

costly-red-campaign-reaps-meager-18-million/115287/ (accessed June 8, 2016).

Global Reporting Initiative (2009) What is sustainability reporting? Available at https://www.globalreporting.org/information/sustainability-reporting/Pages/default.aspx (accessed June 8, 2016).

Gordon, W. (2002) *Brand Green: Mainstream or Forever Niche?* London: Green Alliance.

Gupta, S. & Pirsch, J. (2006) The company-cause-customer fit decision in cause-related marketing. *Journal of Consumer Marketing*, 23(6), 314–326.

Hedberg, C. & von Malmborg, F. (2003) The Global Reporting Initiative and corporate sustainability reporting in Swedish companies. *Corporate Social Responsibility and Environmental Management*, 10(3), 153–164.

Keum, H., Devanathan, N., Deshpande, S., Nelson, M.R. & Shah, D.V. (2004) The citizen-consumer: media effects at the intersection of consumer and civic culture. *Political Communication*, 21(3), 369–391.

Knoll, J. (2013) My China residency and Coca-Cola. Available at http://www.coca-colacompany.com/coca-cola-unbottled/my-china-residency-and-coca-cola (accessed June 8, 2016).

Laroche, M., Bergeron, J. & Barbaro-Forleo, G. (2001) Targeting consumers who are willing to pay more for environmentally friendly products. *Journal of Consumer Marketing*, 18(6), 503–520.

Levy, D., Brown, H. & De Jong, M. (2010) The contested politics of corporate governance: the case of the Global Reporting Initiative. *Business and Society*, 49(1), 88–115.

Lii, Y. (2011) The effect of Corporate Social Responsibility (CSR) initiatives on consumers' identification with companies. *African Journal of Business Management*, 5(5), 1642–1649.

Lucas, H. & Sylla, R. (2003) The global impact of the Internet: widening the economic gap between wealthy and poor nations? *Prometheus*, 21(1), 1–22.

Mainwaring, S. (2011) *We First: How Brands and Consumers Use Social Media to Build a Better World*. New York: St Martin's Press.

Matisoff, A. (2013) Manufacturing malady: the hidden cost of a product. Available at http://asiasociety.org/education/students/global-topics/manufacturing-malady-hidden-cost-product (accessed June 8, 2016).

Mohr, L., Webb, D. & Harris, K. (2001) Do consumers expect companies to be socially responsible? The impact of corporate social responsibility on buying behavior. *Journal of Consumer Affairs*, 35(1), 45–72.

Phillips, J. (2012) The movement to ban McDonald's, Coca-Cola from the London Olympics. Available at http://business.time.com/2012/07/05/olympics-2012-the-move-to-ban-mcdonalds-coca-cola-from-the-london-games (accessed June 8, 2016).

RMHC (2013). Ronald McDonald house: our history. Available at http://www.rmhc.org/our-history (accessed August 26, 2013).

Sood, S. & Rogers, E. (2000) Dimensions of parasocial interaction by letter-writers to a popular Entertainment-Education soap in India. *Journal of Broadcasting and Electronic Media*, 44, 386–414.

Thoits, P. & Hewitt, L. (2001) Volunteer work and well-being. *Journal of Health and Social Behavior*, 42(2) 115–131.

TOMS (2016) Toms Giving Partners. Available at http://www.toms.com/thoughtful-partners (accessed June 8, 2016).

Varadarajan, P. & Menon, A. (1988) Cause-related marketing: a coalignment of marketing strategy and corporate philanthropy. *Journal of Marketing*, 52(3), 58–74.

Wentz, L. (2011) In Argentina, Lay's vending machine turns raw potatoes into bags of chips. Available at http://adage.com/article/global-news/argentina-lay-s-vending-machine-turns-potatoes-chips/229828 (accessed June 8, 2016).

19

Arguing for a General Framework for Social Media Scholarship

Learning Objectives

After reading this chapter, you should be able to:
1   Understand the six paradigms of communication theory.
2   Explain Potter's general framework for mass media scholarship.
3   Identify key intersections of social media scholarship.

Introduction

This book has examined the many ways in which audiences utilize social media platforms to meet their own lifestyles and needs. It has identified ways in which marketers are able to craft social media messages and create strategies to incite behavior change. Chapter 18 examined the field of communication for development and social change. It reviewed the diffusion–participation continuum and examined how users and organizations are able to create *We First* messages for social change to lead to a stronger return on investment.

This knowledge is essential for any social media practitioner looking to make mindful communication decisions in today's digital era. This understanding should not emerge as a silo of information, disconnected from its historical trajectory. Social media practitioners must understand the roots of social media scholarship and how it fits into the overall framework of communication and mass media scholarship.

Strategic Social Media: From Marketing to Social Change, First Edition. L. Meghan Mahoney and Tang Tang.
© 2017 John Wiley & Sons, Inc. Published 2017 by John Wiley & Sons, Inc.

This chapter examines social media scholarship through an inverse triangle of information by examining the six paradigms of general communication theory. This knowledge is crucial in the recognition of the various ways in which communication practitioners have come to understand the role of the audience. Second, we look at mass media scholarship specifically, including a definition and conceptualization of the industry, message production, and its impact on society. Finally, we explore how social media scholarship is unique in the many ways it intersects each of these arenas.

Theory makes it easier to understand why a social media endeavor proves successful or not. A strong understanding of theory will set you apart from other individuals on the social media job market because it allows you the ability to make mindful decisions regarding your audience, and makes you much more valuable than a professional who is only familiar with social media marketing cases and the various tools of social media technology. Let's begin with an examination of the communication discipline as a whole.

The Six Paradigms of Communication Theory

Six paradigms of communication theory are essential to our understanding of effective communication: social psychological theories, psychological models, drama theories, audience-centered theories, contextual theories, and hybrid models. Each of these paradigms posit theories based on their understanding of the role audience members play in the communication transactional process, ranging from passive consumption to active involvement (Sood *et al.*, 2003). Once we understand the differences between them, a better understanding will be gained of the foundation of social media scholarship.

Social psychological theories

Social psychological theories address individuals' psychological beliefs and perceptions about their environment, whereby human behavior is the result of an interplay between the person, culture and society. Perhaps the most prominent social psychological theory is *Bandura's social learning theory* (later developed to social cognitive theory). This theory explains how humans learn through modeling the behavior of others, even modeling behaviors we see through media. Here, people are viewed as self-developing, proactive, self-regulating, and self-reflecting, not just reactive in nature (Bandura, 2004). This is the foundation of most research and communication practices interested in using media for behavior change. Based on this understanding of the audience, social learning theory posits individuals as the producers of social systems, rather than merely products. Individuals are able to comprehend and regulate their environment and make meanings regarding what they see (Bryant & Oliver, 2009). Through these experiences, people process symbols and "transform transient experiences into cognitive models that serve as guides for judgment and action" (Bryant & Oliver, 2009, p. 95). How influential experiences prove depends on personal determinants, behavioral determinants, and environmental determinants.

Social learning theory explains how individuals learn to communicate through modeling the behaviors around us. Most often, our first communication pattern models those of our primary caregivers. However, as we grow up and our world gets bigger, so do our schema for interpretations. We do not just learn to behave based on the behaviors of our parents and primary caregivers. Instead, friends, teachers, and even media role models begin to influence how we behave. As a future social media strategist, it is important for you to understand these schemata of interpretation, because it helps explain how difficult it is to persuade audiences through media messages alone.

Schema theory illustrates how individuals base behavior on existing life experiences. With each new experience, we organize our behavior according to similar events that will be used in subsequent interaction. For example, one of the first relationships most people form is with their mother. When she is happy, babies tend to be happy. One day, the baby may throw a cup onto the floor while mother is feeding. She consequently gets upset and yells, causing the baby to become upset and cry. Based on the premise of schema theory, next time we have the urge to throw a cup on the floor, the baby will remember the schema of the previous negative exchange and learn not to follow through with this disruptive behavior.

As we get older, our primary caregivers become a less and less important part of our schema. Mother may tell a young child never to touch a hot stove. This warning should be sufficient to influence a child's behavior during formative years, but eventually children begin branching out and peers became a stronger presence in their life. If peers begin urging the child to touch a hot stove and the mother is not around, the child may be tempted to touch the stove despite previous cautions. The content of the message and relational history remain the same, but the influence on child behavior changes. With this understanding of social learning theory and the concept of schema, we can see how difficult it is for a simple message to cause direct behavior change. The process is transactional not linear in nature.

Some parenting messages are strong enough to provide children with a schema that will overcome any amount of peer pressure. This is difficult to achieve because children do not always look up to their parents. The process of *symbolic role modeling*, where humans tend to model behaviors from those whom they admire most, is imperative to understanding the effects of communication. By viewing corrective adjustments of others during behavior production, we learn through modeling. Thus, we may not necessarily need to experience those same behaviors in order to make a change (Bandura, 2004). Instead, we see that someone who is similar to us had success when behaving in a certain manner, and those lessons then become a part of our own cognitive process.

Social psychological theories account for the premise that individuals with limited schema, such as children, or individuals with a dysfunctional upbringing may be more prone to model media messages than those with more positive schema to draw from. They suggest that people are more likely to model behavior if they identify with the character they are viewing, and if society would value the outcomes (Bryant & Oliver, 2009). Here you can see how each individual would interact with and respond to media messages very differently from one another. For example, in 2011, Mark Twitchell was dubbed the "Dexter Killer" after stating that he was inspired to murder after watching the fictional television character serial killer in the series *Dexter* (Quigley, 2013). Social psychological theories help explain why one person can watch a violent episode of television and it has no effect, and someone else can watch the same episode with great effect.

Psychological models

Not all communication paradigms are based on the assumption of individuals' psychological beliefs and perceptions about their environment. Psychological models are based on a cognitive processing model. Here, individuals are exposed to a mass communication program and this exposure is used to predict subsequent behavior interactions. It is a much more direct media effects model. A prominent example of a psychological communication model is the *elaboration likelihood model* (ELM). ELM recognizes that media does hold the power to sway audiences in identical manners. The extent to which media is able to persuade depends on whether the messages are effective in changing attitudes and whether these attitudes influence behaviors (Bryant & Oliver, 2009).

According to ELM, people are persuaded through central or peripheral routes of persuasion (Petty & Cacioppo, 1981). The *central route to persuasion* is when a person draws upon prior experience and knowledge counter to the messages that they are receiving. Once feelings regarding the message are determined, the final step involves integrating the new thoughts into their cognitive structure (Bryant & Oliver, 2009). The *peripheral route of persuasion* is when a person's ability to process a message is low, or when they are being a more passive audience (Bryant & Oliver, 2009). Researchers found that people persuaded through peripheral routes are usually only persuaded for short periods of time. Attitude change through peripheral routes tends to be based more on passive acceptance or rejection of simple cues and have a less well-articulated foundation (Petty & Cacioppo, 1981; Bryant & Oliver, 2009). This process is generally referred to in propaganda research.

Herman and Chomsky (1988) developed a *propaganda model* that presents four factors which determine what is newsworthy in society:

- the size, concentrated ownership, owner wealth, and profit orientation of the dominant mass media firms;
- advertising as the primary income source of the mass media;
- the reliance of the media on information provided by government, business and experts, that is funded and approved by these primary sources and agents of power, that use flak as a means of disciplining the media;
- anticommunism as a national religion and control mechanism.

Clearly this model is based on the notion that media has potential to influence and possess great power over audiences. However, social media makes it possible for news stories that do not match these four factors to become viral. The notion of passive audience acceptance or rejection of media messages is outdated, but there are still many benefits to considering the cognitive processes of audiences through psychological models

Drama theories

Drama theories are based on a paradigm that examines the roles people play or the scripts that they follow in their daily lives. The assumption of this paradigm is that audiences have specific emotional reactions to different storylines, and that these reactions influence the way they exchange ideas and opinions on real-life issues. The presentation of a message is intrinsically as important as its content. An example of a drama theory would be Bentley's dramatic theory.

Bentley's dramatic theory suggests that media producers should utilize structure as the framework for creating character archetypes in dramas. This theory breaks theater genre into five categories: tragedy, comedy, tragicomedy, farce, and melodrama (Bentley, 1967). Each of these categories has their own structure and effect on audiences. This includes providing specific and easily recognizable tones, anecdotes and characters (Singhal *et al.*, 2004). These patterns are similar to narrative media created all over the world, in books, theater, television programs, and movies. Tensions between protagonists and antagonists help guide audience members through their own evolution towards the adoption of desired behavior changes. Here, individuals follow patterns of behavior based on the role that they see played out in narratives, in media, and in their daily lives.

Audience-centered theories

Audience-centered theories examine how audiences interact and react to media messages. This paradigm views the audience as having a much more active role in the media selection and interpretation process. An early example of an audience-centered theory is *uses and gratifications theory*, which explains why and how people actively seek out specific media in order to satisfy their specific needs.

As discussed in Chapter 5, uses and gratifications theory has been a major mass communication perspective over the last quarter-century due to its view of the audience as an active agent in the media consumption process, rather than a passive consumer. This perspective stresses the impact of individual differences on media uses and effects by assuming that unique social and psychological circumstances help shape user needs (Haridakis, 2006). It represents one of the oldest continuous programs of research in the discipline of communication (Sherry, 2001).

Uses and gratifications theory also suggests that audiences engage in media through a process named *niche-picking*. Niche-picking refers to the tendency of individuals to choose environments that are most comfortable and of use to their own lives and goals (Sherry, 2001). Audiences are motivated to seek media outlets that gratify their needs for information, entertainment, social interaction, and escapism (Henke, 1985). This media selection is significantly goal directive and purposive. People typically choose to participate in particular media in response to their personal expectations or desires, often leading them to dramatic programs centered on tragic characters. Bryant and Zillmann (1994, p. 453) explain how "seeing misfortunes befall others and seeing them suffer from it thus may make viewers cognizant and appreciative of how good they have it. And such positive feelings accrue to seeing tragedy strike, in reality or in fiction, tragedy becomes appealing." Motivations influence audience media selection, use, exposure and, ultimately, effects (Haridakis, 2006).

Uses and gratifications theory is a critical precursor to audience reception research. The theory presents audience as a goal-directive and active user. It shifts power away from the media text and regards the audience as unique active individuals who interpret texts according to their own life experiences and needs. These are the basic foundations of *participatory audience research* that focuses more on audience dialogue, examines culture identity, and looks at local and unique decision-making processes (Petraglia, 2007).

Contextual theories

Current contextual theories are those that take a social constructivist approach, where meaning is made through the interaction of audience, content, and media and points to the sociocultural context. Rather than viewing the audience as the self-selecting body, outside environments become critical to behavior change. An example of a contextual theory is the *theory of hegemony*, where dominant culture maintains dominant position through the use of institutions such as media (Sood *et al.*, 2003). The basis of contextual theories is that audience involvement is multidimensional and serves as media for prompting behavior change. The more involvement and active role audiences play in the media reception process, the larger potential for behavior change (Sood, 2006).

Contextual theories examine humanistic and critical perspectives focused on power and dominance structures. One of the earliest examples of a contextual theory is the *agenda-setting theory*. Agenda-setting theory indicates the ability of a media source to influence its audiences to think about a particular issue. Media does not tell "viewers what to think" but they are persuasive in "guiding viewers what to think about" (Holbrook & Hill, 2005, p. 278).

Media agenda, public agenda, and corporate agenda are dominant structures often advanced through the agenda-setting process (Carroll & McCombs, 2003). This selection process is what makes agenda-setting potentially persuasive. The process of disseminating information from the press to the public gives an issue salience and is the core mechanism of the agenda-setting process (Kiousis, 2003). Studies have shown that the public's concern over particular issues fluctuates greatly according to the amount of attention it is given from media outlets.

An example of agenda-setting theory was evident during the "summer of the shark" (McCarthy, 2001). On July 6, 2001, a shark bit off the arm of an 8-year-old boy on a Florida beach. This sparked an international media frenzy, and shark attacks became front-page news everywhere. The process of a media outlet choosing to report on shark attacks over other incoming news stories is the process of agenda-setting. Media were not relaying untruthful information or directly warning the public that sharks were more dangerous than before, but that was the message its audience received by the extra coverage.

Audiences were exposed to an overwhelming amount of shark attack stories. Therefore, they prioritized shark attacks as an important issue. However, the number of shark attacks that occurred that summer was actually below average. Media did not provide its audience with a viewpoint through which to examine the incoming messages. Simply by giving more attention to an issue, the public's concern rose. While generally traditional media outlets have served as the gatekeepers of information, everyday audiences are beginning to have more power to set the agenda through social media. This has created many opportunities and challenges for social media marketers like you.

Hybrid theories

Finally, hybrid theories of communication utilize a combination of elements from the other five paradigms. This approach tends to combine linear direct effects models of communication with more active audience participation assumptions, and generally result in a communication intervention or campaign with a limited number of resources and challenges (Phillips, 2011). Chapter 16 introduced the entertainment-education approach to behavior change, a hybrid communication model. While hybrid theories are generally more difficult to monitor and evaluate for causation, they present a strong yield for behavior change when implemented appropriately. This requires a strong understanding of all the other five paradigms.

Each of these six paradigms of communication theory (social psychological theory, psychological models, drama theory, audience-centered theory, contextual theory, and hybrid models) has very different assumptions of how audiences interact with media texts. However, regardless of where you situate yourself as a social media specialist, it is important to note that when communicating, regardless of the platform, messages must be constructed, disseminated and consumed with the intended audience in mind. The more you are able to account for an audience's own individual experiences and preferences, the more powerful your message becomes.

A General Framework for Mass Media Scholarship

The field of media research covers vast areas through various and often-competing approaches. Potter (2013) identified 10 individual definitional elements of mass media. In order to be considered mass media, all 10 of these elements must be met. They are outlined in Table 19.1.

Table 19.1   Synthesized working definition of mass media. Source: Potter, 2013. Reproduced with permission of John Wiley & Sons.

Sender of messages:
- is a complex organization or institution, not an individual
- use standardized practices to mass produce the messages and disseminate them
- have an awareness of specific niche audiences and actively promotes itself in order to attract as many audience members of that niche as possible
- condition audience members for habitual repeated exposures

Audiences members:
- are widely dispersed geographically, i.e., not all in one place
- are aware of the public character of what they are seeing or hearing
- encounter messages in a variety of exposure states but most often in a state of automaticity

Channels of message dissemination are technological devices that:
- make messages public, i.e., available to anyone
- extend the availability of messages in time and space
- can reach audiences within a relatively short time, even simultaneously

Traditional mass media research offers a medium-by-medium examination of print, electronic, and new media (Sterling, 2011), which makes the discipline seem disconnected, with little sense of who we are and what unites us, and does little to examine the deep and changing impact of media on society. Potter (2009) attempts to create a more unified approach to mass media research in his book *Arguing for a General Framework for Mass Media Scholarship*. Through an extensive examination of five decades of research in the field, he identifies patterns and synthesizes interconnections among scholarship. He argues that

> all media research should focus on the ways media channels are used, how audiences choose certain media and media messages, and how they process meaning from those messages, and how those messages shape their knowledge, structures, attitudes, beliefs, emotional reactions, and behavioral patterns over time (Potter, 2009, p. 18).

We should look at media scholarship more broadly, and build a general framework to guide our practice.

Potter's (2009) synthesis identifies four main facets of mass media scholarship: organizations, audiences, media messages, and effects. The *organization approach* examines the institutions and media organizations by defining the business, marketing and employment strategies of media companies and services. This approach examines the structure of various media channels and the relationships within the institution. The *audiences approach* examines audience behavior and the concept of what is an audience. This includes cognitive algorithms, audience filtering of media messages, and the changing meaning and construction of audience. The *media messages approach* reviews the formulas and conventions of media content. This includes the creation of marketing strategy and message design. The *effects approach* examines the multiple effects line of thinking, conceptualizes media influence and effects, and discusses the design of media effects studies (Potter, 2009; Sterling, 2011).

This general framework provides an integrated explanation of mass media as an industry, the messages that are produced and marketed, the audiences for those messages, and the effects of those messages on individuals and larger social structures (Potter, 2009). It is through this lens that the social media concepts of this book have emerged.

Parts I and II of this book examined how individuals utilize various social media platforms, why they choose them, and how they interpret messages given their individual life experiences. We learned the complex process of audience negotiation and the difficulty in inciting persuasion through social media messages. The concepts of diffusion, community, and mobilization were offered to help you balance your need for control with the possibility for behavior change given this knowledge.

Part III of this book focused on how social media practitioners are best able to create messages according to this knowledge to influence human behavior change. Through an understanding of social media business models and marketing strategies, you learned to incite behavior change in audiences in order to meet the objectives of your organization. Part IV of this book discussed how to use this knowledge to create social good and aid behavior change in a globalized stage.

The future of scholarship and communication/marketing endeavors should cross boundaries between different media facets in order to produce more compelling results (Sterling,

2011). Thus, as a social media practitioner, you should be aware that it is important that you understand where your assumptions fit within these frameworks, and keep your social media strategy in an integrated approach. Before completing your social media endeavor, consider the following action plan.

Media Scholarship Action Plan

1 Understand your assumption of the role audience members play in the communication process based on the six paradigms of communication theory.
2 Identify in which of the four main facets of the media communication process your social media endeavors reside.
3 Seek out ways in which your work is able to cross boundaries between various media platforms, alternative facets, and different disciplines in order to produce more complete and compelling results.

Key Intersections of Social Media Scholarship

The previous sections have offered a critical assessment of communication and mass media research. This assessment illustrates that social media scholarship is a dynamic academic discipline. Despite the varying strands of communication studies, there are many points for possible convergence. While mass media has traditionally been seen as its own area of focus, this section calls for social media scholarship to be seen as a more integrative area of study by offering ideas and direction for future social media research.

Each paradigm of communication scholarship has been interested in the impact of social media technologies. Scholars from disparate fields have examined social media practices, implications, culture, meaning of sites, and user engagement through various methodological techniques, theoretical traditions, and analytic approaches (Ellison, 2007).

For example, social psychological theories have examined an individual's perceptions about a particular social media platform (Miller & Morris, 2014; Ruckert *et al.*, 2014); psychological models have examined how exposure to a social media could be used to predict subsequent behavior interactions (Chen & Ku, 2012; Lowry *et al.*, 2012); drama theories have examined the way social media users are influenced in real life by online narratives (Penner, 2014; Ji & Raney, 2015); audience-centered theories have examined why audiences use social media messages (Chen, 2011; Smock *et al.*, 2011); and contextual theories have examined how people make meaning through the interaction with social media content and other social media users (Meraz, 2011; Johnson, 2013).

Though these are ways in which each paradigm of communication scholarship has incorporated social media technologies into their research, it is not the best strategy for advancing our understanding of its impact. Together as a discipline we must challenge the current state of our divided assumptions. A more integrative and hybrid approach to social media scholarship will help us to understand its role more completely.

A strong social media scholarship framework should mirror Potter's (2009) approach and provide an integrated explanation of social media as an industry, the messages that are produced and marketed, the audiences for those messages, and the effects of those messages on individuals and larger social structures.

Much of social media research discusses the benefits of interactivity and participation. However, a reliable, valid, and empirically derived instrument of social participation has yet to be developed. Many of the instruments being used have been designed for traditional mass media technologies. Social media proves different and it is necessary that we have a valid and reliable way to examine audience use and preferences, media structures, and the concepts of diffusion, community and mobilization of social media messages.

It is also imperative for scholarship to embrace a one-to-one model of the communication technology. Not all social media platforms are designed for the one-to-many mass audience. In fact, many of the newest social media applications, such as Snapchat and Messenger, are designed for more personal communication between friends, rather than mass dissemination to a larger audience. This mirrors interpersonal communication structures much more than mass media scholarship. Therefore, future research should integrate this area of communication research into social media scholarship if appropriate. This may require some disconnect from mass media research.

Much more work needs to be done to design an effective monitoring and evaluation system for social media endeavors. Chapter 12 discussed the importance of holistic measurement that includes both quantitative analysis and qualitative audience reception measurement. This triangulation approach will allow a much more nuanced understanding of the audience social media experience, including overall generalizations and distinct outlier behavior.

Additionally, the discipline needs more longitudinal scholarship. Long-term impacts of the technology are unrealized, as the technology is just too new. We have limited understanding of who is and who is not using these sites and why (Ellison, 2007). Future scholarship should include large-scale quantitative and qualitative research, with richer ethnographic research on populations more difficult to access, in order to help us better understand the long-term implications of these tools.

In the classroom, professors must consider the idea of social media scholarship and continue to be open to data sharing, democratization of expertise, and alternative models of peer review and reputation management (Greenhow & Gleeson, 2014). Otherwise, social media will continue to be seen as something unscholarly. We must continue to highlight the relationship between scholarly work, industry practice and society, without pitting scholars who embrace innovative methods against more traditional practices.

Finally, and perhaps most importantly, social media is the most fragmented experience of all the media technologies. It is important to understand that most individuals are accessing social media on the go while multitasking with many elements of their everyday lives. Controlled experimental settings and self-report surveys may not capture the true essence of this mobile and integrated experience. It is important for researchers to design more studies that use noninvasive tracking and observation methods. Online and offline behaviors are interconnected, and it is time that we study them accordingly.

For one researcher to incorporate all these assumptions and alternative designs in a single research agenda would be impossible. However, your role as a social media practitioner is to understand the various communication paradigms, identify where your assumptions regarding the audience and technology align, and actively seek out collaboration with those that think differently. As many mass media programs pair off from the communication discipline, we believe that the future of social media scholarship is strongest when we advance knowledge as a united front.

Case Study: CIRCLE

CIRCLE, or Center for Information and Research on Civic Learning and Engagement, conducts research on the civic and political engagement of young Americans (www.civicyouth.org). This initiative was established in 2001 in an attempt to change public discourse on how young citizens engage in civic and political life with the goal of developing programs that foster civic learning and engagement in democracy.

Oftentimes, public discourse surrounding young citizens posits the demographic as apathetic towards public affairs, having a low sense of efficacy, and filled with negativism (Pinkleton & Austin, 2004). This initiative is interested in utilizing media messages to inspire a more proactive and positive behavior change in young audiences. Based on the transactional model of communication defined in Chapter 1, it is understood that media messages should be constructed not just on the producer's own goals, but based on the needs of the target audience. Additionally, barriers such as competence, access and relational history must be considered.

Because of society's current discourse regarding younger generations, the target audiences of CIRCLE proves interesting. They have been described as having the lowest trends of civic engagement and social capital in history (Putnam, 2001). CIRCLE aims to change public discourse and press coverage about young citizens by altering the way that people think about civic education and engagement. Its research found that today's generation is still participating in civic activities, just in a different manner through social media. Today's digital natives prefer to participate through interdisciplinary and community-based means.

For example, one youth initiative highlighted on the CIRCLE website is Youth Dreams, a group of middle school students. These students felt as though there was a lack of organized activities available to them and decided to create a youth-run center. Through their collective efforts, they have raised over $900,000, served 618 individuals, and completed 17,578 community service hours (Youth Dreamers, 2014). Though this may not be considered civic engagement in the traditional sense, it highlights the potential of project-based, community-building initiatives that do not fit the traditional mold for social change.

Many modern citizens feel fulfilled by engaging in civic engagement through technology. In 2009, over $4 million were donated to charities through mobile text-based campaigns (Choney, 2010). Much of the money donated to Youth Dreamers is done so through the PayPal feature on their website. Individuals also use social media platforms to bring awareness about causes or health issues that are important to them. Social media provides the opportunity to share stories and pictures of initiatives close to their hearts. This is an example of how social media is able to transform social change programs for the better. Moreover, it illustrates how participatory community mobilization through hybrid approaches is the key to positive social change, and is more possible than ever before due to social media.

Discussion questions

1 How might the younger generation target audience of CIRCLE impact behavior change outcomes? How could producers use social media to better market this audience in their communication strategy?
2 It is argued that youth may feel a sense of gratification by engaging in civic engagement through technology, rather than traditional means such as volunteering or voting. Which of the six paradigms of communication theories does this audience selection process most closely align? Why?
3 Much debate centers around how technology influences users in a positive or negative manner. Based on what we know about communication studies models and paradigms, how can you explain the positive impacts of CIRCLE on society?

Summary

The field of communication is huge, with many points of distinction and intersection. Strong social media practitioners need to understand their place within the historical trajectory. By understanding the roots of social media scholarship, one is able to make more mindful decisions about message strategy.

This chapter presents the six paradigms of general communication theory, the definition and conceptualization of mass media scholarship, and the many ways in which social media scholarship intersects each of these arenas to guide future practice and research. Though the field is still too new to conduct a large-scale of analysis such as Potter's (2009) framework for mass media scholarship, many of the patterns emerging are similar. This includes looking at social media as an industry, the messages that are produced and marketed, the audiences for those messages, and the effects of those messages on individuals and larger social structures.

Future social media scholarship should include a more integrative approach across communication paradigms, test new empirical theories and measurements, embrace more interpersonal communication research, design more effective and longitudinal monitoring and evaluation systems for social media endeavors, incorporate social media scholarship in the classroom, and study social media use in more natural, noninvasive and fragmented settings. These changes will put us one step closer towards creating a general framework for social media scholarship.

Now that we have a more thorough understanding of the theories that guide social media strategy and practice, let's turn our attention to the future of social media. Chapter 20 focuses on how marketing strategy and social participation will change in the coming years. Many of the points of distinction outlined in this chapter will become blurred in future practice. Based on this understanding, the structural principles of Web 3.0 technology will be identified, and recommendations for social media practitioners will be offered.

Key Takeaways

1   Six different paradigms of communication theory – social psychological theory, psychological models, drama theory, audience-centered theory, contextual theory and hybrid models – help explain how audiences interact with and are influenced by media texts.
2   The strongest social media strategies integrate hybrid approaches into their campaigns.
3   There are four main facets of mass communication: organizations, audiences, media messages, and effects. Practitioners should cross boundaries between each in today's digital landscape.
4   Integration requires consideration for media industries, social media messages produced, marketing strategies, audiences reached, and societal effects.

References

Bandura, A. (2004) Health promotion by social cognitive means. *Health Education and Behavior*, 31, 143–164.

Bentley, E. (1967) *The Life of the Drama*. New York: Atheneum.

Bryant, J. & Oliver, M.B. (2009) *Media Effects: Advances in Theory and Research*, 3rd edn. New York: Routledge.

Bryant, J. & Zillmann, D. (1994) *Media Effects: Advances in Theory and Research*. Hillsdale, NJ: Lawrence Erlbaum Associates.

Carroll, C. & McCombs, M. (2003) Agenda-setting effects of business news on the public's images and opinions about major corporations. *Corporate Reputation Review*, 6(1), 36–46.

Chen, C. & Ku, E. (2012) Building member's relationship quality toward online community from the elaboration likelihood model perspective. *PACIS 2012 Proceedings*, Paper 126. Available at http://aisel.aisnet.org/pacis2012/126/ (accessed June 8, 2016).

Chen, G. (2011) Tweet this: a uses and gratifications perspective on how active Twitter use gratifies a need to connect with others. *Computers in Human Behavior*, 27(2), 755–762.

Choney, S. (2010) Mobile giving to help Haiti exceeds $30 million. Available at http://www.today.com/id/34850532/ns/today-today_tech/t/mobile-giving-help-haiti-exceeds-million/ (accessed June 8, 2016).

Ellison, N. (2007) Social network sites: definition, history, and scholarship. *Journal of Computer-Mediated Communication*, 13(1), 210–230.

Greenhow, C. & Gleeson, B. (2014) Social scholarship: reconsidering scholarly practices in the age of social media. *British Journal of Educational Technology*, 45(3), 392–402.

Haridakis, P. (2006) Men, women, and television violence: predicting viewer aggression in male and female television viewers. *Communication Quarterly*, 54(2), 227–255.

Henke, L.L. (1985) Perceptions and use of news media by college students, *Journal of Broadcasting and Electronic Media*, 29, 431–436.

Herman, E. & Chomsky, N. (1988) *Manufacturing Consent: The Political Economy of the Mass Media*. New York: Pantheon Books.

Holbrook, R. & Hill, T. (2005) Agenda-setting and priming in prime time television: crime dramas as political cues. *Political Communication*, 22, 277–295.

Ji, Q. & Raney, A.A. (2015) Morally judging entertainment: a case study of live Tweeting during Downton Abbey. *Media Psychology*, 18(2), 221–242.

Johnson, T. (2013) *Agenda Setting in a 2.0 World: New Agendas in Communication*. New York: Routledge.

Kiousis, S. (2003) Job approval and favorability: the impact of media attention to the Monica Lewinsky scandal on public opinion of President Bill Clinton. *Mass Communication and Society*, 6(4), 435–451.

Lowry, P., Moody, G., Vance, A., Jensen, M., Jenkins, J. & Wells, T. (2012) Using an elaboration likelihood approach to better understand the persuasiveness of website privacy assurance cues for online consumers. *Journal of the American Society for Information Science and Technology*, 63(4), 755–776.

McCarthy, T. (2001) Why can't we be friends. Available at http://content.time.com/time/magazine/article/0,9171,1000420,00.html (accessed June 8, 2016).

Meraz, S. (2011) Using time series analysis to measure inter-media agenda-setting influence in traditional media and political blog networks. *Journalism and Mass Communication Quarterly*, 88(1), 176–194.

Miller, B. & Morris, R.G. (2014) Virtual peer effects in social learning theory. *Crime and Delinquency*, doi: 10.1177/0011128714526499.

Penner, J. (2014) On Aggro performance: audience participation and the dystopian response to the living theatre's paradise now. *Comparative Drama*, 48(1), 75–92.

Petraglia, J. (2007) Narrative intervention in behavior and public health. *Journal of Health Communication*, 12(5), 493–505.

Petty, R. & Cacioppo, J. (1981) *Attitudes and Persuasion: Classic and Contemporary Approaches*. Dubuque, IA: Wm C. Brown.

Phillips, L. (2011) *The Promise of Dialogue: The Dialogic Turn in the Production and Communication of Knowledge*. Philadelphia: John Benjamins Publishing Company.

Pinkleton, B. & Austin, E. (2004) Media perceptions and public affairs apathy in the politically inexperienced. *Mass Communication and Society*, 7(3), 319–337.

Potter, W.J. (2009) *Arguing For a General Framework for Mass Media Scholarship*. Thousand Oaks, CA: Sage Publications.

Potter, W.J. (2013) Synthesizing a working definition of "mass" media. *Review of Communication Research*, 1, 1–30.

Putnam, R. (2001) *Bowling Alone: The Collapse and Revival of American Community*. New York: Simon & Schuster.

Quigley, R. (2013) Murderer who was inspired by Dexter is given unlimited access to serial killer TV show from his prison cell. Available at http://www.dailymail.co.uk/news/article-2320301/Mark-Twitchell-Would-serial-killer-given-unlimited-access-Dexter-prison-cell–TV-series-inspired-murder-innocent-man-plot-taken-straight-violent-show.html (accessed June 8, 2016).

Ruckert, E., McDonald, P., Birkmeier, M. *et al.* (2014) Using technology to promote active and social learning experiences in health professions education. *Online Learning: Official Journal of the Online Learning Consortium*, 18(4). Available at http://olj.online-learningconsortium.org/index.php/olj/article/view/515 (accessed June 8, 2016).

Sherry, J. (2001) Toward an etiology of media use motivations: the role of temperament in media use. *Communication Monographs*, 68(3), 274–288.

Singhal, A., Cody, M., Rogers, E. & Sabido, M. (2004) *Entertainment-Education and Social Change*. Mahwah, NJ: Lawrence Erlbaum Associates.

Smock, A., Ellison, N., Lampe, C. & Wohn, D. (2011) Facebook as a toolkit: a uses and gratification approach to unbundling feature use. *Computers in Human Behavior*, 27(6), 2322–2329.

Sood, S. (2006) Audience involvement and entertainment-education. *Communication Theory*, 12(2), 153–172.

Sood, S., Witte, K. & Menard, T. (2003) The theory behind entertainment education. In: M.J. Cody, A. Singhal, M. Sabido & E.M. Rogers (eds) *Entertainment-Education Worldwide: History, Research, and Practice*, pp. 117–149. Mahwah, NJ: Lawrence Erlbaum.

Sterling, C. (2011) Arguing for a general framework for mass media scholarship. *Journal of Broadcasting and Electronic Media*, 55(4), 615–616.

Youth Dreamers (2014) Youth dreamers: be a part of our dream. Available at http://www.youthdreamers.org (accessed June 8, 2016).

20

The Future of Social Media

Learning Objectives

After reading this chapter, you should be able to:
1 Identify changes to the upcoming social media landscape.
2 Explain the possibilities of a Web 3.0 environment.
3 Integrate future social media technologies with caution into your business strategy.

Introduction

A 2012 Gallup survey reports that social media marketing is not as powerful or as persuasive a business force that many companies had initially hoped (Elder, 2014). Despite spending a projected $15 billion by 2018 on social media advertising (Gallup, 2014), research demonstrates how consumers are still primarily turning towards friends and family when seeking advice about the products they buy. Most social media users are not interested in following social media updates regarding products or companies. What do these results tell us about the future of social media marketing? Is the idea of a social media brand advocate just a myth in the industry?

Based on everything that we have learned about the complicated process of using media messages to inspire human behavior change, these findings make sense. Individuals use past experiences as a guide for future action, and friends and family members provide

Strategic Social Media: From Marketing to Social Change, First Edition. L. Meghan Mahoney and Tang Tang.
© 2017 John Wiley & Sons, Inc. Published 2017 by John Wiley & Sons, Inc.

much stronger schemata for interpretation than media content. These findings also demonstrate just how incorrectly social media practitioners have been utilizing the technology to increase their return on investment.

If the focus of a marketing campaign still primarily resides in the quantity of connections, rather than the quality of connections with your consumers, social media is not being utilized to its full potential. "If companies want to acquire new customers, their best bet is to engage their existing customers and inspire them to advocate … customer engagement drives social engagement" (Gallup, 2014, p. 3). Brands must personalize themselves and build a relationship with customers. Social media marketing is not the same as advertising, and so the same century-old principles should not apply.

Just when one company successfully develops a marketing campaign that yields a high return on investment, several other copycat campaigns will undoubtedly emerge. For example, in 2010 Old Spice launched a video response campaign where, over the span of 48 hours, actor Isaiah Mustafa answered real-life questions from audiences on Twitter, Facebook, Reddit, and blogs while standing in a shower. The social media campaign was a hit, resulting in nearly 200 response videos that were viewed over 4 million times (O'Neill, 2010).

Cisco recognized the success of this participatory social media approach and released their own version of the YouTube response project. Their campaign featured "Ted from Accounting." Just like the Old Spice campaign, Cisco asked audiences to send in tweets and then responded to them through personalized videos. The campaign fell short, with only 18 videos uploaded over 24 hours with 2750 views (O'Neill, 2010). This demonstrates how unpredictable successful social media marketing can be.

Just like social connections, companies cannot fake relationships online. Authenticity and trust are crucial to the audience identification process. You can probably tell when individuals in your own life are not being true to themselves. It is easy to detect a fraud. Remember that campaigns exist as part of an ever-changing social media landscape. What worked for one company last month is not likely to work again today. It is important for you to always be forward thinking.

Chapter 19 argued for a general framework for social media scholarship and practice. It is time to turn attention towards the future of social media marketing. This chapter provides upcoming innovations to the social media landscape, discusses the possibilities of a Web 3.0 environment, and provides general conclusions and recommendations for the future of social media marketing.

If nothing else, these Gallup survey results tell us to be cautious about overstepping the promises of social media. Just because the technology makes it easier than ever to form connections, it also makes it easier for audiences to ignore them. Social and behavior changes are difficult to establish, and the only thing worse than developing an unsuccessful marketing campaign is to miss out on the conversation altogether.

The Future Social Media Landscape

It would prove impossible to predict all the new media changes that we will see in our lifetime. You should be cautious with any reference that claims to have all the answers to what a future technological landscape will look like. This section aims to explore some emerging technology trends that today's practitioners should consider when integrating and developing business models. These include mobile marketing, stand-alone applications, wearables, and visual social media. While this list is nowhere near exhaustive, these trends have already proven huge game changers for the industry.

Mobile marketing

Mobile marketing is a two-way or multi-way communication between an organization and its customers using a mobile device (Shankar & Balasubramanian, 2009). Chapter 8 introduced the appeal of location-based marketing through mobile devices. This type of marketing focuses on culture, personalization, interactivity, socialization, and localization (Bauer *et al.*, 2005). Because of the prominent diffusion of mobile technology, which has now reached a level of saturation where there are more mobile phone subscriptions than people on earth (BBC, 2013), high-speed wireless technologies are undoubtedly the future of marketing.

Mobile users are able to access information and communicate with companies at any time and any place (Scharl *et al.*, 2005). Part of the appeal of mobile marketing is based on the concept of *permission marketing*, where users have opted in to receive promotional messages from companies. This approach is very different from the spam and one-to-many model of traditional mass media advertising. Additionally, mobile devices are rarely used by any other person than its owner (Bauer *et al.*, 2005). This makes it a perfect tool for customizing and personalizing brand content. Users are able to select the information that they want to receive, and producers have a better sense of the individual, not mass, audience that their content is reaching.

Stand-alone applications

Given the popularity of mobile marketing, producers of social media content must ensure that it is distributed in accordance with audience needs and expectations. Stand-alone applications are a single-function mobile service that does not need to interact with or be bundled with any other application in order to function correctly. Users tend to select stand-alone applications in order to more efficiently structure online content that they access regularly. Today, mobile applications do not need to be developed based on a website. Popular applications such as Snapchat, Vine, Instagram, and Tinder are all examples of successful stand-alone applications that serve one function for users (Wilson, 2013).

The popularity of stand-alone applications is due to their reliability and ease of use. Additionally, today's mobile users wish to compartmentalize their sharing across different groups as much as possible (Nieva, 2014). Privacy is of greater concern than ever, especially since the line between public and private is becoming increasingly blurred. This change in audience is discussed in more detail in the conclusion and recommendation section. Stand-alone applications make decisions about content sharing easier. Each time a new function is added to software, producers risk slowing down or complicating this process. Today's mobile users enjoy the simplicity of tasks and prioritize usability (Wilson, 2013).

Wearables

Being able to customize content on mobile devices is not enough. A recent trend in the industry is the development of wearable technology. Wearables is the product of convergence between nanotechnology and an expectation of increased mobility from users that allows hands-free interaction worn as clothing or jewelry (De Freitas & Levene, 2003). Users of wearables do not have to pull out and log into a mobile device each time they wish to access content. Instead, the technology is already integrated into something that they are already wearing. Applications for wearables are now even being developed that can be woven into the thread of textiles (Cranny-Francis, 2008). Messages disseminated through wearables are integrated into users' daily lives the same way that an individual speaking to them would be.

It is estimated that the wearables market will reach $6 billion by 2018 (Kelly, 2014). Popular wearable products that have hit the market already include Fitbit, a bracelet that wirelessly tracks fitness goals and other customizable personal health and body metrics; the Sony SmartWatch, a watch that connects to Android smarthphone technology to display SMS, social networking feeds and personal phone calls; and of course Google Glass, a wearable computer that functions through hands-free voice commands that can be worn like a regular pair of reading glasses. These products take advantage of many of the customizable and personal attributes of mobile technology, but with an increase of discretion for wear and use.

Visual social media

While social media is defined by the ability to facilitate dialogue between users, the future of networking resides in users' ability to communicate through visual images, rather than text-based communication. Pinterest is noteworthy for being one of the first social media to promote visual content over text (Ottoni *et al.*, 2013). Video and photo-sharing applications such as Vine, Instagram and Snapchat have also grown in popularity, while social media sites such as Twitter and Facebook have redesigned so that their text-based status update features can be more compatible with videos and photos. The newsfeed that you access on these sites is much more visual now than five years ago.

This push towards visual communication is a response to the fast-paced mobile social media audience. Text-based networking requires more contemplation before acting, which is not as suitable for today's technology (Correa *et al.*, 2010). People are posting messages on the go through mobile technology, which does not facilitate the same format for reading and creating text-based blogs when they sit down in front of personal computers. Consider how much more difficult it is to read a blog or news article on a moving bus than it is in your office. It is important for future social media practitioners to condense their messages with less text and more images in order to support the mobile environment.

Based on these changes to the future social media landscape, it is recommended that practitioners follow a four-step action plan when integrating new media technology into their existing marketing strategies.

Integrating New Media Technology Action Plan

1   Create content based on the principles of mobile marketing: individualized culture, personalization, interactivity, socialization, and localization. Rather than reformatting website content for a more simplistic mobile structure, social media content should be specifically designed for the purposes of mobile marketing, and include more interactivity, customization and personalized updates.

2   Do not try to do too much with mobile application features. Just because a function is offered on your website, it does not mean that it needs to be included in your mobile application. Always ensure that usability and simplicity are the primary drivers for application development. If there is a function of your content that is slowing down or complicating this process, consider removing it or creating a subsequent application where interested users are able to utilize this feature separately.

3   Consider how users of your product access content in their everyday lives. Audiences are likely busy and multitasking with multiple other items. Be sure that your content is less interruptive, responsive to their personalized needs, and provides instant gratification for what they are seeking. Be respectful of your audiences' time.

4   Be as minimalistic as possible with content design choices. All text-based format should follow the micro-blog rule of 140 characters or less. Show, instead of tell, through images or videos whenever possible. Facilitate a forum where users can share their experiences through pictures, rather than stories.

You will notice that each of these new technological functions offer the advantages of customization, mobility, and user-generated content. While these are all functions of a Web 2.0 environment, some argue that their domination is a product of an emerging new media (or new new media) era. This increase in mobility of the Internet has led to an increase in sociogeographic activities, from geo-caching to mobile social networking, described as Socio-Mobile Web 3.0 (Katz & Rice, 2002).

While these features will continue to be built upon, there is much debate about what to call the upcoming third-generation web environment. John Markoff first introduced the concept of Web 3.0 in a 2006 *New York Times* article (Markoff, 2006), but the reference was met with backlash and confusion from other professionals in the industry (Lassila & Hendler, 2007). For simplicity's sake, this book will utilize the terminology of Web 3.0 with the understanding that there is not widespread agreement about what the upcoming web generation will be called. What's important is not how it is referenced, but what it offers to users and producers of media content alike, as well as its influence on society.

Web 3.0: Asynchronous Mass Delivery

Remember from Chapter 2 the differences between a Web 1.0 and Web 2.0 environment. Web 1.0 views the audience as large, anonymous, heterogeneous, and promotes communication across a one-to-many unidirectional model (Pearce, 2009). Web 2.0 brought much advancement for audience interactivity and participation, including the ability for social networking, interaction orientation, personalization, customization, and user-added possibilities (Cormode & Krishnaumurthy, 2008; Wirtz *et al.*, 2010).

These advanced technological features have influenced audiences and society in many ways. We have discussed the shift in power from media producers to everyday audiences. These changes have been significant, and result in a globalized society where individuals are more connected than ever before, which brings new opportunities for online collaboration among users. This trend will only be magnified as we look ahead to the future of social media marketing.

One key function of a Web 3.0 environment identified by Markoff (2006) is the idea of a semantic web. The *semantic web* is a collaborative movement that provides a common framework for data to be shared and reused across applications and community boundaries. Though semantic technologies have been around since 2000, the World Wide Web Consortium is now developing proposed standards for the industry to follow. The function of a semantic web encourages users to find, share and combine information more easily, as well as be more easily interpreted by machines to advance more useful Internet structures (Hendler, 2008). It reorganizes and structures online content so that users anywhere in the world are able to collaborate on projects.

> Whereas Web 1.0 and 2.0 were embryonic, formative technologies, Web 3.0 promises to be a more mature web where better "pathways" for information retrieval will be created, and a greater capacity for cognitive processing of information will be built (Giustini, 2007, p. 1273).

These features allow users to share, produce and expand upon content more easily than ever before, which will undoubtedly influence culture and society just as much, if not more, than the Web 2.0 transition.

One area where users may change behaviors is the way in which we gather and retrieve information. The information age granted opportunities to seek out content based on our own needs and gratifications. If you are at a dinner party and there is disagreement about which celebrity is starring in this summer's blockbuster, any person with a smartphone device is able to look up the information for instant gratification.

Today's users learn by browsing, searching and monitoring the web. The semantic web will change this process. Audiences in a Web 3.0 environment will learn by telling the Internet what we are interested in, ask it what we collectively know, and use it to apply our collective knowledge to address our collective needs (Gruber, 2008). This information will be more customized and reactionary based on our needs. Rather than simply retrieving information from an all-knowing source, the process leading up to the conversation becomes important. Multiple users will be able to provide answers that are more relevant to the culture and environment in which they were sought.

It is unclear just how Web 3.0 will influence society. However, we do know that many of the promises of Web 2.0, especially with regard to power redistribution, have not been maximized. One reason for this may be the exaggerated promises of social media marketing opportunities for businesses. It is important that the same mistakes are not repeated as we look towards the future of the industry. There are many areas in which practitioners should be cautious regarding integrating technology in future strategies, including the use of interruptive technology and audience privacy concerns.

Conclusions and Recommendations

Current technological trends often guide marketing decisions. Marketing practitioners are eager to integrate the newest innovations into their business strategy. Today, this means the increased mobility, interactivity and customization brought by social media. Social media marketing allows increased audience participation. The more your customer is able to engage your product, the better the result. However, it is important to note that even the greatest advances to the consumer experience can become overwhelming and cumbersome when they reach a certain point of saturation.

The tipping point of push

Mobile marketing provides the ability to reach consumers where and when you wish. As a marketer, you no longer have to wait for your customers to turn on the television or radio in order to distribute your message. Consumers are constantly engaging online content, often through social media sites, providing endless opportunities to connect with them. Mobile applications make it easier than ever to reach audiences because, generally, users have voluntarily sought out a media structure that makes it easier to receive notifications about your product.

One way in which marketers have capitalized on mobile technology is through the use of push notifications. *Push notifications* are a feature of mobile applications which users install that periodically disseminates notification messages from notification services. Generally, the architecture of these push notification services have eliminated the needs of application servers to keep track of information, as content producers decide which information is noteworthy for users, and sends interruptive updates to a mobile device (Bell *et al.*, 2011; Namiot, 2013). Consumers tend to agree to these push notifications as part of their user terms and conditions statement.

Maybe you are tired of visiting your bank's online website and logging into your personal account each and every time you need an update. You download the bank's mobile application to set preferences for customizable features, including a daily push notification that tells you the balance of your bank account every morning. Because this is information that you were already likely seeking each morning, you are generally satisfied with the push feature.

As we look ahead at a social media landscape where mobile devices and wearable technology are the norm, there is more opportunity for these push notifications to be sent based on the GPS coordinates of consumers (Sohn *et al.*, 2005). Your bank may be able to tell when you are using a competitor's ATM and send you a push notification to alert you of the proximity of one of their own. Location-based GPS push notifications are designed so that you receive information when you need it most.

Many mobile applications have already taken advantage of these GPS-based push notifications. The coupon and discount service RetailMeNot sends notifications to users when they are in close proximity to a store that is offering a discount through their service. The Starbucks mobile application will send users an update if they are close to a Starbucks café. The location-based check-in application Foursquare will keep track of events and promotions of nearby bars and restaurants. These notifications are useful to customers if they are delivering information that users are interested in and have chosen to receive. However, the more marketers begin to incorporate push notifications into their mobile content, the less influential they will seem.

Increased mobility comes with increased interruption of our daily lives. For the most part, individuals do not like being disturbed when they are in the midst of doing something else. Mobile technology has already made it easy for one friend to interrupt a conversation that someone is having with another friend through phone calls or text messaging. This disturbance will prove even more frustrating when the interruption comes from a marketer rather than a personal contact.

Users are increasingly bombarded with devices that interrupt. Even if content producers are just trying to be helpful, users take purposeful actions to block these alerts (Picard & Liu, 2007). We may have initially thought that we would want to be alerted every time we are near our favorite coffee shop, but these notifications become too exhausting when they are distributed between alerts from our favorite clothing and shoe stores, car dealer and movie theater as well. There is a tipping point to the potential of push notifications. The newness and innovation of being alerted based on GPS location is beginning to wear off, and users will soon regard interruptive mobile technologies in the same manner they do traditional spam marketing.

Be sure to offer users the ability to easily turn off push notifications to prevent your message from becoming a part of the marketing noise. Resist the temptation to send multiple push notifications to users who have opted in, even if you are able, because the end result is that your audience will begin to associate your product with feelings of resentment and annoyance.

Having companies know everything about our purchasing behaviors, preferences and GPS location is scary to most consumers. While it may have been easy at one time to dismiss privacy concerns of mobile technologies, today's consumers are becoming more conscious about the security of their digital imprint. The evening news is constantly filled with stories of Internet privacy gone wrong. It is important for marketing practitioners to begin taking issues of customer privacy more seriously as they design marketing content.

Privacy concerns

The millennial generation is frequently criticized for being flippant about the amount and type of information that they share through social media. Growing up in an age of social media, they are used to sharing stories, photos and videos of everyday interactions. However, research demonstrates that this generation has become increasingly protective of their online privacy (Ma, 2013), a refreshing trend for consumers and producers alike.

As the Internet and social media become less of a new phenomenon, users are learning how to navigate some of its biggest threats. Users want the ability to control when, to what extent, and how information about their lives is communicated to others (Ellison *et al.*, 2011). This requires a strong understanding of media literacy.

Media literacy is defined as the ability of users to critically access, analyze, evaluate, and create messages in a variety of forms (Livingstone, 2004). Audiences must acquire the knowledge to utilize the Internet confidently, competently and safely. Many school programs are beginning to integrate a media literacy curriculum into their lessons (Hobbs, 2010), suggesting that the next generation of web users will be even more concerned and knowledgeable about issues surrounding their privacy and security.

Gone are the days where businesses could post multiple pages of user agreements about their product and expect audiences to blindly accept the terms and conditions without reading. Today's audiences are more cautious than ever about these contracts. Additionally, social media provides endless resources for others to decipher what is really written into the contract even if you do not have the time. The power of social media gives consumers a stronger voice when they don't like the privacy policy implemented by online organizations.

In 2012, the popular photo-sharing application Instagram created a new intellectual property privacy policy. This policy asked users to agree to grant Instagram the right to sell users' photographs without payment or notification, including for advertising purposes (McCullagh, 2012). Several industry blogs deciphered the changes to the privacy policy and cautioned users against agreeing. The outcry became public and viral. Just 24 hours later, Instagram backed down from the policy changes, thanking users for their feedback and letting them know that "We're listening" (Instagram, 2012).

Trust is a critical piece of marketing and you do not want to be caught in a situation where it appears as though you are trying to be sneaky or put something past your audiences without their knowledge. Your audiences should be your primary focus, and every decision you make should be for their benefit.

Companies should never sell customer information to third party organizations. If you do, it is important that you are upfront with users about your intention. Do not be surprised when they go somewhere else though. Ensure that your software is secure and that every measure is taken to protect customers against hackers. The next generation of consumers is willing to switch products or services because of privacy concerns faster than any previous generation (Morgan, 2014). Be certain that your audiences are confident in the security of your organization. If they are not, they will certainly be able to find an alternative space to take their business in today's digital landscape.

By successfully navigating the amount of interruptive technology and privacy concerns integrated in your business strategies, you can better ensure that audiences associate your brand with feelings of trust, respect and commitment. This is key to nurturing your lifelong brand advocates. As the online environment moves towards increasing collaboration, it is important that you see your audience as a critical factors in your own success. There is much to learn from how other businesses manage their audiences. Let's examine how Facebook, one of the longest lasting social networking sites, has been able to constantly revamp their business model and retain users for over 10 years.

Case Study: Looking Ahead at Facebook

Facebook began in 2004 as a social networking site designed to "give people the power to share and make the world more open and connected" (Facebook, 2014). During its inception, Facebook was structured as a virtual space where college students could connect with, or find out more information about, other registered college students. Over time it has transitioned into a multifunctional platform that is open to everyone. It currently has more than 1 billion active users.

The main design of Facebook includes a self-selected user profile picture, an "About Me" section where users can write a brief biography about themselves, and a wall where friends can post comments to each other. Items are disseminated through a Newsfeed that allows users the ability to choose how they would like to receive updates from the individuals that they follow. Many additional features have been added to the site as well, including the ability to poke, like, check-in, share videos, play games, or chat privately with friends.

One of the greatest appeals of Facebook is how every user is able to utilize the social networking site differently from one another. Maybe you are hooked on an integrated social game, while your friend is someone who loathes receiving game requests from others. Some users primarily use Facebook to share news stories, while others only post pictures. When designing a mobile application for users, producers of Facebook had to determine how to provide users the ability to customize content according to their own needs.

Unfortunately, the mobile application has been one of the greatest challenges for Facebook. In 2012, the application held a two-star rating in the United States iTunes store, with over half of the ratings falling below one star (Mobtest, 2012). Users complained the application was slow, inconsistent, and did not work properly. The mobile experience of using Facebook was much less satisfying than accessing the social networking site through a personal computer.

Facebook recognized these challenges and issued a statement explaining how challenging it was to create a profitable business model involving mobile applications, stating

> If users increasingly access Facebook mobile products as a substitute for access through personal computers, and if we are unable to successfully implement monetization strategies for our mobile users, or if we incur excessive expenses in this effort, our financial performance and ability to grow revenue would be negatively affected (Couts, 2012).

The company was struggling with meeting audience expectations, and maintaining a profitable business model.

Nonetheless, the appeal of mobile technology for audiences could not be ignored, especially since over half of the monthly active users who access Facebook do so through their mobile devices (Mobtest, 2012). The company needed to come up with a solution to their mobile problem or risk frustrating and losing users.

In 2012 Facebook bought Instagram, a stand-alone mobile photo-sharing service. The premise of Instagram is relatively simple. Users could take pictures with their mobile phones, filter them through the application, create a brief caption for the photo, and then share with friends that follow them. The features of Instagram are much less customizable than Facebook.

During its inception, the application could only be accessed and used through mobile devices. Users could not use the platform through personal computers. Receiving updates from other users could only be done in chronological order, where users received photos from other users based on the time that they were posted. Users could not sort or rank-order friends in order to structure content. There were no alternative interactive functions, such as the ability to privately chat or share with other specific users. The application also had no integration of content with external software.

Despite its simplicity, Facebook's acquisition of Instagram has proven largely successful. It was estimated that Instagram generated more than $250 million in revenue in 2014, and has been cited as "the most powerful social media platform in the world" (Goel, 2014). Producers have been able to design a mobile application that successfully meets audience expectations and integrates a profitable business model through a relatively simple premise.

Perhaps it is because of Instagram's lack of features that it has grown so popular with users. The mobile application is fast, reliable and easy to use. It is designed very differently from the multifunctional mobile application of Facebook. The appeal of a stand-alone application with fewer functions has not been lost on Facebook creator, Mark Zuckerburg.

During the 2014 earnings call, Zuckerburg explained how roughly half of Facebook's total monthly users utilize a stand-alone service, Facebook Groups, for setting up customized spaces for interactions and sharing (Miners, 2014). By allowing users to directly access the Facebook features of their choice through stand-alone applications, mobile applications could receive direct advertising revenue, and have faster and more reliable software. This stand-alone application initiative is the primary focus of growth for the immediate future of Facebook (Nieva, 2014).

The social networking site has already moved towards removing the private chat feature, Facebook Messenger, from its main mobile application, and asked users to install a separate application if they wish to use this feature instead (Smith, 2014). True to this vision, Facebook has also acquired WhatsApp, a private messaging application service for smartphones, and Oculus VR, a virtual reality gaming platform.

This move towards stand-alone mobile applications for Facebook suggests that while today's users expect to have more options than ever before, an easy, fast and reliable interface structure is still the priority for audiences. The one-stop model of a multifunctional application has lost its appeal with users. If the structure of content is frustrating or difficult to navigate, audiences will go elsewhere for content. Providing audiences the ability to choose which features they most wish to use, and an interface that focuses on these choices, is critical to the success of future social media businesses.

Discussion questions

1   How might a stand-alone application relieve some of the frustrations users feel towards larger applications? As a practitioner, is it better to focus on usability or additional features for audiences?
2   Facebook displays content according to an algorithm that determines the importance of user content. A user's Instagram feed displays content chronologically. Looking to the future of social media, what are some advantages and disadvantages of each structure of dissemination?
3   Facebook's move towards stand-alone applications prove that sometimes less is more. When might a multifunctional application be more appealing to mobile users?

Summary

It may seem discouraging or risky to begin a career in a field as dynamic as social media marketing. However, this book attempts to provide the foundational tools for practitioners to apply to any digital landscape. What is most important is not how technologically savvy or advanced your marketing team proves. Instead, it is your ability to focus on fostering human relationships and connections. A 25-year meta-analysis demonstrates how the most successful health campaigns are those which incorporate theory into their design (King, 1999). The same is true for any campaign that is interested in influencing audience behavior. Theoretical principles should guide every marketing decision that you make.

Part I of this book suggested that social media messaging decisions should be guided by human behavior change literature. The principles of diffusion, community and mobilization should be integrated into every content decision that you make. Find the appropriate balance between audience participation and control over your message based on your business goals. No campaign should begin without a strong audience analysis or end without a strong formative audience evaluation.

Part II further explained how and why online users choose, disseminate and share media messages. It highlighted the importance of creating messages that audiences strongly identify with, as well as the importance of integrating these messages within a media structure that promotes interactivity. If the content of your message does not seem to be working in the ways in which you anticipated, this section offers some structural reasons why. The active within structures paradigm is a nuanced way to view social media audiences and will set you apart from other professionals in the field who are simply trying to disseminate their message to sell a product.

Part III of this book offered tips for increasing business revenue and return on investment through social media marketing and business models. Not only did this section include emerging methods by which businesses are capitalizing on the changing industry, but also offered ways in which these strategies should change the approach to targeting audiences. While media messages traditionally target mass audiences, this section shows the importance of finding your product niche – the smaller the better. Communicating with individuals instead of large audiences will help transform customers into brand advocates for your product.

Part IV of this book applied the theoretical human behavior change principles to prosocial initiatives, such as health campaigns, civic engagement, communication for development, and entertainment-education interventions. Social media offers greater opportunity for equalizing power inequities. One of the most important lessons learned is that the strategy for promoting social change is no different from getting an individual to like your Facebook page or buy your product. Humans make decisions about their everyday lives in the same manner. A strong understanding of behavior change theories will help you persuade any audience.

Part V of this book discussed the importance of integrating a socially responsible message into your marketing strategy. As businesses become more social in nature, users begin to view them as more human. By authentically incorporating a prosocial cause into your social media messages, consumers are better able to see the lifestyle of your brand – the passions and causes that you care most about. This transition from a business to a prosocial brand is imperative for surviving in a world where increased transparency is an expectation from audiences. Finally, Part V also offered alternative recommendations for the future of social media marketing, and suggested that social media is unpredictable and constantly evolving.

While this book offers recommendations for future practitioners, it is not meant to serve as an exclusive reference. Perhaps the greatest responsibility of a social media practitioner is staying up to date with industry news. This field is exciting and offers many benefits, such as an outlet for creativity, flexible hours, and portable offices. Take advantage of the social media industry's largest advantage, the plethora of resources and mentors available.

Social media practitioners are drawn to social media because they love connecting with other individuals. This is the foundation of social media technology, and it should be the foundation of your goals, both professionally and personally. The line between public and private is becoming increasingly blurred. It is important that you take these concepts and apply to branding your social media site. Remember, many of the suggestions offered in this book can easily be applied to your personal social media brand as well. Perhaps it can be used to persuade someone that you are the perfect candidate for the social media position of your dreams.

Key Takeaways

1 There are many changes emerging in the social media landscape, and it is your duty as a practitioner to stay connected to the industry. The future of marketing should include increased customization, mobility and user-generated content through mobile marketing, stand-alone applications, wearables, and visual social media.

2 Regardless of the social media landscape, content and message decisions should be guided by human behavior change theories. The process by which humans make decisions will never change, and a strong understanding of foundational communication principles will prepare you for a lifetime career in the industry.

3 There is much debate about what to call the third-generation web environment. However, regardless of its title, future marketing strategies should be built around the principles of semantic web, user collaboration, and collective intelligence.

4 Practitioners must be cautious about using too much interruptive technology in their campaign design. Today's Internet users are much more concerned about privacy, and this should be the focus of future business strategies as well.

5 Be innovative. Keep calm. And embrace all the opportunities and challenges of social media marketing and social behavior change.

References

Bauer, H.H., Barnes, S.J., Reichardt, T. & Neumann, M.M. (2005) Driving consumer acceptance of mobile marketing: a theoretical framework and empirical study. *Journal of Electronic Commerce Research*, 6(3), 181–192.

BBC (2013) Mobiles "to outnumber people next year", says UN agency. Available at http://www.bbc.com/news/technology-22464368 (accessed June 8, 2016).

Bell, K., Bleau, D. & Davey, J. (2011) Push notification service. Available at http://www.google.com/patents/US8064896 (accessed June 8, 2016).

Cormode, G. & Krishnamurthy, B. (2008) Key differences between Web 1.0 and 2.0. *First Monday*, 13(6). Available at http://firstmonday.org/ojs/index.php/fm/article/view/2125 (accessed June 8, 2016).

Correa, T., Hinsley, A.W. & De Zuniga, H.G. (2010) Who interacts on the Web? The intersection of users' personality and social media use. *Computers in Human Behavior*, 26(2), 247–253.

Couts, A. (2012) Facebook mobile apps: bad on purpose? Available at http://www.digitaltrends.com/mobile/face book-mobile-apps-bad-on-purpose/#!3DavQ (accessed June 8, 2016).

Cranny-Francis, A. (2008) From extension to engagement: mapping the imaginary of wearable technology. *Visual Communication*, 7(3), 363–382.

De Freitas, S. & Levene, M. (2003) Evaluating the development of wearable devices, personal data assistants and the use of other mobile devices in further and higher education institutions. *JISC Technology and Standards Watch Report*, (TSW030), 1–21.

Elder, J. (2014) Social media fail to live up to early marketing hype: companies refine strategies to stress quality over quantity of fans. Available at http://online.wsj.com/articles/companies-alter-social-media-strategies-1403499658 (accessed June 8, 2016).

Ellison, N.B., Vitak, J., Steinfield, C., Gray, R. & Lampe, C. (2011) Negotiating privacy concerns and social capital needs in a social media environment. In: S. Trepte & L. Reinecke (eds) *Privacy Online*, pp. 19–32. Berlin: Springer.

Facebook (2014) About Facebook. Available at https://www.facebook.com/facebook/info (accessed June 8, 2016).

Gallup (2014) The myth of social media. Available at http://online.wsj.com/public/resources/documents/sac_report_11_socialmedia_061114.pdf (accessed June 8, 2016).

Giustini, D. (2007) Web 3.0 and medicine. *BMJ*, 335(7633), 1273–1274.

Goel, V. (2014) Is Instagram another path to riches for Facebook? Available at http://bits.blogs.nytimes.com/2014/02/18/is-instagram-another-path-to-riches-for-facebook/?_php=true&_type=blogs&_r=0 (accessed June 8, 2016).

Gruber, T. (2008) Collective knowledge systems: where the social web meets the semantic web. *Web Semantics: Science, Services and Agents on the World Wide Web*, 6(1), 4–13.

Hendler, J. (2008) Web 3.0: chicken farms on the semantic web. *Computer*, 41(1), 106–108.

Hobbs, R. (2010) *Digital and media literacy: A plan of action*. Geneva: UNAIDS. Available at http://www.knightcomm.org/wp-content/uploads/2010/12/Digital_and_Media_Literacy_A_Plan_of_Action.pdf (accessed June 8, 2016).

Instagram (2012) Thank you, and we're listening. Available at http://blog.instagram.com/post/38252135408/thank-you-and-were-listening (accessed June 8, 2016).

Katz, J.E. & Rice, R.E. (2002) *Social Consequences of Internet Use: Access, Involvement, and Interaction*. Cambridge, MA: MIT Press.

Kelly, H. (2014) Wearable gadgets search for mainstream appeal. Available at http://www.cnn.com/2014/01/08/tech/innovation/wearable-tech-fashion/ (accessed June 8, 2016).

King, R. (1999) Sexual behavioural change for HIV: where have theories taken us? Available at http://www.who.int/hiv/strategic/surveillance/en/unaids_99_27.pdf (accessed June 8, 2016).

Lassila, O. & Hendler, J. (2007) Embracing "Web 3.0". *IEEE Internet Computing*, 11(3), 90–93.

Livingstone, S. (2004) Media literacy and the challenge of new information and communication technologies. *The Communication Review*, 7(1), 3–14.

Ma, A. (2013) An increase in the desire for Internet privacy. Available at http://harvardpolitics.com/hprgument-posts/increase-desire-internet-privacy (accessed June 8, 2016).

Markoff, J. (2006) Entrepreneurs see a web guided by common sense. Available at http://www.nytimes.com/2006/11/12/business/12web.html?ex=1320987600&en=a54d6971614edc62&ei=5090&partner=rssuserland&emc=rss&pagewanted=all (accessed June 8, 2016).

McCullagh, D. (2012) Instagram says it now has the right to sell your photos. Available at http://www.cnet.com/news/instagram-says-it-now-has-the-right-to-sell-your-photos (accessed June 8, 2016).

Miners, Z. (2014) Facebook sees apps in its future … lots of apps. Available at http://www.infoworld.com/d/applications/facebook-sees-apps-in-its-future-lots-of-apps-235316?page=0,0 (accessed June 8, 2016).

Mobtest (2012) Here's why the Facebook iOS app is so bad (UIWebViews and no Nitro). Available at http://blog.mobtest.com/2012/05/heres-why-the-facebook-ios-app-is-so-bad-uiwebviews-and-no-nitro/ (accessed June 8, 2016).

Morgan, B. (2014) Millennials the most privacy-conscious generation, says study. Available at http://www.research-live.com/news/millennials-the-most-privacy-conscious-generation-says-study/4011682.article (accessed June 8, 2016).

Namiot, D. (2013) Local area messaging for smartphones. *International Journal of Open Information Technologies*, 1(2), 8–11.

Nieva, R. (2014) Facebook's Zuckerberg: standalone apps are the plan. Available at http://www.cnet.com/news/facebooks-zuckerberg-standalone-apps-are-the-plan/ (accessed June 8, 2016).

O'Neill, M. (2010) Cisco fails with Old Spice copycat campaign. Available at http://socialtimes.com/cisco-old-spice-campaign_b18558 (accessed June 8, 2016).

Ottoni, R., Pesce, J.P., Las Casas, D.B. *et al.* (2013) Ladies first: analyzing gender roles and behaviors in Pinterest. Presented at Seventh International AAAI Conference on Weblogs and Social Media. Available at http://www.aaai.org/ocs/index.php/ICWSM/ICWSM13/paper/view/6133 (accessed June 8, 2016).

Pearce, K. (2009) Media and mass communication theories. In: S.W. Littlejohn & K.A. Foss (eds) *Encyclopedia of Communication Theory*, pp. 623–627. Thousand Oaks, CA: Sage Publications.

Picard, R.W. & Liu, K.K. (2007) Relative subjective count and assessment of interruptive technologies applied to mobile monitoring of stress. *International Journal of Human-Computer Studies*, 65(4), 361–375.

Scharl, A., Dickinger, A. & Murphy, J. (2005) Diffusion and success factors of mobile marketing. *Electronic Commerce Research and Applications*, 4(2), 159–173.

Shankar, V. & Balasubramanian, S. (2009) Mobile marketing: a synthesis and prognosis. *Journal of Interactive Marketing*, 23(2), 118–129.

Smith, C. (2014) Facebook will force you to install another one of its apps. Available at http://bgr.com/2014/04/10/facebook-messenger-for-ios-and-android/ (accessed June 8, 2016).

Sohn, T., Li, K.A., Lee, G., Smith, I., Scott, J. & Griswold, W.G. (2005) Place-its: a study of location-based reminders on mobile phones. In: M. Beigl, S. Intille, J. Rekimoto & H. Tokuda (eds) *UbiComp 2005: Ubiquitous Computing*, pp. 232–250. Berlin: Springer.

Wilson, C. (2013) Standalone apps: driving the future of mobile technology? Available at http://www.business2community.com/mobile-apps/standalone-apps-driving-future-mobile-technology-0710781#!3bPvc (accessed June 8, 2016).

Wirtz, B., Schilke, O. & Ullrich, S. (2010) Strategic development of business models: implications of the Web 2.0 for creating value on the Internet. *Long Range Planning*, 43(2–3), 272–290.

Index

Strategic Social Media: From Marketing to Social Change, First Edition. L. Meghan Mahoney and Tang Tang.
© 2017 John Wiley & Sons, Inc. Published 2017 by John Wiley & Sons, Inc.